EXPLORING THE WORLD OF MUSIC

An introduction to music from a world music perspective

Dorothea E. Hast
General Editor

James R. Cowdery
Stan Scott

*Produced by Pacific Street Films
and the Educational Film Center*

From
The Annenberg/CPB
Multimedia Collection

KENDALL/HUNT PUBLISHING COMPANY
4050 Westmark Drive Dubuque, Iowa 52002

ISBN 0-7872-7154-3

Printed in the United States of America
10 9 8 7 6 5 4

CONTENTS

PREFACE

Music plays a significant role in virtually every human society. Like language, it appears to be one of our "species-specific" traits. Does this mean that music is as important in human life as language?

Some readers may find this a peculiar question. The practical value of language is obvious, but many people in the modern world consider music a luxury or frill: something which is nice to have, but not absolutely necessary. If this is true, why do even subsistence cultures spend precious time and energy on music? Why is music considered such an essential and powerful part of religion, political expression, work, and play in societies around the world?

Ethnomusicology, the study of music as culture, is to some extent a search for answers to these questions. The quest is not a simple one as it involves encountering cultures on their own terms. Although music seems to exist in every society, its meaning, function, and role differ. Sometimes even the word "music" is problematic. "One of the first lessons that ethnomusicologists learn," the British ethnomusicologist, John Blacking wrote, "is that music is both a social fact and multi-media communication: there are many societies that have no word for 'music' and do not isolate it conceptually from dance, drama, ritual, or costume; and even when music is identified as a specific category of thought and action, there are many different ways in which it is defined and in which different characteristics are regarded as significant."[1]

As ethnomusicologists, the authors of this book take the position that music—its creation, reception, and even its definition—is embedded in culture, and can vary throughout the world as widely as any other aspect of human life. Like Blacking, we believe that ethnomusicology is "an approach to understanding all musics and music-making in the contexts of performance and of the ideas and skills that composers, performers, and listeners bring to what they define as musical situations."[2] This approach provides students with an understanding and appreciation of the sound, power, and meaning of music as it exists within culture. To study music is to study people, community, history, religion, politics, and dance, as well as to study musical styles, forms, and instruments.

A Thematic, Global, Multi-Media Approach

The study of music has traditionally been compartmentalized: theory texts focus on harmony in Western music; orchestration texts on instruments and texture; music appreciation and history texts focus on the history of Western classical music; and ethnomusicology texts focus on cultural areas of the world.

We have pursued a more holistic approach by basing each chapter on one element of music (such as melody, rhythm, texture, and timbre) or one topic (such as music and memory or the transformative power of music). We include Western classical, popular, and folk musics alongside musics from around the world. This is certainly not to deny the importance of area studies. Indeed, we urge readers to consult the many detailed area studies which we cite throughout the text. Our intention, however, is simply to offer the reader access to a broad array of musical ideas and practices through a basic conceptual framework. In this way, we not only present information, but hope to stimulate the reader to think in new and deeper ways about all music.

This book has been specifically designed to be used in several different ways: as a general introduction to world music and the elements of music; as a companion to Western music history and appreciation texts and courses; and as a key component in a unique, new multi-media series and telecourse. The book has been developed to expand upon and deepen the themes presented in the accompanying television series, *Exploring the World of Music,* created by Pacific Street Films in association with the Educational Film Center. While the programs present performances, interviews, and archival footage, the chapters in this book are designed to provide a more in-depth view of issues raised in the programs, and to introduce new material that relates to each topic.

The companion audio CDs augment both the television programs and the book. Each selection of the audio module is keyed and explained. The audio selections give the reader/listener access to fuller and more varied performances to further exemplify musical concepts, styles, and forms discussed. While each of these three components may be used separately, together they offer an integrated, multi-media learning experience.

The Musicians Speak for Themselves

One of our primary sources in the writing process has been the collected interviews conducted for the television series. The musicians and scholars that appear in the series were interviewed from December 1996 to March 1998. Our goal has been to allow these experts to speak for themselves, both on the screen and on the page. The inclusion of their quotes throughout the book will give the reader a more thorough understanding both of musical concepts and of the people who make and study the music. The specialties of the interviewees also provided us with the main cultural areas that are explored throughout the television series and the body of the text.

We also include the voices of many other scholars and musicians who are deeply involved with the musical cultures we explore. We do not pretend to provide a comprehensive compilation and examination of all of the world's music, but we have selected a broad enough range of examples to suggest an overall picture. We have provided an approach that will aid the reader in considering musics not discussed here.

Topics and Elements

Each chapter correlates to its counterpart in the television series. While we have used each program to provide a conceptual outline, we have consciously structured the chapters differently, weaving new information in with material directly relating to the programs. Each chapter includes notation, musical analyses, and figures designed to clarify concepts and deepen understanding of specific compositions and performances.

In Chapter 1 we present the fundamental nature of music as specialized sound grounded in an environment. We discuss definitions of music, the acoustical properties of sound, and relations between musical activity and its setting—from the mountains of Bosnia to the streets of New York City.

The following three chapters address specific aspects of music in relation to culture. Chapter 2 investigates the power of music to enhance and transform experience within religion, ritual, dance, healing, and politics. Chapter 3 considers ways that music provides a vital link to personal and cultural memory, connecting people to their heritage, as well as to past traditions. In Chapter 4, we explore how music is brought from the past to the present and future through teaching and learning.

Basic musical elements are considered in the next three chapters. Chapter 5 investigates the world of rhythm, the time element of music. In Chapter 6, we focus on melody, the use of a succession of rising and falling pitches to tell an abstract musical "story." Chapter 7 examines timbre, the color of musical sound, from the unaccompanied voice to the widely varied sounds of musical instruments.

In the next three chapters we explore how these elements can be combined. Chapter 8 addresses the subject of texture, the relationships of concurrent parts in a musical whole. Chapter 9 focuses on one particular aspect of texture, the simultaneous sounding of musical tones known as harmony. In Chapter 10, we consider overall musical forms, the larger ways that musical experience can be structured in time.

Chapter 11 turns to the contributions of creative individuals, whether they compose music before performing it, improvise it on the spot, or do some of both. Chapter 12 considers the ways that music influences and is influenced by technology, from the early construction of flutes to the rapidly-developing world of electronic sound production, reproduction, and enhancement.

Finally we gratefully acknowledge the help of the following people: Matthew Allen, William Cowdery, Judith A. Gray, Scott Marcus, Mike Moss, Tom Munnelly, and Robert Walser for providing valuable criticism and advice. We would also like to thank Martin Toub, Steven Fishler, and Joel Sucher of Pacific Street Films; Stephen Rabin and Diane Eisenberg for editorial guidance, and Johanne Trew from the University of Limerick Library for her assistance. A special thanks to Mark Slobin, Gage Averill, Barbara Hampton, John Cohen, and Stephen Wild for their helpful critiques of the television programs. In addition, we would like to thank Annette and Tom Munnelly for providing two of us with a computer, e-mail, and companionship during the final stages of writing in Miltown Malbay, Co. Clare, Ireland.

Dorothea Hast, General Editor
James Cowdery
Stan Scott

EXPLORING THE WORLD OF MUSIC
CD AUDIO KEY

CD 1 Songs 1-25

1 - 1
2 - 2
3 - 3
4 - 4
5 - 5
6 - 6
7 - 7
8 - 8
9 - 9
10 - 10
11- 11
12 - 12
13 - 13
14 - 14
15 - 15
16 - 16
17 - 17
18 - 18
19 - 19
20 - 20
21 - 21
22 - 22
23 - 23
24 - 24
25 - 25

CD 2 Songs 26-51

26 - 1
27 - 2
28 - 3
29 - 4
30 - 5
31 - 6
32 - 7
33 - 8
34 - 9
35 - 10
36 - 11
37 - 12
38 - 13
39 - 14
40 - 15
41 - 16
42 - 17
43 - 18
44 - 19
45 - 20
46 - 21
47 - 22
48 - 23
49 - 24
50 - 25
51 - 26

CD 3 Songs 52-64

52 - 1
53 - 2
54 - 3
55 - 4
56 - 5
57 - 6
58 - 7
59 - 8
60 - 9
61 - 10
62 - 11
63 - 12
64 - 13

SOUND, MUSIC, AND THE ENVIRONMENT

About This Chapter

We can analyze music on many levels, beginning with the laws of acoustics. The frequency, amplitude, duration, and timbre of sound waves, acting upon our eardrums, give us music. But in order to have meaning, these sounds must be organized so as to communicate and affect people within their sphere. Every culture in the world has some kind of musical tradition. But while music seems to exist in every human society, its meaning, forms, and functions differ from culture to culture. In this chapter, we examine music as an important component of culture, beginning by asking the question, "What is music?" We then look at sound and the underlying physical laws of all music in order to understand how music is produced and perceived. Finally, we examine the importance of context and the relationship of music, society, and the physical environment.

COMPANION RESOURCES

TELEVISION PROGRAM: Sound, Music, and the Environment

AUDIO SELECTIONS:

1. "Sjajna Zvjezdo." Mirjana Laušević, Donna Lee Kwon, and Tristra Newyear.
2. Imitation of Dog Sound, Tuva
3. Throat Singing in Cave, Tuva

Music seems to exist in every human society, but its meaning, roles, and functions differ markedly from culture to culture. Different societies, and even individuals within a single society, often disagree about what music is. Some languages don't have a word that corresponds exactly to the English word "music." Differences in forms, techniques, instruments, aesthetics, languages, and environments have yielded a wealth of musical styles. How then, from a cross-cultural perspective, can we define music?

We begin by defining music as patterns or sequences of sound, organized by human beings, that are somehow distinct from ordinary speech or every-day sonic occurrences. These musical structures have meanings that must be understood with reference to the societies that produce them. According to ethnomusicologist Anthony Seeger, "music is much more than just sounds captured on a tape recorder."[1] Music is an intentional construction that can be described in many aspects, including its structure and form, its emotional meaning, and its perceived cultural value:

> Music is an intention to make something called music (or structured similarly to what we call music) as opposed to other kinds of sounds. It is an ability to formulate strings of sounds accepted by members of a given society. . . . Music is an emotion that accompanies the pro-duction of, the appreciation of, and the participation in a perfor-mance. Music is also, of course, the sounds themselves after they are produced. Yet it is intention as well as realization; it is emotion and value as well as structure and form.[2]

Like language, music is a system of communication that is embedded in the community, group, or culture from which it arises. Not only must its structures, forms, and rules be understood, but also its function, value, and expressive meaning. Like food, music seems to answer a universal human need. But just as particular foods are esteemed by some cultures and not by others, musical meaning is not a universally agreed upon phenomenon. People around the world make, participate in, and listen to many forms of music for a variety of different reasons. What may seem like noise to one may be deemed the most beautiful music by another.

Depending on its cultural context, music has the power to evoke strong feelings and memories, to intensify religious experience, to bring people to-gether, to move them physically through dance, and to entertain them. As Bosnian ethnomusicologist Mirjana Laušević suggests, music is both a per-sonal and collective creative experience situated within a particular time and place:

> I guess if you try to answer the question what music is, you need to figure out from whose perspective you're looking at. For different people, music means different things. If I need to define what music is for me, it is an expression of life and it is an expression of culture that happens in time and in space. It happens with, around, and for people that you are with, and it cannot be separated from that experience. As an art form that happens in a very specific time, place, and con-text, it is an interaction. It is a creation that expresses your being.[3]

For jazz musician Josh Redman, music is also a creation that expresses his innermost emotions. To a performer, one of the most exciting elements of music is its expressive power to move performers and listeners in ways that cannot be described in words:

> Music for me is a unique and moving experience which is connected to reality, but also transports me outside of reality. I mean, music is transcendent and that is one of the reasons we can never accurately and completely describe what music is. . . . In other words, if every-thing about music had a word or an idea or an analytical concept that we could attach to it, then in a sense there would be nothing mysteri-

*ous or magical or transcendent about music. For me, it's that tran-
scendence, that spiritual involvement and journey in music which
makes it so special.*[4]

Music can be just as vital for the listener as the performer. As one
contradancer in New England states, "Music is as important as air to breathe
with," or another, "When the music soars so do I. It inspires me. It's greatly
satisfying. . . . At its best, I'm lost in the music—transported." Listening to
music—once reserved for live performance situations—now can take place
anywhere that recording technology exists. People use music to relieve stress,
to pass the time while driving, during work-outs at the gym, while doing
housework, or getting to sleep. Walkman culture allows people to create
listening worlds for themselves apart from their immediate surroundings. Listening can be a passionate experience, a passive one, or somewhere in between depending on the focus of the listener and the context for the music
making.

While music conveys meanings, feelings, and images that are understood
and valued differently from group to group and culture to culture, the physical laws of sound are universal. Ethnomusicologist Mark Slobin explains that
vibration is at the root of music:

> *One way to think about music is as a physical fact. Music exists. You
> don't see it, but it's there. It has waves that go through the air and hit
> your ear and do complex physical things. What we do is translate it;
> we translate this energy into a number of its component parts. . . .
> Waves going through the air over and over again sketch the same pat-
> terns if you put them on a screen. . . . This doesn't tell us anything
> about what it means to anybody. But it does tell us a lot about how
> we understand it, how we perceive it.*[5]

THE TECHNOLOGY OF SOUND: FREQUENCY, AMPLITUDE, DURATION, AND TIMBRE

Sound is vibration. On a physical level, it is a result of a disturbance of the
medium that carries it, which may be air (or other gases), water, or solid media such as wood and metal. When carried in air, the vibrations actually
cause changes in atmospheric pressure. A minute disturbance of the pressure,
such as drawing a bow across a string or singing a tune, creates vibrations or
waves, which are transmitted through the air in all directions. These sound
waves are picked up by the ear, transmitted to the brain, and given meaning.
Composer Gerald Shapiro sums up how sound is perceived:

> *In order to have a sound you need three things. You need some object
> which is vibrating, some physical object, such as a flute or a cello. . . .
> Then you need a medium to carry that vibration, usually that's the
> air. But we all have the experience of hearing sound underwater or of
> hearing sound when we put our ear to the door. . . . Obviously, the
> metal of the door can carry the vibration of the sound. A wonderful
> example is the tin can and string telephone that kids make, where the
> sound is carried along on the string between the two tin cans. And
> finally, we need an ear, an eardrum, and a brain to hear the sound
> and to turn it into something that's meaningful to a human being.*[6]

SINE WAVE

The simplest kind of sound is called a sine wave. The initial vibration creates a curve, which rises smoothly to a peak, then subsides, and then dips in a curve equal to the initial rise creating the shape of a backwards letter "S" drawn on its side. However, sound is rarely as simple as a single sine wave. Instead, there are many sine waves occurring simultaneously. These waves can be measured using an instrument called an oscilloscope, which turns sound into visible patterns. When thinking about the musical properties of sound, these wave patterns have four different parameters from which they can be analyzed.

The first parameter is the *frequency* or rate of vibration in time of the sine wave. Frequency is measured in cycles per second, and our ears perceive frequency as a specific pitch—the highness or lowness of the sound. In the Western system, pitches are given letter names and each has its own frequency. For example, the "A" that an orchestra tunes to has a frequency of 440 cycles per second. Pitches are strung together to create melodies.

FREQUENCY

The second measurable parameter of the waveform is its height and depth. This parameter measures the strength of the vibration and indicates the *amplitude,* the loudness or softness, of the sound. In musical terms, amplitude refers to dynamics. Musicians use many different levels of volume, ranging on a continuum from extremely soft to extremely loud. Dynamics are an element of musical expression that are determined partly by the acoustical properties of an instrument or voice, the number of musicians playing or singing, the use of amplification, and the mood that a musician wishes to convey.

AMPLITUDE

The third parameter refers to the *duration* of the sound. How long does the sound last? All music takes place in time, and duration is an essential quality of musical sound. Just as melodies are constructed from successions of pitches, rhythm is created by durational patterns of sounds and silences.

The fourth parameter refers to the complexity and shape of the sound waves—how many waves go into making up the sound and what is their relationship and proportions.

DURATION

This parameter determines the tone color or *timbre* of a sound—why a flute sounds differently from a violin or an oboe. Every sound has a distinctive timbre because of the acoustical phenomenon of the overtone series.

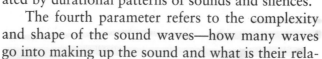

TIMBRE

Each individual tone consists of a fundamental pitch and a simultaneously sounding series of progressively higher overtones, also called partials or harmonics. The fundamental pitch is the actual note sung or played and it is usually the tone we can identify and hear most clearly:

*The lowest frequency of the sound, the fundamental of the sound—
it's a sine wave—is what we hear as the pitch of the sound. And we
say this note is B or a C because it is a certain frequency for its fundamental. Now then, above that fundamental is a string of overtones,
and they are simple multiples of the fundamental. . . . Within any individual note there actually are a whole series of higher, ever higher
overtones which make the timbre of each individual tone or sound.[7]*

The particular overtones of the series that resonate along with the fundamental pitch determine the timbre of the sound. Each instrument has its own
timbre based on the particular overtone structure that it generates. For example, metal flutes sound high and bright because their shape and material
emphasize only the second harmonic, one octave above the fundamental.
Clarinets have a very different sonority because their cylindrical tube construction largely eliminates the even numbered harmonics. Overtones are not
usually heard as distinctive pitches in their own right, rather, their presence
and proportion give a sound its characteristic quality.

Acoustical principles provide a common basis to musical systems around
the world. However, the Western terms used to describe these basic elements
of music—melody, rhythm, dynamics, and timbre—are not indigenous in
many cultures. They provide a common vocabulary because they have been
exported all over the world as basic concepts, but they do not necessarily describe how people think about their own music.

While some cultures have few *explicit* rules governing their musical traditions, most have very definite *implicit* grammars that control the forms that
music takes and the way music is performed. Western music theorists, instrument makers, and sound engineers adopt a technological perspective in which
ratios and measurements are an important concern. But even in societies
where acoustical principles are not articulated and measured as such, musicians are very aware of how music should be created and manipulated so that
it "sounds right" to themselves and to their audiences. These concerns include
technical considerations—how instruments are correctly constructed, tuned,
and played.

Technological concerns and the physical properties of sound production
answer only certain questions about what music is. There are many unmea-
surable and unpredictable aspects of music that have to do with its performance, function, and meaning within an overall culture. Because musical creation and reception are based on individual experience, no two perceptions of
musical meaning will be exactly the same. Nevertheless, musical practices are
strongly rooted in the history, politics, and social forces of any given culture.
Therefore, as ethnomusicologist Timothy Rice suggests, in order to study music, one must understand "how music is individually created and experienced,
how it is historically constructed, and how it is socially maintained."[8]

The context for music making has a great influence on its performance
and reception. From the production of a single sine wave in an electronic
music lab to the performance of an Italian opera in a concert hall, music exists within and creates its own time and space. This context is both a physical
and social space—rooted in place, but imbued with social meaning:

*All music is local and has its local understandings. So it is connected
to place. Any place that music is made is a special place in terms
of how it's being used and what it's importance is to the local people.*

. . . At this level of context we're talking about actual physical locality: [for example,] the dance hall. It's a musical space; it's also a musical context that has rules. When you are in a place where there is music and you are dancing, all kinds of rules apply about behavior between the sexes, about how loud the music should be, about what is the point of the music, about how long it should go on . . . it's a setting, it's an understanding, it's a sensibility . . . so each context of music may be an actual physical space, but it's also a spiritual space or an emotional space as well.[9]

The spaces or contexts where music is made, whether indoors or outdoors, formal or informal, sacred or secular, provide crucial information for understanding musical meaning and the role of music in society.

▄▄ MUSIC IN THE NATURAL ENVIRONMENT

The word "environment" implies all the conditions and influences surrounding and affecting a person and/or group. On the broadest level, we can look at environment as a whole ecosystem, including the entire landscape, soundscape, and social realm in which a person lives. On a more microcosmic level, the word can refer to "worlds" that people are able to enter and leave, such as the shopping mall, university classroom, concert hall, or restaurant. Often these are "artificial" environments which build temporary communities of participants as opposed to natural environments. As urban dwellers, people are capable of entering a variety of such worlds everyday. Music is often an essential part of the decor of interior consumer spaces, consciously manipulated to create atmosphere and to sell products.

Environment can be extremely important in how people relate to their music. The actual physical environment in which a people live determines many aspects of their music, along with their total culture. In many traditional rural economies, the natural environment is the governing force in everyday life, providing the means for sustenance and survival. In such cultures, the importance of nature is often reflected in musical practice, including the construction and use of musical instruments. Ethnomusicologist Ernest Brown gives one example:

The environment has a lot to do with the kind of music that people make. It determines what natural materials are available. For example, if you're talking about a rural society, that society is going to be limited by the material resources that are available. Among the Kung Bushmen from Botswana and Namibia for example, there are some ankle rattles that they use made from the cocoons of a particular kind of caterpillar. If those caterpillars aren't available, if it's a bad year for some reason and the caterpillars die off, then you don't get any leg rattles.[10]

Not only does the environment play an important role in the kinds of instruments the Bushmen use, but also in the style of their musical performance. As a hunter and gathering people living in the harsh surroundings of the Kalahari Desert in southern Africa, the Kung must work together very closely for survival. Their overall social structure is reflected in their music:

The music depends upon interaction and cooperation between a large number of people who make a whole. It's a kind of indivisible whole that they create. When you listen to the music, you can't very easily pick out the individual parts, but it is the whole that makes an impression upon you. And their society is the same way. That is, you won't survive in that environment unless you cooperate and work together very closely and in a very coordinated way with other people.[11]

Music can also be used to influence the natural world. In writing about music among five Shoshone women in Wyoming, Judith Vander describes how certain songs are meant to revitalize nature and promote health. Texts about water ensure the abundance of water which in turn nourishes and sustains ongoing plant and animal life.[12]

The Bosnian Highlands: Ganga and Bećarac

In the mountain highlands of Bosnia, the environment also plays an extremely important role in social life and musical practice. According to Mirjana Laušević, the physical surroundings very much affect daily life and the ways in which people communicate:

©1992 Magellan Geographix℠ Santa Barbara, CA (800) 929-4627

In Bosnian Highlander culture, specifically in Mount Bjelašnica (pronounced "Byel-ahsh-nit-sa"), people will spend a lot of time outdoors since it is a herding culture. They will spend a lot of time on the meadows up in the hills all alone. And they would be up in the hills looking down into the valley. And if somebody is passing through the valley, they certainly want to be heard. And even though they can't be seen, they will voice themselves. They will, in a way, acknowledge their existence.[13]

This rugged and isolated environment makes demands on men and women in different ways, but strength and being fit are valued by both genders. The need to make oneself powerfully heard is reflected in the singing styles—singing loudly means being strong:

And being strong means being beautiful, being right, being the member of the culture. . . . It is very important to show your strength in that vast space in which people are settled, to conquer space with your voice. So in a way, you cannot separate the environment from the culture or from the music.[14]

The song genre that is thought to carry the furthest is called *ganga*. This type of group singing is characterized by very close harmonies which cause

BOSNIAN GANGA SINGERS

the voices to acoustically beat or clash against each other. This loud and powerful music is meant to be sung outdoors by groups of either men or women. A leader starts the song and is then joined by his or her fellow singers, whose accompanying parts are essential to the song. The ganga ends with a scream or sigh which is an integral part of the performance. The singers stand in a semicircle, often touching shoulders. Their long extended breaths, as well as their powerful voices, are thought to reflect strength. People are not singing only for an audience, but rather to and for each other. The setting for ganga singing might be a village fair:

You will have a number of groups of people that will be located in different parts of a meadow. And one group will start singing, just independently. . . . And maybe at the same time, or maybe right after, another group will start singing from wherever they were at that moment. And often groups try to out-sing each other—one group will try to be louder than the other.[15]

Often the natural landscape will be used to augment the sound. For example, singers will face into the valley while singing in order to achieve more resonance.

The different singing styles of men and women reflect both the physical and the social landscape—what it means to be a man or woman. Attributes of masculinity include power and strength achieved through competition and individualism; attributes of femininity involve cooperation, coordination, and neatness. The manner in which songs are performed indicate these gender differences:

Women are expected to sing very neatly. Men are much more loose in the way that they can express their strength. They can express their strength with full volume of their voice. But they can be much more sloppy. Comments that people would make after female singing would be "You embroidered that really nicely," which reflects a certain demand for precision, for neatness, and for beauty that is organized. In male singing what you are exhibiting is strength and endurance. But how you come by that strength and endurance is not necessarily through precision.[16]

Song lyrics also reflect gender differences contextualized within the physical environment. Men's songs are often about men who are rascals or rogues in matters of love. Women's songs may be about the burdens of love or the difficulties of married life, and they may use more natural imagery. One example is called "Shining Star," in a singing genre called *bećarac*. Bećarac emerged as a new genre (circa 1940s) that was influenced by Western tonal harmony, but was still very much in the Highlander idiom. The first verse of the song is translated as follows:

> *Shining stars, do any of you know*
> *where my darling is tonight?*
> *Shining stars, wandering through the sky;*
> *On the earth, my darling and I.*

Mirjana Laušević describes her experience hearing this song for the first time standing on top of a mountain at night with a group of Highlander girls. This experience enabled her to understand more clearly the relationship between the social and physical environment and musical practice in traditional Highlander culture:

We were standing on top of the mountain underneath the stars. And the stars on the mountain are extremely visible, and there are millions of stars right above you and they seem very close. And there are these

ŽABE I BABE TRIO

girls singing. They were singing about a particular man who did not come and they do not know where he is, and he is the boyfriend or the potential boyfriend of one of the women who started the song. It suddenly made so much sense and became so clear—this connection that people find with what is closest to them. And in that case it was the stars. And also this fact that there is nobody else that you ask. . . . In a way it was very symbolic of their experience of the universe, their experience of the environment, and their relationship between environment and their own relationships within that environment.[17]

"Shining Star" sung by Žabe i Babe.

Tragically, due to the war in Bosnia, the Highlanders studied by Mirjana Laušević had their villages destroyed in 1992 and had to be resettled. Therefore, the material presented here is now of historical value.

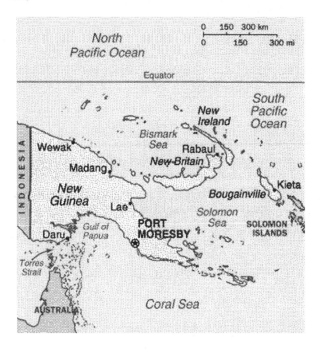

Australia and Papua, New Guinea: Songs from the Spirit World

In some cultures, the use of sound and music represent an even closer link with the natural world, as is the case when the non-human order provides a model for music. Among aboriginal peoples in Australia, for example, traditional music and dance are an important link between humans, nature, and the supernatural or spirit world. Songs are believed to have been created and taught by the ancestors or spirits who emerged from the earth. According to Australian ethnomusicologist Stephen Wild, the ancestors are said to have propagated the world, each spirit creating and populating the landscape of its particular area. They celebrated its creation by singing and dancing. Today Australian aborigines participate in the maintenance of the land by dancing and singing songs tied to sacred geographical sites and the life of the ancestors. Songs are thought to enable performers to draw on powers from the spirits left within the soil. If the songs cease to be sung, then the land will cease to be fertile.[18]

For the Kaluli people of Papua, New Guinea, as described by ethnomusicologist Stephen Feld, birds provide melodic and textual models for human song:

> *This conceptualization of song as bird song and bird talk is only part of the overall importance of birds as an aesthetic trope. Song is inspired by thinking about birds; when performed, it is sung in a bird voice; men wear bird feathers to make themselves beautiful and evocative; dance is patterned as bird movements. . . .*[19]

The Kaluli live in a tropical rain forest, north of Mt. Bosavi on the Great Papuan Plateau, in the southern highlands province of Papua, New Guinea. They are one of four groups who refer to themselves as *Bosavi kalu* ("people of Bosavi"). The total population in the 1980s was about twelve hundred people who lived in approximately twenty communities. Residing at altitudes between 550 and 850 meters, the Kaluli both hunt and cultivate. Their physical environment within the rain forest provides a rich and multi-layered landscape and soundscape filled with many kinds of birds and animals.

Natural imagery fills the texts of songs and give the Kaluli a means for discussing their music. Feld has stated that with only one exception, Kaluli terminology for melodic contours and intervals derives from waterfall terms.[20] Texts are like topographical maps built up through concrete references to places well known to the village, including mountains, streams, waterfalls, rivers, and trees.[21]

Bird sounds embody much of the way Kaluli identify with their environment. Listening to birds is a way of determining time, space, seasons, and weather. Bird songs metaphorize Kaluli feelings and sentiments because birds represent the spirits of those who have died. Birds are also believed to give songs to the Kaluli who then shape what they hear:

> *Composers hear these birds' sounds in their heads and flood their inner sense with the call until it unravels into the melody of a song. These birds give them melodic form.*[22]

Songs from the Tuvan Landscape

For the Tuvans in Siberia, music is also traditionally linked to the natural and spirit world. Like the Kaluli, the Tuvans chronicle place through song texts, which give detailed descriptions of the physical environment. Ted Levin, an ethnomusicologist who has done research in Tuva, as well as arranged concert tours and recordings of Tuvan musicians in the West, discusses how these "sonic maps" personalize the landscape:

> *There are a lot of songs that are narratives of places, that create a narrative journey through some territory. . . . The songs are rich with toponyms, that is, the names of particular places. . . . Many of these songs are really little more than inventories or chronicles of travels through these places, and yet, through these simple chronicles, they create a strong sense of nostalgia.*[23]

TUVAN MUSICIANS

The Republic of Tuva is a sparsely settled region of grasslands, taiga forests, and mountain ridges about 500 miles long and 300 miles wide that lies some 2500 miles east of Moscow in southern Siberia, on the northwest border of Mongolia. The landscape is rugged, isolated, and surrounded by high mountains. Although there are cities and towns, the majority of Tuvans are still pastoral herders of sheep, yak, and reindeer. According to Levin, music is not organized into genres or styles that are shared by a common community. Rather the music has a very individualized performance tradition which is the result of the pastoral lifestyle. People spend a lot of time alone with their livestock, consequently, there are many songs about animals:

There are songs that are used to domesticate a newborn young animal to take the milk from its mother. There are songs that a reindeer herder sings to the reindeer. There are many kinds of chants that are used during the hunt, both to pray to the spirits of the animals that are being hunted and to try to summon those animals to the hunt.[24]

Horses also play a central role in Tuvan life. The Tuvans learn to ride at an early age and they use horses for herding and transportation. Musicians say that the rhythm of music is filled with the rhythm of horses. Their significance is also reflected in other aspects of musical practice. The *igil*, a two stringed fiddle, is made primarily from the horse: the strings are made from horse gut, the skin covering the top of the fiddle is horse skin, the bow is strung with horse hair, and a wooden head of a horse is placed on top of the instrument:

Generically it's called a horse head fiddle. And in fact, a lot of the music that's performed on that instrument is about horses. There are legends and stories about horses that imitate the sounds of horses, so that any Tuvan listener who hears the music can follow the story. It's not a story that is performed with words, but through the melody itself. And a Tuvan listening to that story responds emotionally at the proper time, and it's very common for people to weep if they hear those melodies because they're sad stories.[25]

The Tuvans use imitation of natural sounds, including animal, insect, and water sounds as a basis for their music making. In some cases, they try to imitate the sounds as literally as possible, a technique that Levin called "iconic imitation." In other styles, they use natural sounds as inspiration for a less literal and more imaginative interpretation. Levin believes that throat singing or overtone singing is a result of the Tuvans' search to imaginatively use vocal production to imitate the sounds of nature.

Known as *khoomei* in Tuva, throat singing involves a single vocalist who is able to produce two (and occasionally three) distinct notes at the same time. By adjusting the shape and movement of the lips, tongue, mouth, and larynx, singers can produce one or two overtones as well as the fundamental

Tuvan singer imitating a dog.

pitch. As stated earlier, we normally hear only one fundamental frequency, while other overtones or harmonics serve to "color" the sound, but in throat singing, the overtones can actually be louder than the fundamental. This practice is discussed in more detail in Chapter 7.

Tuvan throat singing in a cave.

Traditional Tuvan music, like Tuvan culture in general, is in a period of change after the break up of the Soviet Union. Tuva was a feudal kingdom under the Manchus in the last century, but by 1921, became a socialist republic known as Tanna-Tuva that was drawn into the orbit of the Soviet Union. In 1944, it officially became part of the Soviet Union, and according to Ted Levin, it was not only drawn in politically, but also culturally:

> *The kind of European models of cultural life that were important to Soviet cultural strategists were imposed on Tuva from the outside. And so the kind of traditional performance life, wherein people really perform for themselves and the spirits of the natural world was replaced by orchestras of folk instruments and choirs and singing in harmony, which is something the Tuvans had never known. It was almost always either a solo tradition or people singing in unison.[26]*

This situation lasted until 1991 with the breakup of the Soviet Union. Tuva was then no longer just a pastoral herding culture, but one with towns and a city of sixty thousand. It was at this time that young Tuvan musicians began to try to recover their musical roots and their own identity. Many are now actively keeping alive old styles and learning from older Tuvans who remember music that is no longer performed. Levin is an active proponent of this work, which he describes as partly empirical, partly intuitive, partly recreated, and strongly linked to the physical environment. He says that music is really the icon of the relationship between the Tuvans and their land:

> *And so by helping them recover that music which was such an important medium of communication and of identification and emplacement of the land, I hope and I think my Tuvan friends and co-work-*

TUVAN MUSICIAN

ers hope that they can really give something back and infuse that culture with a new sense of what it had and perhaps what it lost.[27]

As we have seen in the examples above, nature can have an enormous impact on all aspects of daily life, including artistic expression, in traditional rural and pastoral societies. However, even in complex industrialized and urban cultures, the natural world often serves as a source of inspiration for musicians, even though their actual physical environment may be completely separated from the rhythms of rural or pastoral life. In the North Indian classical tradition, for example, many ragas are based on the seasons and texts use natural imagery to express emotion. In Afghanistan, performers of classical music sometimes like to bring caged birds on stage. Ethnomusicologist John Baily states, "the sound of music plus the singing of birds responding to it constitutes the height of musical enjoyment."[28]

Composers in the Western classical tradition have imitated and interpreted nature in numerous orchestral and choral works. Antonio Vivaldi's famous *The Four Seasons* is an early example of music meant to evoke the rhythms and sounds of nature. In *Spring,* the first of the four concerti, he imitates bird song, breezes, gentle streams, and thunder. Many works inspired by nature and man's relationship with the natural world followed, including Franz Joseph Haydn's oratorio *The Seasons*, Ludwig von Beethoven's Sixth Symphony *(Pastoral)*, Claude Debussy's *La Mer* (The Sea), and Igor Stravinsky's *The Rite of Spring*.

▬ MUSIC IN URBAN ENVIRONMENTS

The urban landscape is a complex site for music making. Whether on a street at a festival, parade, or political rally, or indoors in a living room, concert hall, or recording studio, music and musicians are highly influenced both by the physical space and the social environment in which they are situated.

The influence of particular urban cultures has often been noted by historians of Western classical music. Cities like Vienna, Paris, and Florence seem to have played roles almost as important as those of the composers and musicians who flourished there. Some Western cities have become centers for popular musics as well. In various developments, cities like Detroit, Nashville, and Liverpool have become famous for their "sound," spawning widespread transformations of popular music around the world.

But cities, including non-Western ones, have a more far-reaching influence on musical development than just the nurturing of certain professional practices. As the American ethnomusicologist Bruno Nettl has pointed out, a city can be seen as involving an overall musical system. It is not difficult to see the operation of a musical system in a small village. One can investigate all of the music made there, identifying basic elements of indigenous music making, influences from outside, and so on. This becomes a challenge when dealing with a large city: "the musical 'system' of a city is far more complex, defying quick comprehension."[29]

It is not simply the size of the city which makes it a different musical environment from the village—it is also the diversity of cultural elements. In his landmark collection of essays, Nettl described this difference:

What is it that sets urban musical culture off from that of villages, small towns, and nomadic life? It is wealth, power, education; it is the interaction of different and diverse population groups, rich and poor, majority and minorities, recent migrant and long-standing urbanite; it is the ease of rapid communication, the mass media, literacy; it is crowding and enormous divergencies in living standards and styles. Translated into musical culture, it is in many cases—though by no means in all cities for all repertories—the patronage of wealthy aristocrats and of government agencies. It is the specialization of the professional musician. . . . Perhaps most of all, it is the coming together of different musical styles and genres from many sources.[30]

As Nettl noted, such features are not absent from non-urban cultures, "but the frequency with which they occur in the countryside is low in comparison with what is almost an inevitability of these characteristics in the city."[31]

Urban mixing of local and external musical practices has resulted in many new genres. In the United States, for example, rural Appalachian music—once derided as "hillbilly"—was fashioned in big cities like Nashville into the vastly popular genre now known as "country" music. Blues, the music of poor southern African Americans, developed in cities like Chicago into an urban sound which became the basis for the rhythm & blues of Detroit and other cities, eventually spawning the multifaceted world of today's rock music. Many other developments have also arisen from urban-based mixtures, such as the blending of jazz and east European folk musics now known as "klezmer" music, the combination of jazz with Latin American musics now called "salsa," and so on.

Such musical mixtures may be characterized as *syncretic.* Syncretic musics involve blending congenial elements from different cultures, producing hybrid forms. This practice, known as *syncretism,* is a driving force in cultural developments in any situation where different cultures meet. But again, such processes are accelerated in urban environments where people of various cultural backgrounds find themselves living and working together. Indeed, syncretism can be a way of expressing and celebrating this fact of urban life.

At the same time, the cultural diversity of cities can encourage a choice to guard one's cultural identity carefully, avoiding fusions with other musics. In some cases, traditions become more conservative in the city than they were in their former home. Nettl described such a situation among Poles who immigrated to U.S. cities in the late nineteenth and early twentieth centuries. "The Poles learned the music of other groups around them, both rural and urban. But for a time they also retained their traditional Polish folk music and indeed tried to keep it from mixing with other musics, holding it intact in stable forms while their kith and kin in Poland accepted change more readily."[32]

Particular forces are in play in the music-cultures of non-Western cities; Nettl usefully differentiated two of these as "Westernization" and "modernization." "If Westernization is the process whereby a music becomes Western through the accretion of Western elements, modernization is the process whereby, through similar additions, a music retains its traditional essence but becomes modern—that is, part of the contemporary world and its set of values."[33] The development of *jùjú* music in Lagos, the capital city of Nigeria, can be seen as an illustration of both processes in succeeding stages.[34]

The first stage, roughly in the 1930s and 1940s, involved Westernization. Jùjú trios and quartets used Western instruments like the guitar and banjo, and vocal harmonies gleaned from Christian musical practices, to entertain their cosmopolitan audiences. This music was not simply an imitation of Western genres—the groups also used traditional Nigerian hand percussion instruments, and sang in local languages (usually Yoruba, the language of the dominant ethnic group). Still, in many ways this was a conscious Westernization of Yoruba music, a syncretic way of putting their music into a Western frame.

In the second stage, roughly from the 1950s onward, jùjú became a social dance music with much larger groups and a more traditionally Yoruba orientation. The advent of electronic amplification made it possible to include the Yoruba "talking drums," which would have drowned out acoustic instruments. Traditional principles of Yoruba praise singing and drumming were brought to bear on the musical organization. This syncretic development was less of a Westernization and more of a modernization of the music. While the amplification technology was of Western provenance, the overall musical transformation involved going deeper into traditional Yoruba practices, adapting them to a modern context.

Cities are well known for their concert halls, nightclubs, and other privately-owned musical venues. Another quintessentially urban musical environment is the street itself. For a glimpse of the influence of this kind of context on musical performance and development, we will turn to some examples from New York City.

Modern Minstrels

The idea of street music may be as old as that of the city itself. Street performers plied their trade in the cities of ancient Greece and Egypt, supported by whatever voluntary donations they could generate.[35] Such musicians have thrived for centuries in urban environments throughout the world.

The cities of medieval Europe were host to varying forms of street music, from the *Gauklers* of Germany to the *jongleurs* of France. Throughout Europe, *minstrels*—singers and poets who performed old and new songs on the city streets, often turning out songs for hire—also sang songs of social commentary. As Patricia Campbell has noted, their lives often depended on the whims of those in power. "The common folk loved them and welcomed the glimpse of magic they brought to their grim lives, but the nobles feared such free spirits and regularly persecuted, jailed, and burned them—although they first chose the best for their own households."[36] Unattached minstrels sometimes moved from town to town, providing cross-fertilization of various local styles and participating in the kind of cultural blending which characterizes so much of urban music.

The minstrel tradition has continued throughout history, spreading naturally to the urban environments of the Americas. Since 1970, when Mayor John Lindsay abolished licensing requirements, New York City has become known as one of the more open American cities for street musicians. "During their lunch hour, young professionals gather around Andean and jazz bands in Liberty Park in the Wall Street area," notes American social activist Susie Tanenbaum. "On weekends, young people looking for entertainment with an "edge" congregate in Washington Square Park. Theater and moviegoers cheer breakdancers and standup comics while waiting on line along Broadway in Times Square."[37]

These are comparatively specialized places and audiences. By contrast, music in New York's subway is performed "in an interconnected space traveled by an exceptionally heterogeneous population."[38] This underground rapid transit system, the largest in the world, provides a unique environment for musical experience.

> *The acoustics underground, for example, accommodate both intimate and scattered audience circles. And the labyrinthine structure of such stations as Times Square leads to surprise encounters with musicians. . . . Yet it is also a space that demands a considerable amount of standing and waiting. Perhaps it is in this respect that subway music most differs from street performing. It makes the waiting easier for many riders. It relieves their anxieties and even gives them a feeling of safety in their dismal surroundings.[39]*

Like the minstrels before them, New York's street and subway musicians live to some extent according to official whim. Since the mid-1980s, subway venues have been controlled by Music Under New York, a program affiliated with the Transit Authority's "beautification" efforts, which screens musicians and designates performance spaces and times. Some kinds of music receive more favorable treatment from this program than others, leading to a feeling of an official sponsorship/censorship situation.

Street music above ground is similarly endangered. "Decades after Mayor Lindsay abolished street music licenses," Tanenbaum wrote, "city agencies and private sponsors are attempting to contain unsponsored musicians by regulating them, managing them, and replacing them with official events."[40] Still, as one of Tanenbaum's informants noted, their situation is not entirely as perilous as that of their predecessors:

> *. . . I found him at our appointed meeting place, sitting on a station bench with his head in his hands. He held out a yellow piece of paper—a summons for using an amplifier on a subway platform. The fine was fifty-five dollars. A moment later, though, he bounced back, as he does when he performs. "Do you know what the equivalent would have been in the tenth century?" he asked me. "Decapitation?" I'd learned my lesson. "Or flogging," he concurred.[41]*

Also like their itinerant ancestors, these street and subway musicians perform for whoever happens by; any sense of community they create is fleeting. But some kinds of street performances have a great deal to do with place and community. Rap, for example, developed in New York as a local street-music response to a disastrous consequence of urban planning.

Rap Music and Urban "Renewal"

In 1959, work was begun on the Cross Bronx Expressway, designed by the prestigious city planner Robert Moses. Slicing through the Bronx to connect Long Island and New Jersey, the project was instituted to benefit commerce and commuters—not the working-class ethnic communities which happened to lie in its path. Under Moses's convenient "Slum Clearance" program, about 60,000 Bronx homes were demolished, uprooting some 170,000 people. As the American scholar Tricia Rose has pointed out, "These 'slums' were in fact densely populated stable neighborhoods. . . . Although the neighborhoods under attack had a substantial Jewish population, black and Puerto Rican residents were disproportionately affected. . . . The newly 'relocated' black and Hispanic residents in the South Bronx were left with few city resources, fragmented leadership, and limited political power."[42]

Their situation worsened. Like many American cities, New York experienced a decline in social services and employment in the 1970s. Virtually bankrupt in 1975, the city applied for a federal bailout; President Ford's refusal prompted the celebrated *Daily News* headline, "Ford to New York: Drop Dead." Poor African-Americans and Hispanics in the South Bronx were among the hardest hit by the deteriorating economic situation. Many businesses moved elsewhere, as did most residents who could afford to.

The devastated South Bronx became a political and mass-media symbol of urban blight. Outsiders considered it a cultural nightmare, and its residents were seen as lost, lawless, and barbarous. But, as Rose noted, "Although the city leaders and the popular press had literally and figuratively condemned the South Bronx neighborhoods and their inhabitants, the youngest black and Hispanic residents answered back."[43]

Their answer was *hip hop,* a cultural movement which was manifested in many aspects of life—dress, speech, graffiti writing, breakdancing, formation of alternative families known as crews or posses, and a musical genre called *rap.* This cultural movement was rooted in the local urban environment:

> *Hip hop replicates and reimagines the experiences of urban life and symbolically appropriates urban space through sampling, attitude, dance, style, and sound effects. Talk of subways, crews and posses, urban noise, economic stagnation, static and crossed signals leap out of hip hop lyrics, sounds, and themes. Graffiti artists spraypainted murals and (name) "tags" on trains, trucks, and playgrounds, claiming territories and inscribing their otherwise contained identities on public property. Early breakdancers' elaborate technologically inspired street corner dances involving head spins on concrete sidewalks made the streets theatrically friendly and served as makeshift youth centers.*

> *. . . DJs who initiated spontaneous street parties by attaching customized, makeshift turntables and speakers to street light electrical sources revised the use of central thoroughfares, made "open-air" community centers in neighborhoods where there were none. Rappers seized and used microphones as if amplification was a lifegiving force. Hip hop gives voice to the tensions and contradictions in the public urban landscape during a period of substantial transformation in New York and attempts to seize the shifting urban terrain, to make it work on behalf of the dispossessed.*[44]

Rap lyrics, often articulate the difficulty of urban life, not as a doleful lament, but as a defiant affirmation of the ability to survive the harsh realities of the city. Declaiming their rhymes over powerful beats, sampled noises, and occasional interpolations of other musics, rappers address the social issues which arise from their place in the world, from lighthearted sexual posturing to dark ruminations on gang warfare.

Although today rap is performed to huge audiences in vast public venues, it retains its crucial sense of place. In other cities, local styles have evolved which reflect their own particular environments. And increasingly, individualized local rap styles are developing throughout the world, mirroring even non-Western urban environments.

The City and Beyond

Like rap, other urban popular music genres characteristically retain their sense of place even when marketed and distributed all over the world. As cultural music theorist George Lipsitz articulates, popular music—from reggae to Aboriginal rock—has local meaning emerging from concrete historical experiences, political struggle, and insider knowledge. It also has the power to transcend geographical boundaries and local social issues, creating new meanings for consumers who may be completely unaware of the original intent of the musicians:

> *A poetics of place permeates popular music, shaping significantly its contexts of production, distribution, and reception. New Orleans jazz and sambas from São Paulo circulate freely throughout the world, but they never completely lose their concerns and cultural qualities that give them determinate shape in their place of origin. . . . Like other forms of contemporary mass communication, popular music simultaneously undermines and reinforces our sense of place. . . . Throughout the conduits of commercial culture, music made by aggrieved inner-city populations in Canberra, Kingston, or Compton becomes part of everyday life and culture for affluent consumers in the suburbs of Cleveland, Coventry, or Cologne.*[45]

With recording technology and global marketing, music can serve as an important means of cross cultural communication. Urban technologies have given us both syncretic musical forms and access to music from all over the globe. But divorced from its own environment, music is often appropriated, appreciated, and understood differently by cultural outsiders. One of the consequences of this intercultural exchange is the creation of new settings and new environments for musical performance and reception which in turn gives music altered meaning.

▆▆▆ CHAPTER SUMMARY

We can analyze music on many levels, beginning with the laws of acoustics. The frequency, amplitude, duration, and timbre of sound waves, acting upon our eardrums, give us music. But in order to have meaning, these patterns of organized sound must communicate with and affect those within its sphere. Music is experiential for both performers and listeners. As Anthony Seeger suggests, "Music is an emotion that accompanies the production of, the appreciation of, and the participation in a performance."[46]

Our approach is not to study music in isolation, but rather in the context of the culture in which it lives. As we have seen, music in both urban and non-urban settings is very much linked to a sense of place. In rural or pastoral cultures, the physical environment greatly impacts musical practices. Cities are inevitably more complex sites for the performance and reception of music, but place is still a vital component. In Chapter 2, we will explore further the relationship between music and culture by focusing on the power of music.

STUDY QUESTIONS

1. Describe how music is both like language and food.

2. When thinking about the musical properties of sound, what are the four important parameters of sound waves?

3. What is the overtone series?

4. What are some of the ways music relates to both the social and physical environment in Bosnian Highlander culture?

5. What role does the horse play in the traditional music of Tuva?

6. Describe the term "syncretism" and give one example of a syncretic musical style.

REFERENCED SOURCES

1. Seeger, 1992: xiv.
2. Ibid.
3. Lausevic, interview, 1997.
4. Redman, interview 1997.
5. Slobin, interview 1997.
6. Shapiro, interview 1997.
7. Ibid.
8. Rice, 1994: 8.
9. Slobin, interview 1997.
10. Brown, interview 1997.
11. Ibid.
12. Vander 1988: 22.
13. Lausevic, interview 1997.
14. Ibid.
15. Ibid.
16. Ibid.
17. Ibid.
18. Wild, interview 1997.
19. Feld, 1982: 220.
20. Ibid: 168.
21. Ibid: 191–94.
22. Ibid: 82.
23. Levin, interview 1997.
24. Ibid.
25. Ibid.
26. Ibid.
27. Ibid.
28. Baily, 1997: 56.
29. Nettl, 1978: 8.
30. Ibid: 6.
31. Ibid.
32. Ibid: 9.
33. Ibid.: 10.
34. Waterman, 1990.
35. Campbell, 1981: 9.
36. Ibid: 10.
37. Tanenbaum, 1995: 234.
38. Ibid.
39. Ibid.: 15.
40. Ibid.: 238.
41. Ibid.: 80.
42. Rose, 1994: 31–2.
43. Ibid.: 34.
44. Ibid.: 22.
45. Lipsitz, 1994: 4.
46. Seeger, 1992: xiv.

CHAPTER 2

THE TRANSFORMATIVE POWER OF MUSIC

About This Chapter

This chapter explores the extraordinary power of music as a component of culture. Music from many traditions will be studied in relation to religion, ritual, work, play, and politics. Music is not only an important means of social expression that gives rise to emotions, memories, and pleasure, but it also facilitates transformation on many levels.

KEYWORDS

culture
ethnomusicology
ritual
topical
vocable

COMPANION RESOURCES

TELEVISION PROGRAM: The Transformative Power of Music

AUDIO SELECTIONS:

4. "The Tramp" by Joe Hill.
5. "We Shall Overcome" sung by the SNCC Freedom Singers

Music moves people. It may move them physically, inspiring them to dance or sing; it may also move them inwardly, inducing a heightened state of consciousness. As an invisible force, music can circumvent the rational mind and penetrate the heart, kindling the emotions. It can inspire troops in battle, and rally social forces. It can coordinate and hearten workers. It can be a catalyst for healing. It can bring people together in profound ways, focusing their attention and feelings in a communal experience, reinforcing their connections to each other, perhaps even serving as a bridge to unseen worlds. It can lead one inward, to a meditative experience. It can animate and entertain in times of pleasure, soothe frayed nerves, or lull an infant to sleep.

In all cases, the power of music lies in its connections to other aspects of culture. The idea that music constitutes a "universal language" is an attractive one, but although music's nonverbal communication may reach across linguistic borders, its full power is reserved for those who share its primary cultural context. When we respond to other people's music, our response exists within the framework of our own culture, not theirs.

What is culture? *Culture* may be described as a group's shared ways of experiencing, participating in, and making sense out of their world. In addition to the arts, culture includes languages, religions, belief systems, social organizations, necessary skills, and everyday habits. While ultimately culture is constructed and continually reconfigured by individuals, it is an idea which refers to a group, a community, or a "people." Such collective ways of doing and being are interlinked in complex systems within individual consciousnesses—systems which are far from being fully mapped by researchers. But still, cultures are evident and mighty forces which make it possible for people to live together. They also differentiate groups, in much more useful ways than mere racial features can. According to ethnomusicologist Jeff Titon, "Culture, rather than biological inheritance, accounts for why these people over here think and act differently from those over there."[1]

Ethnomusicologists are scholars who study music in relation to culture. They have construed their occupation in various ways over the years. Alan Merriam defined *ethnomusicology* as "the study of music in culture" in 1960, adjusting this formulation in 1973 to "the study of music as culture."[2] Jeff Titon proposed a different perspective, characterizing ethnomusicology's objective as "knowing people making music."[3] All three definitions have something to offer: the first points to the idea that music is one of the many interlinked elements of culture, the second indicates that music also embodies culture, and the third reminds us that for all its analytical usefulness the concept of culture is still an abstraction. Ultimately we are concerned with what actual people do. However one may conceptualize ethnomusicology, one thing is clear: it is a field of inquiry which approaches music not as a thing in itself, but in its connections to humans and the cultures they construct and experience. It affirms the precept that musical power is intimately involved with human relationships. Individually and collectively, people move music.

Ritual and Aesthetic Power

A musical performance, including the playback of a recording, is situated in time and space. A casual awareness of inconspicuous background music is a valid musical experience, but it is seldom a powerful one, though it may be shown to increase sales by subliminally relaxing shoppers. Usually musical power involves some kind of relationship to ritual.

Rituals, defined broadly, are recurring functional activities that focus minds and energies through their formal repetitiveness, reinforcing feelings and actions which are valued by the individual and community. In common usage, ritual often refers to life-cycle events and religious ceremonies; but the same concept can apply to a wide range of human activities. We can think of ritual as a kind of continuum, running from mundane practices at one end to quite extraordinary ones at the other.

We all have daily rituals, and some of them may include music: washing dishes, preparing meals, working out, or traveling to work or school are examples of structured everyday activities, which for some people involve music—sung, whistled, or hummed, or reproduced electronically. Although we may not think of music in such contexts as "powerful," the fact that so many people own radios and stereos—including portable sets with headphones—indicates that music in daily rituals is important to them. Moving along the continuum, we start to find rituals that have more specific musical repertories, and more powerful experiences. Social dances and weekly religious ceremonies are instances of more specialized and affecting rituals involving music.

TRADITIONAL GREEK WEDDING

Continuing in this direction, we may consider rituals that mark specific yearly occasions. Many cultures have special musical repertories for such seasonal festivities—Christmas, for example, possesses a large body of specialized music, a repertory which runs a gamut from lighthearted children's songs to monumental religious works. Rituals that occur less often, and may provide an even deeper experience, honor landmarks in a life cycle. Weddings, for example, are singularly important life cycle events in many cultures, and they usually involve specific musical repertories, which may even apply to individual subsections of the overall ritual. The musical "bride's lament" is an integral part of many Eastern European wedding celebrations.

Finally, in some cultures rituals may even mark events which are less frequent than a single person's life cycle. In Bali, for example, the great temple ceremony of Eka Desa Rudra is celebrated once every 100 years. No one experiences this ceremony twice. It is considered a ritual of supreme power, and music plays a significant role in the proceedings.

Music also involves aesthetic power. Different emotions can be aroused by music which is stormy and thundering or soothing and peaceful. Bodies can be stirred by infectious rhythms and sensuous sonorities. In many cultures, the ultimate aesthetic experience is one of sublime beauty, which can be uniquely expressed through the limitless abstractions of musical sound. Music can bring beauty to an experience of the divine, or to our everyday world.

In many cultures, an explicit connection is made between aesthetic beauty and ritual effectiveness. Further, the experience of aesthetic beauty in a ritual context may be seen as a way of bringing a proper balance to the world or universe. "Not only are the Balinese gods and deities notorious connoisseurs of the arts, appreciating both embellishment and minute aesthetic detail," writes Edward Herbst, "but also, physical interaction or activity within any environment or space seeks a flow and balanced ordering, an equilibrium that is appreciated as an aesthetic property, sensually, formally, and psychologically."[4]

Some other cultures articulate this aesthetic connection between ritual and the world explicitly. For example, "the Navaho culture includes the concept of *hózhóó* (beauty, blessedness, harmony) which must be maintained, and which, if lost, can be restored by means of ritual"[5] (see also the BaMbuti example below). And as we will see, many other cultures express this idea implicitly, in the ways aesthetic elements—often music in particular—are central to the effectiveness of ritual.

But music, culture, and ritual are all abstract concepts. In the end, music's capacity to move is generated by people, as Titon's formulation confirms.

Very generally, we may consider two ways that people create musical power: through the personal dynamism of an individual, and through the collective energy of a group. A few examples of each will provide a basis for a deeper examination of the potential power of music.

Personal Power

In Ireland and the Irish Diaspora, a particular kind of informal gathering is called a *céilí*. The Irish musician Robin Morton characterized a typical céilí as "a gathering of neighbors in one of their houses, usually in the evening. Often the purpose is simply to exchange local gossip. However, it might easily, and often does, develop into a session of singing, dancing, and storytelling."[6] Such events may occur in pubs as well—what the American folklorist Henry Glassie has called "a céilí in public."[7] Wherever a céilí may take place, it is a situation of fellowship, trust, and intimacy, reaffirming bonds between daily associates, allowing connections of the heart as well as those of the mundane world.

In its confirmation and nourishment of human closeness, the céilí provides a congenial situation for a particular sort of musical power. Moments of deep musical communication may be furnished by musicians who possess a special quality of performance. The Irish singer Joe Heaney recalled that "the old people" of his youth referred to this quality as the *neá:*

> *The old people—oh, honest to God, I mean—in the small places, the country, Gaelic-speaking areas, almost everybody had the neá. You know the first time someone starts singing a song, you know has he got it, or does he not. . . . It means an awful lot. He has the right stuff: he has the neá. It's more than singing, it's more than being able to do a thing, or something. He's doing it the* right *way. You can't go above or below the neá; it's just—it's out on its own.*[8]

A similar concept, *conyach,* is found among some Scottish ballad singers, as recalled by Belle Stewart:

> *Several people could sing the same song, but—we had a something that we called a conyach. And a conyach in a ballad is a feeling. You could sit listening to several people, maybe singing the same ballad, and it didn't do a thing to you, and suddenly someone with a conyach would get up and sing the same ballad, and—God, you were just living it, I mean the—it was something entirely different altogether.*[9]

In the performance of jazz, audiences and fellow musicians are often drawn to individual performers whose personal energies are particularly compelling. Miles Davis was such a musician: his idiosyncratic style and presence were legendary. In an interview with Paul Berliner, trumpeter Lonnie Hillyer recalled a time when he was a "kid back in Detroit" that Davis played for a dance:

> *At one point, people were dancing, and he started to play a ballad. The people just stopped dancing and crowded all around him, listening to this cat play this ballad. You know? Miles STOPPED people from dancing, and I'll never forget that as long as I live. That's mood. And of course, Miles can also make people dance when he wants to.*[10]

Musicians possessing extraordinary personal power and technical prowess may be considered to be in league with supernatural powers. The phenomenal early blues musician Robert Johnson cultivated the notion that he had received his impressive musical abilities through a pact with the Devil, and many people who heard him believed it. The nineteenth-century virtuoso violinist Niccolo Paganini was rumored to have made a similar bargain, as was the pianist Franz Liszt. While the following contemporary account of one of Liszt's performances in Vienna in 1838 dismisses this idea, it attests to his uniquely powerful presence:

> We have now heard him, the strange wonder, whom the superstition of past ages, possessed by the delusion that such things could never be done without the help of the Evil One, would undoubtedly have condemned without mercy to the stake. . . . Just look at the pale, slender youth in his clothes that signal the nonconformist; the long, sleek, drooping hair, the thin arms, the small, delicately formed hands; the almost gloomy and yet childlike pleasant face—those features so strongly stamped and full of meaning . . . through a technique cultivated to the point of perfection, through a touch which he is capable of shading through all conceivable degrees, from the softest breath to the most overwhelming thunderstorm, he brings forth the most stupendous effects; yes, even effects of detail which one would not think of expecting of the instrument . . . his lavishly expended energies seemed steadily to augment, and the flood of tones poured forth in one stream, yet never at the cost of intelligibility, to the last chord, with which were mingled cheers of acclamation that threatened never to end, and for which the expression "enthusiastic" is only an empty unmeaning sound . . . such a tribute of recognition must have affected the virtuoso deeply, accustomed as he was to homage [in France and England], for hot tears rolled down his cheeks.[11]

Group Energies

While many performance situations involve some kind of leader, sometimes the primary source of musical power is group interaction. When people come together for a particular occasion, their individual energies can coalesce into a cumulative force. Political conviction, religious fervor, or just the pleasure of singing and dancing are all possible catalysts for powerful group energies.

Céilís, ballad sessions, and concerts are—in varying degrees—formalized rituals: they involve people congregating at a specific time and place for a specific event. Sometimes informal situations can be transformed into experiences of musical power by the compatible energies of those present. Yvonne Daniel described the aftermath of a formal rumba performance in Cuba, which was followed by a house party:

> By late evening (around ten or later), a small group was singing in harmony, using tabletops and the walls of the house as drums and a couple of spoons as claves. The song lyrics were descriptive of the wonderful time the day had been and the nostalgia for remembered festive times of the past. Gradually the tempo shifted and dancing with real drums in addition to the cajón organization began. There was no set circle around a drum battery, and people danced as

couples, freely, sometimes observing the rules of rumba, sometimes ignoring them to dance improvisationally.[12]

Spontaneous performances of group vocal forms like *ganga* among Bosnian Highlanders can also involve interactive power. For men, the singing is a good-natured male hierarchical contest, as Mirjana Lausevic explains:

When the group of men starts to sing, there will be a leader who will start the song. . . . And then the group will come in. Often what men do is a lot of men will join in. But the singer who has started the song, he needs to out-sing the rest of them. He needs to show his own strength, his physical strength that is demonstrated through the strength in the voice, through the volume of the voice, through the length of the breath. And it's often a game, how many people you can actually out-sing. And then there will be another singer who will say, "Oh, I can do this better, you know." So he will out-sing more singers at the same time.[13]

For Bosnian women, impromptu group singing may generate a different kind of collective power:

Women particularly will point out the fact that music enables a relief of burden, a relief of all the pains and sufferings that they experience in daily life. And it creates a space in which one can indulge in this pain . . . or joy at the same time, that you're not really able to dwell on in your daily duties or in your daily life.[14]

Such informal musical rituals have a special quality: the unceremonious atmosphere can impart feelings of freedom and immediacy, which are not necessarily found in more structured situations. But formal musical gatherings can provide for other kinds of powerful experiences. John Blacking explained the performance of *tshikona*—a music and dance form that requires a minimum of twenty-four participants, each playing a different part—among the Venda of South Africa:

The music of tshikona *expresses the value of the largest social group to which a Venda can really feel he belongs. Its performance involves the largest number of people, and its music incorporates the largest number of tones in any single piece of Venda music involving more than one or two players. . . . Tshikona is valuable and beautiful to the Venda, not only because of the quantity of people and tones involved, but because of the quality of relationships that must be established between people and tones whenever it is performed. . . . The effectiveness of* tshikona *is not a case of MORE = BETTER: it is an example of the production of the maximum of available human energy in a situation that generates the highest degree of individuality in the largest possible community of individuals. Tshikona provides an experience of the best of all possible worlds, and the Venda are fully aware of its value. Tshikona, they say, is Iwa-ha-masia-khali-i-tshi-vhila, "the time when people rush to the scene of the dance and leave their pots to boil over." Tshikona "makes sick people feel better, and old men throw away their sticks and dance." Tshikona "brings peace to the countryside."*[15]

The basic elements of this depiction of social value and musical power could be applied to situations in other cultures. For example, a performance of a nineteenth-century European opera with a symphony orchestra, chorus, and soloists could also be seen as involving "the largest number of people" and "the largest number of tones" in its genre. It may be considered by its audience to be an unrivaled experience of musical power.

Further, both opera and tshikona derive a portion of their power from their enactment of each society's ideal social situation. In the comparatively egalitarian culture of the Venda, each person plays their own equally important role, just as the tshikona musicians each have different, crucially-interconnected instrumental parts. An opera in Western culture also involves individuals playing and singing their own parts, but in addition it requires strings and voices performing in sections enacting the value of teamwork, a conductor exemplifying an ideal of a skillful and admirable manager, and a composer as enlightened lawmaker and leader. Throughout the world, a fundamental element of the power of music-making involves the ways that musical structure and performance reflect important cultural ideals of social organization and interaction while they simultaneously furnish a vital engagement with human emotions.

In addition to affirming human values, group music-making may be experienced as a vital link to the unseen, supernatural, or divine. An elder of the BaMbuti pygmies explained their *molimo* ritual—in which men of the tribe sing around a fire late into the night for several nights in a row—to Colin Turnbull:

> *The forest is a father and mother to us, and like a father or mother it gives us everything we need—food, clothing, shelter, warmth . . . and affection. . . . Normally everything goes well in our world. But at night when we are sleeping, sometimes things go wrong, because we are not awake to stop them from going wrong. . . . So when something big goes wrong, like illness or bad hunting or death, it must be because the forest is sleeping and not looking after its children. So what do we do? We wake it up. We wake it up by singing to it, and we do this because we want it to awaken happy. Then everything will be well and good again. So when our world is going well then also we sing to the forest because we want it to share our happiness.*[16]

Whether it is generated by individual or group energies, musical power derives from the dynamic enactment of valuable human relationships within community. While there is much basis for cross-cultural comparisons, ultimately the association of music with social values, rituals, and traditions is imbedded in specific cultures. From the following examples we gain further understanding of how the power of music is invoked in various cultural contexts.

▬ MUSIC AND THE CREATION OF COMMUNITY

The power of music itself can become the catalyst for forming community. Performances are events marked off from everyday life that combine ordinary and extraordinary social experience and expression. All live performance draws the participants—performers and audience—into a shared experience that creates a temporary community. While music provides neither the mate-

RUSTED ROOT

**JIM
DISPIRITO**

**JOHN
BUYNAK**

**JIM
DONOVAN**

LIZ BERLIN

**MICHAEL
GLABICKI**

rial nor the energy for creating community, it provides an environment in which those elements can work. The social bonding that results often extends beyond the performance itself. There are many such examples in the realm of popular music where fans create networks, friendships, and even fashions based around a band, individual performer, or musical style. Jim DiSpirito, a member of the rock band Rusted Root, describes the kind of community formed around his band:

> *I think that the event for the audience is as important as the music that is being performed on stage. . . . The event is much broader than the musicians standing on stage because people come to a Rusted Root show to meet each other again. They've seen each other at a variety of shows down the road and there's a particular kinship with the people in the audience from trading tapes through just hanging out. There is that sense of community in our live performances because so many people come to multiple shows.[17]*

While the overall event is an important context for socializing and for forming friendships, it is still the music itself that initially brings people together and keeps them coming back for more. DiSpirito describes this phenomenon as an interaction between performers and audience members who almost always dance to their music:

> *Looking from the stage to the audience you can see how the sound pulls people together into a collective because they're all moving to the same pulse. You know, the music is providing something for them to move to and they're in agreement with us on stage. And somehow, we're all in this together because we're providing something musically and they are responding physically and the connection is incredibly apparent.[18]*

Fellow band member Michael Glabicki also describes Rusted Root performances as a ritual that creates a dynamic communication between performers and audience:

> *The way I visualize the performance and how it relates to the community and the ritual that we share together is that we've developed*

a song. As a group we learn to let go our understandings of ourselves . . . and that becomes a microcosm. . . . You then perform the song and try and let go of your walls and your preconceived idea of what the song was yesterday. . . . And then their (the audience's) walls start to go down; it becomes this big like "WOOH" surge of energy up through the ground. . . . You see it in people with black leather jackets on. You see it with people that come in their suits. You see it with thirteen year olds. You see it with seventy-two year olds. They all look at each other and everything is dissolved. (They have) this understanding of who we are, what music is . . . and (we're) just kind of one . . . vibration.[19]

These intense transformative experiences go counter to the "normal" routines of daily life. This atmosphere of release created through the hypnotic absorption of dancing to music occurs at live performances, as well as at clubs or parties using recorded music. The magical combination of highly rhythmic music, movement, and social interaction intensifies the moment as it heightens emotions:

One good measure of good music . . . is precisely, its "presence," its ability to stop time, to make us feel we are living within a moment, with no memory or anxiety about what has come before or what will come after. This is where the physical impact of music comes in—the use of beat, pulse, and rhythm to compel our immediate bodily involvement in an organization of time that the music itself controls. Hence the pleasure of dance and disco; clubs and parties provide a setting, a society which seems to be defined only by the time-scale of the music (beats per minute), which escapes the real time passing outside.[20]

According to DiSpirito, the power of group interaction at Rusted Root concerts is more than pleasurable; he calls it cathartic and healing for the individual, as well as collectively transformative. The combination of the familiar with the unstructured and spontaneous occurrences that happen at live performances bring people together:

I think that music provides some sort of self reflective aspect for everybody. When you get lost in a dance and you're lost in a rhythm, and you're moving, I think that it's a very healing space to be in. . . . Rusted Root's performances are very cathartic for people. I think people come to release. They've been at work all day . . . and they really come to a Rusted Root show to enjoy, to let their hair down and dance, and get around a lot of other people doing exactly the same thing. And I think there's a comfortability level in that type of environment. And I think that's very powerful . . . the environment that's created between the band and the audience provides some sort of emotional venue in which many magical moments happen.[21]

It is these magical moments sparked by musical creation and communication that keep people coming back for more, thereby creating a sense of community.

Other communities organized primarily around the expressive arts of music, dance, or theater revolve around skill and participatory experience—

everybody performs together. The members of a local orchestra or community chorus are drawn together by the activity of playing or singing, as well as by their expertise and love for what they are doing. Both are primarily non-commercial associational collectives, based on interest, affinity, and experience, rather than on more traditional notions of the bounded community—neighborhood, ethnicity, or religious affiliation. According to Mark Slobin, the transformative power of the collective musical experience creates strong fellowship:

> *Music seems to have an odd quality that even passionate activities like gardening or dog raising lack: the simultaneous projecting and dissolving of self in performance. Individual, family, gender, age . . . and other factors hover around the musical space, but can only very partially penetrate the moment of enactment of musical fellowship.*[22]

It is this moment of "musical fellowship" that kindles community and often creates deep and lasting bonds.

Contra Dance and Community

Social dance is another realm in which community flourishes—often created by experiences on the dance floor. Like the rock concert, the intensity of the event creates a temporary collective of participants bound by shared knowledge and experience. As Jane Cowan suggests in her study of dance and gender relations in the Greek Macedonian town of Sohos, the dance experience can be seen as a metaphor for community:

> *The dance metaphor can evoke the wholly positive aspects of belonging to a collectivity. To be a participant in the dance is to be in (and with) the group; it is also to be in the thick of the meanings created. . . . The dance, graphically suggesting a collectivity bound by shared knowledge, skill, and physical connection, is considered an apt metaphor for the community itself.*[23]

New England contra dance events create such a collectivity. Participation in the dance, including playing music, calling, and dancing, forms the social context through which community is created. Not only does every dance event gather a unique and complete community of its own, but through the experience of performing, participants are drawn into wider networks of communication, activity, and association that often grow and develop outside and beyond the dance. The formation of friends, bands, recordings, dance series and festivals, and the composition of new repertoire, are part of a larger context which, to a great extent, is derived from what happens experientially on the dance floor at contemporary dance events.

Contra dance originated in England before the sixteenth century and was called country dance—a generic term for group figure dances in line, square, and round formations. These dances became the most popular urban social dance genre of the eighteenth century. Exported to America, as well as throughout Europe, country dances played an important role in the expressive life of the colonists. By the mid-eighteenth century, the progressive line dances became known as contra dances. In the mid-nineteenth century, contras became less socially fashionable in urban centers as couple dances, such as the waltz and polka, became popular. It was not until the 1960s that contras emerged as a "new" genre in New England as part of the so called "folk revival."

In the 1990s, contra dance is strongly established within a subculture of participatory dance and traditional music forms throughout the United States. Dances take place on a regular basis at churches, town halls, libraries, or other halls that have good wooden floors for dancing. All dances have a live band that consists of at least two or three players, with fiddle and piano as the core instruments. The music repertory comes from a mix of Irish, Scottish, French Canadian, Cape Breton, Shetland, American, and newly composed fiddle tunes. Dances are open to the public at a nominal cost and anyone can join in without attending a class.

The dances are taught by a caller who has the dancers quickly learn and memorize the choreography as they perform a "walk through" without music. Dancers move symmetrically in two lines through choreographed figures (such as "balance and swing" or "circle left") set to tunes, each thirty-two measures in length. One time through the music equals one time through the whole dance progression, which takes approximately thirty to forty seconds to perform. Each individual dance goes on for ten to fifteen minutes, depending on the size of the crowd, so the dance progression may be repeated twenty or more times. When the dance starts with music, the caller cues the dancers until most of them have learned the dance (usually three or four times through the progression). At this point, the caller stops calling and often begins playing with the band until the last time through the dance.

Dances usually include a lot of exhilarating whirling and swinging with intense social interaction and physical exertion. Dancers not only change partners for each dance, but because most of the dances are progressive line dances in sets, dancers interact both with their partner and with all the members of the set while progressing up and down the contra line. The structured and unstructured nature of the dance event creates a setting in which many kinds of transformations occur. One dancer writes about his feelings of transformation during his first contra dance experience:

> *Barely into the dance and in the middle of a swing I realized that I was smiling like a lunatic, that my body felt light as a glider, and that every person in the room—man, woman and child—seemed radiantly beautiful.*[24]

The high degree of repetition within the performance of both the music and the dance, the predominance of fast swings within the dances, and the intensity of physical contact lead many dancers to get "hooked" on dancing. They also talk about the sense of freedom, enjoyment, involvement, challenge, relief from stress, exercise, and aesthetic pleasure they gain from dancing. David Kaynor, a musician and caller from Montague, Massachusetts, describes the buildup of emotional intensity during the course of a dance that creates moments of transcendence for both dancers and musicians:

> *You connect to some timeless stream of human experience that is sometimes promoted by doing something over and over again, almost like a mantra, you go to a different level of experience. . . . Sometimes after playing a tune twelve times, on the thirteenth time everybody will have this incredible thrill . . . all of a sudden something really powerful happens . . . it brings everybody together. It's unpredictable and fleeting. It's like an affirmation of immortal life.*[25]

The fellowship that results from these heightened experiences on the dance floor keep participants coming back for more. Many people begin as casual dancers and gradually become more involved, either in learning how to call, to play an instrument, to organize dance events, or just to dance more often. It's possible to contra dance every night of the week in some cities, such as Seattle and Boston. The image of the contra dance set composed of two lines of dancers moving in symmetrical unison is an appropriate symbol of this community created and maintained around the collective performance of music and dance.

■■■ THE POWER OF MUSIC IN WORSHIP

Embodied in rituals and belief systems, religions help people to make sense out of their universe. Religions regulate life and behavior, as well as answer questions about our relationship to the cosmos, the supernatural and the divine. Whether people worship one god, many gods, nature, spirits, or simply the highest in mankind, religions bring people together in formal ways to enact and reenact ceremonies that commemorate, celebrate, heal, and unite. Because religion is such a fundamental component of culture—linked to identity, ethnicity, customs, and politics—religions also separate people. Many wars throughout history have stemmed from passionate and violent disagreements over religious beliefs.

BUDDHIST PRIEST

Music is often an important component of religious ritual. As stated earlier, rituals often imply collective and formal ceremonial acts that mark important events and transitions, as well as provide a framework for religious practice. Rituals can be once in a lifetime occurrences, such as a baptism, confirmation, graduation, or wedding, or they can be the smaller components that make up one religious service.

Most life cycle events and religious services are made up of numerous small rituals that occur at designated points in the overall proceedings. The Navajo Nightway Ceremony, for example, is composed of a nine-night healing ritual that includes special songs, purification ceremonies, sand-paintings, and prayers that all occur at specified times. On the last night, masked dancers impersonating the gods sing and dance in order to bring supernatural power and blessing for curing the sick person.[26]

Although important for the individual, rituals also hold communities together over time. Because they are customarily repeated, rituals function as traditions that create important links to the past. In religious terms, rituals repeat and revitalize the beliefs, experiences, and ideas of those who have gone before. According to Jewish scholar Samuel Heilman, the repetition of established liturgy in the form of texts, prayers, and songs, creates a common receptacle for the spiritual feelings of each worshipper over time.[27]

In some belief systems, such as in Australian aboriginal culture, rituals in the form of songs and dances invoke the spirits of the ancestors. By reimagining the past through the presence of ancestral spirits, order and balance in the world is maintained in the present.

Because music has the expressive power to take us out of our everyday selves, it often is an important part of extraordinary events. Music facilitates transformation on many levels—whether we are making music or just listening to it. It is, therefore, an important force in religious practice, inspiring spiritual and religious feeling for both the individual and the collective. The role of music in worship can act to heighten emotional experience, to trigger memories, to take people out of their everyday state of mind, to invoke trance, to heal, and to bring them closer to their understanding of the divine. Reverend Henry T. Simmons, Senior Minister of The St. Albans Congregational Church in St. Albans, New York says that music functions as both a collective and individual force in African-American gospel services:

A SHOFAR (RAM'S HORN) IS BLOWN

> *So music serves not only as a rallying point, but it also serves as a therapeutic means. It touches individuals who've been hurt and disappointed by discrimination and life. It gives people an opportunity to cry, to express not only their joy, but also their sorrow—which is very important to maintain one's sense of balance and stability in life.*[28]

Music also functions as a punctuating device in religious ceremonies. Church bells are rung to call Christians to Sunday worship, the blowing of a conch shell invokes a Hindu god or goddess at a puja ceremony, and the blowing of the shofar (ram's horn) marks the beginning of the Jewish New Year, Rosh Hashanah, and the end of the Yom Kippur fast. In Haitian voudou, a neo-African religion that incorporates elements of Catholicism with African religion, the *ason* (sacred bell-rattle) is shaken to begin rituals, to cue musicians, and to mark important points in the ceremony.

The primacy of the sung text to invoke and express religious sentiment is common in many cultures. Religious language itself can be specialized. In some religions, including the Roman Catholic branch of Christianity, Judaism, and Hinduism, a formal liturgical language can be used to the exclusion of all others. In others, such as all the denominations of the Protestant church, the language of worship is the local or vernacular language.

A different case exists in many Native American tribes, where the texts of spiritual songs consist of vocables—sounds that are sung but have no literal meaning. These vocables are not meaningless, however, but create another kind of specialized language that is identifiable both to participants and to the gods who are invoked. The use of music with the vocables gives them meaning and power. In many religions, including the examples above, music in the form of chant or song is used to elevate speech, turning the ordinary into the sacred.

Music in the Christian Church

While music is understood to be an intrinsic part of spiritual practice in many religions, it is regulated, discouraged, or even banned in others. The development of Christianity in the West—from the formation of the Roman Catholic church to the splintering of the Protestant denominations in the sixteenth century, reflects a history of conflicting attitudes toward the role of music in worship. In his fifth century work entitled *Confessions*, St. Augustine described the source of his own conflict—music could both promote the highest of religious sentiment and cause a purely sensuous enjoyment that seemed to be the opposite of religious feeling:

> *So I waver between the danger that lies in gratifying the senses and the benefits which, as I know, can accrue from singing. Without committing myself to an irrevocable opinion, I am inclined to approve of the custom of singing in church, in order that by indulging the ears weaker spirits may be inspired with feelings of devotion. Yet when I find the singing itself more moving than the truth which it conveys, I confess that it is a grievous sin, and at those times I would prefer not to hear the singer.*

St. Augustine's fears about the sinful sensuality of music were reflected in numerous church pronouncements that warned against displays of virtuosity, the use of instruments, and the singing of complicated music in the church setting. Another perspective is expressed seven hundred years later by the twelfth century abbess, composer, and writer, Hildegard of Bingen, who had no such ambivalence about music. Obviously influenced by earlier music theorists, including Boethius and Cassiodorus, music was at the core of her religious life and belief system:

> *So remember, just as the body of Jesus Christ was born by the Holy Spirit from the spotless Virgin Mary, so too the singing in the Church of God's praise, which is an echo of the harmony of heaven, has its roots in that same Holy Spirit. But the body is the garment of the soul and it is the soul which gives life to the voice. That's why the body must raise its voice in harmony with the soul for the praise of God. This is also the command, symbolically of the spirit of the prophets: God should be praised with crashing cymbals, with cymbals of clear praise and with all musical instruments that clever and industrious people have produced. For all the arts serving human desires and needs are derived from the breath of God sent into the human body.*[29]

Hildegard wrote the above as part of a letter to the prelates at Mainz in 1178 after her monastery was placed under indictment which included a ban on singing. Not only did she strongly rebel against this allegation by describing music as the highest way to praise God, but cleverly suggested that a lack of music in the church might be the Devil's work:

> *This is why you and all spiritual leaders should proceed with the greatest caution. Before you close the mouth of the Church—in other words, the choir which sings God's praise—through your judgments . . . you must prove and examine the grounds for these measures with the greatest care. . . . And when you make judgments of this sort, you must constantly be careful that Satan, who deprived humankind of heavenly harmony and the pleasure of Paradise, will not encircle you.*[30]

In the early sixteenth century, a powerful religious movement that splintered the Catholic church began in Germany and Bohemia and rapidly spread across Northern Europe. Martin Luther was at the forefront of this campaign to reform many of the practices of Catholicism, including music. The movement separated the Christian church into two main divisions—Catholic and

Protestant—and later into numerous Protestant denominations. Luther and other reformers believed in a more egalitarian form of worship that included holding services in local languages (rather than Latin) and congregational singing. In reaction to the new doctrines of the Protestant churches, the Catholic church launched a counter-reformation designed to reassert church authority.

The Council of Trent (1545–1563), a general council headed by the Pope, met to assess and reform church practices, including the use of music in the Mass. The main complaints centered on the use of complicated polyphonic music (music with two or more simultaneously occurring parts) that obscured the clarity and power of religious texts, the sensuality of music, the use of instruments, the use of secular music, and the attitudes of the performers. Their final tract on music touches upon these issues, but did not include an outright ban on polyphonic music:

> *All things should indeed be so ordered that the Masses, whether they be celebrated with or without singing, may reach tranquilly into the ears and hearts of those who hear them, when everything is executed clearly and at the right speed. In the case of those Masses which are celebrated with singing and with organ, let nothing profane be inter-mingled, but only hymns and divine praises. . . . They shall also banish from church all music that contains, whether in the singing or in the organ playing, things that are lascivious or impure.[31]*

This attempt to distinguish between music and dance that is "lascivious or impure" and music that evokes the proper religious sentiments continued to be a conflict in Christian worship—from the persecution of the Shakers in the eighteenth and nineteenth centuries for dancing in their church services to the banning of drums in Christian services by European missionaries in Africa and the Caribbean. In the American religious revival movement of the nineteenth century, there emerged two radically different approaches to Protestant worship: the traditional quiet worship of the church and the ecstatic singing, dancing, and emotionalism of the camp meeting. These two styles, and variants in-between, can be found today in Protestant churches across the country. While some people still believe that exuberant music making and dancing have no place in church, others believe that these same elements are essential for proper worship.

Although these differing attitudes may never be reconciled, they are part of a long standing dialogue concerning the role of music in Christian worship—both Catholic and Protestant. What is suggested by the extent of the debate is the enormous power music is thought to wield over the individual and the community within the context of the church. Church elders have rarely denied the beauty or effectiveness of music as a means to heighten religious feeling, but they have attempted

ST. ALBAN'S CONGREGATIONAL MASS CHOIR

to regulate its style, orchestration, and performance to root out the "wrong" emotions. Nevertheless, religious music continuously changes to meet the needs of the congregants.

For Reverend Simmons of the St. Albans Congregational Church, the use of gospel music that engages the whole congregation in active participation is not only the best way to communicate God's love, but a way to communicate hope:

> To me, music is a significant and powerful tool for expressing joy in the midst of sorrow, for expressing life in the midst of death, for expressing joy even in the midst of pain and suffering. . . . We can praise God in the midst of whatever our trials and tribulations are, and we can thank God in a sustained, very powerful, rich, full way. . . . And I see myself as a leader of a celebration, who is not afraid to allow individuals to travel into different compartments in life. And music, particularly music in the black or African-American worship tradition does that. It is, in a sense, the glue that holds the worship, the praise of God together.[32]

MUSIC AND HEALING

In some societies, music is viewed as more than a means of emotional and spiritual expression, but as a form of medicine with healing powers. Healing rituals are an intrinsic part of the overall belief system in many world cultures and music is often a crucial component. As we saw earlier in the chapter, the Navajos have many ceremonies involving singing and dancing that are designed to restore balance and health to both individuals and the whole community. According to Ernest Brown, music in many African and neo-African healing ceremonies is also used to bridge the gap between the natural world and the supernatural world:

> In a healing ceremony, you are asking for help from God in order to heal someone, or you are asking for rain—you are asking for supernatural assistance. Music is something that helps human beings to connect with the spiritual. In Africa they would say that music is something that helps the spirits to connect with human beings. When you want the spirits to come, you play music for them. If you don't play music for them and if you don't give them some offerings of food or drink that they like, they won't come.[33]

In addition to invoking gods and spirits, music is also used to help participants achieve altered states of consciousness or a trance in order to have access to supernatural powers. Whether the trance involves possession—where adepts lose their own personalities in order to be taken over by a divinity—or trance without possession, music often plays an important role in bringing on and maintaining the trance. In many cultures in which trance states are a normal cultural phenomenon, ritual practitioners, such as priests, shamans, or medicine men or women, are the only ones who have the ability to go into a trance. However, as we will see with the Kung people, healing rituals often involve the cooperative effort of the whole community.

The Kung Healing Ceremony

The Kung—also known as the Bushmen—are a nomadic people of hunters and gatherers who reside in Namibia and Botswana in southern Africa. They live in small groups in a mostly desert or semi-arid environment. Weekly healing rituals are an important part of their culture:

> *The Kung live in a very tough environment. It's very easy to cross the line and to get into real trouble through sickness . . . and so the alleviation of sickness and suffering is a regular need that has to be addressed. And the healing ceremonies that the Kung perform are one way of addressing those needs and of restoring balance, harmony, and health to the society and also to particular individuals.*[34]

The Bushmen attribute sickness to the will of the creator God who distributes the forces of good and evil through a secondary god and his messengers, the spirits of the dead.[35] The treatment of illness consists of literally driving out the sickness and bad spirits from a person's body by singing, dancing, and the medicine man's use of supernatural powers while in a trance. Power is thought to reside in medicine songs themselves and in order to activate the power, the songs must be sung as part of the overall ritual. In this context, music can be viewed as a vital form of medicine, as well as a vehicle for transformation.

Within the ceremony itself, singing and clapping are done by women, who typically sit around a fire. Each singer in the group sings melodic fragments in a hocketing technique that ultimately creates a whole melody. Brown further described this kind of singing style as reflecting the Kung's collective lifestyle:

> *You get a kind of composite melody that's not sung by any one person. So it's a very collaborative melody or collaborative form of melodic line. It needs a community in order to have that music happen.*[36]

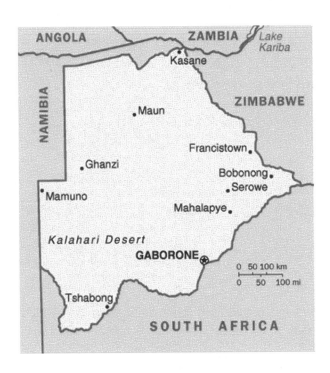

KUNG HEALING CEREMONY

The songs are sung in vocables—non-lexical syllables that are not part of everyday speech, but have meaning for the participants.

The men—wearing rattles on their legs—dance around the women in single file, and sometimes sing. Since over one half the male population are considered medicine men, the males are then able to go into a trance one after another as they dance. Once in a trance, the men do not sing and their trance and dancing are maintained by the singing of the women, who do not themselves go into a trance. As Rouget has described, the treatment begins when one medicine man approaches a sick member of the community:

In the medicine dance, treatment of the illness involves two stages. The first consists of capturing and driving out the illness: the medicine man, in a trance, massages the sick person's body, anoints it with his own perspiration, lays hands upon him, thus drawing the illness out into his own body; he then rids himself of it by ejecting it violently in the direction of the secondary god and his messengers, the spirits of the dead. The second stage consists in driving away the spirits themselves by hurling insults and sticks at them. . . . When entranced, the medicine man is in fact seeing the secondary god and the spirits of the dead, and is therefore able to address them directly.[37]

For the Kung, healing rituals are part of their close association with nature and with the supernatural world. These rituals help to restore health both to individuals and to the society; by curing one person, order and balance are also achieved for the collective. Even though the actual healing must take place through the intermediary of a medicine man in a trance, the ceremony is only able to be performed through active participation by everyone in the community. The power of song to call the spirits, as well as the collective power of the singing, motivates the dance which in turn gives rise to the trance state. According to Rouget, "the curative power of the singing 'boils' and thus attains its full efficacy." Once in a trance, the medicine man is able to directly confront the spirits and to drive out illness.[38]

■■■ THE POLITICAL POWER OF MUSIC

From the beginnings of recorded history to the present day, music has provided a powerful medium for the presentation of political messages. The Psalms of David gave comfort and inspiration to the early Israelites "in the presence of . . . [their] . . . enemies" (Psalm Twenty-Three). The chanted epics of Homer celebrated the virtues and warned of the flaws of early Greek heroes and kings, bolstering Greek national identity in a world of unpredictable deities and rival armies. In the twentieth century, pioneering scholars in the field of oral tradition sought to understand the workings of the Homeric epics by studying the contemporary epic traditions of Yugoslavian singers, Serbian musicians whose songs celebrated the victories of past heroes in battles against neighboring ethnic groups.[39]

Like a once-dormant volcano, this seemingly innocent Balkan musical tradition roared back to life in the early 1990's, not in the form of epic poetry, but in the contemporary guise of music videos portraying machine gun-toting soldiers running through the streets of Sarajevo. Music was such an important psychological factor in the Yugoslavian civil war that rival camps fought pitched gunfights to win control of the television station which broadcast such videos.[40] In battle, nations often derive courage and discipline from patriotic hymns and marches (or now, music videos); in victory, they sing of their heroes, and in defeat, they eulogize their martyrs.

Music also frequently serves as a medium for criticism of government from within a society. The medieval songs of Robin Hood, who robbed the rich, gave to the poor, and fought the tyrant Prince John and his confederate the Sheriff of Nottingham, celebrated one of the earliest "outlaw heroes" in a song tradition that continues in the twentieth-century ballads of Pretty Boy Floyd and Jesse James. Contemporary outlaw songs are also found in traditions as diverse as salsa, reggae, and rap. Just as soldiers serving king or country derive courage from patriotic anthems, protesters struggling against governmental abuses find strength and inspiration in songs, whether on the picket line, in public demonstrations, or in armed uprisings.

Music, and particularly singing, is an especially effective medium for political messages for a number of reasons. Prior to the advent of the mass media in the form of newspapers, magazines, radio, and television, songs served the functions of all these media in many societies. Memorable tunes and rhymes are powerful mnemonic devices or memory aids—when we sing or whistle a few notes, entire verses can easily be called to mind. By adding new words to the melody of a familiar hymn or popular song, political songwriters often find a shortcut to the listener's memory—the familiar tune automatically replays in our minds, reminding us of the new message being carried by a favorite melody.

In some ways, music is closer to the contemporary media of radio and television than to the older medium of print; music, like television, is audible and therefore inescapable. We can choose not to read a newspaper article, but we cannot avoid hearing a song within earshot.

As stated earlier, music also has the power to move people, both physically and emotionally. Marching music literally coordinates the movements and efforts of a group of people. The emotional power of music can bind people into a community, give them courage in the face of danger, and charge them with adrenaline before a confrontation. Music is transformative, and political songs are able to efficiently convey information, deliver opinions, affect our emotions, and motivate us to change our actions. Governments clearly believe music to be a dangerous political weapon, since they often attempt to control music by means of patronage (rewarding artists who support the rulers) and censorship (punishing those who do not).

We begin to explore the political power of music by studying the most obvious genre of political song: the national anthem.

National Anthems and Patriotic Music

The words and tune of England's national anthem "God Save the King" are said to have been composed by the English composer Henry Carey (1690–1743), but rival claims for authorship of the tune have been lodged in both France and Germany. This is truly an "international anthem"; in the United States, "My Country 'Tis of Thee," is one among at least twenty nations to have adopted the melody of "God Save the King" for a national anthem or patriotic song. Germany, Denmark, Austria, Switzerland, and Sweden all have nationalistic songs which employ this melody.

Some of these adaptations have resulted in highly ironic situations; in World War I, British and American soldiers sought courage in the identical melodies of "God Save the King" and "My Country 'Tis of Thee," while German soldiers sang the same tune in their patriotic anthem "Heil dir im Siegerkranz" ("Hail thee in victor's crown").[41] The fact that mortal enemies were all singing the same tune illustrates the chameleonlike nature of melodies, whose affective power owes allegiance to no single party. It is almost as if this tune were a weapon like a rifle or a cannon—all the armies possessed them, and victory went to the power which wielded them most effectively.

While "God Save the King" is a sober prayer on behalf of the monarch, "Rule Britannia" is a more martial anthem of imperial expansion. Composed by Thomas Augustine Arne in 1740 for a masque play about the recovery of Britain by King Alfred from the rule of Danish invaders, "Rule Britannia, Britannia rule the waves," became a popular anthem at the height of the British empire, when Britain did indeed rule much of the sea as well as considerable territory in Asia and Africa.

Although the French national anthem, the "Marseillaise," was adopted as a theme of the French Revolution, its composer, Captain Claude Joseph Rouget de Lisle, was not a revolutionary but a loyal supporter of the Bourbon kings. Composed in 1792 to celebrate the French invasion of Prussia, the "Marseillaise" in 1795 was declared the French national anthem, and performed at every state execution. Its composer, Rouget de Lisle, refused to submit to the edicts of the National Assembly, and nearly suffered the ironic fate of losing his head on the guillotine to the accompaniment of his own composition. Relieved of his employment in the French army, he lived the remainder of his life in poverty, and was only posthumously honored for his musical contribution to the nation.[42]

The "Marseillaise," composed by a royalist, but immediately adopted by the enemies of the crown, subsequently became an international theme of revolution and republicanism, but like "God Save the King," it was occasionally adopted into situations of great irony. In one early German adaptation, the song text exhorted the united armies of Germany to take up their swords and defend their fatherland against the invading army of the French revolutionaries, and in 1798, another German text was set to the "Marseillaise" tune in an anthem dedicated to the newly enthroned king of Prussia.

As a song of revolution, the "Marseillaise" was at times banned in both France and Germany. Before World War I, the German Social Democratic Party adopted it as a rallying song. Decried for its older revolutionary and newer socialist significance, the song was prohibited during the Third Reich. In Vichy France of World War II, the "Marseillaise" was only sung secretly, by members of the Underground resistance movement.

Austria's national anthem, "Gott erhalte," was composed in 1797 by Franz Joseph Haydn, who was inspired to create this musical "weapon" by the threat of Napoleon's rapidly expanding armies.[43] Germany had a number of patriotic songs, including the above mentioned "Heil dir im Siegerkranz," but Germany's most powerful political music was created by Ludwig von Beethoven. Born in 1770, Beethoven enjoyed the benefits of royal patronage as the son of a court singer until he began to make his own career as a composer in Vienna in 1792. There he became the friend of revolutionaries, and chafed against the aristocratic pretenses of patrons who placed themselves above the status of a "mere musician."

Like Haydn, Beethoven sometimes composed music with explicit political purposes. He originally dedicated his third symphony (1804) to the revolutionary hero Napoleon, but later changed the dedication to "Heroic Symphony Composed to Celebrate the Memory of a Great Man" when Napoleon abandoned republican ideals to assume the title of "emperor." Portions of this great work are widely regarded as "program music," that is, music which tells a story, paints a picture, or otherwise evokes feelings associated with extra-musical events. The slow movement in particular is described as a funeral march for the dead of the Napoleonic and all other wars.[44]

Between 1804 and 1816, Beethoven wrote a number of pieces celebrating the German war movement against France. From 1816 until his death in 1827, Beethoven was a vocal critic of the oppressive German regime which ruled after the war. His final, Ninth Symphony (1824) ends with the famous "Ode to Joy," a choral celebration of joy and brotherhood which, perhaps, issued a symbolic challenge to the joyless and despotic government of Germany at the time.[45]

As a consciously political composer, Beethoven moved through a series of postures, first as an ally of benevolent monarchy, then as an advocate of a French revolutionary hero, then as a patriotic defender of his homeland against the French army, and finally as a domestic critic of totalitarian government. After his death, Beethoven's music provided various options for later German political movements that sought to gain validation and popularity by forcing his music and memory into their service. Parties from across the entire political spectrum have tried to invoke such an association.

The Third Reich in particular distorted Beethoven's persona into a "world-conqueror" among composers, and then used public performances of his music to suggest a parallel between him and their own "world-conqueror," Adolf Hitler. Beethoven's music was further manipulated and refashioned into a symbol of "home" to the German people, and Beethoven was touted as an Aryan hero. Populist messages of universal brotherhood in his music were down-played, and his patriotism emphasized, in order to create for the masses a Beethoven who answered the propaganda needs of Nazi Germany.

This emphasis on an Aryanized, re-invented Beethoven went hand-in-hand with a governmental policy which maintained virtually absolute control of public musical performances. Jewish musicians were expelled from performing organizations, and contemporary atonal music was denigrated as part of a Jewish revolutionary plot.

Fortunately, Beethoven continued to be interpreted as something more than an Aryan "superman" outside of the Nazi sphere. Forty-odd years after the end of the Third Reich, when the Berlin Wall was dismantled and East and West Germany re-united in 1989, Beethoven was prominently re-installed on the world stage as an advocate of brotherhood, in a performance of the Ninth Symphony featuring musicians from every major power to have fought in World War II. Under the baton of maestro Leonard Bernstein, this international orchestra and chorus performed the "Ode to Joy" in a concert that was heard simultaneously around the world by means of a telecast from the *Schauspielhaus* of re-united Berlin.[46]

Music of Protest and Resistance

The functions of protest songs are in many ways the same as those of patriotic anthems. They serve to inform, remind, and inspire, giving courage and cohesion to groups of people attempting to achieve particular political ends. The differences lie in the kinds of messages the songs convey and the kinds of movements that utilize them. National anthems usually are sung in order to affirm an existing political order; protest songs are sung in order to criticize, change, or replace such an order. In some cases, a single song, such as the "Marseillaise," served both functions in the course of its career.

To do its job, the tune of a protest or *topical* song must be singable, attractive, memorable, and easy to learn. For this reason, topical songwriters often compose new verses to the melodies of popular hymns or secular music—if the audience and singers already know the tune, they can concentrate on the message that the lyricist is trying to convey. Sometimes the topical song not only borrows the melody but also parodies or builds on the lyrics of an existing song.

Since protest songs challenge the existing social order, they often deal with class struggle, and particularly with the demands of laborers, the unemployed, and the disenfranchised—people whose needs are not satisfied by the status quo. One of the earliest recorded protest songs dates from the march of a "peasant army" against London in 1381, including the lyrics, "When Adam delved and Eve span, Who then was the gentleman?"[47] This reference to the Garden of Eden uses a common theme of topical songs—advocating the return to an original, natural order, which the existing government or society has violated.

The lyrics of protest songs often have a short life. When they succeed in bringing about change, they are no longer necessary, and when they fail to produce change, they are discarded. They tend to deal with transitory issues, the struggle of workers in a particular union action, or the battle for civil rights in a particular time and place. For this reason, topical songs typically do not endure as do the anthems of standing governments.

Topical Songs in the United States

In the United States, topical songs played a central role in the nineteenth-century anti-rent wars and in the abolition of slavery. In the twentieth century, songs encouraging social reform and political change were important in the establishment of universal suffrage, the struggles of immigrant groups, the organization of laborers in virtually all industries, the civil rights movement, and the 1960's anti-war movement.

To a large extent, America in the eighteenth and nineteenth centuries was a singing nation, whose repertory consisted chiefly of Protestant hymns. The melodies of religious songs, therefore, became a common resource of topical songwriters. Researcher John Greenway observed that "Making a union song in the rural South is a simple matter of taking a gospel hymn, changing 'I' to 'We' and 'God' to 'CIO' [Congress of Industrial Organizations]."[48]

Early topical songwriters in America continued the English tradition of printing their lyrics as *broadsides*—single sheets which might be hawked on the street for a penny or posted in public places. Such publications included the song text without musical notation; the tune was usually taken from a popular song, and broadsides occasionally included the instruction to sing the lyrics "to the tune of so-and-so."

As the name suggests, the broadside was often an attack, presenting criticism of a person, group, or government. If songs were the early newspapers, the broadside often played the role of an editorial or letter to the editor. Interestingly, the advent of print media and the publication of newspapers did not replace music as a medium for conveying news or opinion. The same technology that permitted the printing of newspapers also facilitated the circulation of songs, which stirred the emotions much more effectively than printed or even spoken prose or poetry.

Early American broadsides addressed issues related to the United States' transition from a European colony to an independent republic. Marching songs such as "Yankee Doodle" and anthems such as "The Star-Spangled Banner" supported the revolution against British rule. After independence, topical songs accompanied the effort to rid the New World of archaic laws, holdovers from the era of rule by Dutch and then English colonial aristocracies.

Satirical broadsides attacked the imprisonment of debtors, and ballads celebrated the exploits of armed farmers resisting the subjection of renters to virtual slavery under old Dutch feudal laws in the Hudson Valley of upstate New York. In the nineteenth century, immigrant groups encountering segregation in the workplace voiced their indignation in songs such as "No Irish Need Apply."[49]

The Labor Movement

America's first strike occurred in 1786 among journeyman printers in Philadelphia. From that time, unions have sought to improve the working conditions, wages, and social status of their members, often using music as a prominent strategy in motivating their members and promoting their demands. The Knights of Labor, founded in 1869, had limited success in promoting its political agenda, but it was certainly an enthusiastic singing organization.

The Industrial Workers of the World (IWW), founded in the United States in 1905, employed both songs and strikes with more telling effect than the earlier Knights of Labor. The IWW repertory drew heavily on Methodist and Baptist revival music, evangelical and Salvation Army songs, and songs of the hobo "jungles." IWW members, or "Wobblies," sang at every meeting. Important songwriters in the movement included Joe Hill, whose songs addressed the problems of homelessness, unemployment, and prostitution, as well as strike-related issues, and Mac McClintock, author of the Wobbly theme song, "Hallelujah, I'm a Bum." Hill's lyrics in "The Tramp" describe the plight of the unemployed hobo:

> *Tramp, tramp, tramp, keep on a tramping,*
> *Nothing a doing here for you.*
> *If I catch you 'round again,*
> *You will wear the ball and chain.*
> *Keep on tramping, that's the best thing you can do.*

A performance of "The Tramp" by Cisco Houston, an important folksinger who was involved with the labor movement.

Joe Hill became an important Wobbly martyr when he was executed in 1915 on a still-disputed charge of murder; IWW members insisted that the accusation was false, an instance of "white-collar murder" at the hands of enemies of the movement.

Mac McClintock published the IWW repertory in the first "little red songbook" to "fan the flames of discontent" in 1911.[50] In World War I, most leaders of the IWW were imprisoned, ending the effective life of the organization. Labor organizations continued to employ music; the CIO and the United Auto Workers sang, and the Almanac Singers (which at various times included performers Millard Lampell, Pete Seeger, Woody Guthrie, Lee Hays, Cisco Houston, Josh White, Burl Ives, Bess Lomax, Leadbelly, Richard Dyer-Bennett, Sonny Terry, Brownie McGhee, and Earl Robinson) performed at union rallies through the 1940s.

The Wobblies' "little red songbook" was succeeded by many publications of topical songs. The Commonwealth Labor College in Arkansas published the *Commonwealth Song Book*, the Kentucky Workers Alliance published *Songs for Southern Workers*, and the Textile Workers of America published *Labor Songs*. The *People's Song Book* (1948 and 1956), *Lift Every Voice* (1953), *Singout!* magazine (founded in 1950), *People's Songs*, and *People's Artists* propagated political music, either in print or by organizing performances called "hootenannies" or "hoots." Pete Seeger was a principal figure in performing, recording, and publishing topical music, from the Almanac Singers' days up to the 1990s.[51]

The Civil Rights Movement

Although slavery was abolished in the United States in 1863, segregation was the rule in many southern states until the mid-1960s. In segregated areas, African-Americans attended separate schools, dined in separate restaurants, used separate public toilets, and sat in the back of the bus on public transportation. Pervasive social discrimination, unfair job and housing restrictions, the enforcement of unjust laws of disenfranchisement, and poverty were the common lot of African-Americans throughout the country.

The cause for justice for African-Americans began with the first resistance to slavery and continued strongly after the Civil War. Post-slavery movements included Marcus Garvey's back-to-Africa initiative in the first two decades of the twentieth century. Garvey's message of black pride and his philosophy of black self-help and independence electrified African-Americans in urban ghettos all over America.

After the Depression, labor organizations, such as the United Mine Workers led by John L. Lewis, launched a campaign to bring African-American workers into the unions with equal pay. This strategy was adopted by other unions all over the country, including the Congress of Industrial Organizations (CIO), the Steel Workers Organizing Committee, and the United Auto Workers. By the early 1940s, blacks demanding equal job access and equal pay pressured President Roosevelt to establish the Committee on Fair Employment Practices. This executive order allowed almost one million African-Americans to enter the industrial labor force during the war years.

World War II marked a turning point for the civil rights movement in the United States. African-Americans had defended democracy in the war, but were still subject to discrimination and segregation at home. Court cases, such as Brown versus the Board of Education in 1954, only began to address the wrongs of segregation.

The real pressure for social change and racial justice began as a people's movement at the grassroots level. Drawing inspiration from black leaders of the past, Christian doctrine, and the successful civil disobedience campaigns of Mahatma Gandhi in South Africa and India, African-Americans began a highly effective movement of non-violent resistance in the mid-1950s. In

1956, black citizens of Montgomery, Alabama, led by Dr. Martin Luther King, Jr., boycotted the segregated city bus system.

In 1960, African-American college students staged a sit-in at a segregated lunch counter in Greensboro, North Carolina. Their arrest drew the attention of the national media, and sparked a sympathetic movement among university students across the United States. Both in the south, where non-violent marchers faced beatings, hosing, burning, shooting, or jail with no defense other than their courage and songs based on the melodies of traditional hymns, spirituals, and gospel tunes, and in the north, where guitar-wielding students composed and sang songs of solidarity with the civil rights struggle, music played a central role. According to Ernest Brown, spirituals and gospel music kept the growing movement together:

> *Music was a key part of the civil rights movement. Why do I say that? Because if you are alone in a jail cell somewhere in the south in 1962, and you've been threatened with dogs and you've been beaten, the only way you can recover your humanity, the only way you can recover your strength is through singing. Civil rights workers sang those songs in jails, sang those songs on the picket line, and sang those songs in order to uplift their spirits and keep their minds focused on what they were trying to achieve.*[52]

Although the repertory of the southern civil rights marchers in organizations such as the Southern Christian Leadership Conference, led by Reverend Martin Luther King, Jr., and the Student Non-Violent Coordinating Committee (SNCC), drew heavily on African-American religious music, some of the most important songs and musical strategies of the movement were directly influenced by the prior experiences of labor organizers in the south. The Highlander Folk School, founded in 1932 in Tennessee, had long served as a "central clearinghouse" for songs used on picket lines across the nation. Mrs. Zelphia Horton, musical director at the school from 1935 to 1956, adapted the Baptist hymn "I'll Be Alright," retitling it "We Shall Overcome," for use in tobacco worker's strikes in the 1940s. The song is also said to derive from the chorus of a religious composition entitled "I'll Overcome" composed by C. A. Tindley (circa 1905). Horton taught her version of the song to Pete Seeger.

SNCC FREEDOM SINGERS

Photo by Joe Alper, courtesy Jackie Gibson Alper.

In 1959, musical leadership of the Highlander Folk School shifted to Guy Carawan. In April of 1960, Carawan taught "We Shall Overcome" to eighty civil rights sit-in leaders attending a music workshop at Highlander. In the same month, he taught the song to 200 sit-in leaders at a conference organized by the Southern Christian Leadership Conference. Within months, "We Shall Overcome" had become the central anthem of the civil rights movement, sung at every demonstration by singers who swayed from side to side, embracing one another with interlaced arms.[53]

As important as "We Shall Overcome" became, it was only one out of hundreds of songs embraced by the civil rights movement. Each area of the south had its own performers and songs, but the most influential performing group was the Freedom Singers, an ensemble which originally consisted of five SNCC field secretaries. The musical style of the Freedom Singers, unaccompanied part singing by a small group of voices, derived directly from the

A live performance of "We Shall Overcome" by the SNCC Freedom Singers.

gospel quartet tradition, dating back to the nineteenth century and carried into the twentieth by groups such as the Dixie Hummingbirds. The Freedom Singers' repertory is alive today, maintained in performances of Sweet Honey and the Rock, an ensemble including Freedom Singers' founder Bernice Reagon.

The effectiveness of music to promote a message received its ultimate expression when President Lyndon Johnson himself voiced the refrain, "We shall overcome," in a televised statement announcing his support of civil-rights legislation. The song was the vehicle by which the words achieved currency, but it was the message of the words that Johnson was citing. Lyndon Johnson enacted the most sweeping civil rights laws in the history of the United States, but his civil-rights "activism" was overshadowed in the minds of protesters by his subsequent support of the Vietnam War.

The Anti-War Movement

American university students, who had begun to sing and march in support of the civil rights movement in the early 1960s, marched through the decade singing in protest against the United States' military involvement in Vietnam. The most popular protest song of the era, Bob Dylan's "Blowin' in the Wind," served double duty, with verses addressing both issues: "How many times must the cannonballs fly before they're forever banned?" "How many years can some people exist, before they're allowed to be free?"

"Blowin' in the Wind" was one of the earliest and most popular anti-war songs, but like "We Shall Overcome," it was only one of hundreds or perhaps thousands in its genre. Anti-war songs emerged from and addressed a different population than civil rights songs. The latter, based on southern African-American singing traditions, were usually sung in unison or in parts by large groups, often adopting the tunes of traditional hymns and gospel songs. Anti-war songs were more often solo efforts, sometimes including a chorus, but featuring a single voice accompanied by a guitar or a small band.

PETE SEEGER 1960s

Some of the most important voices in the anti-war movement were those of activists seasoned in the labor and civil rights movements, singers and composers like Pete Seeger, whose "Waist Deep in the Big Muddy" voiced his criticism of President Johnson's Vietnam policy before a television audience of millions. But the population most directly affected by the Vietnam War were men, age eighteen through their twenties, and many composers and performers of anti-war songs emerged from this age group.

The first, non-electric efforts were cast in the musical style of the "folk revival" of the early 1960s, but as "folk-rock" and then "acid-rock" captured more of the recording market, anti-war songs moved into new musical territory. The serious, almost religious tone of early songs gave way to biting satire in the recordings of artists like Arlo Guthrie ("Alice's Restaurant Massacree") and Country Joe and the Fish ("It's one-two-three, what're we fighting for?").

PETE SEEGER 1998

The anti-war movement, like the civil rights movement, had a rapid and powerful effect on government policy. The unpopularity of the war brought down one American President and motivated the next to seek a speedy exit from Vietnam, and the popular sentiment that affected these changes owed no little part to the power of music as a carrier of political messages.

We have briefly examined the role of political songs in Europe and the United States. National anthems and protest songs played similar roles in nation-building and the freedom struggles of colonized peoples in Asia, Africa, and South America. To conclude, we will consider an important genre of political song in Latin America: Nueva Canción.

Nueva Canción

Chilean composer, performer, folklorist, and activist Violeta Parra (1918–67) may be considered the "spiritual founder" of nueva canción.[54] Like Pete Seeger in the United States, Parra collected hundreds of traditional ballads, composed songs addressing contemporary political issues in "folk" style, published traditional and contemporary songs, and both performed in and organized concerts of folk and political music. She founded "La Carpa de la Reina" ("The Tent of the Queen"), a center for traditional music. Her children, Isabel and Angel, carried on her work after her death, running an important *peña* or folk music coffeehouse.

The term "nueva canción" was coined to describe a repertory of political songs at a large music festival held in Santiago, Chile, in 1969. The new genre was closely associated with the *Unidad Popular* political party of socialist presidential candidate Salvador Allende. Allende's success in the 1970 election brought political reform and the nueva canción genre to their peak in the early 1970s.

Stylistically, nueva canción emphasized instruments and genres of indigenous Andean music, blended with Hispanic and African musical features. One such genre known as *cueca*, Chile's most popular folk dance, had already served for generations as a vehicle for singing of the struggles of the Chilean working class. Both lyrically and musically, nueva canción songs expressed Chilean nationalism, solidarity with the Andean Indian peoples, socialist ideals, and resistance to social and political domination either by a resident ruling class or by North American cultural imperialism. The United States was viewed with distrust.

The Bay of Pigs invasion of Cuba in 1962, American military action in the Dominican Republic in 1964, and the American world-wide dominance of the mass media made the United States a formidable adversary in the minds of nueva canción activists. Nueva canción was an international genre, which spread throughout Latin America, and American incursions in any nation of the hemisphere were perceived as attacks on the autonomy of all Latin American peoples.

The fate of Allende's government and the singers of nueva canción lend credence to such a view of American intentions in the region. In 1973, when nueva canción had reached its peak of popularity in Chile, a CIA-backed military junta overthrew President Allende. A new totalitarian regime banned political parties, labor unions, mass rallies, overt dissent, and the performance of nueva canción. Victor Jara, a prominent composer and performer in the genre, was tortured and killed; other exponents were jailed or exiled, and the playing of indigenous musical instruments was outlawed.

In this new, extremely repressive environment, musical protest re-appeared in a new genre called "canto nuevo," in which political messages took a more subtle form. The cueca genre, once favored by dissidents, was co-opted by the new regime, which adopted this form to present songs painting unreal images of Chile as a bucolic paradise. Both the musicians and the style of nueva canción were forcibly exported, both to other Latin American countries and around the world. Nueva canción became an important means of political expression in the Nicaraguan revolution during the late 1970s, and international festivals of the genre were held in Cuba, Mexico, Nicaragua, Ecuador, and Argentina, through the mid-1980s.[54] The social and political message of neuva canción continues to attract a significant pan-Latin audience in the 1990s.

▬ CHAPTER SUMMARY

The power of musical expression can give rise to transformation on many levels. Music can enhance religious experience, healing, celebration, social and political protest, and nationalism. It can arouse deep emotions, moving people to ecstasy or tears, and inspire work, play, and dance. Musical experience can be both deeply personal and communal. Because it is rooted in the culture in which it is made, music provides a strong connection between the individual and society. In the next chapter, we will explore the ways in which music, interacting with memory, evokes feelings which play a fundamental role in defining both personal and group identity.

STUDY QUESTIONS

1. How would you define the field of ethnomusicology?

2. Why is music such an important component of culture?

3. Give examples of communities that are formed around music and dance.

4. Describe the roles that music plays in religious worship.

5. What are the conflicts regarding music that have existed within Christian worship over time?

6. What are the functions of protest songs within political movements?

REFERENCED SOURCES

1. Titon, 1997: 254.
2. Merriam, 1977: 197.
3. Titon, 1997: 257.
4. Herbst, 1997: 122.
5. McAllester, 1996: 44–5.
6. Morton, 1973: 179.
7. Glassie, 1982: 81.
8. Cowdery, 1990: 38–9.
9. Cohen, 1982.
10. Berliner, 1994: 256.
11. Weiss and Taruskin, 1984: 363–5.
12. Daniel, 1995: 104.
13. Lausevic, 1997.
14. Ibid.
15. Blacking, 1973: 50–1.
16. Turnbull, 1962: 92.
17. Dispirito. Interview, 1997.
18. Ibid.
19. Glabicki. Interview, 1997.
20. Frith, 1992: 142.
21. Dispirito, 1997.
22. Slobin, 1993: 41.
23. Cowan, 1990: 13.
24. Kotzsch, 1992: 10.
25. Kaynor. Interview, 1989.
26. McAllester, 1996: 29–31.
27. Heilman, 1987: 242.
28. Simmons. Interview, 1997.
29. Fox, 1987.
30. Ibid.
31. Reese, 1959: 449.
32. Simmons. Interview, 1997.
33. Brown. Interview, 1997.
34. Ibid.
35. Rouget, 1985: 140.
36. Brown. Interview, 1997.
37. Rouget, 1985: 140–1.
38. Ibid.
39. Lord, 1960.
40. Laušević, 1993.
41. Nettl, 1967: 34.
42. Ibid.: 70–71
43. Ibid.: 52.
44. Ibid.: 78.
45. Dennis, 1996: 24–25.
46. Ibid.: 144–152.
47. Greenway, 1953: 2.
48. Ibid.: 12.
49. Ibid.: 40–41.
50. Dunson, 1965: 14.
51. Ibid.: 16–17.
52. Brown. Interview, 1997.
53. Dunson, 1968: 29–33
54. Manuel, 1988: 69.
55. Manuel, 1988.

CHAPTER 3

MUSIC AND MEMORY

About This Chapter

Music and memory are closely linked to individual and collective identity. Memories tell us who we are, and music is one of the most powerful tools for evoking memory. Music helps us to recall ideas and events, and serves to make particular occasions memorable. Like the senses of taste and smell, music provides a short-cut to memory, occasionally transporting us mentally back to earlier times. In many cultures, music reminds people of their shared history and shared beliefs; it can also create an active link with the past through rituals which help to form social identity.

Just as music aids memory, memory serves music. Remembering allows us to repeat and recognize melodies, sing, play, and talk, or write about music. This chapter concentrates on the role of music as an instrument and object of memory, shaping and being shaped by individual and collective identity in a variety of cultures around the world.

KEYWORDS

affective memory
authenticity
early music
functional memory
mnemonic
narrative
primary sources
sean-nós
secondary sources

COMPANION RESOURCES

TELEVISION PROGRAM: Music and Memory

AUDIO SELECTIONS:

28. "The Rocks of Bawn"

8. "Walbiri Fire Ceremony"

7. "The Flower of Magheralee"

50. "The Green Fields of Canada"

6. "Pretty Polly"

9. "Oy Comamos"

Memory makes us who we are. As individuals, our identities are based on remembrances of past events, people, and places. Personal recollections of particular happenings and conversations stand in our memories as symbols of our relationships with parents, siblings, friends, teachers, and other associates. We chart our progress through life by recalling such events as signposts along the road of our being and becoming.

Collective memory gives identity to groups of people, to nations, and to the ethnic and cultural communities that both live within and cut across national boundaries. Collective memory, on the personal level, includes the contributions that friends and family members make to our individual understanding of past events. We patch together a story based partly on our own recollections and partly on the testimony of others who shared an experience with us. On a cultural level, collective memory involves passing on the stories of events which we did not personally experience. Collective identity depends on the sense of a common history, which may be passed on by word of mouth or recorded in documents such as the Bible, the Koran, the Magna Carta, or the United States Declaration of Independence.

We may divide individual memory into two types: functional and affective. *Functional memory* includes remembering how to ride a bicycle, memorizing alphabets and multiplication tables, learning to play a musical instrument, recalling important appointments, and mapping out the chronology of our lives in relation to certain key incidents, such as entering grade school, graduating from college, and getting married. *Affective memory* refers to recollections which have a powerful emotional effect on us, sending us into blissful reveries or haunting us with disappointment, anger, or regret.[1]

Music serves as a powerful tool in storing and recalling both functional and affective memory. Billions of English speakers have memorized the alphabet with the help of the alphabet song, sung to the tune of "Twinkle, Twinkle Little Star." Affective memories are often stirred by hearing one's national anthem, familiar hymns, or a song associated with a parent, or with an intense love.

Music may be either an object of memory or an instrument of memory. As an object of memory, music is something that is taught, using *mnemonic* (memory-aiding) devices such as staff notation and solfege syllables (doh-re-mi, etc.), or documented in music history books. Music historians, ethnomusicologists, folklorists, and performers put a great deal of energy into researching, preserving, revising, reviving, and reconstructing remembered—or partially forgotten—music.

As an instrument of memory, music itself is a mnemonic device that helps to store and trigger recollections. The effectiveness of music in aiding memory and stirring emotion is utilized by many cultures in creating and maintaining a sense of group identity. Many ritual traditions use music to define special, sacred, or memorable junctures in a person's life. Such rituals often employ music as a tool for personal and/or collective transformation. Important political events are also marked by performances of culturally charged, affective musical repertory. Both religious songs and national anthems usually serve as audible emblems of cultural identity.

Memory is not static: "The prime function of memory . . . is not to preserve the past but to adapt it so as to enrich and manipulate the present."[2] Both personal and collective memory are highly subjective, and we often revise our recollections in order to correct impressions which today seem incorrect or simply not useful. Music is frequently used as a tool in revising collective memory; songs are used to incite, sustain, and end conflicts ranging from athletic rivalries to international warfare.

Memory is concerned not only with the past, but also with the future. We not only remember what we did yesterday, we also must remember what to do tomorrow. Music is often used, not only to recall the past or to shape the present, but to point to the future. Contemporary syntheses which combine aspects of different musics from around the world seem to be creating a trans-cultural, global network of musical styles and genres.

Music as a Mnemonic Device

According to Mark Slobin, our earliest memories are often associated with music:

> *It's been shown that if you play certain songs to children before they're born, they will recognize those songs after they're born. So there's a very profound imprinting that goes on with music and human beings at the earliest possible stages, before they're even out in the world.*[3]

Slobin goes on to describe the ways in which we "stitch together our lives" by connecting one musical memory to another, referring to contemporary theories about the storage of aural information on replayable "sound tracks" in the brain. He recounts the case study of a woman who consulted a neurologist because she kept hearing songs in her head that she couldn't recognize:

> *They ultimately traced it to songs she had heard when she was young. And it appears that some part of her brain, because of an accident she'd been in, had gotten jiggled loose in a certain way. Some wire had been crossed and she kept hearing those songs. So at a very mechanical level we have in our brains a music track that is running. And, presumably, all the music we have ever heard is lying along that track and can be activated.*[4]

Cultures make use of this cerebral tracking of music to help us remember important information by linking important texts to memorable tunes and/or rhythms. "Thirty days hath September, April, June, and November" is a mnemonic chant by which children learn to recall the number of days in each month. On a more profound level, religious practitioners in many faiths use chant as a device to help remember sacred texts. In religions such as Judaism, with practitioners scattered around the globe, the sacred texts are standardized, but the melodies and rhythms of recitation vary from one place to another according to the aesthetic taste of given regions. "The melodies are very important for the survival of the

PERUVIAN MOTHER AND CHILD

text itself, as a way of keeping the text in memory and as a way of grounding it locally, so that people are connected to that text."[5]

Music often serves to remind individuals and groups of important places in their personal or collective history. Among the Tuvan people in the mountainous region just across the Russian border from northwestern Mongolia, songs provide a guide or map of the Tuvan landscape:

TUVAN SINGER

There are songs that provide in great detail, what I would call a sonic map of a territory. And so the singer, by singing the song, takes you on a trip through this territory. . . . And there's a particular vocabulary that's used to describe landscape in a very detailed way. . . . And the songs are filled with these special terms that refer, say, to the way a mountain slopes down to a stream. Or, for instance, when Tuvans see a mountain range, a ridge, they don't see only a mountain, but they see a human figure. So human figures are personified in landscape. And a lot of the songs also talk about aspects of landscape as if they were aspects of human anatomy. . . .

The songs serve as a way of creating and enhancing oral memory. They serve as an oral record, both of one's travels and of the places that one has lived in and loved and been close to.[6]

These Tuvan "sonic maps" guide the singer and listeners, not literally from one location to another, but through a landscape that corresponds to one's memories of life itself. The personification of mountains and ridges both intensifies memory and gives added emotional significance to the sonic map—each aspect of the terrain takes on human qualities, evoking particular sentimental responses in listeners who know the land and its history.

In many cultures, narrative songs called ballads, like chant and the Tuvan "sonic maps," use melodies to help people remember detailed texts. According to Slobin, tunes that are both familiar and attractive help verses to stick in the mind:

There seems to be a receptor in the mind for tunes. It [a tune] just attaches itself to your mind. And because of that you will remember long stretches of text that you could never remember any other way. So that when you ask somebody, for example, the story of a ballad, they can't tell you the story. They have to start singing it. And then the whole thing falls together.

So a ballad, like any song, is a welded unit. The text and the tune are welded into a particular sculpture, a particular object which is beautifully crafted to serve this purpose.[7]

The function of music in a ballad is not only to help the singer remember the song. The melody also reinforces the mood of the text. Sad songs usually use sad melodies; happy songs use happy melodies. People from different cultures sometimes might disagree as to whether a given melody is cheerful or melancholy, but within a given culture, listeners usually are able to recognize a sad song when they hear it.

The ability of music to evoke emotional responses has to do with the mysterious way in which sound is linked to memory. Talking about a past experience does not usually allow us to relive it in the way that hearing a familiar voice or song can:

Affective memory of the greatest intensity reveals a past so rich and vivid we all but relive it. . . . It is not the introspection that yields these heightened recollections, but the chance reactivation of forgotten sensations, commonly a touch or smell or taste or sound.[8]

Music, then, not only reminds us of past experiences, but also rekindles the sensations and emotions of those experiences, in some measure transporting us back to an earlier time. This happens on a personal level whenever we discover that someone is "playing our song."[9] On a collective level, rituals sometimes use music to transport people back to the mythological beginnings of a particular society.

The Walbiri Fire Ceremony

For the Walbiri, an indigenous people in central Australia, the Fire Ceremony is one such ritual in which song and mythology play a predominant role. Aboriginal creation myths tell of legendary totemic beings or creative ancestors who wandered over the continent in the Dreamtime, singing out the names of everything in nature—birds, animals, plants, rocks, waterholes—and so singing the world into existence.[10]

AUSTRALIAN ABORIGINES

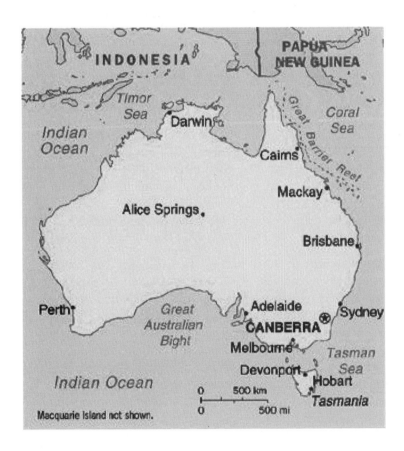

According to the Australian ethnomusicologist Stephen Wild, the creative ancestors were themselves the prototypes of all the living species in the Aboriginal environment, as well as the prototypes of human beings. The ancestors took the forms of plants or animals, such as the crocodile, lizard, or turtle, but still had human qualities.[11] Aboriginal peoples throughout Australia continue to use songs about the ancestors as a way to perpetuate the fertility of the land. Through the singing of song cycles, dancing, painting, and ceremony, they invoke the creative ancestors.

And when they perform as creative ancestors they are indicating their close association with a species and with the land which they occupy . . . in a way, they are participating in the original creative events.[12]

AUDIO 8 Two short songs from the Walbiri Fire Ceremony in which the singers accompany themselves with pairs of boomerangs.

In the Fire Ceremony, the creative ancestor is symbolically showered with sparks as a punishment for not looking after a sacred site which he originally created. In different versions of the ritual, mythology associates it either with the travels of a snake, a rat kangeroo, or a bird. While the song cycles and mythology connected with each ceremony vary considerably, the manner of celebration is always the same, including a period of several weeks of preparatory singing of the song cycle. The last two days of the ceremony involve hours of dancing, singing, the use of a central fire to make torches, and the climax when the torches are set on fire and the dancers are attacked with them.[13] The purpose of the Fire Ceremony is to use ritual to resolve old quarrels within the clan.

Other rituals and ceremonies invoking a culture's mythological beginnings often have a transformative effect, marking rites of passage that literally alter one's social identity. We will now investigate the role of music in one such ritual: the Mouse Ceremony of the Suyá Indians of Brazil.

■ MUSIC, TRANSFORMATION, AND IDENTITY: THE SUYÁ MOUSE CEREMONY

Anthropologist Anthony Seeger documented the Suyá Mouse Ceremony during the rainy season of 1972. At that time, about 120 Suyá lived in a village in Xingu National Park, along the Suia-misu River in the state of Mato Grosso, Brazil. The Suyá speak a language called Ge, which is common to a number of tribes in the Xingu region.[14]

Seeger wrote about the relationship between ceremonial music and time among the Amazonian Indians:

Although we know relatively little about musical traditions in the lowland regions of South America, it appears that whenever music is heard, something important is happening. . . . In the Upper Xingu region, in the state of Mato Grosso, singing is associated with ceremonies taught to men by spirit ancestors when they walked on earth, and music makes possible a return to and renewal from the sacred past. . . . As far as we know, throughout lowland South America music is used to represent and create a transcendence of time and substance: past and present are linked and humans and non-humans communicate and become comingled.[15]

Past, present, human, and non-human are comingled in a fascinating way in the Mouse Ceremony, which reenacts aspects of the myth of the introduction of corn into Suyá life, and serves to initiate a young boy into the collective life of the men of the village plaza. The ceremony also reaffirms a variety of social relationships within the village, and reminds the Suyá of an important origin myth and the values which it imparts.[16]

According to Suyá tradition, the Suyá were introduced to corn and other edible vegetables by a young boy, whose mother had been secretly instructed

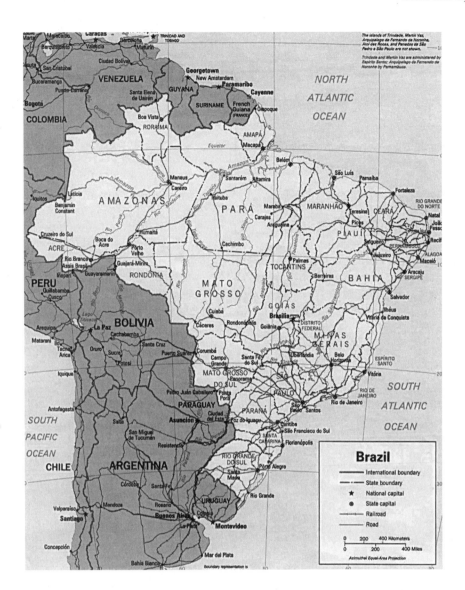

about their preparation by a mouse from the "river of food." The Mouse Ceremony brings this myth to life in the course of a ritual which initiates young boys into their social and ceremonial identities.[17]

The Mouse Ceremony

The two-week ceremony involves all members of the village, but the principal actors are the young boy or name-receiver, his mother, his uncle or name-giver, and a ceremonial specialist, who in this case was the name-giver's elder brother. The ritual begins when the name-giver formally requests his sister's permission to sing over her son, the name-receiver. Receiving permission, the name-giver then learns the appropriate song from the ceremonial specialist, and then proceeds to his sister's house, where he sings over the name-receiver.

For the next two weeks, every day includes some singing by the men of the village. The ceremony is an occasion for re-affirming social relationships and enjoying a communal feeling of euphoria, and the songs sometimes stir strong feelings. In 1972, one woman cried when her brother sang a song formerly sung by another relative, now deceased.[18]

Vocalizations associated with the Mouse Ceremony, both spoken and sung, are stylized in a fashion that sets the ceremonial period apart from nonceremonial times. Formal speech and song remind the village that this is a special time, and sets the mood for the social transformation that the ceremony is meant to achieve.[19]

During the two weeks leading up to the culmination of the Mouse Ceremony, capes are woven from the tenderest leaves of palm fronds. On the day before the actual initiation, the capes are painted, each in a pattern belonging to one of the name groups that provide each young boy with his social identity. At sundown on the final night of the ceremony, every man puts on his cape, ritually transforming himself into a creature which is both man and mouse. The men take the young boys out of the village, into a temporary forest village, from which all the initiated males then reenter the village. They enter the name-receiver's house after dark, through a hole in the back wall of the house (as mice would do), and hum ritual songs over the name-receiver. They then take the name-receiver out to the forest camp; he has now been transformed, given a social identity, and is ready to participate in the activities of the men's house.

After a full night of singing, the men's sisters ritually "wound" the mice by piercing their capes with arrows. Each man performs a song and dance before "dying" by freezing in place. The capes are then removed, and the men doused with cold water. The mice are now dead, and each man has returned to human status. At dawn, the men go to the river, bathe, and throw their mouse ornaments into the river, saying "Go, go back to the river of food."[20]

Singing, Time, and Transformation

During the Mouse Ceremony, the Suyá collective memory of the origin of corn is impressed upon the entire community, and especially upon the young boys, in a most dramatic way. The mythical past and the tangible present collapse into a single moment, and the separate domains of human and animal are conjoined as the men of the village are transformed into dancing and singing mice. The ceremony reenacts certain aspects of the story of the origin of corn: like the young boy in the myth, the name-receiver is initiated by a mouse into the masculine activities of the village plaza. When the men return to human form, the name-receiver has been transformed with a new social identity, the men have enacted Suyá masculine values of verbal ability, strength, self-assertion, and endurance through a night of vigorous singing and dancing, and relationships between men, women, and young boys have been reaffirmed.[21]

The Mouse Ceremony begins with a song, and singing is a central ceremonial activity throughout the two-week ritual. For the Suyá, singing seems literally to shape society. Their village is laid out in a way that conforms to the need to frequently reaffirm social values by the performance of ceremonies, which include music, stylized speech, and dance.[22] The Mouse Ceremony both activates the Suyá memory of a mythical past, and creates new memories of an ongoing cycle of ceremonies, using song as a powerful tool in the creation of both collective and individual identity.

MUSIC AND COLLECTIVE IDENTITY

Irish Traditional Music

What is a folk song? This term has somewhat different meanings, depending on who is using it. A folklorist would probably define a folk song as one which has been passed on from generation to generation, primarily by oral tradition. It may originally have had a single author, but over the generations it has been modified by processes of oral transmission, and ultimately is regarded as the product and property, not of a single composer, but of a larger community. To folklorists, folk songs are in great measure defined by what they are *not*. They are not products of professional musicians attached to royal courts; they are not commercial songs produced for hire. They are, simply, the songs of "the folk"—a concept which has been carried over from the days of feudal society, in which the distinctions between the aristocracy and the peasants seemed clear.

In the modern world, many aristocracies have ceased to function, royal patronage is largely obsolete, and the growth of cities, capitalism, and the middle class has blurred the distinctions that once made folk songs an easily distinguishable genre. In modern commercial terms, a "folk song" might be any song which is sung to the accompaniment of an acoustic guitar, whether it is the product of generations of oral tradition, or a recent commercial creation.

In Ireland, musicians use the term "traditional music" to describe songs and dance tunes which belong, at least stylistically, and in most cases historically, to what folklorists regard as the Irish "folk music" tradition. New songs and tunes are frequently composed, but their creators are careful to tailor them in a recognizably traditional style, and are gratified when their songs or tunes are taken up as—and sometimes mistaken for—products of a generations-old oral tradition.

The building of modern nations around the world has inspired—and drawn inspiration from—a rebirth of interest in traditional music. As a "product of the people," with the power to evoke collective memory, create a sense of identity, and stimulate feelings of love and pride for one's country and culture, folk music has often provided modern nations with an audible emblem of identity. In countries like Ireland, which have fairly recently emerged from colonial rule, traditional music bolsters national pride and provides a sense of cultural grounding, emphasizing the virtues and independence of a newly independent people. A large repertory of Irish song recounts the heroic exploits of nationalist figures who resisted British occupation, often becoming martyrs in the process. Prior to independence—and still today among proponents of a single, undivided Ireland—these songs served to fuel the nationalist movement; after independence, they provided historical heroes for a developing nation.

Irish Traditional Singing

Contemporary Irish culture is the product of many centuries of contact and exchange with a variety of Europeans and later, Americans. The primary players were the Celts, the Scandinavians, and the English, each of whom brought their own languages and customs to this island nation. Christianity was introduced to the Celtic inhabitants of Ireland during the fifth century by European missionaries, mostly from Britain and Gaul; the most famous of these, Saint Patrick, was probably from Wales. During the latter centuries of the first millennium CE, Ireland was repeatedly invaded by the Norsemen of Scandinavia, who in some cases settled, intermarried, and ruled Irish kingdoms.

For much of the second millennium, all or part of Ireland was ruled by the English, who established an Anglo-Irish aristocracy across much of the nation and "planted" Scottish settlers—who themselves were descended from Irish emigrants to Scotland—in the northern county of Ulster. Each of these groups brought their own language, music, and musical instruments to Ireland. Students of Irish culture often feel like archaeologists examining layers, not of ancient ruins, but of the living, composite soil of a contemporary society. Irish traditional singing reveals these layers in striking ways.

The bedrock of Irish traditional song is a repertory and singing style known as *sean-nós*, which literally means "old way." By the early twentieth century, systematic suppression and economic factors had eradicated the Irish language—a Celtic tongue, related to the Gaelic languages of Scotland and Brittany—across much of Ireland. Native Irish speakers still lived in the extreme north, west, and south, the areas farthest from the center of British rule in Dublin.

In 1922, Irish independence ushered in an era of linguistic resurgence, and Irish soon became a required part of the curriculum in all national primary and secondary schools. In 1998, English remains the most commonly spoken and sung language in Ireland, but the Irish language is widely understood, and enthusiastically spoken by a significant minority. The sean-nós singing style has enjoyed a resurgence paralleling the renaissance of the Irish language.

The sean-nós repertory includes primarily lyrical song texts, including nature poetry, love songs influenced by the French *chanson* of the late Middle-ages, and religious songs expressing a somewhat mystical brand of Irish

Catholic belief. The musical style of these songs is quite distinctive: unaccompanied solo singing, long, modal melodies largely independent of European notions of harmonic construction, florid melodic ornamentation, (especially in western Ireland), and a frequently nasal vocal timbre. Both textually and musically, the distinctive features of sean-nós singing mark it as a unique genre of European song, a clear marker of a collective memory that reaches back to the centuries before English colonization.

SEAN-NÓS SINGER

English language songs in the Irish traditional repertory show stylistic features, not only of the older sean-nós repertory, but also of English and Scottish folk song. Irish singers perform hundreds of versions of ballads like "Barbara Allen," narrative songs telling stories of love, jealousy, murder, betrayal, and the exploits of knights, ladies, kings, and queens. These songs are found not only in England and Scotland, but also in the United States. Lyrical, non-narrative songs, including love songs, humorous songs, and tributes to beloved areas of the Irish landscape, are also common. Tributes to Ireland include a large body of emigrant songs composed in England, the United States, and Canada, many of which share aspects of narrative—telling the story of the singer's emigration from Ireland—and lyrical poetry, singing the virtues of the beloved homeland.

Musically, Irish singing in English ranges from fairly simple, syllabic (one note-per-syllable), undecorated melodies to highly ornamented, free rhythm renditions which show the clear influence of sean-nós singing. It is tempting to attribute the plainer, syllabic singing styles to English influence, but this would be an oversimplification. The Irish language repertory includes many syllabic melodies, and English folk song includes styles that utilize a fair amount of ornamentation. It is impossible, after so many centuries of mutual contact and exchange, to chart a clear course for any but the most obvious influences.

AUDIO 28, 29, 7 For two examples of English language singing in Ireland, listen to "The Rocks of Bawn" (audio #28 and #29), sung by the late Connemara singer Joe Heaney, the most renowned modern sean-nós singer, and "The Flower of Magheralee" (audio #7) sung by Pat Kilbride, a younger singer, born in County Kildare, Ireland, but now living in New York.

The Contemporary Musical Landscape

The musical landscape of Ireland in the 1990s is dominated, not by traditional singing or dance tunes, but by both Irish and foreign productions in the international idioms of popular music: rock, country and western, rap, and other genres performed by Irish and non-Irish artists. In spite of the dominance of these popular musical forms, traditional music, particularly dance tunes played on the fiddle, accordion, flute, tin whistle, uilleann pipes, concertina, piano, banjo, bouzouki, mandolin, and guitar, is frequently heard in informal pub sessions, on the concert stage, and through the media of CDs, cassette tapes, records, radio, and television. Although Irish listeners can choose from a variety of internationally available musical styles, traditional Irish music provides a strong marker of cultural identity.

With many styles to choose from, why do some Irish musicians choose to specialize in traditional music? Pat Kilbride describes his first musical inspiration:

I'll never forget the first time that Irish music made an impression on me. I was four years old, and it was a . . . concert, a variety show. You know, there was a guy came down from Dublin to play calypso music—he was actually a West Indian. And there would be a comedian.

And there was one part of the show [which] really struck me. It was a gentleman called Owen Kelly, who died—he was one of the old players around Kildare—and some of his buddies. And they sat on stage with . . . big shiny boots, and their black suits and shiny hats. And they played a tune. I can still hear it; it was a reel. And I've never forgotten. I can hear that music. If I close my eyes today, I can go back to that moment. And ever since then I've loved Irish music.[23]

PAT KILBRIDE

Memories tend to be most vivid when multiple senses are involved. An Irish reel, heard on a sound recording, only reaches the listener through the sense of hearing. Four-year-old Pat Kilbride was impressed, not only by the tune which he heard, but also by the appearance and behavior of the musicians. He mentions their shiny black boots and hats, and from his description of the musicians as "Owen Kelly . . . and some of his buddies," we get the impression of a group of friends, who were clearly enjoying themselves. The overall effect was unforgettable, and provided Pat Kilbride with the initial inspiration for a life of music-making.

Older Musicians

As Pat Kilbride's story indicates, personal contact with older musicians is a key element in the introduction of Irish musicians to traditional music. Senior musicians are usually quite approachable; a strong emphasis on humility and sociability has prevented an Irish "star system" from making musicians into inaccessible cultural icons. Young players often learn by meeting and playing with highly respected exponents of traditional music. Uilleann piper Jerry O'Sullivan describes the respect given to older players in gatherings of musicians:

The elder musicians are given pride of place. They're shown a lot of respect. They're given the best seat. They are allowed to make the decision what piece—what pieces—are going to be played. Generally, you know, people will be deferential and wait for them to suggest something. And people basically let them, in a very benevolent way, let them control the gathering . . . out of affection and out of respect.[24]

Older musicians pass their repertory on to younger players both informally, by playing in musical sessions such as the ones Jerry O'Sullivan described above, and somewhat more formally, in music classes and lessons. Most players also learn Irish traditional tunes by listening to recordings. Going back to early 78 rpm records by artists such as the fiddler Michael Coleman gives younger players a certain sense of history, but to be initiated into the continuing tradition and social context of Irish music, young players seek out the company of senior musicians. O'Sullivan continues:

I think we all, you know, just speaking for myself and other musicians [of] my generation. . . . I think we're lucky enough to realize how much we owe this older generation of musicians. That in many ways we've learned our repertoire from them. We've learned a style of playing from them. . . . Of course there's also the stuff that's found on recorded media, which is fine. But in terms of getting a real sense socially, and in terms of making the whole musical picture fit with the cultural picture, you need a model.[25]

Older players provide models, not only of musical technique, style, and repertory, but also of the social behavior that goes with the music. Irish traditional musicians tend to put a great emphasis on humility, humor, and a strong sense of camaraderie both with other players and with a sympathetic listening audience, which might include singers, dancers, and storytellers, each of whom could contribute something to an evening's entertainment. Such informal gatherings, called *céilís* in the Irish language, provide opportunities for musicians of all ages to enjoy the transmission of tunes, songs, stories, and anecdotes regarding important players in prior generations. O'Sullivan comments on the ways in which such meetings connected younger musicians to a tradition with roots deep in the past:

It's wonderful spending time in the company of older musicians. . . . For somebody like myself, you're much more connected to 100, 150 years ago. . . . They obviously can tell you stories about when they were young. And therefore it sort of brings the chain back even further than their own time. . . . You learn an incredible amount from these older musicians, just from their experience and the people they've met. And more importantly, they're an awful lot of fun to be with.[26]

Emigrant Songs

Like many Irish musicians, Jerry O'Sullivan grew up and learned from traditional musicians in a closely knit Irish and Irish-American community in New York City. Economic hardship in Ireland inspired many generations of young Irish people to seek employment elsewhere, resulting in the creation of an international Irish diaspora, with more people of Irish descent living abroad than in Ireland. Jerry O'Sullivan recalls the huge surge in emigration caused by the great famine, near the middle of the nineteenth century:

In terms of the Irish diaspora, the Great Famine, which happened 150 years ago, in 1847, was a cataclysmic event . . . over two million people starved or emigrated, or died in the crossing . . . A lot came to the U.S., to Canada, to Australia, New Zealand, England.[27]

Emigration, prior to the advent of economical air travel in the mid-twentieth century, often meant leaving one's home and family, never to return. Nineteenth-century trans-Atlantic crossings were both difficult and dangerous, and departures were usually preceded by parties called "American wakes," so-named because parents, siblings, sweethearts, and friends did not expect to see the emigrants again.

As an uprooted people, often living in poverty, the Irish in the New World comforted themselves with the traditions of singing, instrumental music, storytelling, and dancing that they had carried with them from home. They lifted their spirits with lively dance music and humorous songs, and expressed their sorrow by creating a large repertory of emigrant songs, which described the poverty that had driven them from Ireland, the hardships of travel, and the wealth to be had in the New World, all the while expressing a profound nostalgia for Ireland. The memory of emigration is kept alive today by frequent performances of these songs, both in Ireland and abroad.

"The Green Fields of America," also called "The Green Fields of Canada," is a commonly heard song of emigration. The first part of the song describes hardship and oppression at home: living under an absentee landlord in Ireland, being evicted by a bailiff, and being forced, as Catholics, to pay a tithe to the minority Protestant Church of Ireland. It also relates the composer's sadness at leaving Ireland with his family. The third verse documents the results of oppressive living conditions: there is no longer any work for tradespeople, such as weavers, spinners, or coopers (barrel makers), so they are forced to emigrate to find employment. The second part of the song optimistically describes the New World as a paradise, with an unlimited wealth of food, wildlife and natural beauty.

"The Green Fields of Canada"

1

Farewell to the groves of shillelagh and shamrock
Farewell to the girls of old Ireland all around,
May their hearts be as merry as ever I would wish them
When far away on the ocean I'm bound
My mother is old and my father quite feeble,
To leave their own country it grieves them full sore
Oh the tears down their cheeks in great drops they are rolling
To think they must die on a foreign shore . . .

3

The lint dams are dry and the looms all lie broken
The coopers are gone and the winders of creels
Away o'er the ocean go journeymen tailors
And fiddlers who flaked out the old mountain reels
And I mind the time when old Ireland was flourishing
When lots of her tradesmen did work for good pay
But since our manufactures have crossed the Atlantic
Sure now we must follow to Americay . . .

5

And if you grow weary of pleasure and plenty
Of fruit in the orchard and fish in the foam
There's health and good hunting 'way back in the forests
Where herds of great moose and wild buffalo roam
And it's now to conclude and to finish my ditty
If ever friendless Irishman chances my way
With the best in the house I will greet him in welcome
At home on the green fields of Americay.[28]

Irish traditional singers seldom regard a song as an isolated piece of repertory, out of context; they associate it with the singers from whom they learned it, and whatever they know of the history surrounding the song. Jerry O'Sullivan describes the background of "The Green Fields of America":

> *It originally came from the singing of Paddy Tunney . . . He's a wonderful exponent of northern Irish singing. . . . There are a number of people who sing the same song, but in all cases he was the source. And he got it from his mother, Bridget Tunney, going back. This would have been . . . probably before the turn of the century when she learned it.*[29]

O'Sullivan frequently plays the tune of "The Green Fields of America" on the uilleann pipes. Although he renders the song instrumentally, without words, he bases his playing on singing, and keeps the text of the song in mind as he performs. He describes a portion of the text which he finds particularly meaningful:

> *One part of the song that I always thought was very, very sad, and very accurate, is where the singer talks about a lot of the traditional trades drying up in Ireland—the barrel-makers . . . the fabric-makers. You know there's one part of the song, goes "The lint dams are dry, and the looms are all broken."*
>
> *That actually happened, where a lot of the homespun industries were discouraged by taxation, by the government of the time. So that the native Irish industries could not compete with the stuff being imported from abroad. And all these industries were destroyed, and people scattered.*[30]

JERRY O'SULLIVAN

The lyrics to the chorus of "The Green Fields of America" refer to the "sea store," the supply of food which a family would need to carry with them for the six-weeks sea voyage from Ireland to America:

> *So pack up your sea stores,*
> *Consider no longer;*
> *Ten dollars a week isn't very bad pay.*
> *There's no taxes or tithes to devour up your wages*
> *When you're on the green fields of Americay.*

In other ballads, less optimistic than "The Green Fields of America," the sea store is sometimes destroyed in a great storm, and the family depends on the charity of their captain to avoid starving to death during the voyage.

Even Irish instrumental music, rendered without words, carries some imprint of Irish history. Lyrical songs praising a woman's beauty, or the Irish landscape (or both), convey a somewhat deeper historical impression, and narrative songs, particularly those depicting events in the Irish struggle for independence, are explicit expressions of Irish collective memory.

AUDIO 44 In this piece, Jerry O'Sullivan plays "The Green Fields of America" on the uilleann pipes.

BALLADS IN SCOTLAND, ENGLAND, AND THE UNITED STATES

American film-maker and musician John Cohen has made films documenting ballad singing traditions in the United States, Scotland, and England. His research took him from the Appalachian Mountains of the American south to the traveling people of Scotland:

JOHN COHEN

> *After I got interested in the ballads and went down to North Carolina and heard these singers singing so vigorously, I said, "I could go back to Britain to see if the ballad tradition's still alive there, or in what form it is." And I wasn't so interested in the revival of the ballads, you know, where people from the city like myself would learn a ballad and then perform it. I wanted to see if there were any places it was still sung within a family. And, as I searched through, the most vigorous form I found was with the travelers, or the tinkers, or the gypsies in Scotland, who were still singing these very ancient ballads.[31]*

The travelers told John Cohen of their memories of patronage by the British nobility: "When the gypsy people talk about the ballads they say, 'Lord so-and-so allowed us to live on his land. And we had some of the best pipers. And he'd have our pipers come in and play for his festival.'" Many of the ballads sung by the traveling people featured heroes and heroines from the class of landowners who sometimes patronized them. In many parallel traditions around the world, including Irish bardic poetry, members of local aristocracies employed musicians who literally sang the praises of their patrons and their royal ancestors. Such musicians sometimes served as court historians; the jaliya or griots of the Gambia, in West Africa, were the official, professional genealogists and historians of the Mande chiefs. In such cases, narrative songs and stylized speech serve as the collective memory of an entire people or tribe.

For the travelers of Scotland, noble patronage is obsolete, and the struggle to maintain their lifestyle in the face of government pressure to abandon their mobile caravans in favor of conventional, settled life is a constant factor of contemporary life. Ballads and bagpipes are reminders of an earlier era, when singing and musical traditions now surviving among the traveling people were the common entertainments of the society at large.

Musical traditions from Ireland, Scotland, and England, and particularly from eighteenth-century Scots-Irish emigrants to America, had a strong influence on folk music in the United States. Hundreds of ballads from the Anglo-Scottish repertory have been collected in North America, from the Green Mountains of Vermont to the Appalachian Mountains of North Carolina. For Appalachian singers, fiddlers, mandolinists, guitarists, and banjo players, as for Irish traditional musicians, traditional singing and dance music is a marker of regional cultural identity. Personal identity is associated with a particular singer's unique collection of songs and/or tunes.

John Cohen and his band, The New Lost City Ramblers, have introduced generations of urban Americans to the old-time music of the American south. Although he comes from a northern, urban background, John Cohen has

AUDIO 6 John Cohen sings the murder ballad "Pretty Polly," accompanying himself on the five string banjo.

spent many years singing southern ballads and documenting through his films the lives of singers in the southern context.

MUSIC AS AN OBJECT OF MEMORY: RECONSTRUCTION AND REVIVAL IN EARLY MUSIC

Early music specialist and wind player Tom Zajac defines *early music* as "the music that never made it to the twentieth century as a performing tradition." Performers of early music specialize in European repertory dating from the Middle Ages through the end of the Baroque era in the mid-eighteenth century. As instrumentalists, they often perform on "period" instruments, either surviving antiques or, more frequently, modern reconstructions. Both singers and instrumentalists attempt to render early repertory in a way that seems consistent with what we know about performance practice at the time the music was composed. This involves a great deal of detective work on the parts of both performers and scholars who translate and interpret old musical scores and early writings on music. In this case, Medieval and Baroque musical compositions become objects of memory for performers and scholars to bring to life.

Early music repertories, such as Renaissance lute music, are called "broken traditions," because the music has been revived after long periods, sometimes centuries, of neglect. Tom Zajac discusses the challenges in performing such traditions:

> *I think one of the big challenges of performing early music is that it's a broken tradition. If you're a pianist today, you may have a teacher who had a teacher, who had a teacher who studied with Franz Liszt. And there's received knowledge that is passed down from generation to generation. In the performance of early music, there were centuries in between what people performed back then and what they're trying to do today. So in order to get a grip on how to perform this music, we have to do a lot of digging into primary sources and secondary sources.*[32]

NOTTINGHAM FAIR

LUTE

The piano, violin, and trumpet are modern instruments, and learning to play them often involves learning from teachers who provide links in an unbroken line back to the creators of the mainstream classical repertory. In the case of early instruments such as the lute, harpsichord, and baroque oboe, the chain of transmission is broken. Performance practice, like the instruments themselves, must be reconstructed based on the best surviving evidence about early playing techniques.

What attracts modern musicians to early music? The answer varies from player to player. Grant Herreid studied the trumpet in a music conservatory, where he took a course on early music. He was attracted by the sparse textures, pure vocal quality, and novelty of early music performance:

It really resonated inside me somehow. The music was so often sparse, it was very pure. The ways people sang it . . . used much more straight tone. It was very different from regular classical music, and a lot of this early music just seemed to hit a nerve in me, and I was hooked. I'd never heard anything like it.[33]

Paul Shipper was a rock and roll and rhythm and blues singer and guitarist before he discovered early music. Looking for "something more" from music, he found the mainstream classical approach to be "a little staid." The scope for improvisation in early music excited him:

When I discovered early music, and how you can perform it, not just what's on the page, but what's on and off the page—that you were free, to a certain extent, to add and subtract notes that are on the page—the whole element of improvisation just was so appealing that I just had to get involved.[34]

Nostalgia and curiosity about the past are common motivators for performers of early music. Tom Zajac describes early music as a cure for a sort of "cultural amnesia":

There's a sort of a cultural memory that survives, at least for those people of European heritage. I often times think of it as if you could equate the whole history of music to the life of one person, and say when they were eighteen years old they had some weird accident, and they had five years where they had amnesia, had no idea what happened during that time. When they woke up from having that amnesia they would want to know what happened in the past that they can't remember, and they would go back and try and rediscover what took place in their childhood and their early adult lives, until they integrated that early time of their life with what's happening now. And if you look at music that way, you can understand why it's important to know what happened in their musical past, and how we can make sense of it in [the] modern day.[35]

Sparse musical textures, a pure vocal quality, novelty, freedom to improvise, nostalgia, curiosity, community, and an enthusiasm for the detective work of figuring out how repertories and instruments used to be played are all elements that attract musicians who play early music. Another major factor is probably a certain kind of individualism. Each early music revival, beginning in the nineteenth century and continuing to the present day, has in some measure challenged the authority of more mainstream musical conventions. Ethnomusicologist Marc Perlman writes:

> *In musical terms, the clearest way to reject the authority of the mainstream concert world was to reject its 18th- and 19th-century repertory, and an interest in pre-classical music was what gave early music its name. Moving beyond mainstream repertory was as invigorating for the player as it was refreshing for the listener. Old music liberated the performer from mainstream instruments and the authority of mainstream teachers: a training on violin or piano was irrelevant to the viola da gamba or the harpsichord.[36]*

Early Music Practice

The first early music revival dates from the first half of the nineteenth century, when the composer Felix Mendelssohn discovered and popularized the works of Johann Sebastian Bach. Arnold Dolmetsch's work in England during the early part of the twentieth century generated new interest in music, dance, and musical instruments from both the Renaissance and Baroque periods. The most recent revival began in the 1950s, when a popular ensemble known as the New York Pro Musica began performing in major international concert halls and making records. In the 1960s, other musicians, including Christopher Hogwood and Nikolaus Harnoncourt, were highly influential in spurring on the early music movement that continues to grow today. With each new generation of early music performers, research has unearthed new repertory, and new information and theories about how the music was originally performed.

Authenticity—faithfulness to the conventions of the original performance traditions—is a central concern of early music specialists. Clues to early music practice come from a variety of sources. Musical scores provide melodies, rhythms, harmonies, and song texts, but they often contain no indications regarding instrumentation, accompaniment, and interpretive features such as tempo and dynamics. Musicians supplement scores by consulting literature—musical treatises, instrument tutors, diaries, letters, travel accounts, and works of fiction containing descriptions of musical events—and iconographic sources—paintings, illustrated manuscripts, and sculptures. Facsimiles of original scores, and literary and iconographic sources contemporary to the music itself, are primary sources for early music specialists. The writings of modern early music scholars are secondary sources which performers consult in deciding how to interpret early repertory.

Although primary and secondary sources are important resources for early music performers, they inevitably provide an incomplete picture. To fill in the blanks, performers rely on informed intuition. Based on their experience as singers and players, they make educated guesses as to how the music might have been rendered. Ultimately, like the artists who originally performed the music, they must make personal decisions about how they want the music to sound. Tom Zajac describes two kinds of authenticity in playing early music:

> *There [are] . . . two different types of authenticity. I think there's the authenticity where you're trying to find out as much as possible about how that music was played, so you can play it in the same way that it*

*was performed in the Middle Ages or the Renaissance. There's also
. . . what I think of as an authenticity of spirit.*[37]

Authenticity of spirit, for the ensemble known as Nottingham Fair, sometimes means consulting various kinds of modern music practice as a source of
ideas. To understand how Spanish Renaissance musicians might have improvised over a chord progression, or accompanied a drinking song, the members of the group look at contemporary Spanish folk music. Their aim seems
to be not merely to reconstruct a broken tradition, but to bring that tradition
to life in a new way. We will now examine their performance of a late fif-
teenth-century Spanish song, "Oy comamos y bebamos."

Early Music in Performance

"Oy comamos y bebamos" ("Let us eat and drink"), also called "Oy
Comamos," was composed by Juan del Encina (1469–1529 or 1530), who is
regarded as the father of Spanish drama. Encina composed both the words
and the music of "Oy Comamos" for a theatrical entertainment held at the
palace of the Duke of Alba, between 1492 and 1498.[38] The text of the song
exhorts the listeners to "eat, drink, sing, and enjoy ourselves, for tomorrow
we will fast in honor of Saint Antruejo. Well-fed, we will be satisfied, pull in
our paunches, and hang up the wine-skin."[39]

Nottingham Fair begin their interpretation of "Oy Comamos" with a
single recorder, playing the first section of a spirited melody. A second recorder and a tambourine join on the second line, adding harmony and emphasizing the dancing nature of the tune. Then these three instruments are
joined by a small, high-pitched Renaissance guitar, strumming in a festive
style reminiscent of modern flamenco music.

After the instrumental introduction, the recorders are silent, while the
tambourine and guitar accompany four voices singing the text in a spirited,
sometimes boisterous fashion. The second half of the verse is rendered with-

AUDIO 9

As Nottingham
Fair performs
"Oy Comamos,"
the listener
will notice
that the instrumentation and
style of performance are
designed to reflect the
lively meaning of the text.

IBERIAN PENINSULA
1270-1492

out voices; this time, one recorder plays an improvised solo reminiscent of various forms of modern Spanish folk music, accompanied by the other instruments. Finally, the voices repeat the verse. One singer bursts into emphatic speech as the second line is repeated—again reminiscent of modern folk and popular genres. The next-to-last line is rendered a cappella, a dramatic change in texture, before the instruments resume playing to accompany the last line of the song.

The original score of "Oy Comamos" from the *Cancionero de Palacio* compiled in the Spanish court of Ferdinand and Isabella, shows only four vocal lines. The score contains no indication of a guitar, percussion, recorders, spoken performance, or opportunities for improvisation. Why, then, did Nottingham Fair incorporate all of these things into their performance? Grant Herreid addresses this question, pointing out that even modern sheet music omits details of orchestration and interpretation:

> *If I want to go find a piece today in a music store, by a popular singer, I can go find the sheet music and it will be arranged for piano and voice, and the piano part will be somewhat like how it was recorded, maybe. But if I sing it and play it on the piano, it really doesn't sound like it did on the recording. It maybe doesn't have the drums, it doesn't have the other instruments. All the inflections of the singer, the thing that makes, gives the singer a personality, are not indicated in the music.*

> *And so, when we have a piece like "Oy Comamos," which comes from the late fifteenth century in Spain, it survives in a single manuscript, in four vocal parts. . . . It gives us so little information about who was singing, . . . whether it was accompanied by other instruments, whether they used percussion, whether the singer sang with any inflection. All it gives us is the melody, the four different voice parts, and the words, . . . and it sounds very beautiful if you perform it just like that, but we found that we can infuse this music with more life by looking at surviving popular traditions in Spain, or folk traditions, where they use a lot of strumming on guitars, a lot of percussion, castanets, tambourines. And when we use these somewhat anachronistic elements in the earlier music, it makes it sound much more Spanish—it seems to be, and gives it much more life, and it's actually much more fun to play.*[40]

Musicians and scholars suspect that notation in the Renaissance, like modern sheet music, provides only part of the musical picture. Accompaniment on guitar and percussion, and occasional flights of improvised playing, may have been taken for granted by early composers. Since we cannot *hear* the accompaniment style or improvisational approach of fifteenth century Spanish musicians, Nottingham Fair looked to contemporary Hispanic folk and popular music for models. The resulting performance of "Oy Comamos," then, is not merely a reconstructed rendering of a fifteenth century song, but a contemporary synthesis of musical practices from the Renaissance and contemporary Hispanic music.

This kind of synthesis is what differentiates the performance of early music from a historical "reenactment"—such as an American Civil War battle—where the object is to create a complete suspension of the present in order to recreate as accurately as possible the events of the past. In contrasting the

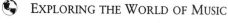

idea of revival with reenactment, Niall Mackinnon suggests that revival requires that the past be entered in some symbolic way "but once so entered, artistic integrity is not so threatened by the intrusion of the present. It is entered . . . but allows continuity through a process of artistic evolution."[41]

■ CHAPTER SUMMARY

In this chapter, we have examined various ways in which music is both an object and an instrument of memory. As an object of memory, music is the subject of historical research and musical reconstruction; as an instrument or agent of memory, it is a powerful mnemonic device, used by people in many cultures to create, preserve, and transform both personal and collective identity. Among the Tuvans of the Russian steppes, music provides sonic maps of both physical and emotional landscapes. Among the Suyá of Brazil, music is used to provide a young boy with his social identity, to remind the community of the origin of corn, and to reaffirm relationships within society and between society, nature, and the realm of myth.

In Ireland, Scotland, England, and the United States, narrative songs which once served as one of the primary modes of communicating and commenting on current events are now sung as markers of cultural identity—or simply because the singers enjoy singing them. Irish traditional music has comforted exiles through three centuries of emigration to the New World, and their struggles are remembered every time an emigration song is sung today.

For contemporary performers of early European music, the reconstruction of broken traditions is not only an exercise in nostalgia, but also the exploration of exciting, and, paradoxically, new frontiers. For each of the cultures we have examined, memory provides the tools to preserve old and synthesize new music, and thus music is a key factor in the maintenance of old memories and the creation of new ones.

STUDY QUESTIONS

1. What is the difference between functional and affective memory?

2. Describe the difference between music as an object of memory and music as an instrument of memory.

3. How does the Suyá Mouse Ceremony affect both individual and collective memory?

4. What are some of the ways that Irish traditional vocal and instrumental music create and maintain social identity for the Irish?

5. What are two approaches to authenticity in the performance of early music?

REFERENCED SOURCES

1. Lowenthal, 1985: 201–204.
2. Ibid: 210.
3. Slobin, 1997.
4. Ibid.
5. Ibid.
6. Levin, 1997.
7. Slobin, 1997.
8. Lowenthal, 1985: 202–203.
9. Slobin, 1997.
10. Breen, 1994: 656.
11. Wild, 1996.
12. Ibid.
13. Peterson, 200–201.
14. A. Seeger, 1987: 2.
15. Ibid: 7.
16. Ibid.
17. Ibid: 27–29, 81–82.
18. Ibid: 104.
19. Ibid: 6–7.
20. Ibid: 107–126.
21. Ibid: 127.
22. Ibid: 130.
23. Kilbride. Interview, 1997.
24. O'Sullivan. Interview, 1997.
25. Ibid.
26. Ibid.
27. Ibid.
28. Tunny, 1991.
29. Ibid.
30. Ibid.
31. Cohen, 1997.
32. Zajac. Interview, 1997.
33. Herreid. Interview, 1997.
34. Shipper. Interview, 1997.
35. Zajac. Interview, 1997.
36. Perlman, 1998.
37. Zajac. Interview, 1997.
38. Brown, 1976: 241.
39. Pope, 1980: 159–161.
40. Herreid, 1997.
41. Ronström 1996: 7.

CHAPTER 4

TRANSMISSION: LEARNING MUSIC

KEYWORDS

acculturation
enculturation
fleádh cheoil
guru-sishya parampara
media landscape
oral, written, aural, and
electronic transmission
solfege

About This Chapter

Transmission refers to the passing on of tradition. The process of learning one's cultural traditions is called enculturation, and this goes on informally from the time a person is born. Musical enculturation includes listening to lullabies, singing nursery rhymes, listening to the radio, singing "Happy Birthday"—the sum total of our informal musical experience. Alongside such informal transmission, musical traditions are also learned formally, in the context of apprenticeships, lessons, classes, and schools.

Societal and technological change transforms processes of transmission, and musical learning has undergone profound changes during the twentieth century. Musical learning in the contemporary world involves three kinds of media: oral, written, and electronic. From remote villages to urban centers, these media interact in a complex new cultural web.

In this chapter, we explore musical transmission as it occurs in a variety of contemporary musical cultures, including classical music in the West and in North India, singing in the Bosnian highlands, Irish traditional music, jazz, and rock.

COMPANION RESOURCES

TELEVISION PROGRAM: Transmission

AUDIO SELECTION:

18. Tabla demonstration in Teental: bols. Ray Spiegel on tabla

The term *transmission* is often used to describe the handing down of tradition from one person to another or from one generation to the next. In the field of ethnomusicology, the term refers to musical communication: the processes by which musical traditions are inherited, learned, shared, and passed on. Alan Merriam, one of the first ethnomusicologists to focus on musical transmission, proposed that we view musical sound as the "end result of a dynamic process," in which learned concepts lead to learned behavior which results in musical structures and presentations.[1]

Learning a musical tradition is an individual experience involving personal choices and the development of cognitive and physical skills. It is also a social process conditioned by collective history and personal memory.[2] Each musician works through socially sanctioned models of form, style, and technique in order to ultimately find his or her own voice. These models are embedded in the fabric of social life, and exist in relationship to other aspects of culture, including politics, economics, gender issues, and aesthetics. Transmission involves who is allowed to be a musician (and in many cultures, musical roles are gender-linked) where musical learning takes place, how and from whom musicians obtain their skills, what instruments are played, and the repertory that is being taught.

While transmission refers both to the teaching and learning of music and to the ways in which music is stored, preserved, and passed on, in this chapter we will focus primarily on the former: the different processes by which musicians learn and inherit their tradition. Scholars have categorized these methods as oral, written, and electronic transmission. *Oral transmission* is the process of learning through imitation directly from an exemplar of a musical tradition; *written transmission* involves the use of notation and/or theoretical texts; and *electronic transmission* involves the use of recordings and computers in the learning process.

Although musicians in some cultures still learn solely through oral transmission, music students in many societies have access to a combination: oral and electronic, oral and written, or the use of all three. Musicians often switch from oral to written to electronic media without any sense that some change is involved.

The teaching and learning of music varies significantly from society to society, but until the recording age, the process had one thing in common worldwide: people learned directly from each other by watching, listening, imitating, and through formal or informal lessons. With the advent of electronic technology in the twentieth century, people were also able to listen to and learn from recordings that froze individual musical performances, allowing people to listen to the same musical material over and over again. Recordings dramatically altered the ways in which music was listened to and stored, and provided a new medium for learning. Nevertheless, musical transmission is still intrinsically connected to people—to the listening, teaching, creating, and collaborating that occurs between musicians, within families, between teachers and students, and between performers and audiences.

The Learning Process

Although we do not all consider ourselves to be musicians, almost all human beings learn music. Much of this learning is informal. Children's games which incorporate singing and movement are common in many African cultures, and lullabies seem to be a global phenomenon. In the United States, children sing nursery rhymes with their parents, game songs such as "Ring Around the Rosie" with their friends, and Christmas carols during the holiday season. We sing patriotic songs in school classrooms and at athletic events, and absorb popular songs from radio and television broadcasts and piped-in music in supermarkets and doctors' offices. This informal acquisition of musical knowledge, along with other aspects of one's culture, is called *enculturation.*

More formal music instruction takes a variety of forms. In many societies, professional musicians have traditionally passed their knowledge on to future performers in guild-like societies, in a master-apprentice style of training. Such guilds have often been restricted to members of families in which music is a hereditary occupation; in such cases, musical knowledge is passed on from parent to child, uncle to nephew, and so on. The modern phenomenon of private instruction in piano, voice, violin, guitar and the like is in some ways an adaptation of traditional apprenticeship, modified to fit the structures of contemporary society.

We may view informal enculturation and formal discipleship as two ends of a continuum which includes a wide variety of approaches to learning music. Students of a demanding piano teacher in America or Europe, or a *sitar* teacher in India, may have to practice several hours per day in order to prepare for their regular lessons. Members of school bands or orchestras may take private lessons on their instruments to acquire the technique to be able to join an ensemble. School choruses and church choirs require the formality of fixed rehearsals and public performances, but the singers are not generally considered "apprentices" of the conductor, and they might not practice the music as individuals between one rehearsal and the next. Rock and jazz musicians may or may not receive formal training from a private instructor, but they often acquire musical knowledge by imitating the playing of performers they observe in concerts and hear via CD's, cassettes, records, and videotapes. We learn music in many ways, and there are respects in which every person's musical education is unique.

The process of learning to sing or play music is very much like the process of learning to speak a language. This insight is central to the somewhat revolutionary educational concepts of Dr. Shinichi Suzuki, one of the most important figures in twentieth-century music education. Dr. Suzuki based his method of teaching the violin on the idea that training in music should parallel, as closely as possible, the learning of one's mother tongue. A thorough study of the "Suzuki technique" is beyond the scope of this chapter, but in thinking about processes of learning music we would do well to bear in mind Dr. Suzuki's basic premise: the acquisition of musical knowledge parallels the learning of spoken—and sometimes, written—language.

We will begin our examination of ways of learning music by considering traditions in informal enculturation.

▬ LEARNING BY INFORMAL ENCULTURATION

Informal learning occurs in a wide variety of contexts. For most people, the family is the first locus of musical education. Children hear lullabies, nursery rhymes, and holiday songs sung by their parents and siblings, joining in as the songs become familiar. Older family members provide models for the behavior of young children, and the children, grandchildren, nephews, nieces, and younger siblings of musicians often absorb musical skills and knowledge by observation and imitation.

In village societies, where the family is part of a closely knit local community, musical neighbors also provide role modeling for young singers and players. For villagers in highland Bosnia, group singing is a sort of social ritual for young people passing into adulthood, and children and young adolescents learn to sing by observing their elders. In Irish communities both in rural Ireland and in urban settings around the world, a natural affinity develops between older "tradition bearers" and young players, who learn both repertory and musical behavior by seeking out the company of senior musicians.

Informal musical enculturation includes listening to music both actively and passively. As active listeners, we may set out consciously to learn a song from a tape or CD. As passive listeners, we are often bombarded with electronically reproduced music at home, in supermarkets, offices, subways, streets, and automobiles. Even when we consciously or subconsciously try to block out background music, it affects us, as when we suddenly catch ourselves in the supermarket, humming along to a song which we were not even aware of hearing.

In some societies, informal learning is the principal means of musical transmission, but even in cultures where formal instruction predominates, enculturation provides the foundation upon which more structured training is built. Lessons and classes may be supplemented by informal sessions of discussion and music-making, which provide important opportunities for deepening and testing skills in a more relaxed setting.

Singing in the Bosnian Highlands

In Bosnian Highlander culture, children often start singing at an early age, but not by formal instruction. Instead they imitate what they hear from their elders in the village in the evening or what they hear at a village fair. Boys and girls start singing together in same sex groups at age six or seven, practicing the adult repertoire that they've acquired by listening and osmosis. Mirjana Laušević observed that this practice of singing is part of later courtship rituals in which group singing plays a fundamental role:

> In patriarchal Highlander culture, men and women do not sing together. Singing is a very important part of courtship rituals. And people will start singing at a very early age, but not in public. They will sing out in the meadows. They will sing up in the hills. They will sing away from the adults. . . . But up to the point when they're ready for courtship and marriage, they will not sing in the village. They will not sing out in the public in front of the adults. So it often happens, for example, a group of girls, when they feel ready for courtship and for marriage, subsequently they will suddenly one night decide to start a song in the village. And it's almost like an initiation rite, in which they will present themselves to the rest of their community, and they'll present themselves through the song. . . . And often mothers would say they were really surprised. But once their daughters started singing in public, they will pay more attention to them. They'll comb their hair, put nice clothes on them, and they'll (give them) jewelry so that they can get the attention that they're trying to get.[3]

BOSNIAN BECÁRAC SINGERS

Learning Irish Traditional Music

In other cultures, informal learning takes place very much within the family environment, functioning as an important component of musical transmission. In Ireland, for example, many musicians talk about the importance of parents, uncles, aunts, and neighbors as the primary source of their repertory, style, and techniques. By extension, musical transmission is considered personal—musicians celebrate the human links in the passing on of a song or tune more than they discuss playing techniques. Because most repertory is learned orally, musicians often cite the particular person from whom they've learned each song or tune in their repertory, including material learned from artists on recordings. Family musical lineages are still most highly valued in this system of personalizing repertory.

Because most music-making used to take place in the home, children learned first by listening to their elders. More formal learning might take place through lessons with a family member or neighbor, but the emphasis was on learning by doing rather than on years of apprenticeship. Recordings also played an important role in the transmission of traditional Irish music. American recordings made during the heyday of ethnic recordings in the 1920s by the great Sligo fiddlers, Paddy Killoran, James Morrison, and Michael Coleman, and the piper Patsy Touhey, have had a great impact on playing styles ever since, in both Ireland and America. In isolated areas in Ireland, recordings often served as a vital means for introducing new repertory and new techniques.

Although published tune collections have long been part of the Anglo-Celtic fiddle tune repertory, the format of these collections has contributed to the continued reliance on oral transmission—passing music down from musician to musician. For the most part, collectors have consistently presented tunes as single melodic lines without indications of performance practice, including instrumentation, ornamentation, variation, and improvisation. Because these aspects of performance practice are what breathes life into a musician's playing, it is generally acknowledged that one cannot learn Irish music from a book. Therefore, while tune collections have served as an important means of preserving and disseminating the ever growing tune repertory, musicians themselves tend to learn orally or "by ear"—from other musicians, recordings, and sessions.

There are, however, many new contexts for the transmission of traditional Irish music in the late twentieth century. While the family and home were, until recently, the locus of informal music sessions and socializing, the pub is now the preferred venue for music making. Both children and adults can study at local traditional music schools or at a variety of one week summer schools, such as the famous Willie Clancy Summer School held each July since 1972 in Miltown Malbay, County Clare.

In the context of the Willie Clancy week, students attend instrumental, singing, or set dance classes every morning, listen to and/or participate in the pub sessions that take place virtually around the clock, and attend daily concerts. There are also two public dances or céilís per day, which feature live bands and set dancing. The week's immersion in music includes formal classes and listening time, but the informal and spontaneous sessions, which bring together musicians of different ages, degrees of skill, and even nationalities, are where much of the learning and sharing take place. Because the school also functions as a week long festival, it attracts musicians from all over Ireland, Europe, Australia, Japan, and the United States, who come just to play in the sessions.

Competitions are also held at the local, regional, and national levels for musicians, singers, and dancers of all ages. Beginning in the early 1950s, these competitions, called *fleádh cheoil* (pronounced "flah kee-ol"), were organized by *Comhaltas Ceoltoiri Eireann* (pronounced "Koltus Keeoltoree Erun"), a new institution founded to promote Irish traditional music and dance, as well as the Irish language. Comhaltas has 400 local branches in Ireland and ten other countries and a pyramidal system of competitions, culminating in an international competition and festival.[4]

There are tens of thousands of people who participate in the competitions each year and many of them are children. For some, these formalized rites of passage are considered an essential means of preserving and promoting the tradition. For others, the organizational model of competitions represents the antithesis of traditional music performance. There seems to be no question that the fleádh cheoils have stimulated a great deal of interest in Irish music, and for many musicians, the contests are regarded, not as serious competitions, but as an excuse to get together and enjoy informal music-making in the sessions that inevitably spring up around any Irish musical gathering.

Transmission in Jazz

Jazz has traveled a long and complex road since its inception near the beginning of the twentieth century. Even from the early years, people have learned to play jazz in a number of different ways. In terms of the use of notation, it is best described as a mixed tradition, in which all players learn some of their art by ear, some never use notation, and some make extensive use of written scores for both learning and passing on their music.

The portion of a traditional jazz performance which is most often notated is the melody or "head," which serves as a point of departure for variation and improvisation. Early players often learned the basic tune by ear, and by definition, their improvisations were not written down. The proliferation of jazz recordings created an interesting paradox regarding improvised solos; once an impromptu performance has been given a fixed form on a record, tape, or CD, it is then possible to study, learn, memorize, and notate it.

By mid-century, the study of recorded solos had become a common means of aural transmission. The creation of jazz programs in universities and conservatories pushed this process still further, and now it is possible to buy books containing note-by-note transcriptions of the improvisations of renowned players such as Charlie Parker or Django Reinhardt. Many students practice exercises from instruction books which guide the reader through the fundamentals of jazz improvisation. They are introduced to the intricacies of swing or bebop style by memorizing the transcribed solos of past masters. These developments are part of a broad shift in the nature of jazz culture, involving, among other things, a change in venues from inexpensive bars to posh concert halls.

An Eclectic Tradition

Jazz has always drawn on popular music. Much traditional jazz consists not of the performance of a repertory unique to the genre, but rather of a special stylistic treatment of popular songs, often called "standards." Early jazz play-

ers improvised on the standards of their day, and contemporary jazz musicians grow up listening to all kinds of music.

Jazz saxophonist Josh Redman recalls that as a young child he heard not only jazz, but also the Beatles, Mozart, Indian, African, and Indonesian music, Aretha Franklin, and the Temptations. It took him some time to discover his particular attraction to his idiom and instrument:

JOSHUA REDMAN

> *Coltrane's music was alive for me from the beginning, Sonny Rollins's music was alive, Charlie Parker's music was alive, Dexter Gordon, Cannonball Adderley—these are musicians that I listened to from a very young age.*
>
> *But as I listened more to those musicians, I began to develop more of a sense of what jazz was as a distinct style, and what made it special, and the more I listened to jazz the more I developed a special relationship to that style of music, as a listener. And then when I started playing saxophone, immediately I found that the jazz style of music, the jazz language, the jazz idiom was the style that I felt the most comfortable with, and the style that I wanted to explore the most as a musician.[5]*

The Jazz Language

Redman goes on to describe the jazz language:

> *Jazz is a language . . . that has been defined and refined over a period of about a hundred years, and anyone who is trying to be an improviser in jazz has to be familiar with that language. . . . The language consists of many different things. It consists of certain melodic fragments, which have almost become clichéd . . . but the language of jazz is also the harmonies, being familiar with the harmonies, knowing how the melodies relate to the harmonies. The language of jazz is also rhythm abstracted from harmonies; you know, there are certain rhythms which are at the core of jazz. The swing rhythm is at the core of jazz.*
>
> *The language of jazz is basically a familiarity with the history of jazz, and the way in which musicians have interacted, and the ways in which they found common ideas to relate to one another with.[6]*

After describing the elements of the jazz language—motifs, harmonies, and rhythms—Redman stresses that familiarity with the genre's history and the ways in which musicians interact are essential components for understanding jazz. We may view history and contemporary interaction as two poles which generate the electricity of jazz today. The player must reach back into history to acquire the language, but he must find something new to say, in a culture of contemporary musicians, to keep the idiom alive and growing.

Modern musicians may learn the elements of jazz in a number of ways. Some players learn jazz by studying for years with private teachers, playing in bands, and eventually enrolling in a program at a university or conservatory. Some begin by learning classical music, and then switch to jazz after they have already acquired some facility on an instrument. Many musicians learn jazz by listening repeatedly to recordings of their favorite musicians and

CHARLIE PARKER

then trying to imitate the style and content of recorded performances. Recent decades have seen a burgeoning of available recordings, so that in some cases we can compare a single player's improvisations on a given piece of repertory over a period of decades of performing. Redman describes the value of such study:

> *To hear how Charlie Parker might have improvised over "Ornithology," one of his tunes, ten, twenty times, to hear the way in which those improvisations changed and the way in which they stayed the same, to hear the way those improvisations may have changed in the course of one studio session, or over the course of fifteen years of Charlie Parker improvising—that can give us more knowledge and more insight into Charlie Parker's process, or the process of any master jazz musician.[7]*

Although the availability of archival recordings and notated materials gives contemporary jazz students an advantage in studying the historical practice of jazz musicians, these materials also make the learning experience for modern players radically different from those of the past masters whose performances they are studying. "Getting it right," for a bebop player in the 1950s, usually meant playing something in a new, daring way, *avoiding* repeating past performances note-for-note. If a player in 1998 succeeds in performing a transcription of a bebop solo forty years after it was recorded, can we then say that she is "getting it right"? The player must balance the principle of historically-informed playing against the enduring jazz ideal of spontaneity. Redman describes this conflict:

> *Right now, as jazz musicians, we are confronted with a virtual glut of material. There are so many recordings of so many jazz musicians out there, there's so much historical information that it can threaten I think, at times, to overwhelm us. And we can get so obsessed with finding that new Charlie Parker recording, you know, with hearing everything from the past, and studying everything from the past, that we lose sight of the ultimate goal of jazz, and the ultimate goal of any music—which is to create something meaningful, and emotional, and honest, in the present.[8]*

Speaking the Language

However one goes about learning the rudiments of jazz, one must ultimately begin "speaking" this musical language by improvising with other musicians. In the context of jam sessions, the player develops a personal voice and style by entering into a musical dialogue with other players. Each improvisation involves learning and listening: sometimes a less experienced player is challenged and instructed by jamming with a more senior musician; other times, the exchange is between near-equals. After discussing the virtues and pitfalls of learning jazz repertory and style by studying recordings, becoming a virtual "apprentice" of recorded masters whom one may never have met or heard in a live performance, Josh Redman talks about the process of transmission as it occurs in person, at the side of other performing artists:

> There's a very important tradition of jazz that has nothing to do with the records, with the recording technology, and that is the tradition of learning at the side of a master musician. You know, not learning from a record which you put on and take off, but learning from a musician who's right there next to you, who's making music with you, who is sharing his or her knowledge and maturity with you.

> There's the tradition of going to the clubs and hearing the music played live, there's nothing to substitute for that, and I think it's important that even with all the information that's out there technologically, with all the recordings that are out there, we never lose sight of the fact that ultimately jazz is about human beings interacting, telling each other stories both verbally and musically, and sharing with each other as people at a particular time in the present tense.[9]

Interacting with other improvising musicians often creates strong emotional ties between the players. The musician must learn the language, the motifs, harmonies, and rhythms of jazz in order to be able to communicate, but for many players the essence of jazz lies not in its history, but in the act of communication. Josh Redman says, "Ultimately jazz is about the interactions of the different members of the band, the community of the band, and the way in which the band members relate to each other as musicians." In these relationships, transmission is a constant, multi-directional process, in which each player both learns and teaches. Within the "community of the band," Josh Redman says:

> The connection that you have to make in order to play music, the act of cooperating with someone musically, the act of communicating with someone musically so that you can together make a meaningful, coherent statement, that's a very spiritual act, and it's a form of spiritual education in a way.[10]

Transmission in Rock: Rusted Root

Jazz, which began as an African-American musical genre near the turn of the twentieth century, has had a profound effect on music around the world. American and European classical composers began borrowing harmonic, rhythmic, and melodic elements of jazz during the first quarter of the century. Popular music owes much of its formal vocabulary to the contributions of jazz musicians, and listeners and performers around the world have become devoted aficionados and exponents of the jazz tradition.

Rock and roll, America's second major contribution to the world's popular musics, also sprang from an African-American musical genre: rhythm and blues. During the 1950s, the first rock recordings of artists such as Bill Haley and the Comets, Buddy Holly and the Crickets, and Elvis Presley introduced white Americans to the musical language of rhythm and blues—a twelve-bar, three line song form, with an infectious beat and an ensemble usually consisting of voice, guitar, bass, piano, and drums.

Like jazz, rock is an eclectic, improvisational genre. Early recordings stuck close to their rhythm and blues roots, but over the decades, the rhythms, forms, and timbres of rock have been adopted by musicians across the popular music spectrum, so that today it is very difficult to draw a clear line dividing rock from other genres such as country and western. Rock lyricists have frequently moved out of the familiar subject matter of light-hearted love songs into "serious" composition, expressing themes related to politics, civil rights, religion, and philosophical issues, and rock composers draw on a myriad of musical influences, from J. S. Bach to the music of west African drum ensembles.

The "Media Landscape" of Rock

Unlike jazz, which underwent a transition from primarily live oral transmission to a learning process that frequently involves the extensive use of recorded performances as models, rock was "born and brought up" in the age of a mature and dominant recording industry. Jim DiSpirito, drummer with the popular rock band Rusted Root, remembers learning to play the drums while listening to recordings on headphones:

JIM DiSPIRITO

I always have this really nice memory of when I first started to really get into music, and started to think, "Boy, I'd sure like to play, you know, . . . that would be fun. And I remember you know, sitting on my bed with my drumsticks and my black t-shirt on, and puttin' on headphones, 'cause you know my parents were in the next room, and listening to AC-DC records and Led Zeppelin records. And, you know, just smacking the bed as hard as I could with these drumsticks, . . . and dust is flying all over the place. And just like going through record after record and like, a whole evening would pass and I would . . . take the headphones off and not even realize any time has passed. And . . . for me that was as close to a spiritual experience as I ever found, even more than going to church. It was something that I knew, like if it could take me out of time and it could take me away from all the pressures of being a kid, then . . . there's some real magic there.[11]

The proliferation of private listening devices, including headphones and portable tape and CD players, has transformed processes of transmission. Each student has the potential of living in multiple soundscapes, including live performances (the only medium available until the late nineteenth century) recorded music played in a common listening space, such as a home, office, store, or car, radio and television broadcasts, and the extremely private space enclosed between a pair of headphones. Students who wish to learn to play rock often take lessons with experienced music teachers, but much learning goes on in other contexts, and no rock musician may be said to be the exclusive product of apprenticeship to a single master.

As Jim DiSpirito says,

The media landscape is very different than in India, where the oral tradition specifically comes from one teacher and the information is passed orally. Modern American culture is much more eclectic, . . . because the student, a guitar student has so many different teachers, if you will, to choose from, given that so much is really learned through sound recordings."[12]

Like jazz musicians, rock players often learn to improvise by first memorizing solos from commercially available recordings, and as in jazz, this process seems to contain inherent contradictions. If improvisation is the goal, then why do we try so hard to reproduce a performance, note for note? If personal expression is the aim, then why do we work so diligently at mimicking the playing of other performers? These questions are particularly intriguing in the context of another issue: the association of rock with rebellion against conservative cultural values, and particularly against the constraints of Western classical music.

Finding One's Own Voice

For the most successful students of rock and roll, mimicry seems to be an early phase in their musical growth, followed by the search for an original voice. Rusted Root vocalist and percussionist Liz Berlin describes her learning process, not as one of imitating other vocalists, but as an effort to break through her early classical training to develop new vocal timbres and techniques:

LIZ BERLIN

> I think that I learned to play rock music by making it up, trying to make something new. I was raised with a classical voice training, and, you know, sang a lot of classical music when I was younger, and then—you know, when I learned to play the guitar, moved on to folk music, and started making up folk songs. But then when I joined the band it was just a whole new spectrum. . . . A lot more was possible and, I really, sort of rebelled against a lot of my training, to try and find places in my voice that were new and interesting. And places that, you know, I had to create sounds that I didn't hear on the radio at the time.[13]

The contrast between imitating recorded performances and trying to create something new illustrates a fundamental principle that rock musicians share with performers in many genres. They create their art in the context of a dynamic polarity between emulating the sound of admired performers and searching for one's own unique style.

Perhaps the notion of rock as rebellion against earlier classical training reflects something of the cultural roots of rock and roll. Rhythm and blues developed out of African-American traditions, which had always included an important place for improvised singing and playing. European classical music, and particularly the playing of Renaissance lutenists whose instruments were forerunners to the modern guitar, also has an old tradition of improvised playing, but by the twentieth century the art of improvisation had largely vanished from the Western classical tradition. When African-Americans played rhythm and blues, this was an expression of a continuing tradition, but when white Americans first took up jazz, and then rock and roll, the artistic freedom of the music represented a new frontier for many of the performers.

Returning to Jim DiSpirito's early practice sessions, drumming on his bed while listening to recordings, we find an example not only of modeling one's playing after that of recorded artists, but also of a search for a personal style. Rather than playing a single passage over and over to try and mimic every aspect of a drummer's playing, he played along with the recordings, "sitting in" as an extra member of the band. In this context, one inevitably combines the process of imitation with that of creating something new. He refers to this learning process as "learning through remembering," "learning by accident," and "pooling it from your being." Such expressions suggest that the source of musical knowledge is ultimately neither tangible, nor external like a record, tape, CD, score, or teacher, but an inner resource located in the memory and being of the musician.

"Birthing" a Song

Transmission refers not only to learning to sing or play an instrument, but to all the ways that music "travels" from person to person. In the Western classical tradition, we think of music as originating with a composer, who then transmits his compositions to the performers via the medium of a written score. They then transmit the music to the audience via the medium of performance.

In some cultures, such as those of the Kaluli of Papua, New Guinea or the Suyá of Brazil, repertory is thought to originate, not with human composers, but with extra-human agents such as animals and spirits. Even in the West, not all composers are comfortable with the idea that they are the single author of a given composition. Michael Glabicki, songwriter with Rusted Root, says "I often feel I'm being led to a song, [as] opposed to creating a song or writing a song." He goes on to describe this process in some detail, beginning at the point that the song has begun to have a shape of its own:

MICHAEL GLABICKI

> *At that point, that's where the struggle comes in, because it becomes even harder at that point to have something sitting in front of you and still remain unattached from it. . . . I continue at that point to bring it into the world, to birth it, to have it grow up in front of me without having influence over it. And I am not the owner of it; I am the keeper of it.*[14]

Continuing with the imagery of "birthing," Michael Glabicki observes that "often as you raise a child, it's not the parents that raise the child, it's the community around the child. So I'm always open to being shown ways to help that song grow. And that's bringing it to the band." When he brings a new idea for a song to the band, Michael Glabicki conceives of the song as "sitting in the center of our circle, and we are sitting around it. I have a certain perception of it, being the songwriter, that I see from here. You know, I can see maybe a little bit more than everybody else." As the musicians begin to experiment with accompaniments, harmonies, variations, and improvisations, the band "discovers" the song, taking the songwriter's original contribution as a point of departure in the creation of a new entity which is independent of any single author.

For Rusted Root, the creation of the song continues in performance, with the audience providing the ultimate contribution. Glabicki describes this process:

> *At the point of performing it, the audience gives to it. . . . You can visualize it as a tree. Back to when I receive a seed of it, I bring [it] till it's about this big, you know. And then I present it to the band, and then we work on the foundation of it, the trunk and the stronger branches of it. And then at that point we start to go into the thinner branches and the leaves.*

And then when you perform it, it starts to change all different sea-sons, and change colors, and leaves change, and leaves become bigger and more textured, and then the wind starts to come and create a pic-ture around it. And . . . then it becomes this wholesome world view, how this tree relates to this person, this person, and this other tree, and this other tree, and then it gets much bigger. . . . You truly realize that there's something bigger happening, and you know that, you know it's not your song anymore, it's gone.[15]

We may envision the creation of a Rusted Root song, then as a circular process, with various parties contributing in a process of mutual exchange:

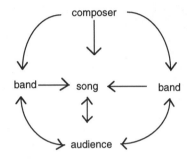

To be sure, not all rock songwriters take the non-possessive stance ex-pressed by Michael Glabicki, but several aspects of the process he describes—nurturing the nascent composition, collaborative creation, and the ultimate completion of the process in performance—are common to the experience of many rock and roll musicians.

LEARNING BY APPRENTICESHIP

In the tradition of apprenticeship, professional musicians learn their art by be-coming disciples or apprentices of a master-teacher. In a number of societies, apprentices are either literal or symbolic sons or daughters of their teachers. The actual children of the master benefit from twenty-four hour contact with their teacher and his art, absorbing nuances of musical behavior not only in formal lessons, but also by observation and osmosis. Non-relatives who be-come disciples of such a teacher often move into the mentor's home for several years, so that they too can have the advantage of full-time immersion in the life and art of a musician.

North Indian Classical Music: The Guru-Sishya Parampara

Traditional discipleship in Indian classical music takes the form of the *guru-sishya parampara* (master-disciple tradition). Historically, musicians in India prior to the twentieth century tended to come from three streams of society: families for whom music or dance were hereditary occupations; members of the aristocracy who practiced music as amateurs; and "musician-saints," for whom music was a path to God. Aristocratic and "saintly" musicians were often highly-respected members of society, but professional musicians were usually regarded as low-caste artisans employed by the temples or courts. Professionals might earn great respect for their artistry, develop a reputation as highly spiritual performers of religious music, and even become gurus of aristocratic patrons who became their musical disciples, but they still were regarded as "beyond the pale" by much of Indian society.

Whether a music student was a young aristocratic amateur or the child of a professional performer, the traditional setting for music instruction was the *guru-kula,* literally meaning the "master's household." Disciples or "sishyas" would undergo a formal initiation ceremony, in which a thread tied around the student's wrist symbolized his adoption as a life-long student and member of the guru's musical "family."

From this point on, the sishya moved into the guru's home, where the disciple performed domestic chores such as cooking, shopping, and cleaning, all the while observing the teacher's practice and instruction of advanced disciples. After some time, the guru might decide the student was ready to begin formal training. Lessons took place at the teacher's pleasure, at any hour of the day or night. After several years, when the student had reached an advanced level, he would accompany his guru to performances, carrying instruments, tending to his teacher's comfort, and playing or singing with the guru on stage, learning the art of performance at the mentor's side.

Female performers in the courts and temples were often born into families of professional musicians, or sometimes were "offered" as children by non-musician families to temples as "servants of God," to be trained as temple performers. Women played an important role in the transmission of music in the courts and temples, both as virtuoso performers, and sometimes as unacknowledged teachers of younger performers. Formal training took place in discipleship to a male guru, but informal musical enculturation often took place in the company of the sishya's mother or aunts. The low social status of professional musicians prevented most upper-caste girls from entering musical discipleship until the twentieth century, when courtly patronage came to an end and a new, urban middle-class became the main patrons, students, and eventually, professional performers of Indian classical music.

Foreseeing the extinction of courtly patronage, Indian musicians and musicologists in the early twentieth century began holding public concerts, establishing music schools, and publishing books of musical repertory, theory, and history, to ensure the survival of the music after its traditional patronage base no longer existed. These strategies, and the development of the Indian recording and broadcasting industries, seem to have been successful in introducing Indian classical music to a newly developed culture of middle-class listeners and performers.

Contemporary students seldom live with their gurus, and service in the teacher's home has largely been replaced by the payment of tuition fees, but other aspects of the guru-sishya parampara survive. Devotion to the teacher, a close, almost familial affection between guru and disciple, and a strong emphasis on oral, rather than written instruction, remain the foundations of musical instruction in India, and these qualities often persist even in institutional training. Serious performers still regard several years of intensive, personalized instruction as an indispensable part of a professional musician's education, and students who aspire to become professional performers often supplement classroom teaching in a music school or university by taking lessons with their personal gurus.

New Contexts for Transmission

Around the turn of the twentieth century, Indian classical musicians began performing in Europe and America. This activity intensified dramatically in the late 1960s, when several American universities began employing Indian musicians on their teaching faculty. The eminent North Indian instrumentalists Ali Akbar Khan and Ravi Shankar each established music schools in California, where Ali Akbar Khan resides and teaches to this day. Some American disciples of the faculty of the Ali Akbar College of Music have been studying for close to thirty years, and a number have made inroads as professional or semi-professional performers in India. Cross-cultural discipleship in the jet-age has created some interesting variations on the tradition of the guru-sishya parampara, as illustrated in the following quote from Ray Spiegel, an advanced American disciple of tabla maestro Ustad Alla Rakha:

> *When I got a chance to be near him (Alla Rakha) I would go . . . to the airport, and learn in somewhat of an old-fashioned method, which is not paying tuition but going and doing work or seva, service to the guru. . . . So I had no money, but I would go and meet him and sleep on the floor of his hotel, and take care of errands and help out with driving, cooking, shopping, cleaning—anything.*
>
> *And when he felt like it, he would teach me. These lessons were not formal. He never wrote anything down for me. In fact I never sat in front of him with drums. He only would recite compositions to me, and then I was expected to remember them, and at a later time write them down. . . . So it requires a lot of memory, and you have to be on your toes at all times, because you don't know when you're going to get a lesson. It could be in a restaurant, it could be late at night while he's in bed, it could be in the car in rush hour traffic in New York City on the way to the airport. But when it occurred to him to teach, that's when it was time for me to learn. So I did that for about, almost twenty years.*[16]

The substance of Ray Spiegel's training—serving the guru, learning at the master's pleasure, living at times in the guru's household, memorizing com-

RAY SPIEGEL AND USTAD ALLA RAKHA

positions verbally before either playing or notating them—corresponds to that of the traditional guru-kula, but the settings—hotel rooms, taxis, and airports—represent a radical departure from the ways of the past.

Ways of Learning

Ray Spiegel illustrates the tabla bols for the 16-beat rhythmic cycle known as teental.

Ray Spiegel was able to memorize compositions without actually playing them at the time of learning because Indian musicians and dancers use a system of mnemonic syllables in learning rhythms, drum strokes, choreography, and melodies. For tabla players, these mnemonic syllables, called *bols,* meaning literally "words," represent particular drum strokes. "Dha, dhin, na, tin, tete, kata, gadi, gena"—these are examples of bols that tabla players use to memorize drum compositions set in the *talas* or rhythmic cycles of Indian classical music.

Singers and players of melodic instruments such as the sarod, sitar, and bamboo flute use a set of mnemonic syllables called *sargam,* which are exactly analogous to the *solfege,* "do, re, mi," of Western music. Singers may first learn a song using the syllables "sa, re, ga, ma, pa, dha," and "ni," before actually singing the melody with its poetic text. Instrumentalists often learn to sing instrumental compositions called *gats* in sargam before attempting to play them on their instruments, and instrumental teachers frequently teach melodies by singing, rather than playing. This approach helps the student to internalize a composition before actually attempting to play it, and it emphasizes a key concept in Indian musical aesthetics. Indian aestheticians regard vocal music as the fountainhead of the arts, and instrumentalists are expected to emulate the motion and phrasing of the human voice in playing their instruments.

Before an Indian musician can begin learning actual compositions for voice, melodic instruments, or drums, he or she must gain a basic mastery of the notes and fundamental instrumental techniques. Singers and instrumentalists begin by practicing exercises called *paltas,* which train them to produce a variety of melodic patterns throughout their vocal or instrumental range. They then proceed to simple compositions in basic *ragas,* the melodic modes of Indian classical music. These compositions are often followed with numerous *tans,* fast passages created by the guru to provide the sishya with examples of correctly formed improvisations.

Students may memorize hundreds of such prototypes, creating a stockpile of rhythmic and melodic patterns which the disciple will later draw upon in his or her own spontaneous creations. Eventually, this training is intended to bring the student to a level of mastery and maturity in which she can compose and improvise melodies that correctly reflect both the complex melodic and rhythmic grammar of Indian classical music and the performer's own, individual creative imagination. Sarod player Buddhadev Das Gupta describes the training process from the guru's perspective:

> When you teach music, any kind, vocal or instrumental, you have first of all got to make your disciple or pupil go through the notes. And he has got to get the notes correct, then various combinations of notes which are called paltas, *in our terminology. And then he is started off with a simple* gat *in a relatively uncomplicated raga.*
>
> At first, all his lessons, just like a school boy, are written down in a book. Gradually, just like learning a language, when he has got all

BUDDHADEV DAS GUPTA

the words and sentences and grammar all stacked up, here he goes over to improvisations or impromptu playing. This stage may take, you know, years for somebody to attain. But ultimately you have to free yourself from the slavery of the book and written-down instructions. And then only you are really a performing musician.[17]

Each guru teaches not only a repertory of compositions and the basic rules of raga and tala, but a stylistic approach that is peculiar to his own particular family or teaching lineage, which in North India is called a *gharana*. Every Indian classical musician, therefore, must create a personal style, which at one time adheres to the melodic and rhythmic grammar of the broad tradition, reflects the stylistic approach of his particular lineage or school, and reflects his own, personal creative approach.

Western Classical Music

Western classical music, like Indian classical music, received its early patronage from courts and religious institutions. Singing was an essential part of worship both in Jewish synagogues and in the Christian church, and cantors and choir-masters held important places in the liturgical hierarchy. Music was also an important aspect of courtly life, where musicians were employed to play martial music before battles, to sing ballads celebrating the triumphs and virtues of their patrons, and to play dance music for royal entertainments. The quality of a court's musicians reflected the glory of the resident patron, so musicians were commonly retained as regular members of aristocratic establishments. Musicians, like other artisans, formed guilds which in some measure controlled the transmission of musical knowledge, and professional musicians naturally tended to pass their knowledge and profession on to their children.

Musicians, such as Johann Sebastian Bach, learned the theory and technique of performance and composition from the masters of preceding generations. They applied their knowledge as employees of either the Church or the courts, often moving from one church or court to another in the course of their careers. Although musicians often passed their knowledge on to their children, discipleship did not take on quite the formal character it had in India, nor did stylistic schools and teaching lineages become linked with a single court as they did in the gharanas of North India.

The eighteenth-century creation of the modern nation-states, a new emphasis on individualism, and the development of industries based on the division of labor had profound effects on the culture of Western classical music. With the crumbling of the aristocratic order in the revolutionary environment of late eighteenth-century Europe, musicians came to embody a new, democratic ideal of individualism, while at the same time appropriating some of the charisma and respect formerly reserved for the nobility. The "labor" of music-making became increasingly specialized and hierarchical, with pride of place reserved for composers, conductors, and virtuoso soloists. Composers, such as Ludwig von Beethoven, whose predecessors had been regarded as craftsmen in the royal "workshop," rose to a position of independence and prominence. The composer was no longer a mere craftsman, but an artist with a distinct and individual voice.

Most modern students of the piano are probably unaware that they themselves are links in one or another historical chain of transmission reaching back perhaps to the time of Beethoven. Masters of the piano, such as Franz Liszt, imparted not only repertory and technique, but also a distinct and personal stylistic approach to their students. Their students in turn passed on something of that approach to succeeding generations, down to the present. These chains of transmission may be regarded as stylistic schools, but in a much freer sense than that of the nineteenth-century North Indian gharanas. In India, transmission was carefully controlled by families in an active guild system under viable courtly patronage. In Europe, the guilds and the courts were essentially things of the past.

Learning the Piano

Modern Western classical pianists undergo a kind of training which in some ways parallels the master-disciple tradition of classical Indian music. The pianist, like a sarod player, undergoes many years of private instruction, in which he or she first acquires a basic knowledge of the notes, practices technical exercises, learns simple and then more complex compositions, and gradually absorbs the aesthetic approach of the teacher or teachers, ultimately going on to develop a style of his or her own.

For most Western classical pianists, formal musical training begins in childhood, in the form of weekly private lessons with a piano teacher. The piano, unlike orchestral and band instruments, is not often used in school music ensembles, so young piano students concentrate on solo repertory and seldom becoming involved as pianists learning or performing in institutional settings. Many young pianists in the United States compete in local or statewide competitions, whose organizers attempt to set broad technical standards for the grading of young performers, but many students never become involved in competing, and piano teachers are free to teach unencumbered by a prescribed curriculum. Serious students may continue to study for their entire lives, and those with professional aspirations often major in music at a college or music conservatory.

Mary Jo Pagano, who teaches piano in New York City, describes her approach to training young students:

*I mainly teach young children up till they're ready to go to college . . .
I have to cover notation. I have to teach them how to read the music.
I have to teach them their hand positions, how to execute things.*

*My focus is a little bit different in, say, a nine year old, than in a sev-
enteen year old. I teach them how to be relaxed, and how to use their
arm weight, and to produce good sound and try to bring out the
melody as opposed to the accompaniment.*

*I'm also very concerned that they begin at a very, very early age [to
learn] the musical concepts. A phrase is understandable by a small
child, but a lot of people forget to mention that. So I really try to talk
about phrasing, as early as five years old—so that it's not something
that they kind of have to learn later. That it becomes the language,
because music is a language, and if you don't learn to speak in sentences, if you get caught up in the little words or the little notes, then
you don't have music.*[18]

Like sarodist Buddhadev Das Gupta, Mary Jo Pagano begins by teaching
her students the basic notes and the way of producing them on her instrument, but unlike Indian classical musicians, her beginning pedagogy also emphasizes notation. This fundamental difference
reflects a basic distinction between Indian and
Western classical music—Indian classical music
is largely improvised, but the Western classical
piano repertory consists of a large number of notated pieces.

In Indian classical music, the guru teaches
repertory and interpretation all at once, by demonstrating phrases, which the student then imitates. The guru teaches the entire fixed portion of
the repertory by rote, note by note and phrase by
phrase. In Western classical music, the teacher
tends to present repertory and interpretation in
two phases: first, giving the student access to the
repertory by training them to read music, and
second, showing the student how to bring the
music to life by demonstration (playing for the
student) and discussion.

MARY JO PAGANO AND STUDENT

For those Western music students who do not proceed beyond the beginning stages of study, the notes on the page may remain just that—isolated
sounds, which ultimately make no sense together. Therefore, Pagano tries
from the very beginning stages of study, to instill in her students a sense of
phrasing, the way in which notes combine to create meaningful melodies.
Like many good teachers, she combines the two phases of instruction in
Western classical music in a single, integrated process.

Learning to interpret musical scores does not end with learning how to
read notes and rhythms. In every performance, musicians must make decisions about tempo (velocity—fast, slow, or somewhere in between), dynamics (loud or soft), attack (accented or unaccented), note duration (short, dis-
connected notes, or smooth melodic lines) phrasing (the grouping of notes
into meaningful melodies), timbre (tone quality—piercing and bright, or

warm and dark), and the balance between the different simultaneously sounding parts in a multi-voiced texture.

Composers during the Middle Ages and Renaissance gave no indications regarding these aspects of their music, so modern musicians must study the history of early music practice to be able to make informed decisions about how to interpret early music scores. Baroque composers such as Vivaldi, Bach, and Handel began to give indications of tempo and dynamics. Classical composers such as Mozart wrote in still more interpretive directions, and many twentieth century composers, such as Igor Stravinsky, gave detailed and explicit instructions as to how they wanted each note in their scores to be played.

Western classical musicians spend their lives studying score interpretation, in part because there are endless ways of playing a single piece of music. The composer's indications tell us only so much; the rest is up to the performer. Violinist Timothy Ying compares the freedom of a Western classical musician, playing from a written score, with that of an improvising jazz musician:

I think one of the misconceptions that people have about Western classical music is that because the notes are written down, there's somehow less freedom in performing it than there is in an art form like jazz, where there's actual improvisation going on. And it might seem like that at first, but actually, there's a tremendous amount of artistic expression going on within this music. Because even though you have that limited parameter of following these specific notes . . . there's an infinite variety in the number of ways that a given passage can be played.

For instance, you can have the same passage of music, and one person could play it very nobly and heroically, and then another person could play that very same passage of music and bring out the more thoughtful and reflective quality of it. And the interesting thing is, both of those qualities are there in the music, but these two performances bring out different aspects of the same masterpiece. So it's like taking a gem, and looking at it from first one way, and then you look at it from another way. And it's still the same gem, but you're seeing different aspects of it—different facets of it. And that's the wonderful thing about hearing two different people play the same piece.[19]

Teachers often use metaphors, like Timothy Ying's example of the gem which can be viewed from different directions, to discuss musical ideas with their students. Mary Jo Pagano recalls that her piano teacher, Leon Fleisher, used the image of a house to explain his approach to musical form:

I remember him often saying, "Don't begin with the detail. Begin with the large structure. You don't want to build your house around the furniture. You want to have the house, and then you want to put the furniture in the house."[20]

The "house" which Leon Fleisher described is the entire structure of a piece of music. At an advanced level of study, the pianist strives to understand all the aspects of this structure, so that she knows exactly how each musical detail contributes to the whole.

Ultimately, although Western classical musicians learn their music from printed scores, the music has no real "life" on the page. The musician brings it to life by making it audible, and for performer and audience alike, the thrill is in the hearing. In this respect, Western classical music is no different than musical traditions in which transmission happen primarily through oral means. Some teachers of Western music, such as Dr. Shinichi Suzuki, believe that rote learning should play an important part in the early training of classical musicians, and advanced students, for whom score-reading has ceased to be a problem, may do most of their learning by listening to the playing of their teachers and other performers. Mary Jo Pagano comments on the primacy of sound in learning music:

> You can't learn it [musical technique] from books. And most importantly, unlike other disciplines, music is . . . sound. And to describe a sound in words is so much more difficult than a demonstration by a great artist. Once you hear it, whatever those words were that the teacher was trying to explain to you . . . it becomes completely apparent, because you can hear it.[21]

■■■ CHAPTER SUMMARY

Musical transmission refers to all of the ways in which music is passed on from one person to another, one generation to another, or one culture to another. Musical enculturation, the process of learning one's own music culture, usually begins informally, with listening and perhaps singing among relatives and friends, at home or in one's local community. In many cultures, formal musical education is based on a master-apprentice model, in which one becomes a performer by undergoing prolonged training under the guidance of an established artist. Aspects of traditional apprenticeship persist in the form of private instruction and institutional learning in settings ranging from local music schools to university music departments and conservatories.

Musical learning has been transformed internationally by the spread of electronic media, which allows contemporary musicians to hear and study the performances of musicians over a century of recorded music around the globe. The spread of recording technology has greatly increased the pace of *acculturation,* the learning of music across cultures. Listeners who first hear the music of India, Ireland, or the European classical tradition by the media of records, tapes, and CD's, are sometimes inspired to study the performance of new musics, and it is not uncommon to find Germans playing Irish music, Japanese playing European classical music, or Southeast Asians playing rock.

Alongside such cross-cultural adoptions of musical style, many contemporary genres consist of syntheses of several traditions, resulting from the mixing of immigrant populations around the world. The meaning of the term "world music" varies greatly, depending on who is using it, but it is significant that it was coined shortly after the mid-point of the twentieth century. Internationally, contemporary musicians and listeners are members of an increasingly global web of music cultures.

STUDY QUESTIONS

1. How does informal enculturation differ from formal musical training?

2. What are the main features of the guru-sisya parampara?

3. Compare the training of a Western classical pianist with that of an Indian sarod player.

4. How is learning to play jazz like learning a language?

5. How has the transmission of Irish traditional music changed over the last century?

6. What is the role of the media landscape in the training of rock and roll musicians?

REFERENCED SOURCES

1. Merriam, 1964: 145.
2. Rice, 1994: 301.
3. Lausevic. Interview, 1996.
4. Henry, 1989: 68–69.
5. Redman. Interview, 1997.
6. Ibid.
7. Ibid.
8. Ibid.
9. Ibid.
10. Ibid.
11. DiSpirito, 1998.
12. Ibid.
13. Berlin. Interview, 1998.
14. Glabicki. Interview, 1998.
15. Ibid.
16. Spiegel. Interview, 1997.
17. Das Gupta. Interview, 1997.
18. Pagano. Interview, 1997.
19. Ying. Interview, 1997.
20. Pagano. Interview, 1997.
21. Ibid.

CHAPTER 5

RHYTHM

About This Chapter

This chapter provides an introduction to the subject of rhythm. Rhythm in music involves the patterning of sounds in time. Because all music unfolds in time, rhythm can be viewed as the duration of a whole piece or performance. The term can also be defined as the smaller patterns and durations that animate and structure the music—moving melodies and coordinating different parts together. Rhythm can be free, allowing the performer to play or sing without a fixed beat, but more often, rhythm involves a regularly recurring series of pulses or beats. The beat is what you can clap or tap your foot to. Beats are usually arranged in groupings or patterns of stressed and unstressed pulses, as in the meters of European-American classical and popular musics and in the cycles of North Indian and Javanese music. In the musics of the African diaspora, polyrhythms create a more complex grouping of beats among different musical parts.

KEYWORDS

meter
measure
ostinato
polyrhythm
pulse
syncopation
tala
tempo

COMPANION RESOURCES

TELEVISION PROGRAM: Rhythm

AUDIO SELECTIONS:

10. "Scotland the Brave"
11. "Wedding Waltz"
12. "John Howatt"
13. "The Tar Road to Sligo"
14. Symphony No. 5 in C minor by Ludwig von Beethoven: First Movement
15. Jor in Rag Kamod
16. "Hifumi Hachi Gaeshi"
17. "The Comet"
18. Tabla demonstration in Teental: bols
19. Tabla demonstration in Teental: khali
20. Tabla kaida in Teental.
21. Gat in Rag Kamod
22. "Soft Black Jersey Cow" (excerpt)
23. Rumba guaguancó (excerpt)
24. "Ratos e Urubus . . . Larguem Minha Fantasia"

The word rhythm refers to time and the organization of events in time. On a cosmological level, the earth, its moon, and the other planets each manifest a periodic rhythm, and it is the regular, predictable nature of such movement that allows us to divide decades into years, years into months, months into weeks, weeks into days, days into hours, hours into minutes, and minutes into seconds. The science of astronomy is dependent on rhythm—we would not know where and when to aim our telescope at a particular star or planet if these celestial bodies—especially our own planet—did not move in repeating temporal cycles. On a microcosmic level, our bodies manifest rhythm in the regular pulsing of our hearts, the alternation of inhalation and exhalation, the motion of our walking or running feet, and the functioning of the "internal clock" which tells us when to sleep, when to wake up, and when to become hungry.

Rhythm is perhaps the most essential ingredient of music—the motivating force that moves and structures music through time. The term can be used in several ways to designate everything that happens temporally within the confines of a composition or performance. Because all music unfolds in time, rhythm in its most general sense can be viewed as the duration of a whole piece or performance from start to finish. It can also be defined as the smaller patterns and durations that animate and structure the music—moving melodies and coordinating different parts together. On an even more micro level, rhythm can be viewed as the rate of vibrations of a single tone. As we saw in Chapter 1, every tone is a product of the periodic oscillation of a vibrating object.

In terms of structuring a piece or performance, rhythm can be free, allowing the performer to play or sing without a fixed beat. As we will see later, the alap or introductory section of a North Indian classical music performance begins with this kind of free rhythm. More often, rhythm involves a regularly recurring series of pulses or beats. The beat is what you can clap or tap your foot to. A strong beat is characteristic of dance music all over the world, from rumba to ballet, disco to Irish step dance. Beats are usually arranged in groupings or patterns of stressed and unstressed pulses, as in the meters of European-American classical and popular musics and in the cycles of North Indian and Javanese music. In the musics of the African diaspora, polyrhythms create a more complex grouping of beats among different musical parts.

▄▄▄ PULSE, METER, AND RHYTHM

Western musicians usually begin their formal rhythmic training by learning to count evenly spaced pulses in *measures* or *bars* of four beats. We say that musical time organized into such regular, repeating patterns is *metrical*—that is, it conforms to a *meter,* in this case, of four pulses. While pulse can be defined as regularly occurring beats of equal weight, like the ticking of a clock, meter groups pulses into recurring patterns of strong and weak beats. Each repeating unit of this pattern is called a bar or measure and these are marked off from one another in musical notation by bar lines. Western music is often composed in meters of two, three, four, six, nine, or twelve beats per measure; European and American dance music provide many examples.

Marches provide an example of a meter in two, with a stressed pulse on one and an unstressed pulse on two. This kind of pattern, in which alternate beats are stressed strong—weak—strong—weak is called *duple meter*. The rhythmic feel of marches is closely related to walking, and therefore, the music is often used to facilitate and inspire dances with walking steps and marching of all kinds.

RHYTHM EXAMPLE 1: "SCOTLAND THE BRAVE"

A performance of "Scotland the Brave."

Example 1 shows the first eight measures of "Scotland the Brave," a traditional Scottish march. In this and the following three examples, numbers under the first two measures illustrate the meter.

When beats are grouped in threes with a stressed pulse on one, we have triple meter. Waltzes provide a good example of dance music in triple meter. Two well known compositions in triple meter are "The Star Spangled Banner" and "My Country 'Tis of Thee."

RHYTHM EXAMPLE 2: "WEDDING WALTZ"

A performance of "Wedding Waltz."

Example 2 shows the first eight measures of "Wedding Waltz," composed by the American fiddler and guitarist George Wilson.

Two beat and three beat measures are, in a sense, the basic units underlying meter in Western music: others are a combination of these. For example, two groups of two beats can be combined into a single measure to create four beats per measure. The strongest beat is on one and a secondary accent on three. This patterning in four is the meter for perhaps ninety percent of rock and many other kinds of popular music. Although written in units of four, much music in this meter (called 4/4) is perceived in two; music divided into measures of two or four beats is therefore said to be in *duple meter*.

RHYTHM EXAMPLE 3: "JOHN HOWATT"

A performance of "John Howatt."

Example 3 shows the first eight measures of "John Howatt," a traditional Scottish reel in 4/4.

Compound meter involves larger groupings of beats divided into regularly recurring patterns of strong and weak. Compound meters consist of a certain number of main beats, each subdivided into subsidiary beats. The most common example involves two main beats, each one subdivided into three: **1** 2 3 **4** 5 6/**1** 2 3 **4** 5 6. The meter is divided into units of six beats (and called 6/8), but the overall rhythmic feel is in two. It is therefore referred to as compound duple meter. The Irish jig is a dance type that is composed in compound meter, either in groupings of six (6/8) or groupings of nine (9/8) that have three strong beats. Other familiar American children's songs in 6/8 include "Row, Row, Row Your Boat" and "Three Blind Mice."

RHYTHM EXAMPLE 4: "THE TAR ROAD TO SLIGO"

A performance of "The Tar Road to Sligo"

Example 4 shows the first eight measures of "The Tar Road to Sligo," a traditional Irish jig in 6/8.

Because the meter often stays the same throughout a piece of music, it provides a rhythmic structure for all the musical content of the piece. The arrangement of long and short durations within each measure vary and it is these rhythms that animate the melodies and harmonies. Thus the measure becomes a conduit for all the events that move the music through time. Joseph Kerman described this contrast:

> *In most Western music, duple, triple, or compound meter serves as the regular background against which one perceives the actual rhythms, which are almost always much more complicated. As the rhythm now coincides with the meter, then goes its own way, all kinds of variety, tension, and excitement can result. Indeed, it is the interaction of rhythm and meter that supplies much of music's vitality. Meter is background, rhythm foreground.[1]*

The famous first movement of this work provides an excellent example of the contrast between meter and rhythm. The first movement is in duple meter throughout. In terms of the rhythmic foreground, the piece is dominated by a single rhythmic and melodic motif that appears as the famous opening theme.

RHYTHM EXAMPLE 5: BEETHOVEN'S FIFTH SYMPHONY

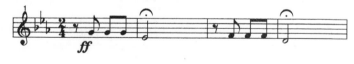

A performance of the first movement of Beethoven's Fifth Symphony in C minor.

Example 5 shows the first four measures of Beethoven's Fifth Symphony in C minor.

LUDWIG VON BEETHOVEN

This theme surfaces over and over again in the movement—at different pitch levels and dynamic levels, in different parts, and even turned upside down. It also becomes joined together immediately after the first statement of the theme. The restatement of this motif in different keys set against the background of duple meter creates consistency, tension, and excitement in the music.

While meter is background and rhythm foreground in much of Western classical and popular music, we have not mentioned the overall speed of the music how quickly or slowly it is played or sung. The term *tempo* refers to this aspect of performance. We say that a song is meant to be sung slowly and expressively or that a tune is upbeat. The tempo of a piece indicates how fast the basic pulse moves through time. Western classical composers have often used Italian terms such as *adagio* (slow) and *allegro* (quick) to indicate tempo.

Unmetered Pulse and Free Rhythm

Not all music has a regularly recurring pattern of strong and weak beats. Music may have a pulse which is non-metric; that is, it may maintain a regular beat without being organized into regularly recurring measures of a particular number of pulses. An example of this kind of rhythm is the *jor* section of a melodic improvisation in the classical music of North India.

Buddhadev Das Gupta plays the jor section of his alap in Rag Kamod.

Music may also be performed in "free rhythm," without a steady, measurable beat. Such music is not a-rhythmic, because it still presents sounds organized in time—not in measures or pulses, but according to non-metric principles such as the length of an exhalation, the duration of a violinist's bow-stroke, or the completion of a word or a phrase in a line of sung poetry. Such free rhythm is exemplified in the solo *shakuhachi* tradition of Japan, in which the player's breath determines the length of the musical phrase. Both the technique of the flutist's inhalation and exhalation, and the silences between phrases, are important in shakuhachi playing. The exhalation determines dynamics and tone colors in the musical phrase; typically the sound grows fainter toward the end of the exhalation. Some notes have more stress than others and there is a sense of gravitational pull forward. Nevertheless, it is impossible to tap out a regularly recurring beat or pulse. Tomie Hahn, an ethnomusicologist and shakuhachi player, states that breath determines the rhythm of the phrase as well as the whole piece:

> So we have the inhale and then the note and the end of the phrase. . . . The breath . . . is what each phrase is built upon. And in between each phrase we have silence and then the taking in of the breath. This is actually the pace of all the units and how they connect all the little phrases that build up the piece into a larger rhythmic form.[2]

A performance of "Hifumi Hachi Gaeshi," a traditional Japanese shakuhachi piece in free rhythm.

Music in free rhythm is often performed by a soloist—a singer or instrumentalist who doesn't have to coordinate with other performers. When two

TOMIE HAHN, SHAKUHACHI PLAYER

or more musicians play or sing together, it is essential that they have markers to keep them synchronized. One important reference is the presence of a regular recurring beat or grouping of beats. On the other hand, an unaccompanied soloist, such as a ballad singer, can convey his or her message with more flexibility in terms of both rhythm and expression.

Free rhythm has also been an important component of some twentieth century avante-garde music and modern jazz. John Cage, the pioneer of chance music, is perhaps the best known composer of music based on random and unpredictable sounds. In attempting to give up traditional structures and processes of music, Cage's compositions are often free in terms of predetermined length or overall rhythm and in the ways that performers perform their parts.

Cyclical Thinking

Western music is often conceived of as a linear phenomenon. The use of staff notation, with its horizontal lines that are read, like most Western languages, from left to right, reinforces this conception. In India, Indonesia, and the Middle East, meter is often organized not into visually conceived lines, but into time cycles which may best be represented as circles, much like the face of a rotary clock. These repeating rhythmic structures may be as short as a single measure of two or three beats, or they may combine large numbers of shorter metrical units into cycles of hundreds of pulses, which may take one or more minutes to complete. In Java, music played by the gamelan—an orchestra made up primarily of metallophones and knobbed and hanging gongs—is in rhythmic cycles almost always based on some factor of two, including cycles of 8, 16, 32, 64, or 128 beats. These cycles are regularly marked at key points by different sized gongs. The largest instrument in the ensemble—a hanging gong called the Gong Ageng —always plays the last and most important beat of the cycle.

In India, time cycles are central not only to musical thinking but also to commonly-held assumptions about the nature of human existence. In many societies, the rhythmic organization of music reflects cultural ideas about the structure of society and/or the cosmos. The relationship of time cycles to the music of North India will be discussed later in the chapter.

Syncopation, Swing, and Polyrhythm

In many kinds of music, rhythmic interest is heightened by the occasional emphasis of "weak" beats—such as beats two and four in 4/4 time—or notes which fall between the pulses—places within the measure which normally do not receive an accent. The accenting of such "off-beats," called *syncopation,* may anticipate a strong beat by placing an accent just before it, or delay the emphasis by placing it immediately after a strong beat.

In jazz, syncopation and a more subtle form of off-beat emphasis known as "swing" animate performance. Although no two jazz musicians may agree on exactly how to define "swing," it is "a combination of two things: rhythmic interpretation and rhythmic unity." According to saxophonist Josh Redman, swing is the essence of jazz:

A performance of "The Comet" by Rave Tesar, demonstrating swing rhythm and syncopation.

> *One of the things that defines jazz and makes it jazz is the swing rhythm. . . . Swing is a subdivision of rhythm which is, in a certain way, off-center, it's uneven. If I play a series of eighth notes very straight [right on the beat], there's no swing involved. Now if I put a swing feel on those eighth notes, they're going to become uneven, one is going to be a bit longer than the other, and the shorter is actually going to have a certain accent that the longer one doesn't have. So the rhythm comes alive, it dances a little bit, and that is the essence of the swing rhythm. . . . I like to define it more as a feel. It's sort of a relaxed intensity; there's an edge there, there's forward motion, but at the same time there's a coolness to it.[3]*

Syncopation and swing generate rhythmic excitement, but do not usually go so far as to obscure the basic meter of a piece. In much African traditional music, interlocking, repeating parts called *ostinatos* create multiple accents and a shifting sense of meter, in which it is neither possible nor absolutely correct to say that a particular piece of repertory is in 3/4 or 4/4 time. The individual parts in a Ghanaian Asante *Kete* ensemble, for example, do not all share a common beginning point in time. Each instrument is, in a sense, in its own meter, resulting in a combined rhythm which can be felt as having several possible beginnings.[4] We call this metric ambiguity *polyrhythm*, defining it as the simultaneous sounding of multiple rhythmic frameworks.

The simplest example of polyrhythm is called "three-against-two," in which one player—or one hand—plays three evenly-spaced beats in the same time that a second player—or hand—plays two, also evenly-spaced, pulses. You can learn to clap this simple polyrhythm by filling in the beats and counting "and" after each beat, subdividing each measure into six equal parts (six being divisible by both two and three). The right hand claps on one, two, and three; the left on one and the "and" after two. The resultant, composite rhythm is shown in example 6:

RHYTHM EXAMPLE 6

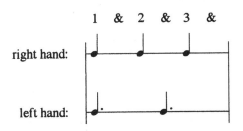

This way of counting organizes both hands into a basic measure of three beats, but in true polyrhythm, you should be able to feel each measure in either three or two equal parts (or both at once). To more fully understand this concept, give a strong accent to the "one" and the "and" claps of the left hand, which divide the measure into two halves. To get an even stronger sense of this polyrhythm, you may practice dividing the measure into two parts by counting "*one*-and-a-*two*-and-a," clapping with the left hand on "one" and "two" and with the right on "one," the "a" before "two," and the "and" after "two." When you have mastered the parts, you will be able to switch between feeling the triple pulse in your right hand and the duple pulse in your left.

The challenge is not physical but conceptual; the hands perform identically whether one is counting in two or in three. This metrical ambiguity characterizes much African music, and creates an important role for the listener—who may also be a dancer, singer, or hand-clapper. African music in many traditions has no role for a passive audience, but requires all present to participate, and the shifting perception of accent and meter provides the listener with the opportunity and need to "frame" the music according to a spontaneous and continually changing perception of its rhythmic organization.

▄▄▄ RHYTHM IN SOUTH ASIAN CLASSICAL MUSIC: NORTH INDIA

We use the term "South Asia" to describe the region encompassed by the modern nations of Pakistan, India, Nepal, Bangladesh, and Sri Lanka. South Asia presents a complex overlay of cultures, the product of many centuries of migration, trade, travel and conquest involving a broad array of cultures, religions, and ethnic groups.

By 2500 BCE, a well-organized urban civilization had developed in the Indus River valley of present-day Pakistan. By 1500 BCE, nomadic herdsmen from Central Asia called Aryans had begun to take control of the region. Over the course of several centuries, the Aryans established a dominant culture, with a classical Indo-European language (Sanskrit), a religious literature (the Vedas), a pantheon of gods and goddesses—the basis of later Hindu-

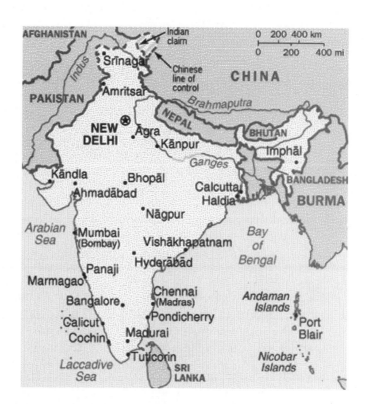

ism—and a social hierarchy which came to be known as the varna-jati or caste system. This dominant culture faced repeated challenges both from indigenous, Indian-born religions (Jainism and Buddhism), and from conquerors and missionaries from the West (Islam and Christianity).

Such cultural contacts sometimes resulted in war and the establishment or overthrow of foreign rule, but as often as not, the conquerors themselves underwent a process of "Indianization" which resulted in the creation of hybrid forms of language, religion, art and music. North Indian—also called *Hindustani*—classical music is one such form, resulting from the adoption and development of Indian court and temple music in the largely Muslim courts of North India, beginning in the thirteenth century and continuing into the twentieth.

Early treatises describe Indian classical music as a gift from the gods, derived from religious chant, and the form, content, and intent of modern Indian music continues to embody basic principles of Hindu cosmology. Central among these is the idea that everything in the universe moves in repeating cycles. Human life itself is considered to be a cycle including birth, death, and rebirth, and the entire universe also proceeds through unending circles of creation, dissolution, and recreation.

Tala and Alap

Rhythmically, the cyclical aspect of all existence is reflected in the concept of *tala,* which is the most important rhythmic principle in Indian classical music. In both North and South India, classical songs and instrumental compositions are set to repeating rhythmic cycles called talas. North Indian talas may be as short as three beats or as long as one-hundred-and-eight. The longer patterns are commonly subdivided into smaller sections of two, three, four, or five pulses.

While tala is an important aspect of Indian classical music, the opening portion of a performance, called *alap,* is performed in free rhythm. This alap is frequently subdivided into three portions: 1) *alap:* graceful, unhurried melodic movement in which there is no obvious pulse; 2) *jor:* a medium tempo pulse is established, but no tala structure is applied; and 3) *jhala:* the pulse becomes quite fast, but still is not confined within a tala cycle.

Once the melodic soloist—either a singer or an instrumentalist—has completed the alap, he or she usually proceeds to a composition set in tala. At this point, the soloist is joined by a drummer, who provides accompaniment by outlining the rhythmic shape of the time cycle on the paired drums known collectively as *tabla.*

TABLA DRUMS

The most common tala in North India is *teental,* a cycle of sixteen beats divided into four measures of four. The first beat of the cycle is called *sam* (pronounced "sum"). This accented beat functions as a point of departure and return for the structured improvisations that make up a large part of

Hindustani music performance. Musicians often show *sam* by clapping on the first beat of the cycle. The midpoint of the cycle, which falls on beat nine—the beginning of the third measure of tala—is called *khali,* and is shown by a "wave" in which the palm of the hand is turned upwards, the reverse of a clap. The fifth and thirteenth beats, which begin the second and fourth measures of tala, are shown by hand claps. The musician must always complete the cycle by returning to *sam* at the conclusion of a performance or practice session. An entire cycle of teental, then, may be counted and clapped as follows:

clap (*sam*)
1   2   3   4

clap
5   6   7   8

wave (*khali*)
9   10   11   12

clap
13   14   15   16

clap (*sam*)
1

Ray Spiegel demonstrates teental, by counting, clapping, reciting, and playing the tabla.

The tabla player is often restricted to a supporting role, showing the basic tala structure by playing a repeated, basic pattern, called the *theka* of the tala. Every theka is represented by a series of spoken syllables, each of which represents a stroke or combination of strokes on the drums. One common theka pattern for the sixteen-beat teental is as follows:

clap (*sam*)
Dha   Dhin   Dhin   Dha

clap
Dha   Dhin   Dhin   Dha

wave (*khali*)
Dha   Tin   Tin   Ta

clap
Ta   Dhin   Dhin   Dha

clap (*sam*)
Dha

Ray Spiegel demonstrates khali by counting and playing the tabla.

By playing the theka clearly, the tabla player provides an improvising soloist with audible "signposts" that help the soloist to tailor his improvisations properly within the tala. The clearest signpost occurs from beats 9 through 12 ("Dha Tin Tin Ta"), when the low sound of the bass drum is absent. The third measure of the cycle, in which the bass sound disappears, is called khali or "empty."

The tabla player often fills in the theka with subtle ornamentation, clearly maintaining the basic shape of the tala, but sometimes he is given the opportunity to play a solo for one or more cycles. Both melodic soloists and drummers often display their mastery of rhythm by concluding a solo with a *tihai,* a rhythmic figure which, performed three times in succession, concludes on *sam.* In audio example #20, Ray Spiegel plays a tabla composition called a *kaida,* a set of variations on the theme, and a concluding tihai. The kaida and tihai are represented by the following syllables:

Kaida
dhati dha-tere kitataka terekita
dhati dhaga tina kena
tati ta-tere kitataka terekita
dhati dhaga dhina gena

Tihai (the entire tihai is played 3 times to end on sam)
dhati dha ga dhina gena
dhati dha-tere kitataka terekita dha -
dhati dha-tere kitataka terekita dha -
dhati dha-tere kitataka terekita dha -

Ray Spiegel performs an improvised tabla solo (*kaida*) in teental.

Songs and instrumental compositions in Indian classical music are set in tala cycles such as teental. We will explore one teental composition in Chapter 6 "Melody" and Chapter 10 "Form."

▬ POLYRHYTHM IN THE AFRICAN DIASPORA

The cultures of Africa and the African diaspora are especially rich areas for the study of polyrhythm. Along with call and response form, polyrhythmic texture is one of the most salient features of almost all of the musics of these cultures. Through an investigation of a few African-American examples in North, Central, and South America, we can begin to sense the tremendous diversity of rhythmic expression in what the collector and author John Storm Roberts has called the "black music of two worlds."[5]

The connection between these two worlds involves one of the most heinous passages in recorded history: the slave trade. For over three centuries, until the countries of the New World abolished slavery in the mid-1800s, slave ships plundered the coast of western Africa, kidnapping countless inhabitants and condemning them to lives of forced labor, mainly in North, Central, and South America. Most slaves were taken from the regions of sub-Saharan West Africa. In the United States, members of different ethnic and language groups were routinely mixed together to discourage cooperation and communication between the captives. As a result of this and other forms of suppression, relatively few African cultural practices survived unchanged in America; for the most part new cultural practices arose, rooted generally in sub-Saharan West African practices but adapted to the harsh new circumstances of slavery in an unknown land.

Little is known about the music of the slaves, except for reports of singing at work, worship, and recreation, and indications that a number of slaves were taught to furnish European-style music for the entertainment of their captors. But contemporary accounts only reproduced song lyrics—and those only occasionally—and very general and ethnocentric descriptions of performing styles. For specific musical details, we can only turn to those few examples in oral tradition which are said to come from the slavery era.

One such example is *Jibber.* According to Bessie Jones, who learned it sometime in the early twentieth century from her paternal grandfather, an ex-slave, "People say Juba, but it's really jibber."[6] Jibber is a polyrhythmic song which can be performed by one musician: the handpatting pattern sets up a triple rhythm while the vocal part is in a duple rhythm, creating a constant three-against-two polyrhythm. While Jones referred to Jibber as a game, there was clearly more to it:

> *Many of the games used to be what you call "talking to the white man in song." Like where my grandfather was in Virginia, they used to have the slaves eat out of a trough on Sundays. They used to have a big thing where they would bring mush from all the houses around and put it in there, then add all the leftovers from through the week, and sometimes fresh roasted rabbit or pig, and gather the slaves around to play games and eat that food. . . . Jibber was the ends of food that they used to have in that trough. . . . These games were for talking to them white folks direct, because the slaves didn't like the way they were being treated.*[7]

RHYTHM EXAMPLE 7: JIBBER

Example 7 shows the handpatting and vocal parts for one verse of Jibber. "Jibber kill the alley cat" means that the leftover food isn't even fit for a stray cat to eat. "Get over double trouble" refers to the wish to escape from slavery; as Jones put it, it means "Someday I'll get to cook my own food."[8]

To perform Jibber yourself, start with the handpatting rhythm. With your left hand held just over your right, strike your right thigh with the palm of your right hand. Now bring your right hand up so that its back strikes the palm of your left hand. Now strike your right thigh with your right palm again, while you move your left hand to your left thigh. Repeat the same pattern there: left palm to thigh, left backhand to right palm, left palm to thigh while moving your right hand back to your right thigh. Now work on getting the rhythm steady—right palm, right back, right palm/left palm, left back, left palm. You are producing a triple rhythm, two groups of three beats. Once you can keep this pattern going, start adding the vocal part. It's tricky at first, but eventually you'll be able to reproduce this polyrhythmic game song from the slavery era of the United States.

Although polyrhythms are usually social in nature, involving at least two musicians playing different rhythmic patterns, Jibber shows that one resourceful person can produce polyrhythmic music. Polyrhythms can also be played on a single multi-toned instrument. One of several West African examples is the *kora,* a spiked harp with a large gourd resonator. While kora performances may involve various practices, pieces are always based on a repeating polyrhythm known as *kumbengo* which supports singing and/or instrumental improvisation.

African-American blues musicians approached the guitar in similar ways, layering repeating polyrhythms in different registers of the instrument to accompany their songs and improvisations. This kind of polyrhythmic solo playing fed into the development of ragtime guitar and piano playing, which in turn inspired the virtuoso piano music of the 1930s and 1940s known as "boogie-woogie." Another African-American development, the drum set, allowed a solo drummer to produce polyrhythmic layers on an array of percussion instruments.

But the most widespread examples of polyrhythm involve various instruments played by more than one musician. Although few African-American polyrhythms can be traced to specific African pieces, African organizing principles can be found in many of the African-American musics of the New World. There are few North American examples of percussion ensembles dating from the slavery era. Many slaveholders in the southern United States forbade drumming among their slaves for two reasons: 1) concerns over the sanctioning of "pagan" rituals and 2) the fact that drums could be used to send subversive signals through the African practice of using them to replicate speech. But some polyrhythmic drumming practices survived into the twentieth century in that region, as we will see below.

Slaveowners in South and Central America tended to be more indulgent of ensemble drumming, and we will turn to these regions later for two further explorations of African-American polyrhythmic traditions. Finally we will look at developments in African-American popular music in the late twentieth century, when polyrhythmic practices became salient in the development of funk music, leading to the growth of the richly polyrhythmic genre known as rap.

Mississippi: Fife and Drum

Although the largely pre-revolutionary Black Codes had a chilling effect on drumming among slaves in the southern United States, leading to the banning of drums in some areas, such practices were not wiped out entirely. Throughout the slavery era, informal accounts such as letters and diaries bear witness to polyrhythmic drumming practices in various parts of the region. There are also plenty of accounts of drumming among slaves in the northeastern United States, where the Black Codes had less influence. Black fife and drum bands existed even before the Revolutionary War in the north, and participated in that war as well as in the Civil War. Presumably these bands played in the characteristic European-derived military style. But as time passed, southern African-Americans evolved very different ways of playing these instruments.

On a trip to Mississippi to record folk music in 1942, the American folklorist Alan Lomax heard about Sid Hemphill's group, located and recorded them. This remarkable African-American ensemble of multi-instrumentalists could perform as a string band on fiddle, guitar, banjo, mandolin, and harmonica; as a full brass band; or as a fife-and-drum band. Their repertory included music to appeal to white audiences, from barn dances to the latest popular tunes. But they also played polyrhythmic music on their drums, with Hemphill blowing short repeated phrases on panpipes—one-note reed pipes attached in a scalar sequence—whooping and shouting in between. Listening to Lomax's recordings, it is difficult to imagine that one is listening to the same musicians from one song to the next—the string band selections sound like any good white country band of the period, while the panpipe and drum music sounds like it could have been recorded in Africa.

Panpipes are no longer played in the region, but local fife and drum music could still be found in some agricultural areas of rural Mississippi when the American folklorist David Evans visited there in the late 1960s and early 1970s. The music was mainly performed at summer community picnics, often on Saturday afternoon after a baseball game. A few people might dance, but mainly the picnickers just enjoyed the music, the food, and the chance to socialize. Othar Turner, an outstanding player of this music, described the feeling of such occasions:

> *Laughin', talkin', just associatin' with one another—just fun. Little kids go out and dance behind the drum. We have all of that, just a real of what you call a good time. Just for enjoyment, just to keep from bein' at home alone, just goin' out for a little enjoyment, that's the way we do. We all meets there, white peoples come there just like colored, right there, sit down there laughin' and talkin'. . . no clownin', cussin', hootin' and hollerin', no gun, no cuttin' and shootin'. Everybody bein' lovin' and peaceful—we always want that. Just to enjoy.*[9]

Although Turner and his friends refer to the music as "fife and drum," they call the wind instrument a "cane." It is indeed a piece of fresh cane stalk, cut from a local creek bottom and reamed with a hot poker, with five or six finger holes and a breath hole burned into it. The drums are the usual commercial instruments found in marching bands: one or more snare drums and a bass drum. While the music is essentially instrumental, the cane player may stop to sing a few lines of a blues or some other song; otherwise he improvises on short repeating phrases, varying them with different decorations,

sometimes throwing in a long, undecorated note reminiscent of a vocal whoop. The musicians sometimes dance with their instruments, even occasionally performing stunts such as the cane player doffing his hat with one hand while continuing to play with the other. The musicians refer to their own dancing and antics as "marching," recalling the military origins of this instrumental grouping.

RHYTHM EXAMPLE 8: "SOFT BLACK JERSEY COW"

Example 8 shows the basic polyrhythmic cycle for "Soft Black Jersey Cow" as played by three of Turner's associates. The cane line shown is one of several possible ostinatos. In most drumming traditions the lowest-pitched drum plays a slower rhythm while any higher-pitched drums play quicker, more improvisatory parts, but that norm is inverted in this performance: the snare drum plays a relatively unchanging part somewhat reminiscent of the *clave* of some Cuban musics, while the bass drum is both more active and more improvisatory. The bass drum part shown here is the general pattern, which the player elaborates on or departs from in various ways.

A performance of "Soft Black Jersey Cow." At one point in this performance the cane player sings two humorous verses about the cow in the title: "mama gonna milk you or either kill you dead," derived from a local children's song, and "had no milk and butter since old Jersey been gone," derived from a country blues in which the lost cow symbolizes a former lover.

Cuba: Rumba

The largest and most populous island in the Caribbean Sea, Cuba is a land of severe economic hardship—but also of great cultural abundance, including a bountiful musical environment. Historically, this creative richness is mainly

the result of contacts between Hispanic and African peoples—the former initially as conquerors and settlers, the latter subsequently as their slaves—over the last few centuries. The indigenous *Taino* people of Cuba were exterminated by the Spanish in the decades after Columbus first reached the Caribbean; today their cultural impact on the whole region is minimal.

The spectrum of Cuban musics runs from practices directly derived from Africa, such as those of the *santería* religion, which is founded in beliefs, rituals, and music of the Yoruba of Nigeria, to genres rooted mainly in European-based traditions, such as the popular, politically-oriented *nueva trova* songs. Cuba's musical influence is felt all over the Caribbean, and since the nineteenth century it has spread to Europe and other parts of America. By the mid-twentieth century many of the popular musics of urban Africa were derived from Cuban models. And, as we will see later, one Cuban genre—*son*—evolved into a music whose impact extended even further.

Rumba apparently developed in the 1860s, in the black, lower-class urban areas of Havana and Matanzas provinces. Centered in the large, crowded residences known as *solares*, where many poor Afro-Cubans were forced to live, its songs spoke of hard times in both love relationships and social injustices, while its music affirmed the inner vitality of the heart, like much of the music of oppressed peoples. In the solares, rumba was a communal music which could involve any number of percussionists and chorus singers. The lead singer improvised lyrics on topics ranging from local news or the personalities and proclivities of those present to broader themes of troubled or happy love, the inequities of racism, and the bitterness of poverty. Initially the instruments were often just empty wooden crates of various sizes, bottles, spoons, and so on—whatever people could find that made a strong sound.

From the solares rumba disseminated throughout the island, evolving many different local idioms, both in music and dance. Soon it was being exported to other parts of the Caribbean, to Africa, and to Europe and the United States, fueling the "Latin Dance" fad of the 1930s. The ballroom style, sometimes known as *rumba de salon*, may involve elegant dancers in tuxedos and evening gowns, accompanied by a full Western orchestra—a far cry from the culture of the solares! But despite such class-crossing, and the

LOS MUÑEQUITOS DE MATANZAS

Photograph by Mary A. Overby.

Cuban government's overt manipulation of the genre for propagandistic purposes, rumba essentially remains a music and dance of the heart.

Today three forms of rumba survive in oral tradition, each with its own characteristic rhythmic cycle and dance form: *yambú*, *columbia*, and *guaguancó*. While rumba music may be played for general social dancing, the traditional dance forms are improvised by one couple (yambú and guaguancó) or by a solo male dancer (columbia) within a circle of onlookers who may participate with handclaps and encouraging shouts.

The columbia is a display of the soloist's grace, skill, and inventiveness. It may involve humorous miming movements evoking sports events, drunkenness, fighting, and so on—or it may be purely abstract, with subtle or flamboyant movements, sometimes involving manipulating knives or other handheld objects. In all cases, the excitement of the columbia derives from both the creativeness of the dancer and his ability to move instantly and flawlessly from quick, off-center movements to a state of perfect balance.

The yambú and guaguancó depict the ageless game of flirtation, the woman alternately inviting and resisting the man's advances, the man successively showing off, imploring her, or even teasing her with a sharp pelvic thrust or mimed assault, which she must repel gracefully, usually by protecting herself with a swish of her long skirts. These couple dances always stress good-humored sophistication and virtuosity, avoiding vulgarity. They require intense concentration and split-second timing, as well as technical and improvisational skill, belying the apparent nonchalance of the performers. Yambú, which some musicians consider the oldest form of rumba, is comparatively low-key and stately, while guaguancó is quicker and flashier. **Example 9** shows the basic polyrhythmic cycle for rumba guaguancó.

RHYTHM EXAMPLE 9: RUMBA GUAGUANCÓ

An excerpt from a rumba guaguancó performance by Cuban street musicians.

The core instruments of the rumba ensemble are three standing barrel drums, usually called *conga*, *segundo*, and *quinto*, from the lowest in pitch to the highest, and a pair of sticks called *clave* which may be played by the lead singer. The quinto player improvises almost constantly; the other parts are relatively unchanging, anchoring the group with the characteristic polyrhythm of each rumba type. Other hand-held percussion instruments may be involved, but the four core instruments are essential.

Brazil: Samba

Brazil is the largest country in South America, and it is one of environmental contrasts—from the humid rain forest surrounding the Amazon River to the arid desert of the Northeast to the lush grasslands of the South. It is also

home to manifold cultures. Some Native American groups live in much the same way they did before Europeans ever arrived; sprawling cities pit glamour and technology against teeming slums and appalling poverty; and some villages in the Bahia region very closely resemble their counterparts in West Africa. In fact, there are more people of African descent living in Brazil than in any other country outside of Africa. Yet the national language is Portuguese, a distinction Brazil shares with but a handful of other countries.

The country's cultural diversity is reflected in the panorama of its music, which runs a gamut from the comparatively conservative traditions of the Amazonian and Bahian regions to the wildly eclectic urban genre known as MPB—*música popular brasileira*, "Brazilian popular music"—which seems to borrow musical sounds and ideas from every corner of the earth while still retaining a clear Brazilian essence. Between these extremes are a number of indigenous forms which have sprung largely from connections between cultures from Europe and Africa. To many people, the genre which functions as the primary wellspring of truly Brazilian music is *samba.*

Apparently samba developed in the African-American community of nineteenth-century Rio de Janeiro, one of Brazil's most important seaports. By the early twentieth century it was a distinct form, differentiated from other urban Brazilian genres by its greater reliance on such African elements as call and response singing and polyrhythmic accompaniment, influenced to some extent by the musical practices of Brazil's syncretic *macumba* religions. Samba has taken several different forms, from the intimate, soulful melodies of *samba-canção* to the boisterous *samba-enredo* of Carnaval. It can involve a voice and one or two instruments, a large group of singers with a massive *batucada* percussion ensemble, and just about any kind of assemblage in between.

The heartbeat of samba is the *surdo* rhythm, emphasizing the third beat of each four-beat group with a low-pitched accent which might be played on the large *surdo* drum, any other comparatively low drum, or in the low register of a guitar or other accompanying instrument. Various cross-rhythms may be played above this rhythmic basis, by smaller percussion instruments, in the higher registers of the guitar, or on the *cavaquinho*, a small four-stringed guitar-like instrument.

Samba is also a dance form, which has many regional variants. Some forms are presentational, with improvising soloists alternating within a circle of spectators like the forms of rumba discussed earlier; some are relatively informal couple dances; and the competing groups of Carnaval perform extravagant, carefully-rehearsed choreography.

Carnaval is a pre-Lenten festival. In the Christian calendar Lent is a period of austerity, and several cultures have evolved traditions of exuberant celebration just before this time of fasting and repentance—one well known example is the Mardi Gras in New Orleans. Since the nineteenth century,

Rio's version of Carnaval has included parades, percussion and vocal music, and dancing, in addition to nonmusical pleasures, such as drinking and general merriment.

In the early twentieth-century *escolas de samba* ("samba schools") arose: community centers, usually in poor neighborhoods, whose annual function was to organize music and dance groups for Carnaval. Often they are also year-round social centers, and they may provide other community services as well, such as medical assistance or day-care. Today there are over fifty escolas de samba in Rio alone, and the centerpiece of Carnaval is their competition. Each escola spends most of the year creating elaborate costumes and floats and composing, choreographing, and rehearsing their samba-enredo group.

While it is dear to the hearts of many Brazilians, Carnaval is also a mammoth tourist event. The samba-enredo competition has sometimes appeared to be corrupted by political interests, and some escolas de samba are suspected of connections to money laundering from drug trafficking and other illegal activities. Some *sambaistas* are disillusioned about what Carnaval has become, seeing it as an empty exercise in mindless euphoria, turning the pleasures of the poor into political propaganda and exploiting the music of the people for the enrichment of cynical manipulators. On one occasion, this disillusionment found a voice in an unexpected way.

In 1989 the members of *Beija-Flor*, an escola de samba which had been famous for its particularly opulent costumes and extravagant performances, astonished all of Rio by appearing at Carnaval dressed in rags and garbage, singing a song which addressed the disparity between reality and fantasy in samba-enredo: "*Ratos e Urubus. . . Larguem Minha Fantasia*" (Rats and Vultures. . . Let Me Have my Costume). "In life I am a beggar," they sang, "but I am the king of the revelry . . . if you stay the rat will catch you; if you fall the vulture will eat you!" Although the group's presentation was the audience's clear favorite that year, Beija-Flor missed the first-place designation by one point, losing to a group whose presentation was not socially charged.[10]

RHYTHM EXAMPLE 10: RATOS E URUBUS, LARGUEM MINHA FANTASIA, BASIC CYCLE

AUDIO 23 Beija-Flor's recording of "Ratos e Urubus."

Example 10 shows the basic polyrhythmic cycle of "Ratos e Urubus." As in any large batucada, the pulsing surdo part is divided between two sizes of surdo, the lowest ones sounding on the decisive third beat. The *agogo*, a double cowbell, provides a syncopated rhythmic cycle, interlocking with the *tambourims*, small pan drums held in one hand and played with a stick in the other. The *caixa* snare drum plays a steady stream of eighth notes, accenting the first and fourth of each group of four; the *reco-reco* scraper characteristically accents just the first of each eighth-note group.

Funk and Rap

In the mid-1960s African-American popular music was dominated by two generic categories: rhythm & blues, a youthful development of the forms and practices of older electric blues styles, and soul, which, while its lyrics were secular, drew more on the conventions of gospel music. There was much intermingling of the two—for example, Ray Charles's celebrated "What'd I Say" used a twelve-bar blues form, but featured gospel-style call and response singing. But the distinction widened as rhythm & blues increasingly was marketed as "rock & roll," expanding its territory into white America while soul remained more of a distinctly African-American genre. Many of soul's most accomplished singers, such as Aretha Franklin and Sam Cooke, came from a solid background in gospel music, using its declamatory style and upbeat music to fashion a sound which to many fans symbolized the contemporary growth of "black pride" and the Civil Rights Movement.

James Brown, one of the popular young soul singers of this period, developed a new genre, grounded in gospel and soul but also seeming to have a tap root stretching back to Africa. As the American critic Robert Palmer put it, "Brown, his musicians, and his arrangers began to treat every instrument and voice in the group as if it were a drum."[11] Perhaps influenced by Cuban and other Caribbean genres which could be heard in the United States, Brown and his band pioneered a highly polyrhythmic music which became known as funk. While American popular music had previously been essentially homophonic, funk was a polyphonic music in which both voices and instruments produced interlocking rhythms and melodic lines. Over this pulsating web of sound, Brown could sing or speak rhythmically, setting up further polyrhythms and showcasing his improvisatory virtuosity.

Following the success of Brown's innovations funk became a genre in itself, further popularized by groups like Sly and the Family Stone, Parliament, and Funkadelic. The rise of disco in the 1970s overshadowed funk's popularity, ushering in a period in which polyrhythm played a less significant role in African-American music. But by the end of the decade a new genre that had been developing in poor urban neighborhoods started to gain more and more attention. With the release of Sugar Hill Gang's "Rapper's Delight" in 1979, rap music burst out of the ghettoes and into the national—and subsequently international—spotlight.

To a certain extent, rapping grew out of an African-American form of spoken oral poetry known as "toasts." Taking their generic name from their function at drinking parties, these rhymed couplets are often a humorous satire on the conventional "here's to your health" kind of toast. They are stylized insults, usually obscene, often denigrating the subject's parentage, sexual mores, and so on. Toasts may be traded in an improvisatory, competitive interaction, a game known as "signifying" or "the dozens."

Some longer toasts are stories—involving, for example, a signifying monkey who manages to repeatedly insult a lion while avoiding its claws—until the tale's end, or a legendary black man named Shine who survives the Titanic disaster by swimming home ("When the news hit the street that the Titanic had sunk / Shine was standin' on the street corner, one-half drunk"), always in strings of rhymed couplets. Another important influence came from the rhythmic declamations of the "beat poets" of the 1950s and 60s, particularly the African-Americans collectively known as The Last Poets.

Today's rappers may compose their raps carefully, or they may improvise; one can even find a contemporary version of "the dozens," with rappers competing in rhymed insults. Whatever the situation, rapping combines rhetoric, rhythm, and rhyme in a celebration of verbal virtuosity. Although some forms of rapping are stylized to the point of sounding like chants, by definition rap is never literally sung to a melody.

The non-vocal components of rap are most often polyrhythms derived from funk conventions, though these are usually articulated through technological manipulation rather than by live instrumentalists. Rap musicians are well aware of their musical heritage, and often include digital samples from older funk recordings in their polyrhythmic creations. Indeed, it has been noted that James Brown's recordings may be the most often-sampled sources in rap music.

In all of these African-American group examples, polyrhythmic practices symbolize a particular kind of cultural value: the participants know and stick to their roles, yet each is a distinctive contributor to a larger whole which comprises more than the sum of its parts. Polyrhythmic groups portray a vision of individuality and cooperation in a vibrant society, enacted in sound.

▬ CHAPTER SUMMARY

Rhythm, in its broadest sense, is fundamental to our world. From the rotation of our planet to the beating of our hearts, it pervades our experience. People use musical rhythm to articulate this central fact of living, celebrate it, and to organize and synchronize bodies, minds, and spirits. And perhaps more than any other aspect of music, rhythm connects us not only to what people think, feel, and do, but also to the pulses, cycles, and tempos of the natural world.

STUDY QUESTIONS

1. What is the relationship between pulse and meter?

2. What is duple meter? What is triple meter?

3. Define the following terms:

   syncopation

   swing

4. What general rhythmic term applies to each of these genres?

   alap

   march

   rumba

   samba

   gat

   jig

5. What musical characteristics do rumba, samba, funk, and rap have in common?

REFERENCED SOURCES

1. Kerman, 1987: 19–20.
2. Hahn. Interview, 1997.
3. Redman. Interview, 1997.
4. Koetting, 1992: 85–93.
5. Roberts, 1972.
6. Jones, 1983: 44–5.
7. Ibid: 44–5.
8. Ibid: 44).
9. Evans, N.d.
10. Searles, 1990.
11. Palmer, 1992: 168.

CHAPTER 6

MELODY

About This Chapter

In this chapter we will examine the nature of melody, the "singable part" of music. Our earliest musical memories usually have to do with the simple tunes of common songs such as Christmas carols or nursery rhymes. When you remove the words from these songs, what remains is the melody. Pitch, the frequency (highness or lowness) of a sung or played sound, is the raw material from which melodies are made. Melodies, or tunes, organize pitches into sequences which have a distinct contour and rhythm.

Each music culture has its own ways of organizing pitches into melodies. In some cultures the rules of melody-making are unspoken, learned by ear, and taken for granted by the members of a community. In other cultures, melodic systems have developed an elaborate and explicit musical grammar, which is discussed by theorists and practitioners. This chapter will introduce you to some of the ways that musicians create and think about melodies in a variety of cultures, including the European classical, Arabic, Irish, and North Indian musical traditions.

KEYWORDS

diatonic
interval
maqam
mode
modulation
motif, motive
octave
pitch
raga
scale
tonic

COMPANION RESOURCES

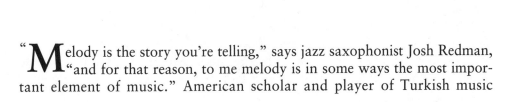

TELEVISION PROGRAM: Melody

AUDIO SELECTIONS:

25. "Sonata in A Major" by Wolfgang Amadeus Mozart: First Movement.
26. "Dikrayati"
27. "Crossing the Shannon"
28. "The Rocks of Bawn" (1st verse), 1963
29. "The Rocks of Bawn" (1st verse), 1973
30. "Were You at the Rock?"
21. Gat in Rag Kamod, Teental

"Melody is the story you're telling," says jazz saxophonist Josh Redman, "and for that reason, to me melody is in some ways the most important element of music." American scholar and player of Turkish music

Frederick Stubbs continues: "It's like a story because it has a beginning, it has a plot, and it has an ending." Melody tells its story through changing pitch, a succession of rising and falling tones.

A drone is not a melody: its *pitch* never changes. The regular rise and fall of an emergency siren has meaning as a signal, but few people would call it a melody; in its incessant regularity, it is more like a drone. It doesn't tell a story. Neither does the signal of a two-note doorbell or cuckoo clock. The children's song "Rain, Rain, Go Away" can be sung using just two pitches—the same two that doorbells and cuckoo clocks often use—but we might be more willing to call it a melody; this is probably because the words and rhythm give a feeling of shape to the overall utterance. Still, most people consider it a very simple, childish melody—it barely squeezes into the category. If we add one occurrence of a third pitch, as many children do, it already sounds more melodic.

Some melodies are very short. A celebrated example is the four-note theme from which Ludwig von Beethoven built the entire first movement of his Fifth Symphony. Melodies might be quite long as well. Some Arabic and Turkish melodies take several minutes to perform, and the melody of a Central Javanese gamelan composition can stretch even longer without repeating. What they all share is pitch, which can be described as the vibrating frequency of a tone.

In the Western common system, the pitch called "A" vibrates at or near 440 cycles per second. The pitch vibrating twice as fast—880 cycles per second—is also called "A," but it is said to be an octave higher. When women and men sing the same melody together they often sing in octaves, the higher women's voices sounding an octave above the men's. Still, it sounds like they are all singing the same melody; tones which are an octave apart are perceived as sharing a basic pitch identity.

Perhaps for this reason, many of the world's music systems involve the octave as a frame for placing other pitches, which may divide the octave in various ways. Such subdivisions of the octave are called *scales*. In the West and in a number of other cultures, seven basic pitches or "steps" divide the octave into a diatonic scale. In fact the word *octave* ("eighth") refers to these seven steps plus the next note, which is an "eighth" or octave above the starting pitch. Several other systems involve five steps, making a pentatonic scale; still others may use more or less. Steps may have names—such as the solfege syllables doh, re, mi, fa, sol, la, ti or the letter names A, B, C, D, E, F, G in the West. Some other cultures also use solfege syllables to identify pitches in a row or scale: in India, the steps dividing the octave are called sa, re, ga, ma, pa, dha, and ni.

Western musicians also recognize a twelve-pitch scale called the *chromatic scale*, in which five of the diatonic steps are subdivided. This set of pitches represents all the white and black keys on the piano within one octave. Until the twentieth century, these chromatic pitches were always regarded as somewhat auxiliary to the prevailing diatonic scale pitches. As we will see later in this chapter, Indian and Arabic music systems have somewhat similar concepts.

In general, Western musicians do not regard scales as having meaning in themselves, beyond the overly simplified observation that melodies in major scales sound happy or serene and those in minor scales sound sad or agitated. American composer Gerald Shapiro refers to a scale as "a kind of bag of

A demonstration of two important Western diatonic scales, major and harmonic minor. These are notated in **Appendix 2**.

notes from which you can choose the notes of your melody." In the music systems in some other cultures, scales are not used as abstract sets of pitches. Indian *ragas* are considered to possess inherent meaning, as did Arabic maqamet in an earlier period; the composer or improviser does not simply choose pitches from a collection, but is entrusted with the responsibility of unfolding and developing a complex and rich aggregation of meanings that are considered to be already inherent in the melody form.

But whatever the specifics of the system, melodic meaning begins here, with the relationships of pitches to each other and often to the framing octave as well. Individual melodies might move up and down a scale smoothly by steps, or may leap past one or more steps to another pitch. They may slide between pitches, or use pitches which lie between the basic steps, sometimes dividing one step into minute subdivisions. But pitches only start to have meaning as melodies when they are heard in relationship to each other through time.

Pitch relationships are called *intervals*. We have already discussed the interval of an octave, or eighth. Other intervals are also referred to numerically: two notes which are one step apart constitute a *second*, notes two steps apart form a *third*, and so on. Two notes of identical pitch constitute a *unison* ("one sound"). When notes sound simultaneously, the interval is said to be *harmonic*; when they sound sequentially, the interval is *melodic*.

A demonstration of melodic and harmonic intervals. These are notated in **Appendix 1**.

The smallest interval in Western music is the *half step*, also known as a *minor second*. It can be visualized as the distance between two adjacent frets on a guitar fingerboard, or as immediately neighboring keys on a piano. The steps of diatonic scales are all either half steps or whole steps (comprising two half steps, a major second). The intervals of the chromatic scale are all half steps.

If you program a computer to move randomly between the pitches of a given scale, it is unlikely that the result would sound like a satisfying melody. A melody must have a coherent form. Different cultures have different criteria for creating a pleasing form, but pure formlessness is seldom regarded as music. There must be some formal considerations if any melody is to cohere and satisfy. Such considerations may involve clear subdivisions, giving a melody a feeling of inner relationships somewhat like the relationships between words in a sentence, sentences in a paragraph, paragraphs in a chapter, and so on. Or, perhaps more frequently, these formal practices might resemble elements of poetry—small-scale relationships like assonance, consonance, and rhyme; larger-scale relationships like metric patterns, stanzaic patterns, and so on.

Western musicians have developed a terminology for the structural elements of melody. The shortest unit, of course, is a single pitch. A relatively small group of pitches which repeats, perhaps with some variation, is called a *motive* or *motif*. Some people would argue that the four-note theme of Beethoven's Fifth Symphony is not a melody at all, but a motif which is used to build larger structures in the piece. A grouping of a small number of pitches which does not repeat motivically is called a phrase member, and two or more phrase members constitute a phrase. In turn, two or more phrases constitute a complete melody.

Another Western children's song can provide a brief example. This melody has carried many different sets of words; in English, at least three sets are fairly well known: "Twinkle, Twinkle, Little Star," "Baa, Baa, Black

Sheep," and "The Alphabet Song." The first pitch (sung twice) immediately establishes a reference point for any following pitches. The second pitch creates an interval called a fifth: it is the fifth scale pitch above the first. The melody then moves up a step, returns to the fifth above the first pitch, and pauses there. This pause carries a little bit of tension: the melody doesn't sound finished yet. Then the melody continues down stepwise, finally returning to the first pitch with a feeling of resolution.

MELODY EXAMPLE 1: "TWINKLE, TWINKLE, LITTLE STAR" MELODY

Although this melody normally continues on from here, we can view this section as a little melody in itself: in Stubbs's words, it has a beginning (the rising fifth), a plot (a pause followed by stepwise movement back down), and an end (returning to the initial pitch). Like most melodies, it involves both stepwise motion and leaping motion—the fifth at the beginning. It has a specific rhythmic shape as well: a rhythmic pattern is repeated, six quarter-notes followed by a half-note.

The midpoint pause separates the melody into two parts, increasing the tension which is resolved at the end. The words sung to this melody sometimes mirror this feeling with a question and answer: "Baa baa black sheep, have you any wool? / Yes sir, yes sir, three bags full." The French text Wolfgang Amadeus Mozart referred to when he wrote his twelve variations on this melody has a somewhat similar structure—in this case the pause separates two clauses of one sentence: "Ah, vous dirai-je, Maman, / Ce qui cause mon tourment?" ("Ah, shall I tell you, Mama, / What is causing my torment?")

The beginning of a melody Mozart composed for another set of variations can give us a chance to look at further kinds of melodic relationships. It starts with a brief melodic idea—a step up, a step back down, and an upward leap of a third—which can be called a motif. What follows is a varied repetition of this motif, moving it down one scale step. The phrase member which follows presents a contrast, rising and falling mainly in stepwise motion, but ending the whole phrase with that questioning sound which indicates that the story will continue. Then the original motif and its variation are repeated, and the following phrase member provides another contrast, echoing the stepwise rise and fall of its counterpart in the first phrase, but ending with a real feeling of resolution. In the ensuing variations this melody is transformed in several ways, but these basic relationships are always preserved.

A performance of this theme-and-variations movement from Mozart's Piano Sonata in A Major.

MELODY EXAMPLE 2: FIRST EIGHT MEASURES FROM THE FIRST MOVEMENT OF MOZART'S A MAJOR PIANO SONATA, NO. 11 (K.331).

Many music-cultures make use of the idea of melodic variation, either in the kinds of large-scale systematic variations written by composers like Mozart or in more spontaneous and small-scale improvisational practices such as those associated with Irish traditional music, discussed later in this chapter. Variation can involve a very subtle level of musical communication. Once you know the basic melody, you can perceive every nuance of its variation, drawing you into an appreciation of the tiniest details of the composer or improviser's art.

Indeed, whole music systems, such as those of India and the Arab world which are described below, may be based on elaborate melodic prototypes which can be unfolded in various ways through composition and improvisation; knowledgeable audience members can recognize and understand a musician's individual approach to these prototypes in relation to the many other performances they have heard of them. Although these melodic systems have their own names—*raga*, *maqam*, and so on—scholars sometimes refer to them cross-culturally with the term *mode*, borrowed from similar melodic prototypes which were used by medieval composers of Western church music.

WOLFGANG AMADEUS MOZART

MELODY IN WESTERN CLASSICAL MUSIC

The earliest examples we have of European music are notated melodies of sacred chants. These melodies are based on the mode system, which involves scales derived from the Western diatonic scale with differing "final" pitches—*finalis* in the Latin of the early scribes. Since these modal scales have been found in common practice among many of Europe's folk musicians, some scholars have suggested that local folk music provided the elemental basis for some of the more elaborate modal melodies of traditions like that of Gregorian Chant, while other melodies apparently were rooted in earlier traditions of Western Asia and Northern Africa. Throughout the medieval and Renaissance eras (until approximately the mid-sixteenth century), composers in religious and courtly traditions used modal scales in their melodic practices, but eventually the modal system was largely superseded by the tonal system, which involved two basic scales called major and minor.

For centuries, Western classical musicians have also worked with the idea of simultaneous melodies which might contrast with or complement each other. Early modal developments in counterpoint ushered in polyphonic systems involving two or more concurrent melodies, and composers delighted in crafting forms in which several voices or instruments produced distinct melodies that blended into a harmonious whole. Such multi-melodic practices enriched a compositional tradition which continues to thrive and develop today.

In the twentieth century, many Western classical musicians began to reconsider their ideas about melody. Some immersed themselves in folk or popular musics, convinced that the melodic practices of non-classical musicians had much to offer. Others cultivated contacts with the melodic traditions of non-European cultures.

Another restructuring of melodic thought came from the serial practices developed by Arnold Schoenberg and his associates, in which the twelve tones of the chromatic scale are arranged into tone rows—abstract melodic prototypes that may be articulated in different ways, layered polyphonically, and varied through transposition (being raised or lower), retrograde (being played backwards), and inversion (being played upside-down). In such practices, the "melody" of the tone row is not necessarily meant to be consciously perceived as such. Its constant presence and manipulation is intended to give compositions an inner coherence that goes beyond earlier concepts of melodic usage.

Such ideas have led to a complete rethinking of the nature and role of melody in some spheres of Western classical music. Indeed, some composers and musicians have abandoned the ideas of scale and melody altogether. All of these twentieth-century developments are controversial; only time will tell whether a consensus can be reached about whose melodic ideas will survive beside those of Mozart and Beethoven.

▬ MELODY IN ARABIC MUSIC: MAQAM

Melodic systems in the art music of Turkey, northern Africa, and the Middle East share a common basis in the concept of _maqam_ (Turkish _makam_) or melodic mode. The Arabic maqam system is practiced primarily in the eastern Arab world from Egypt to Lebanon and Syria. The influence of Arabic culture reaches from Spain to Indonesia, owing to the rapid spread of Islam during the centuries following the death of its founder, the Prophet Muhammad, in 632 CE. Instruments and elements of musical style travelled with Islam throughout the Muslim world, from southern Europe to North India and Indonesia.

The _maqamat_ (plural of maqam) of Arabic music share significant features with European scales and modes and Indian _ragas_. All three systems cre-

MIDDLE EAST

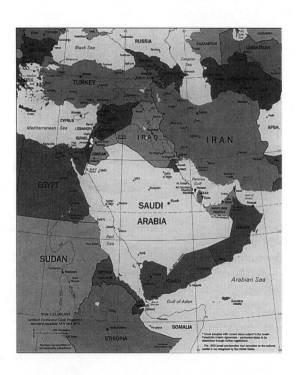

ate melodies from a set of seven pitches within an octave. In Arabic music, these notes are called "rast, dukah, sikah, jaharkah, nawa, husayni, awj"—although Western solfege syllables are now commonly used by Arabic musicians. All three systems further divide the octave into smaller intervals, including higher or lower variants of each of the main pitches, and all three systems impose a particular hierarchy on the notes in a particular scale, mode, maqam, or raga—that is, some notes are more important than others. One particular note functions as what Western theorists called a *finalis*—the final note in a composition or improvised performance. In Western harmonic practice, this final note is called the tonic or keynote, and English-speaking Arab and Indian musicians often use the word *tonic* when referring to the concluding tone of a maqam or raga.

Recognizing the similarities between Western, Arabic, and Indian music is helpful in two ways. First, it alerts us to notice parallels when we encounter them. Second, it provides a framework for examining differences. Knowing that these are octave-based systems which share the principle of note hierarchy, we are prepared to investigate the different ways in which scales, modes, maqams and ragas divide the octave and emphasize particular notes. We may also be on the lookout for major characteristics that the systems do *not* share—such as the harmonic structure of Western music, the fact that Arabic maqams often change their note content from one octave to the next, or that in Indian classical music the tonic never moves (or modulates) from the note "sa."

It is also useful to bear in mind that melodic systems change over time. Western classical music before the time of Johann Sebastian Bach (1685–1750) employed a number of different tuning systems, and when modern listeners hear early music performed in its original temperament (or tuning), they may at first feel that the notes are out-of-tune. Prior to the eighteenth century, the twelve half-steps in the Western chromatic scale were not all equidistant from their neighboring tones; some half-steps were larger than others. The rapid modulations (or key-changes) in the music of Bach's time necessitated the creation of the equal-tempered scale, in which equidistant half-steps allow the composer to move freely from one key to another without creating unwanted dissonances.

Arabic and Indian music also have changed in recent centuries, and arguments about the proper intonation or tuning of particular notes provide a rich ground for debate in both traditions. The influence of Western music has been an important factor in these changes—exposure to Western music theory and equal-tempered instruments like the piano, organ, and the Indian harmonium, a bellows-blown, keyboard instrument, have created new challenges and controversies in non-Western music cultures.

The Notes of Arabic Music

We may begin to understand the notes of Arabic music by comparing them to the notes of the Western major scale. Like Western musicians, Arabic musicians have a seven-note "natural scale," but unlike Westerners, they subdivide the octave, not into twelve half-steps, but into twenty-four "quarter-tones," which are needed to express the subtle intonational nuances of Arabic music. Thus, Arabic musicians recognize "half-sharps" and "half-flats" between the half-steps of the Western chromatic scale. In Western music, the space between the notes C and D is two half-steps; in Arabic music, the same interval includes four quarter-tones. E half-flat and B half-flat are included in the Arabic fundamental scale, which is built on the note "C" (Arabic "Rast").

Listeners who are unfamiliar with Arabic music will find it difficult to conceive of the sound of "E half-flat" or "B half-flat" without hearing the notes played or sung. To illustrate the principle, you may take a common Western instrument such as a piano or guitar and play the three notes, "C, D, E," or "doh, re, mi." These three notes, separated by two whole steps, are not only the initial pitches in a Western C major scale, but also the first three notes in the Arabic maqam known as *Ajam*. Now play the three notes, "C, D, E flat" or "doh, re, mi flat." These three notes, separated by one whole step and one half-step, are the initial pitches in a Western C minor scale and the first three notes in the maqam known as Nahawand. Now sing the notes "C" and "D," and then try to sing a third note which sounds approximately halfway between "E flat" and "E". This is the third note in maqam Rast, the fundamental Arabic scale. Arabic listeners, who have grown up hearing these intervals, find them as natural as Western listeners find the notes of the major and minor scales.

Simon Shaheen illustrates the use of "E half-flat" in the "Melody" television program. As he points out, with practice Westerners can learn to hear, sing and play the quarter-tones of Arabic music.

The Nature of Maqam

A maqam is not a tune or a song, but, somewhat like a Western key, provides the tonal material for a great many songs and instrumental melodies. Early writers associated specific maqamat with particular planets, signs of the zodiac, seasons, times of the day or night, elements, humors, temperaments, virtues, classes of people, colors, odors, raw materials, alphabetical letters, poetic meters, and healing properties, but more recent theorists have tended to dismiss these associations, restricting modern discussions to more tangible aspects of musical form.[1]

Although the maqamat are theoretically infinite in number, the number in current use is limited. The repertory of popular Arabic singers includes a core of about twelve frequently performed maqamat and another dozen which receive occasional performances. "Serious" composers in the academic world commonly supplement these approximately two dozen maqamat with an additional fifteen, and occasionally compose in another twenty to thirty less common ones. The total number of maqamat in current use, then, is about seventy, although scholars over the last two centuries have documented the existence of up to one hundred and nineteen distinct modes.[2]

The repertory varies between different parts of the Arabic music area. The maqamat also have changed over time, partly as a result of contact with Turkish, Persian, and European music, and partly due to changes in the status of music in modern Arabic culture. In Egypt, Arabic music has been transformed from a poorly respected profession to a mark of high culture which every student must encounter in school; one result of this "elevation" of the music has been a simplification of its theory and repertory to make it accessible to a broad population of amateur students.[3]

Prior to the twentieth century, the maqamat were described not as scales, but as melodic formulae, each with its own starting-note, ending-note, and typical, defining melodic phrases or song-like tunes. Modern Arabic music theorists define each maqam, not as a melodic formula, but as a scale, in which the final note also functions as the most important tone. Each maqam is a "weighted scale," in that some notes may be regarded as strong, some weak, and others of moderate importance.[4]

Composers are free to create melodies without being confined to a pre-scribed order of pitches, but both composers and improvisers must observe certain conventions in ordering their compositions and performances. Arabic music theorist Touma writes that each maqam consists of a number of pitch regions, each "centered on a principal note around which the neighboring notes effect a rotary embroidery." Each of these regions comprises a "phase in the development of a maqam." Touma concludes that "the totality of these phrases constitute the form of the maqam which is defined by the succession of pivot-notes."[5]

The Maqam in Performance

In practice, the notes of each maqam are seldom rendered simply. The melody is enriched by the use of various slides, shakes, trills, tremelo (the rapid repetition of a single note), and grace notes. Early Western music, and melodic systems outside of the Western classical tradition, often employ such devices; while Western classical composers often rely on harmony to add flavor to their music, Arabic, Indian, and Irish traditional musicians use melodic ornamentation to add spice to their playing and singing. According to Simon Shaheen, musical ornamentation often reflects a preference for "dressing up" in other areas of life, such as visual art, calligraphy, clothing, and cooking.

SIMON SHAHEEN PLAYING THE 'UD

> *You hardly listen to Arabic music or Arabic melody without this art of ornament. And it is obvious in our way of life, for example, the way we dress traditionally—like this vest, it's very ornamented. When we prepare our food, the food on the table should be very much ornamented; otherwise nobody would touch it. And the same thing with music.*[6]

Arabic musicians add variety to their music not only by ornamenting the notes of a particular maqam, but by *modulation* from one maqam to another in the course of a composition or improvisation. In some cases, such modulation involves changing the key-note, from C to G, for example. In other cases modulation to a new maqam involves altering the structure of the scale by raising or lowering one or more notes by a quarter-tone or half-step.

In the instrumental composition known as "Dikrayati," both the key-note and the scale structure alter in the course of a modulation during the first section of the piece. We may describe the composition as having the form A-B-A. The A section begins in the

THE SIMON SHAHEEN ENSEMBLE

maqam known as *Nahawand,* which corresponds to the Western scale of C minor. Partway through this segment, the melody modulates to the maqam

The Simon Shaheen ensemble plays the composition "Dikrayati."

known as *Bayyati*. In this modulation, the key-note moves up from C to G, and the note A is raised by one quarter-tone. The *'ud* player then plays a short improvisation called a *taqasim*, in which he eventually modulates back to the original maqam, Nahawand.

The ensemble then plays a sprightly B section in Nahawand, and then returns to section A, concluding their performance on the key-note C. The recapitulation of section A does not include the original modulation to Bayyati maqam—the melody ends just before the point where that modulation occurred in the first statement of section A. The following time-line will help you to recognize important points in recorded selection Audio #26.

Audio Example #26: "Dikrayati"

0:00	0:07	0:17	0:29
A section begins in Nahawand maqam on note G	first phrase ends on note G	second phrase ends on note F	third phrase descends to low G

0:36	0:37	0:44	0:58
melody rests on key-note C	rising scale climbs to high C, modulates to Bayyati during descent to G	series of phrases ending on G, key-note of Bayyati maqam	series of phrases ending on high C, returning to G

1:20	1:41	2:30	3:09
'ud taqsim begins on G, modulates back to Nahawand, concludes on C	B section, faster	return to slow A section	piece concludes on note C, in original maqam

FIGURE 1: SIMON SHAHEEN ENSEMBLE PLAYS "DIKRAYATI" (AUDIO 26)

▬▬ MELODY IN IRISH MUSIC

According to Irish-American uilleann piper Jerry O'Sullivan, "With Irish music, the most important thing is the melody." Broadly speaking, Irish traditional music can be divided into four categories or genres that are all based on single sung or played melodic lines: dance music, instrumental slow airs (usually based on song melodies), songs in the English language, and sean-nós singing, a repertory of songs primarily in the Irish language. Sean-nós, translated from Irish gaelic as "old style," is considered to be the oldest form of musical expression in Ireland. While the songs in both Irish and English are traditionally sung by one performer, the dance tunes are played in groups as well as by solo players.

Dance Music

The body of traditional dance music is played on instruments such as the fiddle, uilleann pipes, concertina, accordion, flute, tin whistle, mandolin, banjo, and bouzouki. These instruments are primarily used to play the melody or tune while guitar, piano, and bodhrán, an Irish frame drum, are often used to play accompaniments. Tunes include jigs, reels, hornpipes, and marches, most of which conform to a basic structure of two eight bar sections. In performance, each section or strain is played twice before the entire tune is repeated again.

Musicians and scholars talk about the "bare bones" or "skeleton" of the tune, an unembellished version using only the basic notes, melodic shape, and rhythm that give a tune its own identity. Irish players don't actually perform this skeletal melody. Performances differ from player to player because, as fiddler Brian Conway says, "There's room for imprinting your own personality, your own creativity within the structure of Irish music." Individual renditions of tunes will vary according to a variety of factors, including the player's source for learning the tune, and his or her instrument, technique, and style. Many musicians insist that a tune should never be played the same way twice. However, as Brian Conway says, "The challenge is to alter it in such a way as to enable you to sit in and play with somebody you've never met before who also plays that tune. And then do it in such a way that doesn't sound discordant, that it doesn't sound chaotic. That's the beautiful thing." Jerry O'Sullivan describes the process as follows:

FIDDLER BRIAN CONWAY

In Irish music, when you're using variation in a piece, it's a subtle type of thing where you can change notes. If you change the melody a little bit you can put in different notes. You can change the rhythm a little bit. And that's okay as long as the variations you put in wouldn't make another player uncomfortable, or make his job difficult, or obscure the main melody. If it becomes too different, then it's a problem. However, the idea is not to have the same exact performance twice around. It should be a little bit different every time you play it.[7]

These subtle variations don't get in the way in group playing. As Brian Conway stresses, the context for Irish music is often social and informal:

Irish music is a social music because it brings people together. House sessions are a major component of traditional Irish music. Houses are where people would congregate in Ireland, and even in my house [in New York] when I was growing up because both my parents were from Ireland, we had an Irish session almost every Friday where people would congregate. They would play tunes, sharing new tunes and old tunes. It's a wonderful opportunity to meet with people. And because the music is so predictable within its structure, people can sit down who have learned tunes from different sources and play a tune together. It's a wonderful aspect of the tradition that continues on today.[8]

The fiddle is one of the main melody instruments used by Irish musicians. Its presence in Ireland can be traced back at least two hundred years. The instrument is structurally the same as the standard violin, but it is held in a variety of ways. Some players rest it against their chest, shoulder, or upper arm; others tuck it under their chin. The method of holding the bow also varies enormously from player to player. Traditional players generally play only in first position on the fiddle, giving them a range of just over two octaves.

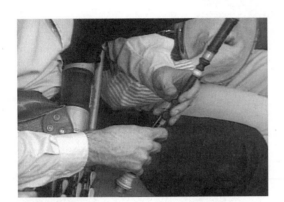

UILLEANN PIPES

The uilleann pipes are a distinctly Irish member of the bagpipe family. The Irish word "uilleann" means elbow and refers to the fact that the piper must pump a bellows under his or her left elbow rather than blow in order to power the instrument. The standard uilleann pipes that developed early in the 1800s has a chanter (a holed pipe that provides the pitches), three drones, and three regulators. The regulators make the instrument fairly unique among bagpipes. While the drone pipes each provide one constant note tuned to the tonic, each regulator has four or five keys. If switched on, the regulators can provide more of a harmonic accompaniment to the tune. The piper must be very dexterous in order to pump the bag, finger the chanter, switch the regulators off and on, play the regulators with the right wrist, and keep all the pipes in tune. The sound of the uilleann pipes being played is much quieter than the Scottish war pipes and the instrument is meant to be played indoors in a seated position.

Analysis of a Tune

The tune "Crossing the Shannon" is a typical reel that has a two part structure. Like the majority of fiddle tunes in the Anglo-Celtic tradition, "Crossing the Shannon" (**Example 3**) has a first or "A" section that is played and

JERRY O'SULLIVAN, BRIAN CONWAY, AND PAT KILBRIDE

then repeated, followed by the second or "B" section which is also repeated. This fixed structure is 32 measures long. In Irish music sessions, musicians tend to play a tune through two or three times at which point they switch without break into another tune. This technique of making medleys expands the melodic material in a single performance.

MELODY EXAMPLE 3: "CROSSING THE SHANNON" (IRISH REEL)

While we can think of melody in Irish traditional music as the tune, we can also look at the smaller melodic units that make up the whole. Typically melodies are composed of phrases that create musical thoughts. In "Crossing the Shannon," each grouping of four measures creates a complete thought or phrase. If we look more closely we can see how those four measures fit together. First of all, measures one, two and three begin in exactly the same way, while measure four is different. Taken together, measures one and two present part of an idea that is responded to or answered in measures three and four. At this point the melody comes to a brief moment of rest marking the end of the phrase. However, the last two eighth notes in measure four, called the upbeat, propel the melody forward to begin a new phrase. Measures five and six are identical to measures one and two followed by two new measures of music that end the second phrase and section A.

In breaking down the melody in both section A and section B in "Crossing the Shannon," we see that repetition plays an important role. For example, measures one and five are identical as are measures two and six. On an even smaller level, the motive that begins measure one also begins measures two, three, five, and six. The identical motive also begins measures nine, eleven, and thirteen in the B section. Therefore, repetition within the body of the tune can be seen on a micro level each time the motive reappears. The combination of repetition and contrast within the larger phrase structure creates a sense of both unity and movement. Repetition occurs on the macro level when the tune is repeated over and over again in performance.

As stated above, musicians alter the fixed structure of the tune in performance by their use of ornamentation and variation. These methods of improvisation are subtle when compared with techniques used in more highly extemporaneous genres, such as jazz or North Indian classical music. In jazz, the players will often start with a fixed tune or song, but during the course of

A performance of "Crossing the Shannon" and "The Duke of Leinster." The tunes are played by Jerry O'Sullivan on uilleann pipes, Brian Conway on fiddle, and Pat Kilbride on guitar.

their performance, will move completely away from the original melody. In Irish traditional music, the tune is always recognizable. The musician's artistry lies in his or her ability to alter or vary the tune each time it is played. As fiddler Brian Conway says, "There are just plain notes, but that doesn't make a performance."

While other musicians may appreciate all the minute changes they hear in a particular rendition of a tune, all listeners can perceive the vitality and expression in the playing. Although subtle, the variations a musician uses may be perceived by the listener because of the use of repetition. Even though musicians are working within the framework of a fixed melody that is repeated in performance, their use of ornamentation and variation keeps the music spontaneous and new.

Song Traditions in Irish and English

The human voice is perhaps the oldest and most accessible musical "instrument." Most of us use our voices primarily to speak, but spoken utterances have a great deal in common with singing. Speech has rhythm, tempo, dynamics, and timbre (tonal color). More importantly for the subject of this chapter, speech requires the creation of rising and falling patterns of pitch—speech therefore has melody.

In most cultures there is a marked difference between everyday speech and song. Song takes the natural intonation patterns of speech and formalizes them into melodies. But melody when combined with language evokes added meaning and emotion. In quoting lyricist Yip Harburg, singer and composer Pete Seeger said, "Words make you think, music makes you feel, and a song makes it possible to feel a thought."[9]

In some song traditions, the text fuels the melody: the words are carefully rendered so that their full meaning comes across to the listener. In other traditions, the melody seems to take precedence over the words. Irish traditional songs in both the Irish and English languages fall more into the former category. Because many of the songs are ballads—songs which tell a story—the texts are set in conventional verse or strophic form in which their meanings are clearly rendered. Jerry O'Sullivan describes the singing of ballads:

> The singer, with these songs, is telling a story, literally. Some of these can be ten, twelve verses long. And sometimes they're talking about love themes. . . . Some of them are about disasters, boating disasters or different types of disasters. But in all cases, it's a very emotional thing—very very emotional, a very intense emotional type of thing.[10]

SEAN NÓS SINGER

Each ballad may have many stanzas that are each comprised of four lines. While the text changes in each stanza in order to unfold the story, the music stays the same so that the same four lines of music are repeated over and over again. Nevertheless, it is rare for any two stanzas to sound exactly alike.

Singers use some of the same devices employed by dance musicians to alter their performance, including ornamentation and melodic variations. But because many of the songs are in free rhythm and performed by one person at a time, there is more room for rhythmic freedom—changes in word stress and timing.

By spontaneously making these choices during a performance, the singer makes the song his or her own. Joe Heaney, one of Ireland's finest exponents of both sean-nós and English language songs, described this process:

> *And I do a song my own way, you know. I get a song off you or somebody, now I sing that song my own way. . . . Now I'm not saying this is the way that was decorated by somebody else. It's the way I do it, and every time I do it I probably do it different; but I do it in the same way. I don't take anything away from it, in fact I try to better it every time I do it, you know. . . . I love to sing it, and I love it so much that I don't want to leave it. I just want to hold on to it as long as I can when I'm singing it. That's the way to treat a good song.[11]*

Two recorded examples of the first verse of "The Rocks of Bawn" show how Joe Heaney could sing the same song differently on two occasions. The first recording was made in 1963 (**Example 4**) while the second was made in 1973 (**Example 5**). Notice how the second version is much more highly ornamented than the first.

The story of the song takes place at the time of Oliver Cromwell in the late seventeenth century. Cromwell was responsible for seizing Irish properties, sending the original owners "to hell or Connaught"—Connaught being so rocky as to be virtually unfarmable. The title of the song refers to a specific place name, but is emblematic of the whole western region and the particular social, agricultural, and historical situation. The third verse is spoken by the bailiff, the agent of the absentee landlord, cursing Sweeney for being unable to pay the rent. The last verse contains a special irony, as Sweeney decides that his only hope for a future is in the army of his oppressors.

28, 29
Joe Heaney's recordings of the first verse of "The Rocks of Bawn" from 1963 and 1973, respectively.

MELODY EXAMPLE 4: "THE ROCKS OF BAWN" (FIRST VERSE) SUNG BY JOE HEANEY IN 1963

MELODY EXAMPLE 5: "THE ROCKS OF BAWN" (FIRST VERSE) SUNG BY JOE HEANEY IN 1973

Come   all   you loy - al he-roes,   where - ev - er   you may be:

Don't   hire with   a - ny   mas - ter   'till you know   what your   work will   be,

For   you   must rise   up ear - ly,   from the clear   (e) day - (l) light 'till   the   dawn,

I'm   a-fraid   you'll   ne'er   be   a - ble   to   plow the   rocks of   Bawn.

"The Rocks of Bawn"

Come all you loyal heroes, wherever you may be
Don't hire with any master 'till you know what your work will be
For you must rise up early, from the clear daylight 'till dawn;
I'm afraid you'll ne'er be able to plow the rocks of Bawn.

And rise up gallant Sweeney, and give your horse some hay
And give him a good feed of oats before you go away
Don't feed him on soft turnip, put him out on your green lawn;
For I'm afraid he'll ne'er be able to plow the rocks of Bawn.

And my curse attend you Sweeney, you have me nearly robbed:
You're sitting by the fireside with a dudeen in your gob,
You're sitting by the fireside from the clear daylight 'till the dawn;
I'm afraid you'll ne'er be able to plow the rocks of Bawn.

My shoes they are well-worn now, my stockings they are thin;
My heart is always trembling, I'm afraid I might give in.
My heart is always trembling from the clear daylight 'till the dawn;
I'm afraid I'll n'eer be able to plow the rocks of Bawn.

And I wish the Queen of England would send for me in time
And put me in a regiment, all in my youth and prime.
I would fight for Ireland's glory from the clear daylight 'till the dawn;
But I never return again to plow the rocks o'Bawn.

Many of the melodies to particular songs are played on instruments as slow airs. According to Jerry O'Sullivan, the important thing in playing slow airs is to try to imitate the style of the singer:

You try as closely as you can, and it's difficult because a musical instrument is different from the voice. But still you try to do what the singer does as much as possible. . . . You try to imitate the singer's phrasing, their rhythm, even their variations. Because their timing is based on the words that they sing, and the words are different in each verse, it will be a little different every time around.[12]

Brian Conway plays "Were You at the Rock" as a slow air on the fiddle. This beautiful love song in the Irish language is also called "Have You Been at Carrack?"

MELODY IN NORTH INDIAN CLASSICAL MUSIC: RAGA

The most common word for music in Indian languages is *sangit,* a term whose original meaning encompassed singing, instrumental music, and dance. The classical music of India is properly called *raga sangit,* that is, music which conforms to the conventions of the Indian *ragas* (modes or melody-types). While raga sangit is performed in both North and South India, the political and cultural histories of the two regions—especially the impact of Islamic, Turko-Persian culture in the North—has led to the creation of two separate systems of ragas. Our focus here is the classical music of the North.

The Notes of Indian Classical Music

Like Western classical music, raga sangit employs a heptatonic (seven-note) scale. As discussed earlier, the notes are called "sa, re, ga, ma, pa, dha," and "ni."

Indian solfege is like the Western "movable doh" system, in which "doh" is not fixed at any particular pitch. An Indian vocalist places "sa" at a frequency which suits the range of his or her voice, and Indian instrumentalists tune their instruments to the pitch at which they seem to sound best—or, when accompanying a singer, to the keynote chosen by the vocalist. Unlike Western and Arabic musicians, Indian classical musicians virtually never alter the keynote, once it has been established in a performance. "Sa" remains stable, and except in "light-classical" genres, musicians do not modulate from one raga to another.

Buddhadev Das Gupta, a master of the North Indian plucked instrument called *sarod,* states that "our music has the same twelve notes that occur in your piano keyboard in one octave." The first and fifth notes of the scale (sa and pa) are considered unchanging. The other five notes can be moved up or down by approximately one half-step, creating a twelve-tone set corresponding to the Western chromatic scale. Indian musicians further divide the octave into microtonal intervals, which in India are called *srutis.* Ancient theoretical texts divide the octave into twenty-two srutis, but the original placement of these microtones is a matter of conjecture. In modern times, the term sruti is used by musicians to indicate that a particular note should be sung or played a little higher or lower in a particular raga, or to describe the delicate shades of pitch in a glissando (glide) from one note to another.

BUDDHADEV DAS GUPTA PLAYING THE SAROD, ACCOMPANIED BY RAY SPIEGEL ON TABLA AND IRA LANDGARTEN ON TANPURA

The Nature of Raga

"Indian music is totally melodic, but we cannot just go on producing any melody that comes to our mind. It is guided by certain rules and framework," says Buddhadev Das Gupta. The "rules and framework" of Indian classical melody relate to the concept of raga. Each of the several hundred ragas in contemporary use provides a unique recipe for the creation of composed and improvised melodies. Every raga has a specific set of characteristics: a scale including five, six, or seven permitted (and required) notes, an ascending pattern, a descending pattern, a note hierarchy in which two particular scale degrees receive particular emphasis, and a set of prescribed motifs (short pieces of melody) which, taken together, create the "path" of the raga. In addition to these technical qualities, each raga also possesses extra-musical attributes: a prescribed time or season of performance, a prevailing mood, and, in some cases, legendary "magical" properties, such as the power to invoke rain, healing, or fire. A raga is not a composition or a performance, but each raga provides the raw material for hundreds of composed melodies and thousands of improvised performances.

Rag Kamod is a popular North Indian raga. Every raga has a prescribed time of performance; Rag Kamod is meant to be sung or played between six and nine at night. Every raga has a pair of particularly important notes, called the *vadi* and *samvadi*. Musicians often describe the vadi as the "king" of the raga and the samvadi as the king's "minister." In Rag Kamod, the vadi is pa, and the samvadi is re. Every raga has specific ascending and descending patterns; in Rag Kamod, the ascent and descent are crooked, creating melodies with interesting turns that Buddhadev Das Gupta describes as "kinks":

> *Music has, let us say, three kinds of movements: going up from down, coming down from up, and a mixture of the upward and downward movements. So our ascent, or upward movement, may not be a straight one. . . . The rules of the raga may preclude you from just lining up straightforward in sequence. It may have kinks in it. Now, this rule for ascent and descent has to be stuck to always, even when you are improvising.*[13]

We may observe in **Example 6** that the ascending and descending forms of Rag Kamod do indeed reveal "kinks," crooked patterns such as "dha pa, ni-dha-sa," and "ga ma pa, ga ma re sa." One of the challenges Indian musicians face is the strict observation of such crooked motion, even when improvising at great speed.

MELODY EXAMPLE 6: RAG KAMOD: AROHA AND AVAROHA

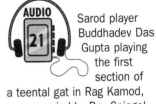

Every raga has its own unique melodic personality, and Indian musicians often compare the features of a raga to the characteristics of a human being. As Buddhadev Das Gupta says:

> Out of these several "dos" and "don'ts" there finally emerge a set of basic phrases which are just like the ears, nose, eyes, lips of a human countenance. These basic phrases, when you go through them, they paint the face of the raga before you. Now our music is such that you can start either from the nose or from the eyes or from the ears, but you have to draw the entire face eventually.[14]

Audio 21: Sarod player Buddhadev Das Gupta playing the first section of a teental gat in Rag Kamod, accompanied by Ray Spiegel on tabla.

Musicians "draw the face" of a raga in improvisations which often use a brief, more-or-less fixed composition as a point of departure and return. A short instrumental composition set in a particular raga is called a *gat* (pronounced "gut").

While reading a transcription of the performance of Rag Kamod (**Example 7**), we may discover some of the ways in which this composition reveals important melodic characteristics of the raga in which it is composed.

MELODY EXAMPLE 7: GAT IN RAG KAMOD

In the first measure, emphasis is given to the minister-note and king-note, re and pa. The first, fourth, eighth, and ninth measures feature two characteristic melodic "kinks" of Rag Kamod, ma-re-pa, and ga-ma-re-sa. The entire composition is set in the rhythmic cycle known as teental, with *sam* falling on the first beat of the gat. Here, rhythm serves melody, giving added emphasis to the minister- and king-notes by placing them on the strong first and third beats of the first and last measures.

▬▬ CHAPTER SUMMARY

We began this chapter with the idea that melodies are like stories, with a beginning, a plot, and a conclusion. Perhaps we find melodies memorable and meaningful because their form is similar to that of speech. Melodic systems are very much like languages. They have vocabularies (pitches organized into frameworks such as scales, modes, maqams, and ragas), grammars (the rules of the systems), idioms (genres and styles within a music culture), and structural units like spoken or written phrases, sentences, and paragraphs (motifs, phrases, and sections). Motifs which are common to an entire genre are like the cliches or common usages of a spoken language.

While melodic systems are similar to languages, we should remember the ways in which they are *not* like speech or literature. A single melody, when combined with one set of words in a patriotic song like the English "God Save the Queen," has a different meaning when sung with the text of the American "My Country 'Tis of Thee." Speech is verbal and often literal; it speaks *about* things and events. Melody is non-verbal and often abstract. Melodies are *like* stories, but they do not always *tell* stories. Part of the appeal of music is its ability to move us in ways that have little to do with intellectual understanding. The plot of a melody does not need to describe anything outside of itself, and its meaning may simply be in the beauty of its construction.

Comparing music with speech, melody can be related to the rise and fall of a speaking voice. Speech is given meaning, not only by the use of words, rhythm, and changing pitch, but by the tonal quality or *timbre* of the speaker's voice. Similarly, musical meaning is created not only by rhythm and melody, but by the tone colors of singing voices and sounding instruments. In Chapter 7, we will consider the subject of timbre—the aspect of sound that gives each voice and instrument its unique tonal personality.

STUDY QUESTIONS

1. What is a melody?

2. What are motifs and phrases?

3. What is a maqam?

4. How are Irish dance tunes structured?

5. What is a raga?

6. Describe the differences between scales, maqamat, and ragas.

REFERENCED SOURCES

1. Marcus, 1987: 747–9.
2. Wright, 1980: 523.
3. Marcus, 1987: 330–347.
4. Ibid: 448–567.
5. Touma, 1977: 52–4.
6. Shaheen, Interview. 1997.
7. O'Sullivan. Interview, 1997.
8. Conway. Interview, 1997.
9. Pete Seeger, Interview 1997.
10. O'Sullivan, 1997.
11. Cowdery, 1990: 31.
12. O'Sullivan, 1997
13. Das Gupta, Interview, 1997.
14. Ibid.

CHAPTER 7

TIMBRE: THE COLOR OF MUSIC

About This Chapter

This chapter provides an introduction to the concept of timbre or tone color in music. Across the globe, a rich variety of instrumental and vocal traditions create an astonishing assortment of tone colors. The tonal quality of any given instrument or voice is influenced by a number of factors, including method of sound production, instrument construction, playing technique, and aesthetics. The chapter explores methods of sound production and then focuses on musical instruments in several cultures. The chapter concludes with a comparison of vocal timbre in Tuva, Bosnia, Ireland, and in the Western classical tradition.

KEYWORDS

aerophone
chordophone
electrophone
gamelan
idiophone
material culture
membranophone
organology
overtone series
vibrato

COMPANION RESOURCES

TELEVISION PROGRAM: Timbre: The Color of Music

AUDIO SELECTIONS:

14. Beethoven's *Symphony* No. 5 in C minor, First Movement
31. North Indian tanpura played by Ira Landgarten
21. Buddhadev Das Gupta, Performance in "Rag Kamod"
20. Tabla solo performed by Ray Spiegel
16. "Hifumi Hachi Gaeshi"
32. Tadao Sawai, "Tori No Yo Ni"
26. "Dikrayati." Simon Shaheen, violin; Najib Shaheen, 'ud; Bassam Saba, nay; Michel Merhej, daff.
62. 'Ud taqasim in Maqam Nahawand.
33. Modulatory taqasim.
3. Tuvan Throat Singing in Cave
1. Bosnian ganga "Sjajna Zvjezdo"
29. "Rocks of Bawn" sung by Joe Heaney (1st verse)
7. "Flower of Magheralee" sung by Pat Kilbride
6. "Pretty Polly" sung by John Cohen

139

*T*imbre, like pitch and rhythm, is one of the fundamental elements of music. Pitch refers to a note's frequency, its highness or lowness, rhythm to its duration, and timbre to its tonal quality or color. In describing a sound's timbre, we often resort to words normally used to identify non-musical qualities such as appearance or temperature; a voice or instrument can sound dark or light, warm or cool, mellow or metallic, smooth or rough, covered or open, deep or thin. Distinctions of timbre refer not to the fundamental pitch of a note, but rather to the coloration that distinguishes the various sounds of a single pitch played on different instruments. The note "A" sounds differently on a flute than on an oboe or violin; the pitch on all three instruments may be identical, but we hear differences in timbre.

Every sound has a distinctive timbre because of the acoustical phenomenon of the overtone series. As discussed in Chapter 1, each individual tone consists of a fundamental pitch and a simultaneously sounding series of progressively higher overtones, also called partials or harmonics. The fundamental pitch is the actual note sung or played and it is usually the tone we can identify and hear most clearly. The particular overtones of the series that resonate along with the fundamental pitch determine the timbre of the sound. Each instrument has its own timbre based on the particular overtone structure that it generates.

The shape of an instrument and the material from which it is made emphasize particular partials. Metal flutes sound clear and bright because their shape and material emphasize only the second harmonic, one octave above the fundamental. Wooden flutes often sound richer and warmer, because the resonant properties of wood emphasize a wider range of partials. Clarinets have a very different sonority because their cylindrical tube construction largely eliminates the even numbered harmonics. Similarly, the open "G" string of a violin sounds brighter and thinner than the same pitch sounded on the open "G" string of the larger viola. The size of the latter instrument alters the weight given to particular partials, darkening the sound.

SIMON SHAHEEN

Timbre is not static; a single note's overtones fluctuate in intensity as the tone starts up, is sustained, and decays. Even though we usually hear one pitch as a single entity, the shape that each note takes as it is played can be divided into three parts: a beginning or attack, a middle or constant state, and an end or decay.[1] Many plucked instruments, such as guitars, mandolins, and banjos, have a sharp attack with almost immediate decay, while wind and bowed instruments tend to have a softer attack, a sustained period, and a decay controlled by the performer. The clashing of cymbals, with their resultant sustained ringing, has a very different sound shape than the striking of a woodblock, with its nearly instant decay.

Different cultures have distinct aesthetic preferences for particular sound qualities: the tone colors produced by the highly trained singers in the Peking Opera differ considerably from the timbre of either Western opera singers or ganga singers from Bosnia. The Balinese preference for the tone colors produced by bronze or iron percussion instruments played together in the gamelan is quite different from timbres found in the Trinidadian steel band. In Zimbabwe, the buzzing tones of the mbira are considered essential to its overall sound.

Even the same instrument can produce contrasting timbres depending on the player or on its cultural context. One saxophone player may produce strikingly different tone colors than another using the same instrument; an Irish fiddler's playing may sound considerably unlike the playing of either a Western classical, Arabic, or North Indian violinist.

According to ethnomusicologist and instrument maker Fred Stubbs, timbre is related to tradition, technique, and structure, as well as to individual expertise and sensitivity:

> . . . the real place that timbre lives [is] inside the instrumentalist's heart and head. If the instrumentalist doesn't hear the timbre in the instrument and the music, then the audience won't hear it either. I guess I'm trying to say that music is composed of more than formulae, but also of this ineffable kind of expression that might be at the heart of many musics.[2]

FRED STUBBS

Timbre is perhaps the most personal element in music, the quality that allows us to distinguish between the voices of individual singers or the unique tonal "signatures" of particular instrumentalists. Jazz musician Josh Redman talks about the timbral qualities that caused him to choose the saxophone as his artistic voice:

> I recognized early on that the saxophone would be the way I could sing, that would be my voice. . . . I felt a connection with the instrument, and it's hard to describe it beyond that because I think the connection that you feel with music, and with an instrument, is oftentimes beyond literal or verbal description. . . . I think one thing that really attracted me to the sound of the tenor saxophone was its incredible emotional range. It's an instrument that can be very very gentle and poignant and sensitive and vulnerable, yet at the same time, very, very powerful and passionate, and at times almost violent, very robust, very raw. And I like having those expressive options, and I like having them integrated into the sound of one instrument.[3]

Timbre can also be viewed as the particular palette of tone colors produced by one instrument or voice or the tone colors that result from a group. The timbres of a symphony orchestra are very different from those of a wind quintet or a solo violin. Some cultures seem to prefer listening to one player or singer at a time, some favor ensembles where each instrument or voice has a similar timbre, while others create ensembles with instruments of different sonorities. Many cultures employ different sizes and kinds of groupings of musicians depending on the function, style, and context of musical performance. In each case, timbre is an essential component of the culture's overall musical aesthetic.

Instruments are themselves an important aspect of musical culture—part of what ethnomusicologists term "material culture." Aside from the human body which can be used as an instrument for singing, clapping, snapping the fingers, whistling, or percussive dancing, the objects used as instruments in a culture are often based on local natural resources, such as wood, clay, bamboo, reeds, gourds, silk, and skins. The large calabash gourds that make up the body of the North Indian sitar are plentiful throughout India; the rattles common in many Native American traditions are made from the small gourds that grow in North America. Many drums throughout Africa are made from hollowed-out trees; flutes from every corner of the globe are made from bamboo or wood. The availability and use of specific natural substances help to determine what instruments will be made, and therefore, what timbres will be indigenous to a particular culture.

The work of the instrument maker is to transform these raw materials into a music-making tool, which is why instrument construction is closely allied to technology. The advent of bronze production in Southeast Asia, for example, greatly impacted the creation of large orchestras of gong-chime instruments made out of bronze. In Trinidad, instrument makers in the 1940s transformed cast off man-made materials in the form of oil drums into sophisticated instruments.

MAKING A STEEL DRUM IN TRINIDAD

All makers require technical skills in order to correctly construct and tune their instruments, but many are also artists. Instruments are often highly decorated with precious materials and considered works of art in themselves.

Instruments are also often believed to be sacred objects. Among the Akan in Ghana, drums are believed to be sentient beings imbued with the spirit of the tree from which they were made. Instrument makers must ask for a blessing from the tree before cutting it down to make the drum. In Java, the great gong is the most highly revered instrument and gong makers and their craft are associated with magical powers. The other instruments of the gamelan are also considered sentient beings. The Australian ethnomusicologist Margaret Kartomi compares two special objects of Javanese culture—percussion instruments and rice:

> *Indeed, percussion is to the instrumental culture what the staple crop rice is to the food culture. . . . Taboos are operative against walking over instruments or sitting on bags of rice, because spirits are believed to reside in them. Indeed these spirits, when properly appeased, are thought to beautify the sounds of the instruments or to affect the quality of the rice they inhabit.[4]*

The qualities ascribed to instruments—whether they are thought of as tools, works of art, sacred objects, or all three—determine their place in a given society. Because of their importance, musical instruments have been

CENTRAL JAVANESE GAMELAN

classified in most cultures. While sound production is the basis for instrument construction, people have classified instruments in ways that embrace many other aspects of culture. In the following pages we will use the mechanics of sound production as a springboard to understand how several cultures have classified their instruments.

SOUND PRODUCTION AND INSTRUMENT CLASSIFICATION SYSTEMS

Every musical sound has four parameters, of which timbre is one. The sound also has pitch—its highness or lowness; it has amplitude—its relative loudness or softness; and it has duration—how long it lasts in time. When we think particularly of timbre, we think of the instrument or voice that produces the sound. It is perhaps the easiest of the four parameters to recognize and identify because it is linked to something tangible: a sound producing agent.

In order to make a sound you need three things: a physical object which is vibrating, a medium to carry the vibrations or sound waves, and an ear to hear the sound and turn it into something meaningful. In order to create music, the physical object must be an instrument or voice capable of vibrating and resonating. The sounds of a violin, for example, are produced by strings set in motion by the player's bow, the instrument's resonating body, sound holes, and a bridge:

> When you listen to a violin, you're hearing chemical energy in the violinist's muscles transformed into sound. The energy enters the violin by scraping a bow against strings. Not much sound comes to your ear directly from the strings, where the surface area is too small to push at very much air. But the strings are strung across a bridge . . . and this transmits the string vibrations to the body of the violin, where a much greater surface area presses against more air to make more sound. The violin body transmits best the frequencies it resonates at, while damping all others. Some of a violin's characteristic sound, its timbre, is attributable to its strings, and some to the resonance of its body.[5]

A vibrating sound source can be produced in a finite number of ways: besides responding to the friction of a bow, stretched strings may be plucked or struck; air may be forced through a tube at a higher pressure than the air outside, causing the tube to vibrate; a stretched skin may be hit, rubbed, or scraped; a solid object may be shaken, hit, scraped, rubbed, or whirled; and finally, the sound may be produced electronically. The human voice consists of a sound producing agent in the form of reed-like vocal chords, an air supply from the lungs, and resonating cavities—the mouth, nose, throat, and chest. These four categories of sound production—string, wind, percussion, and electronic— are the basis of musical instrument construction and classification all over the world.

THE TRIANGLE, AN IDIOPHONE

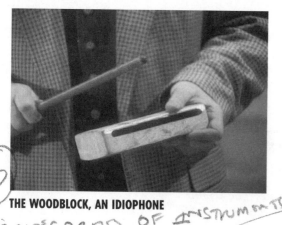

THE WOODBLOCK, AN IDIOPHONE

In the early twentieth century, a number of European acousticians and musicologists used these categories of sound production to classify musical instruments from different parts of the globe. Because of growing interest in *organology*—the study of musical instruments—and the formation of world instrument collections in museums in Europe and the United States, there arose a need for a classification system that could be used to document any instrument. The German musicologist Curt Sachs, in collaboration with Erich von Hornbostel, devised one such scheme in 1914.

The Sachs-Hornbostel system has been more widely used than any other during the twentieth century.[6] The categories were divided according to the physical characteristics of sound production into *chordophones*—instruments with one or more strings stretched between fixed points; *aerophones*—instruments in which air is the principal means of vibration; *membranophones*—instruments which vibrate by means of tightly stretched skins or membranes; and *idiophones*—instruments sounded by the substance of the instrument itself. In response to rapidly changing technology, Sachs added *electrophones* as a fifth category in 1940. These five general divisions—chordophones, aerophones, membranophones, idiophones, and electrophones—were further divided into increasingly narrow subcategories.

While the Sachs-Hornbostel system is used internationally by museums and music scholars, there are a wealth of other instrument classification systems that exist worldwide. Some of these schemes are subject to extensive written theory while others exist as part of an oral tradition. The Chinese have perhaps the oldest documented tradition that may date back to 2000 BCE. An early four part system and a later eight part scheme classified musical instruments by the substance from which they were made and in relation to nature and religion:

> *The earliest known principle by which the Chinese classified musical instruments or sources of sound (yin) was according to the materials of which they were made. The choice of character was based on the link in the sphere of cosmological thought and ritual between these materials and the seasons, the winds, the abundance of grain, and, by extension, human welfare, wealth, and political power. [7]*

The eight-part system, known as *pa yin*, included instruments made of metal, stone, silk, bamboo, gourd, clay, leather, and wood. These were ranked in terms of their extra-musical benefit to the human spirit:

> *The early ideas about instruments were based on the elemental belief in the "breath" or "spirit" that enabled sounds and instruments to serve as manifestations of nature as well as prognostic aids, performing magical services that could benefit the harvest, divine the enemy's morale, and so on. Instruments made from the eight materials each controlled one of the dances performed at ritual mimes that in turn could summon one of the eight winds.[8]*

The ancient Greeks and European theorists in the Middle Ages and Renaissance also classified musical instruments in terms of their effects on nature and the human spirit. The Greek notion that music was directly associated with the movement of the planets—the music of the spheres—was used by Pythagoras to illustrate harmonic proportions, as well as to explain the cathartic and ethical power of music. The Greeks had a three-part classification system dividing instruments into strings, winds, and percussion, but considered the first two to be more beneficial to man:

> Moreover, as the sounds of stringed and wind instruments were considered to be analogous to the music of the spheres, these instruments were believed to influence the human soul through its sympathetic responses to them. . . . These associations and analogies persisted in Greek culture for about a millennium and were eventually transmitted into medieval European thought as well.[9]

Medieval theorists also viewed music as an edifying force and linked it to cosmological beliefs. Perhaps the greatest exponent was Boethius who categorized musical sound into a three-part structure: *musica mundana* which included sounds made by the movements of the planets, the elements, and the changes of the season; *musica humana* which was music humans could hear; and *musica quae in quibusdam constituta est instrumentalis* which related to music theory and its application to instruments.[10] Like the Greeks, the medieval theorists believed in the superiority of the human voice, and ranked the three classes of instruments in order of importance—winds, strings, and percussion. Music was intimately related to Christian doctrine and its moral affect on the human spirit.

The earliest extant classification system that distinguishes instruments by their physical sound is found in the Sanskrit treatise, *Natyasastra*, composed in India between the second century BCE and the sixth century CE. Instruments are categorized into four divisions indicating the physical sound producing characteristics of the instrument's body: stretched (chordophones), covered (membranophones), hollow (aerophones such as flutes and reeds), and solid (idiophones, such as bells and cymbals). Each of the four categories are further subdivided into major and minor limbs. Unlike its Chinese, Greek, and early European counterparts, this fourfold scheme is unrelated to cosmological belief. It is still in use in India today, and is believed to have influenced Sachs and Hornbostel in the creation of their system in the first decade of the twentieth century.

These examples describe only a few of the instrument classification systems that have developed historically or are in use today. For the purposes of this book, we will use the Sachs-Hornbostel scheme in order to look at instruments and instrumental timbre in several world cultures. We will then conclude the chapter by devoting a separate section to timbre in vocal musics.

▰ TIMBRE IN WESTERN CLASSICAL MUSIC: INSTRUMENTS IN THE SYMPHONY ORCHESTRA

The contemporary symphony orchestra is divided into four basic groups: strings, woodwinds, brass, and percussion. Each group is further divided into sections: strings include first and second violins, violas, cellos, and double-basses; winds include oboes, flutes, piccolo, clarinets, bass clarinet, English horn, bassoons, and contrabassoon; brasses include trumpets, French horns,

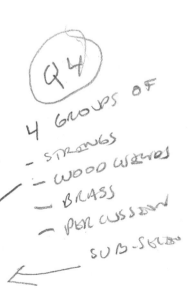

ORCHESTRAL STRINGS

trombones, and tuba; and percussionists play a variety of struck instruments including timpani (kettle drums), woodblocks, and keyed percussion such as the glockenspiel. Sections are seated together to facilitate tuning, as well as timbral blending, with the quieter instruments, strings, seated nearest to the audience and the loudest, percussion, brass, and winds, seated behind. Large modern orchestras may be composed of eighty or more players, with up to sixty-eight string players, twelve wind players, nine brass players, and four percussionists.

The symphony orchestra has changed over time. The typical Baroque orchestra at the time of Bach, Vivaldi, and Handel was essentially a string ensemble of under thirty players with a harpsichord or organ used for accompaniment. Woodwinds were sometimes added, but they were not a fixed part of the orchestra. Brass and timpani were used mostly for festive occasions. By the Classical era (1750–1825) the orchestra, although much smaller than its contemporary counterpart, had the same standardized instrumentation that it has today. In the nineteenth century, the orchestra was expanded to reach its present form.

Chordophones: Stringed Instruments

The main chordophones in the symphony orchestra are the bowed members of the violin family—the violin, viola, violoncello, and double bass. This family emerged in its present form in the early part of the sixteenth century. Almost every European country has made claims to the invention of the violin, but there is little doubt that it was preeminent in Italy at this time. The accepted modern form of the violin was in place by 1710, largely due to the work of the northern Italian instrument maker, Antonio Stradivari. The violin has since become an important instrument in many traditions outside the European classical world, including in North and South Indian classical music, Arabic classical music, and many European and American folk and traditional genres. The word "fiddle" is often used to colloquially refer to the violin, and is actually the more common term in many folk traditions.

The violin consists of four strings that are tuned in intervals a fifth apart. The framework of the body has a six rib structure that corresponds to the six main curves of the instrument. The shape and height of the archings, the wood used, the finished thickness of the wood, and even the final coats of varnish are fundamental factors influencing its tone quality. Different combinations of oils and resins give violins different degrees of hardness and flexibility; a good varnish is supposed to allow the instrument to speak with its full voice.[11] The table or front of the violin has two sound holes called "f holes"; the back is constructed from one or two pieces of matching maple. The strings are attached to four tuning pegs—usually made from rosewood or boxwood—and run down the unfretted neck of the instrument over a bridge that is held on only by the pressure of strings. In order to produce different pitches, players stop the strings on the neck with their left hand fingers while holding the bow with the right hand.

The modern violin bow is concave shaped and strung tightly with horsehair. Resin is applied to the bow in order to make it glide more evenly over the strings. The player's method of bowing is a critical component of the resultant timbre. Violinists can play on a continuum from long smooth strokes to short staccato strokes. They can even produce more than one pitch at a time by bowing two strings simultaneously. Players can also dispense with the bow in order to pluck the strings with their fingers. This method of articulation is called *pizzicato*.

The violin's wide range and rich palette of tone colors make it into an extremely versatile solo and ensemble instrument. This flexibility is one reason why the violin has become a staple instrument in so many diverse cultures. Its range and warm tones can be compared to the human voice, and yet it is capable of producing extremely harsh and strident timbres if required. The instrument also blends well with other violins—ten or more players in an orchestra's violin section often sound like one voice.

The other instruments in the violin family are in progressively lower ranges. The viola is several inches longer than the violin and is in the tenor range. Its timbre tends to be more mellow than the violin, although it is capable of loud and powerful passage work. The violoncello, commonly called the cello, has the richest sound of the violin family. Cellists play in a seated position with the large body of the instrument between their legs. The cello is used for solo playing as well as for accompaniment. The bass—also called the string bass or double bass—is the largest member of the family. It is usually played while standing or sitting on a stool. While it is conventionally bowed for classical repertory, it is most often plucked when used in jazz.

Violins, violas, and cellos are not only the most plentiful instruments found in the modern symphony orchestra, they are also commonly grouped together in the string quartet. The string quartet features four musicians—two violinists, one violist, and one cellist. Composers since the early nineteenth century have been inspired by the timbre and texture of this particular combination of string instruments and have written many works for string quartet.

Aerophones: Wind Instruments

Wind instruments depend on a column of air pushed through a tube at a higher pressure than air outside; the resulting column vibrates like a string. The air column's fundamental frequency depends on its length, but the overtone structure varies with the shape of the column. Instruments with a conical bore—saxophones or oboes—have an even distribution of overtones; the cylindrical bores of flutes and clarinets suppress some overtones; and the flared bell shape in brasses tends to favor high frequency overtones.

The column of vibration is initiated in different ways according to the instrument. In flutes, the player's breath interacting with the sharp edge of the mouth hole causes the column of air in the tube to be set in motion. In oboes and clarinets, the vibration is caused by the movement of a reed—a thin sheet of cane that vibrates between the lips. Clarinets and saxophones use a single reed which fits into a mouthpiece, while oboes and bassoons have double reeds that when held directly in the player's mouth, vibrate against each other. Players of brass instruments activate the vibration with their lips pressed against a cup or funnel shaped mouthpiece. The shape of the mouthpiece also affects the timbre of the instrument.

In the symphony orchestra, wind instruments are divided into woodwinds and brass. The three woodwind instruments—flutes, clarinets, and oboes—have approximately the same range, but quite different tone colors. The modern silver flute has a very clear quality due to its limited overtone structure. The clarinet, usually made of ebony, is capable of warm, rich, and mellow tones that often resemble the human voice. It has the most expressive and dynamic range of the woodwinds. The oboe, with its double reed structure, has a much more crisp and penetrating sound than the clarinet.

Each of these three instruments has higher and lower counterparts in the orchestra, including the piccolo, the smallest and highest member of the flute family, the small E-flat clarinet, the bass clarinet, and the English horn—a larger oboe which plays in the viola range. The bassoon is in the cello range and with its double reed, has characteristics similar to the oboe. The instrument's long tube is bent back on itself and the reeds are brought close to the player's mouth by means of a narrow metal tube. The double bassoon or contrabassoon is more rarely employed in the orchestra; its range is an octave below the bassoon.

The brass instruments in the symphony orchestra include the trumpet, French horn, trombone, and tuba. The loudest of the wind instruments, they are made of metal and have long tubes that are coiled. Brass players create the pitches of the overtone series by adjusting the pressure of their vibrating lips within the mouthpiece of their instrument. The trumpet is the highest of the brass; it is made with a funnel shaped mouthpiece and narrow bore that flares at the end into a bell. The modern trumpet is constructed with three pistons or valves that when deployed allow air to pass through additional lengths of tubing, thereby giving players access to all the pitches of the chromatic scale. The bright color of the trumpet can be changed by inserting different shaped mutes into the bell.

The modern French horn is constructed from a long coiled tube, and like the trumpet, has valves to add additional tonal possibilities. It has a lower and more mellow tone than the trumpet, and is used to play solo parts and to enrich the overall web of color in the orchestra. It has also a great dynamic range and as with the trumpet, mutes can be used to change its tone color.

The trombone has a cylindrical bore and a cup-shaped mouthpiece, and is operated by a sliding mechanism rather than valves. The length of the instrument is increased by means of the slide which gives the instrument a larger range of pitches. Both the tenor trombone and the bass trombone are found in the contemporary orchestra. Trombones have a wide range of tone colors, ranging from noble, solemn, and voice-like to staccato, hard, and powerful.

The tuba is the lowest of the brass instruments and is constructed with a wide conical bore and a cup-shaped mouthpiece. The tuba family first came into existence in the mid-nineteenth century. Wagner's use of the instrument in the late 1860s established its place in the symphony orchestra. Both the tenor and bass tubas are operated with valves, but do not have the pitch range of the other brass instruments. Like other bass instruments, they are typically used to play accompaniments rather than solo parts.

Percussion Instruments: Membranophones and Idiophones

Percussion instruments include membranophones—the many forms of drums that are constructed with some sort of stretched skin over a resonating body—and idiophones, instruments whose bodies create sound without the aid of strings or skin. Idiophones can be struck with mallets, such as xylophones, glockenspiels, woodblocks, triangles, steel drums, bells, and all the bronze or iron gongs and barred instruments of the central Javanese gamelan. Other idiophones can be scraped—such as the Latin guiro, or shaken—such as the maracas or rattle. Some idiophones and membranophones are tuned to exact pitches, while others have no fixed pitch.

The timpani have been the main percussion instruments in the symphony orchestra since its inception. The contemporary timpani consist of a set of three to five tunable kettledrums played by one player. The drum body is a large bowl of metal over which a skin or synthetic head is stretched. The chief use of the timpani is to provide punctuation and tone color. Before Beethoven's time, the drums were used dramatically and ceremonially in loud passages in combination with brass. The refinement of the instrument in the early nineteenth century gave composers the opportunity to use it in new ways. Hector Berlioz was perhaps the first composer to thoroughly investigate how different drum mallets affected tone color on the timpani. Because they are tuned to precise pitches, timpani are used to play bass lines and more occasionally, melodic passages. Players often have to change the tuning of their instruments within a single piece.

Up until the twentieth century, percussion instruments played a relatively small role in the orchestra. Composers used percussion mostly for punctuation, to highlight or intensify certain passages, and for novelty. By the 1940s, some composers who were influenced by many musics from non-Western cultures, as well as by jazz and popular music, began to write compositions using a lot of percussion in the form of marimbas, vibraphones, xylophones, bells, gongs, cymbals, and drums.

Tone Color and Composition

Each instrumental group of the orchestra may be regarded as a separate "choir" of instrumental voices, with its own distinctive timbre—the woodwinds create a particular timbre when sounded together, as do the brass or strings. Instead of hearing individual instruments, one hears a composite sound that has a definite tone color. In orchestrating their compositions, composers use timbre by contrasting one section against another and one choir against another. The possible interplay and contrast between the sound of a solo instrument, one or more sections, individual choirs, and the entire orchestra provide unlimited possibilities for the use of timbre in orchestral composition.

Beethoven's Symphony No. 5 in C minor, First Movement. As you listen, notice how changes in timbre help to create movement and mood, including the use of the timpani and alternation between instrumental choirs.

Composers have written for all kinds of smaller ensembles that make use of the instruments of the contemporary symphony orchestra. The separate choirs of the orchestra—strings, woodwinds, and brass—have served as inspiration for composers in the form of the woodwind quintet, string trio, string quartet, and brass quintet. Many other combinations of instruments have been used in chamber music. Unlike orchestral music, chamber music is composed for a small group of musicians—generally two to nine—in which each musician has his or her own part. While the timbres of a large group tend to blend together, the tonal nuances of each instrument can be more readily distinguished in chamber music performances.

TIMBRE IN INDIAN CLASSICAL MUSIC

In many cultures, small ensembles are the primary means of musical expression. In the performance of North Indian classical music, small groups, including one or two instrumental or vocal soloists, a percussionist, and a musician playing a drone instrument called the tanpura, are common.

Indian musicians and dancers regard vocal music as the fountainhead of the arts, and in important respects Indian melodic instruments are designed to imitate aspects of the human voice. Plucked instruments such as the *veena, sitar,* and *sarod,* bowed instruments such as the *sarangi* and violin, and blown instruments such as the bamboo flute and *shahnai,* are constructed to emulate the pitch range, volume, ornaments, and timbre of Indian classical singing. Drone instruments such as the stringed *tanpura* are designed to accompany both singing and instrumental music, as are percussion instruments such as the *tabla, pakhawaj* or *mrdangm,* and hand-held cymbals.

Classical Instruments of North India

strings:		winds:	drums:
plucked	*bowed*	*blown*	
sitar	sarangi	shahnai (reed "oboe")	tabla
sarod	esraj	bansuri (bamboo flute)	pakhawaj
surbahar	violin		
Rudra-vina		*bellows-blown*	
slide guitar		harmonium	
tanpura			

Many additional varieties of stringed instruments and hand percussion are used to accompany folk and devotional music.

The traditional settings of classical music performances, solo or small ensemble recitals for audiences of knowledgeable listeners in the temples and courts, lent themselves to an intimate style of singing. A singer did not need to sing loudly, but subtle pitch inflections, ornaments including glissandos (slides), shakes, and grace notes, sophisticated rhythmic play, and an individualistic vocal timbre which emphasized the emotion of the sung text, were (and remain) high priorities.

The twentieth-century advent of concerts in large public halls more or less coincided with the introduction of microphones and electric sound amplification, so Indian singers and instrumentalists have been able to retain their emphasis on an intimate approach appropriate to what in the West would be called chamber recitals. This "chamber music aesthetic" applies to all Indian classical instruments except outdoor instruments such as the powerful South Indian *nagaswaram,* whose reedy sound accompanies religious processions which may be attended by thousands of devotees.

Chordophones: Plucked Instruments

Statues and portraits of Saraswati, the Hindu goddess of learning and the arts (particularly music) depict her as a musician, holding the *veena,* which may be regarded as the quintessential Indian classical instrument. A plucked, fretted lute, the veena is capable of producing pitches in the full three-octave range that is theoretically (and, in some cases, literally) used by Indian classical singers. A very ancient instrument, the veena remains to this day the most popular fretted instrument among South Indian classical musicians.

In North India, the veena—also called *been*—has largely been supplanted by the *sitar,* the most common fretted instrument in North Indian classical music. The sitar seems to have become the instrument of choice in North Indian court music during the eighteenth century.[12] The great virtuoso Ravi Shankar introduced the sitar to many listeners in the West via concert tours and recordings, beginning in the early 1960s. Millions of Westerners became familiar with the sound of the sitar during that decade when popular bands like the Beatles began incorporating the instrument as an intriguing "new" timbre in rock recordings.

A number of structural features of the sitar give it a timbre which contrasts markedly with those of Western plucked instruments like the guitar, banjo, and mandolin. The sound of a vibrating string on a guitar or sitar is transmitted to the resonant body of the instrument by a wooden, bone, plastic, or metal bridge, which sits on the instrument's sound-board, directly beneath the taut string. On most Western instruments, including not only the guitar but also the mandolin, banjo, and the violin family, the point where the string crosses the bridge is a narrow ridge, less than an eighth of an inch across. This one-pointed transit gives the instrument a very sharp, clear sound. When the bridge becomes worn or damaged, causing the string to travel across an unusually wide or depressed surface, the result is an undesired muted or buzzing timbre, and the bridge requires repair or replacement.

In contrast, the sitar has a very wide, almost flat bridge. The string crosses a surface of half an inch or more. The bridge is carefully shaped into a gentle curve, which is designed to add a buzzing timbre to the sound of the string. This kind of buzzing, which Western instrument makers work very hard to prevent, is a desired quality in the sound of a sitar. This buzzing is an important part of what Indian musicians call the *jawari* or "voice" of the instrument, and when the bridge becomes worn, repair is required to restore the instrument's jawari.

Guitars, mandolins, violins, violas, cellos, and double basses all transmit their sound to the listener in part through round or f-shaped holes in the surface of the instrument. Sound vibrations bounce from the back wall of the instrument through the soundhole and towards the listener. The sitar, like many other Indian stringed instruments, has no sound hole. Unlike the guitar, which has a single resonating hardwood body and a solid wooden neck, the sitar has a gourd resonator at its base, a hollow, resonant wooden neck, and in many cases a second gourd resonator attached near the upper end of the neck. Thus, the resonance of the sitar has a different quality than that of

TANPURA

SAROD

PAKAWAJ

NORTH INDIAN INSTRUMENTS

SITAR

TABLA

SARANGI

a guitar. The sound of the sitar seems to permeate the performance space, instead of bouncing from the instrument towards the audience.

Readers who are familiar with the guitar know that the instrument sounds particularly resonant in certain keys, such as E major or E minor, A major or A minor, D major or D minor, and G major. The reason for this lies in the principle of sympathetic vibration. When a particular note is sounded near to a string tuned to the same pitch, or one of its prominent overtones, the second string will vibrate "in sympathy" with the sounding note. The open strings of the guitar are tuned to the notes E, A, D, G, B, and E. When the note E is played on the guitar, two additional open strings (E and B) vibrate in sympathy with the plucked string. The same phenomenon occurs when the notes A, D, or G are played.

Sitar-makers takes advantage of the principle of sympathetic vibration by including nine or more sympathetic strings in the construction of the instrument. Most sitars have seven playing strings, which run over a set of curved metal frets. These are the strings which are played to produce melodies and rhythmic drones in the course of a performance. The sympathetic strings lie *beneath* the frets. They are tuned to the notes of the raga being played, and are rarely plucked in the course of a performance. Their function is to enhance the resonance of the playing strings by vibrating in sympathy with the sound of the plucked notes.

The buzzing timbre of the sitar, the fact that its long neck functions as a resonating chamber, the indirect diffusion of its sound, and the resonant quality of its sympathetic strings result in a very different timbre than that of Western plucked instruments. Readers who are unfamiliar with the sound of the sitar may seek out commercially available recordings by internationally renowned artists such as Ravi Shankar, Vilayat Khan, and Nikhil Banerjee.

The North Indian *tanpura* shares many structural and timbral qualities with the sitar, including a wide bridge, a gourd resonator at its base, and a hollow, resonant neck. Unlike the sitar, the tanpura has no frets or sympathetic strings. The function of the tanpura is not to provide a melody, but to sound a continuous accompanying drone by the sequential plucking of its four, five, or six open strings. The buzzing of the strings is enhanced by the placement of slender threads of cotton or silk between each string and the bridge.

A North Indian tanpura played by Ira Landgarten.

The North Indian *sarod* is, like the sitar, a plucked, melodic instrument, used by soloists in the performance of Hindustani classical music. Like the sitar, the sarod has a hollow, resonant neck, and utilizes sympathetic strings to enhance the instrument's resonance. Unlike the sitar, the sarod has a tight goatskin head beneath the bridge, rather than a wooden soundboard, and a fretless, metal fingerboard, rather than metal frets, mounted on its neck. The sound of the sarod is more percussive, clear, and metallic than that of the sitar.

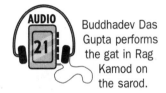

Buddhadev Das Gupta performs the gat in Rag Kamod on the sarod.

Wind Instruments: Bansuri and Shahnai

The North Indian bamboo flute, or *bansuri,* is very simple in its construction, consisting of a piece of bamboo close to two feet in length, closed at one end and open at the other, with a soundhole near the closed end, six finger holes, and occasionally one or more unfingered tuning holes near the open end of the instrument. The bansuri is a transverse flute, that is, the player blows across the soundhole from the side.

The Hindu god Krishna is often pictured playing the bansuri, and many songs and stories tell of the seductive power of his playing. The flute is considered a highly romantic instrument in India. The timbre of the instrument is high and "pure," but perhaps warmer and darker than that of most metal flutes.

The *shahnai* is an end-blown reed instrument, with a piercing tone quality and open finger holes that allow performers to slide gracefully from note to note, emulating the glissandos and ornaments of North Indian classical singing. Like the South Indian nagaswaram, the shahnai is associated with temple music, and is frequently played for weddings.

Percussion Instruments

Contemporary performances of North Indian classical music are usually accompanied by the paired hand drums called *tabla.* The right hand drum in a pair of tabla, called the *dahina* or *tabla* (the same name used for the drums as a pair) consists of a tapered wooden cylinder from nine to twelve inches high, with a diameter at the upper, narrow end of four and three-quarters to six inches. The left hand drum, called the *bayan,* is a hemispheric kettle drum eight and three-quarters to eleven inches high, with an upper diameter of eight to nine inches.

Both drums are covered with heads of goatskin, with a narrow second skin placed over the first in a half-inch band around the rim of the drum. On each head is mounted a black dot, two and three-quarter inches in diameter, composed of paste and iron filings, called a *siyahi* ("ink").[13] The main skin on each drum, which is visible between the rim and the centrally placed siyahi, is called the *sur* ("note" or "keynote"). The second skin, which is mounted around the rim of the first, is called the *kinar* ("bank" or "edge").

Both heads are held taught by leather thongs, which are threaded through the edge of the head and strung back and forth between the top and the bottom of the drum. The kinar and sur of the right hand drum are tuned precisely to the keynote "sa" by the manipulation of wooden pegs placed under the thongs and the gentle hammering of a leather rim around the outside circumference of the head. Under the skilled fingers of a master drummer, the kinar produces overtones which emphasize the "sa" one octave above the "sa" played on the sur. The sound produced on the kinar is called "na"; the sur produces "tin." The siyahi produces a bell-like, ringing tone called "tun," with overtones that ring one whole-step above "sa." The siyahi may also be muted, producing a short, unpitched, "dry" sound called "te," without the ringing quality of "tun."

The skin of the bayan is tuned less precisely and more loosely than that of the dahina. When allowed to ring, the bayan produces a deep, bass sound called "ge," which can be made to imitate the inflections of speech by adjusting the pressure of the heel of the left hand against the vibrating head. The bayan may also be made to produce muted, "dry" sounds called "kat" or "ke."

Indian percussion instruments include a wide variety of cylindrical drums such as the mrdangm, pakhawaj, and dholak, frame drums such as the daff and kanjira, and cymbals of bell metal such as the manjira.

Percussionist Ray Spiegel illustrating the timbre of the tabla. Listen to the ringing, almost bell-like quality of the dahina, and the vocal, bass sonority of the bayan.

▬▬ TIMBRE IN JAPANESE TRADITIONAL MUSIC

In much of Japanese traditional music, performance is centered around a solo instrument or a small ensemble consisting of voice, shakuhachi (an end-blown bamboo flute), koto (a rectangular zither), and/or shamisen (a three-stringed plucked lute). Unlike the hierarchical structure in North Indian classical music which features a soloist accompanied by two other musicians, Japanese musicians play and sing the same part within the small ensemble. Timbres also differ markedly. In North Indian sitar and sarod performance, the presence of drone and sympathetic strings create both a continual web of sound and a buzzing tone color. According to ethnomusicologist and shakuhachi player Tomie Hahn, Japanese aesthetics call for more clarity and simplicity of line and subtlety of tone color:

One of the concepts in Japanese music that I believe is really different than in other styles of music around the world is the beauty of simplicity. In a sense, the clean, very clear, yet subtle line is really to be appreciated as an aesthetic. . . . We can even see this in architecture . . . and in gardens, in bonsai, this really clear line. This is something very obvious in the single line of the shakuhachi where we see, actually can hear the shapes of the sound. . . . In the ensemble when shakuhachi and koto or shamisen are playing together we will have these beautiful simple lines passing by . . . yet there are nuances particular to each instrument.

Particularly in Japanese music this [timbre] is something we really love—that full palette of sound. To have everything from a really rough [tone color] to a very clean, beautiful, clear, clear sound. We want all of this variety and this is what colors the music. This is what makes the subtleties ring throughout the piece.[14]

The Shakuhachi

Of all the instruments in Japanese traditional music, perhaps the shakuhachi displays the widest range of tone colors, which are achieved through the player's breathing and articulation:

> *In shakuhachi music, the subtleties are what is to be appreciated and various timbral changes. . . . Shakuhachi has such a palette of different color sounds. For example, we have a strong bell-like sound on the one hand, a very large round sound, and then we have no pitch way on the other side, just air coming out of the shakuhachi. What we want is everything in between, the entire palette of sound.*[15]

"Hifumi Hachi Gaeshi" played on the shakuhachi.

The shakuhachi is thought to have come from China in the eighth century with Buddhism. It was later adopted in the seventeenth century by itinerant Buddhist monks who used the instrument to play for alms and as an aid in meditation. The production of a single tone was believed to bring the player closer to enlightenment. According to Hahn, "Within one note there is a whole microcosm, a whole world of sound. The subtleties are endless." This appreciation for the timbral possibilities of one tone explains why each articulation—including silence—is so important in the aesthetic of shakuhachi playing.

The instrument is made from bamboo that has large joints, and both the stalk and root are used. The bamboo is heated in order to straighten it out and shape it with the bell given a slight upward curve. The bamboo is then stored for six months which allows water and oil to evaporate. It is then hollowed out with a rasp and finger holes and a mouthpiece are cut. A piece of water buffalo horn or ivory is inlaid into the blowing edge, and finally, the bore is given five coats of black or red lacquer.

The instrument is played vertically with the lower lip almost covering the mouthpiece opening. The stream of air strikes the horn inlay of the mouthpiece and enters the flute. Very little air is needed to produce a tone, but excess air is sometimes desired to create the airy and strong explosive sounds that are characteristic of the playing style.

The Koto

The koto is the Japanese member of a family of long zithers with movable bridges assumed to have originated in China. The wooden body of the koto is long and rectangular and the instrument is played sitting or kneeling on the floor. It has thirteen silk strings that are strung horizontally at equal tension. The desired pitch of each open string is determined by placing a movable bridge made of ivory, bone, or plastic, at a specific point under it. Different tunings are created by moving the bridges. Players traditionally stop the string above the bridge with the fingers of their left hand to create additional pitches. They use ivory, bone, or bamboo picks on the thumb, forefinger, and middle finger of their right hand to pluck the strings. The main playing finger is the right hand thumb. In contemporary music, the left hand is also used to pluck the strings, giving the instrument an almost harp-like sound.

THE KOTO

A contemporary composition for solo koto by Sawai Tadao entitled "Tori No Yo Ni."

The koto has an astonishing range of subtle tone colors that are achieved by the player's plucking techniques. Musicians can play a very scratchy style across the strings, or with the picks they can repeatedly strike one string after another to make a continuous, beautiful, almost water-like, flowing sound. With their left hands, they can bend or hammer on the string in order to produce a pitch without plucking.

Sawai Tadao composed the solo koto piece "Tori No Yo Ni" in 1985. The composer used the image of flying as his inspiration. He wrote, "How would it feel to fly free in the sky as a bird flies? Humans have invented airplanes, but we are not free to feel the clouds as we pass through them." Sawai achieves the sense of flying by having the player repeatedly play one string after another, using both hands to pluck the strings. Listeners will notice changes of timbre—even when a single note is repeated—and should keep in mind that tone color and dynamic range are closely related.

TIMBRE IN ARABIC CLASSICAL MUSIC

Much of Arabic art music is performed by a soloist or by a small ensemble of musicians. In Arabic music, as in India, vocal music is often regarded as the fountainhead of the arts, and in important respects, instruments are designed to imitate aspects of the human voice. Both the singing and instrumental styles include a high amount of ornamentation and little or no vibrato.

The ensemble of 'ud (a short necked lute), qanun (a plucked zither), violin, and nay (an endblown flute), accompanied by either the darabukka (a goblet-shaped drum) or daff (tambourine) is used to play the principle of form of Arabic art music known as *nawba*.[16] While all the melody instruments play the same musical line, this combination of blown, bowed, plucked, and struck instruments provides a wide palette of musical timbres.

The 'Ud

The 'ud, ancestor of the Western lute, was and still is considered the cornerstone of Arabic music and "the Sultan of Musical Instruments."[17] Played both as a solo and an ensemble instrument, the 'ud is a short necked lute with a

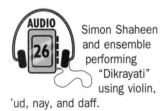

Simon Shaheen and ensemble performing "Dikrayati" using violin, 'ud, nay, and daff.

THE VIOLIN AND 'UD

THE 'UD

pear shaped construction that has a long history in the Arabic world. The word "'ud" literally means wood. Musician Simon Shaheen describes the instrument:

> *The 'ud is actually the most prominent instrument in Arabic music and it is as valuable as the piano is for the Western composer. It has five double strings and one single low string. And it has a finger board that is fretless, and this is how the quarter tone quality is produced. . . . The fact that we don't have frets on the finger board like on the guitar or the lute makes it possible to produce the microtonal qualities or any qualities of sound.*[18]

Like all lutes, the 'ud is a chordophone that has a neck that acts as a string bearer. The strings are strung from near the base along the full length of the neck. All lutes have both a resonating body with soundholes and a neck, although instruments differ according to relative length of body and neck, shape of the back, number of strings, and whether they have frets or not. The 'ud has a narrower neck than the Western lute, three large circular soundholes, and a tortoiseshell plaque.

The documented history of the 'ud goes back to the fifth century, when the instrument was reported to have a skin top and three strings. This skin top was later replaced by a wooden top, and by the end of the sixth century, the 'ud had four strings and four frets. In the ninth century, the 'ud was reported to already have five strings. It was the instrument most discussed by the classical theorists in the ninth and tenth centuries who combined Greek, Persian, and Arabic concepts to contemplate both the technical aspects of music—scales and modes—and the cosmological. The 'ud was portrayed as a microcosmic representation of man's physical, mental, and spiritual states.

The work of al-Kind, the first important theorist whose work survives today, analyzed intervals and scales in terms of fretting on the 'ud, as well as cosmological concepts derived from the Greeks, comparing the 'ud's original four strings to the zodiac, the elements, the seasons, and four humors. The fifth string was thought to symbolize the soul.[19]

In the ninth century, the 'ud was brought to Spain which was part of the Islamic world. It appeared in other parts of Europe by the thirteenth century where it developed into the lute, one of the most important instruments of the European Renaissance. The word "lute" evolved directly from the Arabic "al'ud." The Renaissance lute was shaped like the 'ud, but had frets and was played with the fingers rather than with a plectrum.

Today, the 'ud is usually played in the context of a small ensemble, as accompaniment to a vocalist, or as a solo instrument. It is the most widely used instrument in both art and popular music ensembles throughout the Islamic world. It is plucked with a feather-like plastic plectrum, a modern substitute for the eagle feather quills originally used. The strings are plucked in regular or irregular upward or downward motions. The player must know both repertoire and plucking techniques which help to give the instrument its wide variety of timbres. 'Ud players change between the high and low registers, repeatedly pluck the high open string to create a drone, and simultaneously play one or more melodies.[20]

The Nay

The nay, an endblown flute made from cane, is a Persian term meaning pipe, and versions of the instrument are found from North Africa to western

THE NAY

China. The instrument is used throughout the Arab world as both an ensemble and a solo instrument. Nays are constructed in different sizes, but in all cases, musicians blow against the sharp edge of the pipe opening to make a sound. According to Fred Stubbs, it is the mouthpiece that differentiates one type of nay from another:

The Turkish nay is different from the Iranian nay or the Arabic nay because of its embouchure. This mouthpiece is what actually touches the lips, and it's a little bit more complex than the Arabic style. The Arabic style ends without a cap and the Persian nay has a metal sleeve on it. . . . The Turkish nay is the only one to have a mouthpiece usually made out of ox horn. . . . It is this shape that is said to give the Turkish nay its particular tonal timbre.[21]

The nay generally has six finger holes on the front and one in the back. Through overblowing, musicians can get a range of three octaves. The lips and head position must be changed while blowing and opening or closing the finger holes.

In Turkey, the nay is a central symbol for the Mevlevi Dervishes, a Sufi order whose patron saint is the great poet Rumi who died in the fourteenth century. Stubbs said, the Mevlevis' recreation story about the nay is symbolic of the human condition:

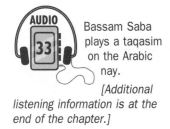

Bassam Saba plays a taqasim on the Arabic nay.
[Additional listening information is at the end of the chapter.]

The nay is first cut from the reed bed and then it is pierced with the number of holes in the human body. And at the moment that the nay is made hollow or empty, which happens by means of a hot poker, it is said that the nay then begins to scream or sing or to cry out to be reunited with the beloved. And so the nay is a powerful instrument for the Mevlevis. It's not a magic instrument. Playing the nay expresses something about the human condition. It expresses that the human condition is temporary, and that our natural condition is to long for a reuniting with our source, with the universal power, with God. . . .[22]

▬▬ TIMBRE IN MUSIC FROM SUB-SAHARAN AFRICA

The many countries that lie south of the Sahara Desert utilize an enormous variety of musical instruments. All types of chordophones, aerophones, membranophones, idiophones, and electrophones are represented, ranging from traditional hand-crafted string, wind, and percussion instruments to mass-produced imports from the West. In many popular urban genres, indigenous instruments are used in combination with acoustic and electric guitars, electric bass, synthesizers, brass instruments, and accordions, to create contemporary musical fusions such as Nigerian *jùjú* and *chimurenga* from Zimbabwe.

The Mbira

Although there are countless varieties of drums of all shapes and sizes found throughout sub-Saharan Africa, other instruments are equally important. One of the most popular is the *mbira*, also known as the *sanzi, likembe, kalimba,* or thumb piano. The range of this keyboard-type idiophone, belonging to a general class of instruments called lamellophones, extends from South Africa to Ethiopia in the east and the Gambia in the west, but it is found in greater concentration in Zaire, Zimbabwe, Mozambique, and parts of Angola.[23] There are many forms and sizes, but all mbiras have basically the same layout and four elements in common: they contain a soundboard, a natural means for amplifying the sound, a set of keys, and a method of producing a buzzing quality.[24]

According to Paul Berliner, the buzzing timbre is considered an essential and pleasing feature of the music played on the mbira:

> *This quality is appreciated by African musicians in the same way that Westerners appreciate the sound of the snares on a snare drum or the fuzz-tone on an electric guitar. It may be seen as analogous to the mist that partly obscures the mountains and small figures of certain Chinese silk-screen paintings: the mist is an integral part of such paintings, establishing mood and feeling, and the figures are not supposed to be seen more clearly. The same is true for the buzzing that accompanies the pure sound of the mbira.*[25]

The buzzing can be produced in different ways, including by placing metal beads around the keys or by attaching shells and more recently, bottle caps, to a metal plate on the soundboard. When the keys are played, these devices vibrate sympathetically, creating a continuous drone-like buzz.

The overall timbre of the mbira differs according to the materials used in its construction. The body of the instrument is usually a rectangular box made from a single block of wood that is hollowed out. The keys are fixed to the soundboard and attached to the back of the bridge. They can be made from iron, copper, steel, brass, stems, bamboo, wire, or nails and range in number from as few as three to as many as fifty-two. For added sound, the instrument is often placed on or in a resonating chamber such as a gasoline tin, bark trough, or gourd. Large instruments are often placed in bowl-shaped calabash gourd resonators.[26]

The instruments are played in a variety of contexts ranging from pure recreation to religious events. Among the Lemba, a Bantu tribe from the

Transvaal, the mbira, known as the *deza sanza*, is considered a sacred and symbolic object which represents the Lemba ancestors.[27] Although often used as a solo instrument to accompany a single singer, mbiras are also played in combination with other instruments. Mbira ensembles exist throughout sub-Saharan Africa, including groups of more than fifteen players that play at the religious ceremonies of the Shona in Zimbabwe.[28]

The Xylophone

The xylophone is another keyboard-type idiophone that is found throughout sub-Saharan Africa. The instrument has many different names, including *balafon, madimba, mbila,* and *akadinda,* depending on the region where it is found. Most xylophones have wooden keys that are played using wooden mallets; resonators are often used to deepen the timbre and amplify the sound. The instrument's size, shape, and materials vary from region to region. Timbre is affected by the wood chosen for the keys, as well as the size and type of resonators or their absence. Instruments without resonators are appropriate for solo or group playing in an intimate setting. Xylophones are also played in many different instrumental combinations and social settings, ranging from single players to entire orchestras.

The simplest version may be the leg xylophones that consist of three or four bars placed on the extended legs of the player.[29] Log xylophones, found throughout Central Africa, consist of two logs that act as support for the keys. Some of these instruments may be long enough to enable two or three musicians to play together at the same instrument. The akadinda, a twenty-two keyed instrument from Buganda, is played by six people—three on each side.

The most common type of xylophone has calabash resonators that are fixed under the keys. According to Bebey, the distinctive timbre of this type of instrument comes partly from the construction of the resonator: a hole in each calabash is covered with a substance made from a spider's web, a thin piece of fish skin, or a bat's wing, and attached with resin.[30]

One example of this type of xylophone is the *balo* or *balafon* from Guinea, Mali, and the Gambia. The balafon usually has eighteen to twenty-one rosewood keys that are arranged on a bamboo frame over gourd resonators of graduated size. Its history is often traced back to the thirteenth century and it has been used by the *jalis* (discussed below) ever since. The well known Malian singer, Salif Keita, recently added the balafon to his electric band.

The Kora

The kora is an instrument unique to the Manding people who live in Senegal, the Gambia, Guinea, and Mali. While chordophones, including harps, are found throughout sub-Saharan Africa, the kora is an interesting combination of parts. It is classified as a spiked bridge harp which has a skin-covered gourd sound box with twenty-one strings that come off the neck in two rows perpendicular to the soundboard. The strings cross over notches in a high bridge and the long neck passes completely through the soundbox. Like the mbira and many other African instruments, traditional koras often have a metal plate with jangles attached to the bridge. The metal vibrates sympathetically when the strings are plucked, thereby creating a buzzing sound. Because the buzz gets overemphasized when the kora is amplified, the plate is now often removed for recordings and broadcasts.[31]

The kora's tuning is divided between the two rows of strings so that the playing technique often involves the alternate plucking of notes by the left and right hands. The melody results from the interlocking of the two parts. Traditionally the strings were made of twisted hide, but today they are made of nylon in graded strengths. According to Roderic Knight, the bright, clear timbre produced by the nylon strings has helped to make the instrument popular far beyond the areas in which it is indigenous.[32]

THE KORA

The kora is traditionally played by *jalis*—hereditary musicians who function as historians, genealogists, and praise singers. The jali uses the kora, balo or balafon, and the *kontingo* (a five-stringed plucked lute with a skin head) to accompany songs. In the past, the verbal skills of the jali were considered important for the maintenance of society:

> *For example, praises and genealogy were incorporated into songs, and oral history told to the accompaniment of instrumental music. The jalis (Mandinka:jalolu) held important positions next to various leaders and influential people of the state because of their exclusive knowledge and ability in the verbal arts. They were essentially the personal court musicians of these people and they were highly respected and well paid for their important contributions.*[33]

While there is a large body of repertoire for the solo kora, most of the repertoire involves singing. The importance of speech and song are evident in performance:

> *At different points in a performance* jalolu *may tell stories in everyday speech, chant narrative songs associated with specific heroes, sing tunefully, or declaim highly formulaic praises and proverbs. The preferred timbral quality, a forceful chest resonance sung with a tensed throat, evokes the strength of the Mande heroes in sound itself.*[34]

The importance of song in the music of the jalis is evident throughout sub-Saharan Africa where the human voice is often the primary instrument. When instruments are used, they often imitate the contour and even the meaning of tonal languages. Pitched drums can be used to convey complete phrases, messages, or verbal formulas, such as proverbs or praises. The hourglass drum of the *Yoruba*, for example, reproduces all the tones of speech by the musician's regulation of the leather thongs attached to the skin of the drum.[35]

TIMBRE IN VOCAL MUSIC

The human voice, perhaps the most mysterious and complex of all musical instruments, works somewhat like a set of bellows-blown bagpipes. The singer inhales through the nose and/or mouth, holds and compresses the air in the lungs, and expels the pressurized air between the vocal cords, which function as a pair of vibrating reeds. By coordinating the flow of air, the tension of the vocal cords, and the shape of the lips, soft palate, tongue, and air passages, the singer controls pitch, volume, and timbre.

Tone color in the voice, as in all instruments, results from the phenomenon of the overtone series. The singer's body is a wind instrument, but unlike a flautist or clarinetist, the singer can actually control the shape of the resonating spaces within his or her instrument to emphasize desired partials. The chest, throat, mouth, nasal passages, and sinuses act as a set of resonators, amplifying the reedy buzz created by the vibrating vocal cords. The throat, tongue, soft palate, and cheeks are used, either consciously or unconsciously, to shape the resonant space and create desired timbres. Posture, breathing, and the shaping of the throat affect the resonance of the chest cavity.

Although the sinuses and nasal cavities are not directly shaped by muscular action, by the action of his or her muscles the singer can direct sound into or away from these resonators. All parts of the resonating system are therefore under the singer's direct or indirect control, resulting in an enormous variety of possible tone colors. The singer can, in effect, turn her instrument into a flute, saxophone, or clarinet at will, by simply altering the shape of the resonant spaces within his or her own body.

Singers control the timbre of their voices by shaping vowels and hummable consonants. The vowels "ee," "ah," "eh," "oh," and "oo" each require a different shape of the lips, tongue, and cheeks, and this reshaping of the resonant cavity alters the emphasis within the overtone series, creating changes in tone color. Hummable consonants, such as "mm," "nn," "ng," "ll," and "zz" also can be manipulated to create various timbres.

For the sake of discussion, we divide the sound of a single sung note into separate domains of pitch, duration, timbre, volume or intensity, and attack (accented or unaccented), but these are all artificial distinctions, aspects of what the ear correctly perceives as a single sonic event. Our perception of vocal timbre is, therefore, affected not only by the functioning of the overtone series, but by every other aspect of singing. We may be fooled into thinking we have heard a change in timbre when what we really have perceived is a change in volume or pitch, but even this is not the whole story. The timbre of a singer's voice actually does change, not only when he or she alters the shape of a sung vowel, but also when he or she makes changes in pitch, volume, or attack.

The actions of the vocal instrument are mostly invisible—we cannot observe the workings of the lungs and throat as we can the fingers of a violinist, the lips of a trombonist, or the hammers striking the strings of a piano. The manipulation of pitch, volume, and timbre is largely intuitive, a set of skills partly inborn, partly acquired by enculturation, and only occasionally subject to premeditated control on the part of the performer.

As children, we imitate the sounds around us—the honking of car horns, the shrieking of sirens, the mooing of cows, the bleating of sheep, and the voices of our parents, without thinking about how to make such sounds. Speaking and singing share, to a great extent, the unconscious nature of the other functions shared by the vocal organs—breathing, eating, and drinking. Singing teachers in the West have developed a vocabulary for discussing vocal technique, but even the most carefully coached performer of European art songs absorbs a great deal of her art by observing and listening to exemplary singers.

Cultural preferences for particular vocal timbres are, like the entire process of vocalization, essentially intuitive. We learn how a singer's voice should sound by hearing singers, and the preferred timbres of our own musical culture are acquired early and usually taken for granted. The automatic nature of this conditioning is apparent when we hear singing from an unfamiliar culture with aesthetic values different than our own. To a child reared on Italian opera, country and western singing may seem unpleasantly nasal, but to a young fan of country and western music, operatic singing may at first sound mannered and pretentious. Fortunately, such prejudices may be overcome by listening and attempting to understand the aesthetic preferences of less familiar cultures.

Overtone Singing: The Throat-Singers of Tuva

Tuva is a high table-land surrounded by mountains in Central Asia, just over the Russian border from northwest Mongolia. The nomadic herders of Tuva have developed a fascinating vocal style in which the singer sequentially emphasizes different partials of the overtone series, all the while maintaining a steady drone on the fundamental pitch. At any moment, the vocalist is producing two distinct notes, creating a melody out of the changing upper harmonics.

The principle of throat-singing, the selective emphasis of overtones that are always present in the voice, is the same as that of the Jew's harp, which is, significantly, the most popular musical instrument in Tuva. Westerners who are unfamiliar with overtone-singing may have encountered the Jew's harp, which consists of a two-part armature housing a thin piece of metal. The armature is held against the player's upper and lower lips. The player repeatedly plucks the thin metal strip, and by altering the shape of his mouth, changes the overtones which ring along with the fundamental pitch produced by the vibrating metal. A skilled Jew's harpist, like a Tuvan throat-singer, can create clear, rapidly moving melodies by simply adjusting the resonant space in his or her mouth.

According to Ted Levi, Tuvan throat-singing both imitates and interacts with the mountainous, riverine landscape of the Tuvan countryside, and the horse-centered lifestyle of the Tuvan people:

A Tuvan singer maintaining a constant drone on the fundamental while creating a clearly audible melody with the upper partials. Once you have heard this kind of singing, you may begin to notice the presence of harmonics even in the voices of conventional singers.

> *There are kinds of throat-singing that imitate water, that imitate birds, that imitate the growl of a bear, or the cawing of a crow, that imitate the sound of boots rattling in stirrups on a horse. And in addition to these kinds of throat-singing, there are many other forms of music in Tuva that are also imitative in different ways, songs that use the echo of cliffs in a sense to interact with the spirit of the cliff and draw out the echo. Those are also forms of music that, whose inspiration is place, a sense of place.[36]*

Now we will consider vocal timbre in a second genre which draws much of its inspiration from a sense of place: the "ganga" singing of the Bosnian highlands.

Timbre in the Ganga Singing of the Bosnian Highlands

Vocal timbre is affected, not only by the shaping of internal space within a singer's mouth, throat, and chest, but by the external space of the environment in which the individual sings. A singer is greatly influenced by the context of performance, whether it be in a concert hall, living room, or in the mountains outdoors.

Before the breakup of Yugoslavia and the violent destruction of many villages in the Bosnian highlands during the early 1990s, Bosnian villagers, like the nomadic herders of Tuva, tended their livestock in the wide-open spaces of a mountainous terrain. Their vocal style reflects both the broad, outdoor character of the highland landscape and the intimate nature of village society.

The influence of the landscape is perceptible in the sheer volume and penetrating timbre of their singing, a full-throated, somewhat nasal production that seems designed to be audible across valleys and in neighboring hills. The rhythmic nature of ganga—interludes of loud singing alternating with long silences—suggests that space is left for the hills to echo the voices of the singers. The intimacy of Bosnian village society is reflected in the posture of a small ensemble of singing women, standing close together and touching one another, so that their powerful individual voices blend into a single resonant whole.

Their choice of intervals—notes spaced only a single scale degree apart—guarantees the presence of "beats," the acoustical phenomenon of a rapid, regular pulsation which results from the placement of two or more notes in close harmonic "conflict" with one another. The sound waves set up by a single voice create beats when they interact with waves set up by a second voice singing only a whole- or half-step apart, rather like the bobbing caused by the intersection of the wakes of two motorboats passing one another on a body of water.

Ganga singing illustrates the fact that vocal timbre is affected, not only by the space in which the singers perform, but by musical texture—the presence, or absence, of simultaneously sounding voices or instruments. The "beats," which are an essential part of the timbre of ganga singing, cannot be produced without the presence of at least two voices. Singers, listeners, and even musicologists often confuse the concepts of timbre and texture, in part because the two phenomena are so dependent on one another. The timbre of a single voice is inherently different than that of two or more voices. A difference in *texture*—the addition of one or more voices—results in a difference in *timbre*—the overtone series created by those voices as they interact.

Bosnian ethnomusicologist Mirjana Laušević singing a ganga entitled "Sjajna Zvjezdo" with Donna Lee Kwon and Tristra Newyear, members of the ensemble known as Zabe-i-Babe.

Timbre in Irish and Appalachian Folk Singing

The timbre of singing may be heavily stylized, as in Tuvan throat-singing or Bosnian ganga, or it may be almost conversational, emulating the contours and tone qualities of informal speech. The narrative song traditions of England, Scotland, Ireland, and North America employ a highly conversational style of singing, in which the first priority is given to verbal clarity. The singer's basic responsibility is to tell a story, in a dialect and accent which can be understood and appreciated by local listeners.

Modern folk-singers often perform traditional ballads on the concert stage, but prior to the mid-twentieth century the setting for a performance of such songs was usually a fairly small room, for an audience of friends and family members. Ballad singers often belonged to the communities in which

In this example, Joe Heaney sings the English language song "The Rocks of Bawn" in the sean-nós style. His distinctive tone quality has provided an influential example for an entire generation of sean-nós singers in contemporary Ireland.

they sang, and they were not usually paid for performing. Housewives, farmers, and other local people provided their own, home-made entertainment before the days of television, commercial recordings, and radio broadcasts. Singing reinforced a sense of local identity for both singer and listeners, who might also take a turn at singing in the course of an evening's fun. In such a setting, with no need to project the voice across a valley, or to the last row in a large concert hall, the singer could give maximum attention to telling the story. This emphasis on storytelling did not encourage the display of exaggerated histrionics, however, understatement was an important aesthetic value.

In these narrative traditions, then, singing closely reflects the sound of everyday speech. Remembering that vocal timbre is a result of the formation of vowels and singable consonants, it is clear that tone quality is dependent on pronunciation, and that dialect and accent must therefore be central in determining a community's preferences for particular kinds of tone color. The timbre of North American, Irish, Scottish, and English folk singing reflects the hundreds of local accents of particular communities and singers in a network of inter-related music cultures.

The singers of Connemara, in western Ireland, developed a particularly interesting singing style in which vocal timbre plays a distinctive role. The most famous exponent of this style, known in Irish Gaelic as *sean-nós* ("old-style") singing, was Joseph Heaney. Sean-nós singers perform primarily in the Irish language, in a style which emphasizes the use of delicate melodic ornamentation and, in many cases, a strong nasal vocal timbre.

The deep, reedy quality of Joe Heaney's singing has come to exemplify the Connemara sean-nós tradition to many modern listeners, but we should remember that each singer is an individual, and that each person's vocal timbre, while it reflects aesthetic preferences of the culture in which he lives, is also as personal as a signature or fingerprint.

Many narrative songs from Ireland, Scotland, and England traveled with immigrants from those nations to the Appalachian Mountains of the United States, where they fed new song traditions, eventually adding a southern American "twang" to the singing timbre.

Compare the timbre of Joe Heaney's voice to that of Irish vocalist Pat Kilbride, in his rendition of "The Flower of Magheralee."

John Cohen sings the American ballad "Pretty Polly." John Cohen's pronunciation, and resultant tonal quality, is strongly influenced by the voices of ballad singers from the southern Appalachian Mountains, and it is tempting to believe that the timbre of the entire tradition is colored by the predominantly treble qualities of the banjo and fiddle, the two most common traditional instruments in the region.

Western Classical Singing

Timbre is perhaps the central concern in the training of Western classical singers. Performers of European art song have adopted the term *chiaroscuro* (clear-dark) from the vocabulary of art history, to describe the ideal round and rich timbre of a classically-trained vocalist.

If we compare the singing of an opera singer with that of a balladeer from the Appalachian Mountains, we notice some striking contrasts. The opera singer must be able to sing loud enough to be heard in a large hall over a full orchestra and chorus; the balladeer needs only enough volume to be heard by a small audience in a living room or kitchen. The opera singer strives to blend both "bright" and "dark" timbres in each note; the balladeer tends to emphasize primarily the bright side of the tonal spectrum. The opera singer performs with a wide, cultivated vibrato, a minute fluctuation of both volume and pitch in every sustained note; the balladeer's voice may or may not include vibrato, but it usually is not consciously cultivated.

Classical singers are divided into four basic voice types, based primarily on their natural pitch range. Men with low voices sing bass, men with high voices sing tenor, women with low voices sing alto, and women with high voices sing soprano. Within these categories, there are sub-groups based on features such as timbre, range, flexibility, and stylistic approach. The "dramatic soprano," for example, tends to have a darker voice and more declamatory style; the "lyric soprano" has a lighter voice and a more easygoing style of production, and the "coloratura soprano" has a very high voice with remarkable speed and flexibility.

All singing is stylized, removed to some extent from the conversational quality of everyday speech. If the Appalachian balladeer represents the informal end of the stylistic spectrum, then the opera singer must represent the formal end, in which stylization removes pronunciation and timbre far from the realm of natural speech. This does not mean that the balladeer's performance is unstudied. On the contrary, the folk-singer must work to realize the aesthetic values of his genre, just as the lyric soprano works to create a beautiful performance within the parameters of Western art song.

The large, robust sound and strong vibrato of the contemporary opera singer are not desirable in every performing context of Western classical music. Singers who specialize in early music, from the Baroque and especially from the Renaissance eras, often perform with small ensembles or the accompaniment of a single, quiet instrument such as the lute or guitar. A loud, operatic style, replete with a wide vibrato, would sound overbearing in such a musical context, so early music specialists tend to cultivate a quieter style, in which vocal flexibility and precise intonation are more important than volume.

The volume and vibrato required of an operatic soloist are also considered inappropriate in the context of choral singing, where the primary consideration is the ability of the vocalists to blend their voices in a well-coordinated ensemble. Like the orchestra, choral singers united together to create a composite sound in which no single voice stands out.

Finally, we should remember that, although Western classical singers tend to strive for an ideal blend of "light" and "dark" timbres in their singing, each singer is an individual. The aim of classical vocal pedagogy is not to produce thousands of singers who each sound the same, but to allow each singer to develop his or her unique voice within the accepted parameters of the tradition. In this respect, the widely variant timbres of Tuvan throat-singing, Bosnian ganga, Appalachian balladry, and Italian opera represent a variety of solutions to a single problem—that of giving voice to artistic inspiration within the aesthetic values of a given peoples' culture and history.

■■■ CHAPTER SUMMARY

In describing the experience of hearing music, we often employ visual metaphors. "Tone color" is the most common way of describing the element of music known as timbre. Physically, sounds do not have "color," but each voice and instrument has a distinctive tonal quality based on the combination of overtones it generates. Timbre is perhaps the most personal aspect of music; no two singers or instruments sound alike, in part because of the unique overtone "signature" of every sounding body.

Composers use a broad "palette" of timbres to create particular effects, just as painters use color. Every culture has its own set of timbral preferences; the desired buzzing quality of an Indian sitar is very different than the crisp, clear sonority of a guitar or mandolin.

The human exploration of sound is a continually evolving process. Musicians and audiences are constantly defining and redefining the sounds which we call music. While some musical instruments seem to have remained fairly stable over hundreds of years, others have changed dramatically. The remarkable invention and dissemination of the steel band in Trinidad during the last fifty years demonstrates how quickly musical traditions can be transformed.

With the invention of electronic instruments and computers in the twentieth century, our capabilities for producing, reproducing, and storing sounds have completely changed. Recording technology was developed by the late 1890s and electronic instruments were already developed in the 1920s and 1930s, including the electric guitar that was on the market by 1936. Recordings, radio, television, electric instruments, and computers have altered how and where we create and listen to music. It has also generated a vast realm of new timbral possibilities. This relationship between music and electronic technology will be discussed in detail in Chapter 12.

ADDITIONAL LISTENING

AUDIO #33 BASSAM SABA PLAYS A TAQASIM ON THE ARABIC NAY

Bassam Saba slowly explores the third and fourth degrees of the scale, exhibiting the unique double-octave sound characteristic of traditional nay performance. He achieves a timbre that includes one and the same note in two different octaves at the same time. The tone colors range from a fairly pure sound—especially in the high register—to the breathy or airy sounds that often result when the musician breaks between high and low octaves.

STUDY QUESTIONS

1. What gives each sound its own distinctive timbre?

2. What three things are necessary in order to produce a sound? — P. 143

3. What are the five categories of instruments in the Sachs-Hornbostel — P. 144 system?

4. What are the major sections in the contemporary symphony — P. 145 orchestra?

5. What are some of the timbral qualities of the North Indian sitar that give it a different sound than the guitar?

6. What timbres are valued in the performance of the Japanese shakuchachi?

7. What factors affect the production of vocal timbre?

REFERENCED SOURCES

1. Reck, 1977: 257.
2. Stubbs. Interview, 1997.
3. Redman. Interview, 1997.
4. Kartomi, 1990: 88.
5. Jourdain, 1997: 37.
6. Kartomi, 1990: 171.
7. Ibid: 1990: 37.
8. Ibid: 50.
9. Ibid: 121.
10. Ibid: 140.
11. Slowett, 1992: 15.
12. Miner, 1993.
13. Kippen, 1988.
14. Hahn. Interview, 1997.
15. Ibid.
16. Wright, 1980: 523–5.
17. Touma, 1996: 110.
18. Shaheen. Interview, 1997.
19. Wright, 1980: 516.
20. Touma, 1996: 113.
21. Stubbs. Interview, 1997.
22. Ibid.
23. Berliner, 1981: 10.
24. Ibid.
25. Ibid: 11.
26. Ibid: 10.
27. Bebey, 1975: 81.
28. Berliner, 1981: 15.
29. Bebey, 1975: 84.
30. Ibid: 85.
31. Knight, 1976: 3.
32. Ibid.
33. Ibid: 5.
34. Locke, 1996: 107.
35. Bebey, 1969: 94.
36. Levin. Interview, 1997.

CHAPTER 8

TEXTURE

About This Chapter

This chapter provides an introduction to the subject of musical texture. Texture refers to how music is organized into one or more simultaneously sounding parts and the ways in which these different parts relate to each other. Western music scholars have classified musical texture into four main categories: monophony, heterophony, polyphony, and homophony. While musicians and composers around the world don't necessarily think in these terms, they can be used as a starting point to discuss texture in all music. The chapter will examine the role of texture in several world music cultures.

KEYWORDS

clave
concerto
exposition
fugue
heterophony
homophony
monophony
polyphony
program music
son

COMPANION RESOURCES

TELEVISION PROGRAM: Texture

AUDIO SELECTION:

36. Plainchant: "Benedicamus Domino"
16. "Hifumi Hachi Gaeshi"
37. "Chidori no Kyoku"
38. Highlander Men's Ganga
39. "The Train to Bre"
40. "Ahora Vengo Yo"
34. "Kasatriyan"
41. "Kreasi Beleganjur Padma Mudra"
42. Fugue in G minor, BWV 578, by J. S. Bach
43. "Spring" (1st Movement) from *The Four Seasons* by Antonio Vivaldi

The word *texture* often refers to our senses of touch and sight. We feel rough or smooth objects with our fingers. We notice the difference between silk, cotton, or wool in the clothes we wear. We see textures in our environment and in nature, such as the smoothness of snow, the craggy grandeur of rock formations, and the fluffiness of clouds. Texture can also refer to how something is made or constructed. The texture of a piece of woven cloth is created by the weaver's use and arrangement of specific threads. The size and quality of the thread in conjunction with the looseness or tightness of the weave determines the overall texture of the material.

Texture in music most clearly relates to this idea of structure and method. If we use fabric as an analogy, we can say that the weave or texture of music is created through the use of various combinations of instruments or voices, ranging from a solo voice to a large ensemble or orchestra. As in weaving, texture in music is established through the structuring of parts that exist in relationship to each other to create a whole. This structuring occurs differently from culture to culture. According to Mark Slobin, texture is an important component of musical taste and aesthetics:

Any music is a set of preferences. . . . People really have strong preferences in terms of something like texture. There are large regions where people really only like to hear one or two things happening at a time. They perhaps like to hear a really dominant sound and something accompanying it. And that's mostly what they like. There are other places where people seem to feel that's not enough or that's limited in some way. They want a really complex texture with a lot of different things going on at the same time. These are preferences. It's basically about an aesthetic. And traditionally, people have had very strong aesthetic feelings in terms of texture as much as anything else they do with their music."[1]

The subject of musical texture can be divided into two broad areas: (1) the organization of music into one or more simultaneously sounding parts, including sung or played melodies, chords, and percussion and (2) the ways in which these different parts relate to each other. Since qualities that distinguish one kind of voice or instrument from another include tone color and pitch range, texture in music is closely connected to concepts of timbre and melody.

Texture also refers to the density of sound. A symphony orchestra will have a denser, thicker sound than a string quartet or a solo violinist. In the West, music is often described as thick and full when many parts are being played together and thin or transparent when few parts are played together. Rhythm, tempo, and dynamics, the loudness or softness of music, affect how we perceive density of sound. If the music is played loudly it often seems fuller and richer; conversely, music played softly, even within a large ensemble, can feel thinner.

Dance can add an additional texture to a musical performance. The percussive rhythms of the dancer's feet in traditions as diverse as tap, clogging, Irish step dance, North Indian Kathak, and South Indian Bharata Natyam add another musical line to the overall texture of the performance.

Western music scholars have classified musical texture in ways that refer to the number of parts and to the manner in which these parts relate to each other. While musicians and composers around the world don't necessarily think in these terms, they can be used to discuss texture in all musics. The four main categories include *monophony, heterophony, polyphony,* and *homophony.* It is important to note that while these classifications suggest a model for analyzing texture in music, they are not air tight categories. Some musics will be difficult to place in any one category, while others will employ three or four within one performance.

Monophony: Music in One Part

Monophony can be defined as music in one part—a single unaccompanied line. There are many cultures that have rich monophonic musical traditions that give voice to the solo performer. By playing or singing unaccompanied, the soloist has enormous freedom in interpreting the music. Monophonic textures occur in both sacred and secular music.

Perhaps the most common form of monophony occurs as part of religious practice. Single line chants are found in many of the world's religions, including Judaism, Hinduism, Christianity, Islam, and Buddhism. Chants are not considered music in some religions, but they are melodic utterances that are meant to heighten religious experience and render speech sacred. Chants may be personal renderings of religious texts or formal performances by religious professionals, such as priests, cantors, and monks. They may be sung by a single person or in unison within a group. Chant forms range from recitations on a single tone to those that use six or seven pitches and are highly ornamented.

Plainchant is a tradition that comprises the earliest music of the medieval church in Europe. Plainchants were originally sung by priests, nuns, and monks as part of a fixed daily schedule of worship. Over 3000 melodies survive today, each with its own significance in the Catholic liturgy. This repertory is called "plain" because it is monophonic and without fixed rhythm. It was often called Gregorian chant after Pope Gregory (540–604) who assembled and standardized the basic chants of his time. Because many chants were composed after Pope Gregory's lifetime, the repertory is now commonly referred to as plainsong or plainchant.

An example of a plainchant that uses six pitches. Notice the weight given to the first and final pitch (d) throughout the melody.

"BENEDICAMUS DOMINO" (PLAINCHANT)

Be - ne - di - ca - mus Do   mi - no.

Solo shakuhachi playing in Japan is another example in which monophony is used for spiritual expression. The shakuhachi, an endblown flute made from bamboo, is traditionally linked to Zen Buddhist philosophy and aesthetics. The main solo repertoire for the shakuhachi comes from the wandering monks of the Tokugawa period (1600–1867). Pieces are played slowly in a free rhythm that is influenced by the breath of the player. Great changes in dynamics and tone color—within the piece as a whole and within a single phrase—are characteristic of the playing style.

Monophonic textures are also found in many secular music traditions around the world. What these traditions have in common is the power of the solo singer or instrumentalist to convey a message, whether in the home or in the concert hall. Unaccompanied solo song forms are found in every corner of the globe, ranging from lullabies to laments to ballads. In Ireland, solo instrumentalists play slow airs derived from the rich unaccompanied song traditions in both the English and Irish languages.

Here you can hear the richness of the single line of music embellished by subtle fluctuations of pitch, ornamentation, and a wide variety of playing techniques by Tomie Hahn. Such fluidity of timbre and rhythm are made possible because the music is performed by a single player.

Heterophony: Variations on a Single Musical Line

Heterophony occurs when two or more musicians simultaneously sing or play the same melody in different ways. These differences can range from small discrepancies in unison singing—such as in a church congregation—to more pronounced variations in ornamentation or rhythm. According to ethnomusicologist David Reck, heterophony "is the weaving of melodic strands around a single core of a melody; it is melody-based (rather than harmonically-based) and its strands, happening simultaneously, all relate to the central melody in some way: they may be variations of it, they may ornament it, they may scan or punctuate its important notes.[2] Heterophonic textures are found in many musical traditions in Asia, The Middle East, and Europe.

A good example of a heterophonic texture can be found in the performance of traditional Irish dance music. The tunes found in the repertory consist of melodies that are played solo or in unison. These tunes are usually in two sections that are both repeated during performance. Each tune is played over and over again before musicians switch to another. While there are formal parameters of each tune that make it recognizable, musicians usually have their own slightly different versions. These different renditions occur because the music is usually learned orally and passed along from musician to musician.

As discussed in Chapter 6, many players pride themselves on never playing a tune exactly the same way twice in performance. Therefore, when musicians get together in a playing session, there will always be slight variations in the playing of a single tune. These variations include differences in ornamentation and in melodic contour. Other differences in playing occur simply because each instrument has its own characteristic playing techniques, fingerings, and sound.

Irish traditional music often takes place in an informal social setting, such as in a pub or in a living room. The communal setting for the music is reflected in the playing style. However, while all the musicians agree to play essentially the same thing at the same time, there is still enormous scope for individuality. Musicians really listen to each other and value different versions of a tune or the melodic variations that spontaneously occur within a session. Players often ask each other where they learned a specific tune and there is enormous interest taken in how and from whom individuals acquired their repertory. The heterophonic textures that occur within the informal group playing demonstrate the respect musicians have for a common shared repertory and for individual expression. Spontaneity and the acquisition of a deep knowledge of the tune tradition are both considered essential qualities for a good player.

Heterophony can also occur on a more formal level in ensemble playing. For example, when the Japanese shakuhachi is used as an ensemble instrument combined with voice and koto, a thirteen stringed zither with movable bridges, the resultant texture is heterophonic. While voice and instruments follow a single melodic line, slight variations in melody and rhythm occur because of specific playing or singing techniques.

AUDIO 37 — The koto plays essentially the same melodic line as the shakuhachi, but follows slightly later. The shakuhachi player (Tomie Hahn) and koto player (Masayo Ishigure) also play different ornaments around a single note and move at times in slightly different rhythms. While these variations do occur among the two parts, there is always an evident central melody.

Polyphony: Multi-Part Music

The term polyphony is generally used to describe any multi-part musical tradition, and examples of rhythmic polyphony, melodic polyphony, and a com-

TOMIE HAHN PLAYING THE SHAKUHACHI WITH MASAYO ISHIGURE PLAYING THE KOTO.

bination of the two can be found around the world. Polyphony results when two or more lines of music are played or sung simultaneously. Music with a polyphonic texture can create a rich layering of sound.

In much polyphonic music there is often a fluctuation in the density of parts during a piece or performance. As in the case of a round or canon, one sung or played part will enter alone followed by other parts entering at pre-scribed intervals. A round, such as "Row, Row, Row Your Boat," is a strictly imitative form—all the parts imitate the first one. At its most complex, after all the parts have come in, there will be a dense polyphonic texture. As the piece nears conclusion, the texture will thin again as one part at a time drops out until only a single part is left.

NOTATION OF "ROW, ROW, ROW YOUR BOAT"

Ganga, a popular type of song performed throughout Bosnia and Herzegovina, is another example of a polyphonic genre that changes density within performance. As discussed in Chapter 1, ganga singing occurs in either men's or women's groups that usually form at an early age and continue well into adulthood. The nature of the close part singing, involving drones (long sustained notes on a single pitch), adjacent intervals, and accompanying patterns of vocal fluctuations called "cutting," creates a loud, powerful sound that is well suited to the mountainous environment. The metaphors used by singers to describe the texture of their singing reflect both the close-knit unit of the village and the social ideals of power and strength.

The term polyphony has a specific meaning in Western classical music, describing much of the multi-part music of the Middle Ages and Renaissance in which all the sung or played parts are of equal importance. Each part functions as an independent entity providing aproximately the same amount of interest. The compositional technique of writing a polyphonic texture that has two or more simultaneously sounding melodies is called counterpoint, although the two terms are often used as synonyms. Imitative counterpoint is a common form of Renaissance polyphony in which each independent melodic line in a composition enters at staggered intervals with the same theme as the first.

Composers after the Renaissance and to the present day continue to employ polyphony in their music. While some genres, such as the Baroque *fugue*, are completely polyphonic, other multi-part musical genres feature contrasting textures even within a single movement. Examples of polyphony in European art music will be explored later in the chapter and in the next chapter.

Homophony: Multi-Part Music with One Dominant Part

A piece of music with multiple parts in which one voice affirms the principal part and the remaining voices serve as accompaniment is called homophonic. In general terms, homophony is a form of polyphony in which one or more simultaneously occurring parts function as a support for a dominant part. In Irish traditional music, for example, the addition of a chordal guitar accompaniment makes the overall texture homophonic, although the melody players may be creating a heterophonic texture between themselves. The dance tune stands out as the dominant part backed up by the chordal support from the guitar.

Most music in the Euro-American classical and popular repertories has a homophonic texture. Composers in eighteenth-century Europe, including Franz Joseph Haydn and Wolfgang Amadeus Mozart, developed the use of homophony by strong memorable melodies supported by straightforward harmonic accompaniments. Twentieth-century popular musics, including show tunes, country, and rock also have, for the most part, a dominant melody line supported by chordal and percussion accompaniment. Homophony also plays an important role in church music: Protestant hymns have a prevalent texture in which the hymn melody, usually found in the soprano part, is supported by the alto, tenor, and bass lines.

When considering music cultures around the world, such a definition creates complications if indigenous concepts of polyphony and homophony don't exist within the specific culture. For example, while most West African drumming traditions can be considered polyphonic because of the many lay-

AUDIO 38
One man sings the first phrase, followed by the other singers in parts. The vocal lines are extremely close together, sometimes only a minor second apart. The parts all rise at the end of the phrase in a kind of whoop followed by a pause. The first singer then comes in again to begin the next part of the song.

ers of interlocking percussion parts, the lead or master drummer's improvisations on top of the other parts could be viewed as creating a kind of homophonic texture. We look to indigenous musicians for clues and find that the improvised line may not be considered the most important. Among the Ewe in Ghana, for example, the repetitive bell part is considered the glue holding all the other parts together.[3] Therefore, it is important to understand the flexibility and limitations of these Western-imposed categories in analyzing music from other parts of the world.

In considering homophony in the West, the dominant line is always melodic. This part can be supported by counter melodies, chords, and percussion.

We will now take a more detailed look at the role of texture in several musical cultures from around the world.

In this piece written by Stan Scott, Scott sings the dominant melodic line while playing a chordal guitar accompaniment. The melodic line is also supported by countermelodies played on the fiddle by Becky Tracy and alto recorder by Dora Hast. During the instrumental break, both fiddle and recorder begin by playing the melody in unison supported by the guitar; in the second half, the recorder plays a counter melody while the fiddle continues playing the melody.

TRINIDAD: THE STEEL BAND

Originally created in the urban ghettos of Trinidad, the steel band has now become an important symbol of national identity on the island. The spectacular annual *Panorama* competitions held at Carnival time attract bands from all over the island and spectators from all over the world. Bands are also found throughout the Caribbean, as well as in Great Britain, the United States, and in parts of South America, Asia, Africa, and Europe. The instruments have been used in music education in England since the 1970s, and more recently, in schools and universities in America.

The versatility, range, and sonority of the instruments and the rich texture of the ensemble have inspired composers and arrangers to orchestrate all kinds of music for the steel band. While the most popular tunes are arrangements of indigenous calypso songs, repertoire ranges from pan-Latin dance musics to Western classical music. Texture plays a vital role in the music because of the similar sonorities of the steel drums or pans. While the instruments have different pitch ranges, they all have a similar tone color. Therefore, arrangers make great use of texture in order to create contrast, vitality, and excitement.

The most common and predominant texture for steel band music is homophonic—a dominant melody played on the lead instruments supported by many underlying parts, including a rhythm section. Because so many different genres of music are represented in the steel band repertoire, there are also arrangements of monophonic and polyphonic pieces, as well as compositions that includes all three textures within one piece.

History of the Steel Band

The name "Trinidad" is often used to refer to both Trinidad and Tobago, two islands in the southeast Caribbean, seven miles off the coast of Venezuela. They were settled in the 1500s by the Spanish; by the end of the eighteenth century, French landowners from other islands came in large numbers bringing their slaves with them. The two islands were subsequently under British rule from 1797–1962. Today there is a rich layering and blending of social and cultural traditions. The history of settlement on Trinidad—both through forced and voluntary immigration—make it one of the most culturally and ethnically diverse places in the world.[4]

The history of the steel band is linked to the history of Carnival in Port of Spain, Trinidad. This festival, which has become the largest of its kind in the Caribbean, took on special significance after the abolishment of slavery in 1834. Originally of French Catholic origin, Carnival had previously been a holiday celebrated by the ruling class during the period immediately before Lent. It was a time for boundary crossing and inversions of the social order, marked by masquerade balls, dancing, and promenading.

After emancipation, Carnival became an important venue for Afro-Trinidadian expressive culture—a lively and often disorderly event featuring "cannes brulees" (cane burning), torch light processions, stick fighting, masquerades, singing, loud drumming, and occasional outbreaks of street fighting. In the 1850s and 1860s, the British attempted to suppress what they considered the subversive and unlawful activities at Carnival by banning processions. The government enacted further legislation in 1884 that effectively banned drumming on the island. This restriction on the use of drums is thought to have gradually led to the development of the steel band.

As Carnival continued to exert a strong influence on Afro-Trinidadian culture, musicians were forced to find other means for making music. *Tamboo-bamboo* bands formed in which musicians used hollowed-out bamboo sticks of various lengths to produce sounds. The bamboo sticks were either struck together or against the ground to produce various pitches. Bottles and spoons were also used to produce higher pitches and rhythmic accompaniment. Soon musicians began to add further accompaniment in the form of discarded metal objects and containers, such as metal buckets, paint cans, dust bins, brake drums, frying pans, and pitch oil pans. By the early 1930s, metal instruments became more and more dominant in the tamboo-bamboo bands. This preference for metal sounds finally resulted in the appearance of an all-steel band in 1937 that was an instant hit at Carnival.[5]

A series of innovations in the late 1930s and 1940s led to the twin discoveries that a single piece of metal could be bent to produce multiple pitches and that fifty-five gallon oil barrels could be used to make beautiful sounding instruments. These barrels were plentiful and free, discards of the oil companies in Trinidad. The instruments were soon called steel drums or pans, and were cut from the barrels into different sizes, each capable of producing more than one pitch. The first pans were worn around the necks of the performers, but by 1960, pans were placed on movable stands that enabled musicians to play larger instruments and more than one at a time.

The Steel Band Today

The contemporary conventional steel band consists of a wide variety of pans in different sizes. Instrument making and tuning has become a respected art demanding special skills. Fierce competitions between bands have led both to innovative instrument construction and a lack of standardized tuning from band to band. Instruments are made in five steps:

1. The head of the instrument is pounded into a concave shape.
2. The position of each note is marked on the head by a steel punch.
3. The metal is tempered by heat.
4. The drum barrel is cut to the required length.
5. The instrument is tuned.

Conventional steel bands may employ over one hundred and twenty musicians using up to three hundred different instruments. The whole group is divided into major sections for each size pan in the steel drum family, ranging from high to low. The highest instrument is called the *lead* or *tenor* and is capable of producing up to thirty-two different pitches. It plays the melody in approximately the soprano range. This melody is supported in various ways by the rest of the ensemble creating a thick homophonic texture.

The double tenor is a set of two drums slightly larger than the tenor and used to play harmony. Other pans are used primarily to play rhythm, including the second and the double second pans. The guitar pan consists of two drums that are used to play strumming patterns. It is approximately fourteen to sixteen inches in depth as compared to the tenor which is about six inches in depth. The cello pan is in the tenor voice range and is played in sets of three.

The largest instruments in the ensemble are the bass pans that consist of full size oil drums. These pans are played in sets of six or nine. Each instru-

TRINIDADIAN STEEL BAND

ment has a range of two to four notes and is arranged on a stand either vertically or horizontally. These instruments provide the underlying harmonic structure in the form of bass lines.

In addition to the pans, the steel band usually includes an "engine room," a rhythm section made up of drum set, conga, bongos, maracas, and a piece of heavy iron (often a brake drum). The iron keeps the pulse for the whole group; its loud sound cuts through the entire band. The interlocking patterns of the skin drums and hand held percussion instruments create a dense and vibrant underlying texture for the ensemble, as well as providing a variety of different tone colors. The engine room musicians may take solos at various points in the overall performance of a composition.

When all these instruments are put together, the overall musical texture is rich and complex. The sound of over one hundred instrumentalists playing steel drums in combination with other percussion instruments is powerful, exhuberant, and festive. With the emergence of women players in the 1970s, the formation of school bands, and the presence of at least fifty large adults bands on the islands, the steel band movement has become a vital national art form in Trinidad. Through recordings, performances, emigration, and the creation of new bands, the steel band tradition has also extended far beyond the borders of Trinidad.

▬ LATIN AMERICA: SALSA

Is New York City part of Latin America? It is if the subject is *salsa* music, which developed among Nuyoricans (New Yorkers of Puerto Rican descent), immigrants from Cuba and other parts of Central and South America, and American jazz musicians in the mid-twentieth century. This hybrid genre was initially referred to in the United States just as "Latin music"; but in the 1960s its cultural context was changing, and its name changed accordingly.

Salsa literally just means sauce, but its usual meaning—hot sauce—already carried the metaphoric connotation of invigorating Latino spices, in music as well as in cuisine. Responding to the increasing pride in Latino identity in the New York *barrio*, the Spanish-speaking part of the city, salsa became a vibrant, celebratory music of cultural empowerment and affirmation.

The genre has disseminated all over Central America and parts of South America, making it almost a "Pan-Latino" music. And now it can be heard in many other parts of the world as well, from Europe to Africa to East Asia.

Salsa derives largely from the Cuban *son*, a genre founded on a basic form called *largo-montuno*—a brief song followed by an extended vocal call-and-response section over characteristic harmonic and rhythmic ostinatos—and a core rhythm known as *clave*. Like the rumba clave rhythms discussed in Chapter 5, the *son* clave has two parts, one with three accents and one with two; a given piece can begin with either part, yielding a "three-two" or "two-three" clave.

CLAVE RHYTHMIC CYCLE (TWO VERSIONS)

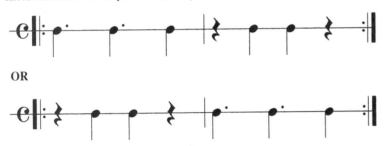

OR

This rhythm is characteristically played on its namesake wooden sticks, though in practice it can be produced on just about anything from clapping hands to a spoon tapping on an empty bottle.

In the 1940s, *son* was evolving in New York City from a relatively informal collective music into a carefully organized ensemble music with arrangements influenced by big-band jazz. The montuno section featured extended vocal and instrumental improvisations, the latter again drawing on certain jazz practices, as well as composed instrumental sections.

The fundamental *clave* rhythm started to become something felt rather than explicitly heard, as it was adorned with more and more layers of rhythmic improvisation and sometimes not played at all. Off-beat bass parts, combined with a rhythmic basis which often existed only in the players' minds, produced an infectiously danceable music to those who understood, consciously or not, the implicit clave cycle. Outsiders, by contrast, could be so dazzled by all the syncopation that they couldn't find "the beat"; even the great jazz trumpeter Dizzy Gillespie confessed to occasional rhythmic disorientation when jamming with Cuban musicians. Already this was a new, dynamic music which lent itself to a kind of ethnic pride: if you didn't have the clave, which literally means "key," you couldn't get inside.

Cuba had long been a source of inspiration for many Caribbean musicians, and when the island became politically and economically isolated following Fidel Castro's revolution, New York City became an important international center for Cuban music. And Latino circumstances and perceptions there were changing: the rise of the Civil Rights and Black Power movements of the 1960s inspired young Latinos in the barrio to strive for more social and political power, and to embrace and honor their ethnic identities. The evolution of Cuban music in New York became a revolution, as a wave of musical creativity was unleashed by these cultural developments.

Young Nuyoricans, immigrants from other Latino cultures, such as those of Venezuela and the Dominican Republic, and even some non-Latinos brought ideas and practices from their own backgrounds, pouring many new sounds into the largo-montuno mold. The term "Latin music" sounded old-fashioned, and the music was no longer strictly Cuban; *salsa* arose as a term for this new musical aggregate, pushed to a certain extent by recording and performing venues, and it stuck.

Some salsa devotees feel that the music has gone into a creative decline since the more socially-conscious days of the 1960s and 70s. Others point to the persistence of serious-minded songwriting among some *salseros* and recent cross-fertilizations with rap and other musics as evidence that salsa is still vigorous and relevant in people's lives. Any popular music, they argue, develops a bland, predictable side as some musicians and entrepreneurs seek the broadest possible commercial base. But whether it is serving as a force for Latino identity and expression or just as excellent dance music, salsa is currently thriving throughout and well beyond the world of Latino culture.

Texture in Salsa

Generally, a salsa group can be described as comprising three sub-groups, similar to those of big-band jazz: the rhythm section, which supplies rhythmic and harmonic accompaniment; the horn section, which plays composed segments and provides improvising soloists; and the vocal section, usually a soloist and at least two backing vocalists, known as the *coro*. Some of the vocalists may also play hand-held percussion instruments. A typical band consists of ten to fourteen people.[6]

The rhythm section includes piano and bass, either of which may temporarily move to the foreground for an improvised solo, as well as certain important percussion instruments: congas (a pair of tall standing drums), timbales (a pair of shallower drums on a stand plus two cowbells and often a suspended cymbal, the whole resembling an abbreviated drum set), bongos (a pair of small drums held between the seated player's legs), and often another cowbell and maracas (shakers) which might be played by one of the vocalists.

Some rhythm sections include the *tres* or *quatro*, a kind of small guitar with three or four unison pairs of strings, in addition to or instead of the piano. The horn section most often includes one or more trumpets and trombones; less often, a saxophone, flute, or violin might be part of this section. These sections, and their various members, create changing textures which delineate the formal structures of the overall performance. Overall, salsa texture would be described as homophonic, although the music always involves a richly polyrhythmic accompaniment.

For example, in "Ahora Vengo Yo" by Ricardo Ray and Bobby Cruz, at the beginning the audience is already clapping the clave cycle. The piano and bass start up a melodic theme which will return at various times throughout the performance, and they are joined by the rest of the rhythm section. After a trumpet solo, the largo section begins: a short song in which the singer humorously complains that people in Puerto Rico criticized him for being in New York, but then failed to welcome him when he returned. The montuno section begins as the singer launches into an *inspiración*, improvising phrases about the good life in Puerto Rico—basking in the sun, drinking rum, enjoying the gentle breezes and fine music—as well as extolling his situation in New York by praising the band and the dancers.

Rhythmically polyphonic textures like those of salsa are considered ideal for dancing in many cultures. In such ensembles each member performs a distinct role, resulting in a texture which metaphorically affirms social unity while valuing individuality, as does the highly structured yet personally nuanced dancing that often goes with polyrhythmic music. Certainly this is true of salsa musicians and dancers, who respect each other's abilities to express their personalities and aesthetics within standardized systems. And even if it is felt inwardly rather than sounded outwardly, the clave is the foundation that supports all participants, the single most essential element of salsa texture.

"Ahora Vengo Yo" performed by The Fania All-Stars.

▬ INDONESIA: THE CENTRAL JAVANESE GAMELAN

"Unity in Diversity" is the hopeful motto of the Republic of Indonesia, which comprises thousands of populated islands between Australia and mainland Southeast Asia. Java is not the largest of these islands, but it is the seat of political and economic power. Still, its cultural dominance is limited: numerous cultures and peoples—with over two hundred distinct languages—thrive on these islands, united by some similarities and distinguished by many differences.

One general term used in various parts of Indonesia is *gamelan*, which might be translated as "musical ensemble." Such ensembles involve sets of instruments tuned to each other, and not to any standard "objective" pitch, like Western instruments. These instruments might be made of bronze, bamboo, wood, or other materials, and often a gamelan includes more than one kind of instrumental set. One very widespread instrument type is the *gong*—an Indonesian word which refers to a hanging metal disk with a knob in the center; when this knob is struck, the gong resonates with a clear pitch,

Indonesia

unlike the flat-surfaced "gongs" commonly found among Western percussion instruments.

Within each type of gamelan, particular kinds of instruments play particular textural roles; usually there is some kind of basic melody, played by certain types of instruments in unison or octaves, while other types play various formulaic elaborations or countermelodies, and still others provide punctuating accompaniment. Some kinds of gamelan also include singers. A gamelan may be considered a living being: it may have a name and the instruments are given the same kinds of respectful treatment accorded to people, such as never stepping over an instrument, or otherwise exposing the soles of one's feet to it.

Central Javanese gamelan is generally found in and around the aristocratic cities of Surakarta and Yogyakarta, roughly in the middle of the island. Whether it is played by esteemed professionals at royal courts and music schools, or by villagers who come together at the end of a working day for pleasure and community service, the music is considered auspicious. Certain types of gamelan are strictly used for ceremonial purposes; others may function primarily as a component of various kinds of theater/dance forms, including the very popular shadow-puppet theater, or as an accompaniment to social events.

Traditionally, there is no such thing as a gamelan "concert," in the Western sense of a formal presentation before a silent audience. Gamelan performances, with or without theater or dance, often take place in an open pavilion, making it possible for some people to come closer to listen and watch, while others might remain at more of a distance to socialize, smoke, or eat while they enjoy the event.

Most pieces in the large repertory of Central Javanese gamelan date from antiquity, and are not identified with a composer's name. However, in the twentieth century several Javanese gamelan musicians have begun to compose new pieces, sometimes involving innovative formal structures, techniques, and textures. Certain Western composers have also taken an interest in creating new music for gamelan, and some Western groups, such as New York City's Gamelan Son of Lion, are devoted to playing new music on Central Javanese gamelan instruments.

Western institutional ethnomusicology and world music programs have brought whole sets of instruments from Indonesia, along with expert teachers, and the number of Western players of this music is growing. In some cases, "town gamelans" have arisen in Britain and the United States. Gamelan—perhaps especially Central Javanese gamelan—is starting to become a worldwide phenomenon. Such developments are alarming to some lovers of this music, who decry the abandonment of traditional practices and performance contexts in favor of more modern ones. But at the moment it appears that recent developments in the gamelan world have not supplanted the older usages, which continue to create power and meaning within the culture of Central Java.

Texture in Central Javanese Gamelan

Central Javanese gamelan music may generally be described as polyphonic, though there is more to its texture than a single word can encompass. In various instances, the texture may be thought of as comprising simultaneous layers of homophony, heterophony, homophony, and polyphony. At other times—particularly in the ever-changing music which accompanies shadow-puppet performances—textures may alter dramatically, from the solo singing of the puppeteer accompanied by a single instrument to the full, throbbing sonorites which underscore battle scenes.

The repertory involves two basic playing styles, often referred to as "loud" and "soft." In both styles the central melody, or *balungan*, is played mainly by one-octave keyed metal instruments. Other instruments create elaborations of the balungan, and various kinds of gongs are struck to punctuate specific points in the overall form. Each section of a piece ends with a stroke on the *gong ageng*, the lowest-pitched instrument in the ensemble. The "loud" playing style involves only metal instruments, with the exception of the *kendang* drum which leads the tempo. This style can be considered homophonic because it involves one melody with accompanying parts; it can also be considered heterophonic because different instruments play the melody in different ways.

"Soft style" pieces involve further melodic layers, resulting in a polyphonic texture. A group of male singers may sing a unison melody; sometimes men and women sing together in octaves. A countermelody to the balungan is played on the *rebab* (a two-stringed spike fiddle), and formulaically elaborated by a solo female vocalist and certain "soft-playing" instruments such as the wooden-keyed *gambang*, the *gendèr* with bronze keys suspended over resonators, and the bamboo *suling* flute. This overall texture can be altered in dynamics and density: for example, on a signal from the kendang the balungan and punctuating instruments may gradually slow down and settle into a more deliberate tempo, playing more softly, while the "soft playing" instruments play more quickly, filling the pauses between balungan pitches with more elaborate melodic figurations and playing a more prominent role in the ensemble sound.

Kasatriyan is an example of the "soft" playing style of Central Javanese gamelan.

Although most of the instruments in a Central Javanese gamelan are played throughout a piece's duration, various kinds of formalized adjustments can cause subtle changes in overall timbre and texture, contributing to a sense of flow and timelessness which is never static. To one who knows the tradition well, there are many levels of musical communication to relish. And to the many who are not familiar with such concerns, the music of the gamelan still provides the inspirational experience of a complex and beautiful musical texture, imbued with auspicious spiritual power.

A CENTRAL JAVANESE GAMELAN IN THE UNITED STATES (WESLEYAN UNIVERSITY)

◼ INDONESIA: BALINESE GAMELAN BELEGANJUR

The relatively small island of Bali is home to a dazzling array of artistic practices, and music is no exception. Though many of their instruments are structurally similar to those of Java, which lies just to the west, the Balinese create very different musical textures with them. From the dynamic, lightning-fast music of the *gamelan gong kebyar* to the stately, haunting flutes of *gamelan gambuh*, the world of Balinese music is one of kaleidoscopic variety.

In Bali, music is seldom a profession in itself, nor is it a solitary avocation; rather, it is a community undertaking. Often the center of such activities

KREASI BELEGANJUR

Photo: Michael Bakan

is the *banjar*, a community organization with a meeting hall which houses musical instruments and provides rehearsal space. Many other community activities are supported by the banjar as well, all of which involve the kind of group collaboration which is highly valued in Bali. Here music is not just pleasing sound—it is also a public affirmation of social values like cooperation, responsibility, and hard personal work toward a collective achievement.

One of the many types of gamelan which might be supported by a local banjar is *gamelan beleganjur*, which could be translated as "gamelan of walking warriors." The name points both to the fact that this is a processional music, and to one of its earliest functions: accompanying warriors into battle. With its thundering drums and gongs, and the vibrant resonance of gong-chimes and cymbals, beleganjur inspired soldiers while terrifying their enemies.

Gamelan beleganjur has also long been used for various rituals: accompanying processions bearing offerings for temples or cremation towers for funerals, aiding in exorcistic purification rites, and so on. It is perhaps the most widespread form of gamelan in Bali, and is considered crucial for many religious functions. Unlike the many kinds of Balinese gamelan that are intended for aesthetic enjoyment or used as accompaniment for theater and dance performances—forms that often involve many changes of musical texture, tempo, and mood—traditional beleganjur provides a constant pulse of multileveled, exuberant concord. Through various signals, the lead drummer can adjust the tempo or signal an invigorating outburst of drums and cymbals, but in general the texture remains unchanged, an ever-flowing river of sonorous energy.

Less is known about the history of beleganjur than other Balinese genres, but it appears that the basic formal, structural, and textural aspects of the music have not undergone radical transformation until recently, when a new context prompted the development of a new style.

In 1986, a beleganjur contest was announced as part of an annual festival in Denpasar, Bali's capital city, commemorating Bali's illustrious past. Notices were sent out to all the local banjars, stating that entrants would be judged on the extent to which their performance embodied youthful, heroic masculine energy. They were also encouraged to include movement or choreography, and to arrange their music with changing sections of differing character, showcasing virtuosity. Following the success of that event, beleganjur contests sprang up all over Bali. The resulting presentational "contest style," *kreasi beleganjur* quickly became immensely popular among young Balinese men, often to the neglect of the older ritual-oriented style of performance.

To the chagrin of some older Balinese, kreasi beleganjur is now performed on many ritual occasions, in what they see as an unacceptable incongruity between flashy presentational music and sacred devotional practice. Others feel that the good results of getting young people excited about indigenous music outweigh any imagined offenses; Balinese arts, they argue, have accommodated new influences throughout history, ensuring a constant flow of creativity.

There are controversies within the kreasi beleganjur world as well. The combination of movement/choreography with an ideal of youthful masculine energy has led to some very sassy dancing; sometimes proprietary boundaries are broached, as when an otherwise outstanding group was demoted by judges for their "pornographic" presentation. It appears that some contest results have been politically tainted, with rewards going to the banjars of districts which supported incumbent politicians. And the vitality and presentationality of kreasi beleganjur make it a prime target for jingoistic exploitation by both the tourist industry and political propagandists.

Perhaps the most controversial development of all is the emergence of women's beleganjur groups. While the Hindu-Balinese religion does not explicitly ban women from any artistic activity, beleganjur's categorical identification with masculine energies makes it impossible for some Balinese to accept the idea of female involvement. Yet this development is directly in line with Indonesia's prevalent political agenda of modernity, which includes a mandate for the "emancipation" of women. As the American ethnomusicologist Michael Bakan put it, "the act of women playing beleganjur is defiantly un-Balinese, yet quintessentially Indonesian."[7]

But women's beleganjur is not necessarily just politically motivated. "Since childhood, I had a feeling I really wanted to play [beleganjur] music," one woman told Bakan. "I saw the boys playing and I thought, 'I really want to try.' But initially the head of the village didn't allow it." Now some banjars proudly support women's beleganjur groups, despite the uneasiness such activities cause to more conservative Balinese. As Bakan noted, this ancient music of "walking warriors" now flourishes on battlegrounds of culture.

Texture in Gamelan Beleganjur

The standard beleganjur group involves twenty-nine people: twenty-one musicians and eight gong-carriers. The instruments fall into four general categories: drums, cymbals, gongs, and gong-chimes—small hand-held gongs. Each of the gong-chime players plays only one pitch, and their interlocking patterns create a four-pitch *reyong* ornamentation based on the two-pitch *ponggang* melody.

The result is undoubtedly a good texture for rhythmic walking: full and lively, with a strong marching beat provided by the drums and punctuating instruments. Beleganjur's texture also makes it an appropriate accompaniment for sacred rituals. Its tumultuous resonances, overlapping and pulsating with power, fend off evil or meddlesome spirits, while its jagged cross-

GAMELAN BELEGANJUR: GONG-CHIME PARTS

The beginning of a performance of kreasi beleganjur. Notice that various rhythmic patterns are played just by the cymbals and drums before the gong-chime parts enter.

rhythms confuse demons, who can only move in straight lines. At the same time, its throbbing energy inspires ritual participants, even aiding the souls of the deceased on their perilous journeys in the afterlife.

TEXTURE IN WESTERN CLASSICAL MUSIC

There are many different textural possibilities within the Western classical tradition. Composers have written instrumental and vocal music for many kinds and sizes of ensembles, ranging from a solo singer or instrumentalist to a symphony orchestra. But while there are many possibilities for orchestration, the prevalent texture in the music is polyphonic and homophonic. Monophony exists in the European tradition, both in unaccompanied instrumental and vocal pieces and in the large body of plainchant melodies dating back to the Middle Ages. But more often, composers have used monophonic textures as contrast within compositions that have a prevailing homophonic texture.

The prevalent texture in classical music up to 1600 was polyphony. The melodic lines of Renaissance polyphonic music were considered to have equal weight. Each musical part was an independent entity, rhythmically and melodically whole. Around the end of the sixteenth century composers began to think more vertically—using chords and harmonies to support a dominant melody. Homophonic textures in music were developed during the Baroque and Classical eras. The history of these developments in musical texture will be disccussed more fully in the next chapter.

Homophony and Polyphony in Baroque Music: Fugue and Concerto

Although homophony was explored in the Baroque era, composers continued to use polyphonic textures. *Fugues,* one of the most important forms developed in this period, are imitative polyphonic compositions usually built on a

single theme. They were often written as single movement works for keyboard instruments. The basic structure of all fugues follows a similar pattern that begins with the exposition—the section in which the theme, called the subject, is "exposed" at staggered intervals in all the voices. The subject is announced first in a single voice, then it appears in the second voice while the first continues with new melodic material. This process goes on until all the voices (usually three or four) have stated the theme in its entirety.

After the exposition, the subject will be stated again at various intervals in each of the voices. Passages called episodes appear in between; usually the music in the episodes is derived from the original theme. The fugue develops by the alternation of theme and episodes in all the voices.

In many other instrumental compositions of the Baroque period, composers used a basically homophonic texture, but employed polyphony as contrast within a single piece. The concerto and concerto grosso, the most important orchestral genres of the Baroque, provide many examples.

The Baroque concerto was scored for one solo instrument with orchestra, while the concerto grosso was written for a small group of soloists with orchestra. Both genres typically consisted of three movements of contrasting mood and tempo: a slow second movement—often in constrasting key—was usually sandwiched between two fast movements. Composers of the era (including Johann Sebastian Bach, George Frideric Handel, and Antonio Vivaldi) explored textural contrast in the concerto form by pitting the sound of a soloist or soloists against the sound of the whole orchestra. The solo instrument or instruments were treated in a virtuosic manner that set them well apart from the rest of the ensemble.

Johann Sebastian Bach's Organ Fugue in G minor BWV 578 is an excellent and clear example of a four voice fugue.

[Additional listening information is at the end of the chapter.]

BACH ORGAN FUGUE IN G MINOR: OPENING

The resultant texture alternates between thick (the "tutti" sound of the whole ensemble) and thin (the sections for one or more soloists). The typical format of a concerto movement consists of four tutti sections alternating with three solo ones. The tutti sections are usually homophonic, supported by the chordal accompaniment of the harpsichord—the main keyboard instrument of the period. In contrast, the solo passages can be polyphonic, homophonic, or more rarely, monophonic.

This kind of textural contrast can be explored in more detail by looking at the first movement ("Allegro") of Antonio Vivaldi's "Spring," one of four

Antonio Vivaldi, "Spring" Concerto, First Movement.

[Additional listening information is at the end of the chapter.]

violin concertos comprising his famous orchestral masterpiece, *The Four Seasons*. Vivaldi's work is programmatic—instrumental music that is representational rather than abstract. Program music is intended to be narrative or descriptive of a particular scene, story, or image. In this case, Vivaldi was inspired by the sounds, rhythms, and imagery of the changing seasons. He was perhaps the first composer to write program music in the concerto form.

Four explanatory sonnets accompanied the publication of *The Four Seasons* in 1725. Vivaldi apparently added them after writing the music, but their authorship is unknown. Each line of text appears in the score indicating the details of the scene that the music is supposed to depict. Letters preceding the lines are also found in the score at the corresponding passage.[8]

In "Allegro," the first movement of "Spring," Vivaldi used the typical concerto format, alternating tutti sections with solo sections. The accompanying sonnet describes the events of the movement:

A *Spring has arrived and merrily*
B *the birds hail her with happy song*
C *and meanwhile, at the breath of Zephyrs, the streams flow with a sweet murmer*
D *thunder and lightning, chosen to proclaim her, come covering the sky with a black mantle*
E *and then, when these fall silent, the little birds return once more to their melodious incantation.*

▬▬▬ CHAPTER SUMMARY

While there are many examples of music from the European classical tradition that fall neatly into the categories of monophony, polyphony, or homophony, the texture in most music changes during the course of the composition. Just as in many other musical traditions, composers use different textures as a way to add tension and variety to their music. It is important to realize that a piece of music doesn't have to fit into any one mold. Since it is often difficult to analyze accurately the texture of a piece of music, theorist Jay Swain conjectures that it may be better to understand the "prevailing texture":

> *Because the texture can change so rapidly and because it is often a matter of judgment, not precise like the length of a note, it is often the* prevailing texture *that is described. That means naming the texture present most of the time in a passage or piece. In this way we can make a useful observation about a piece without worrying about every small detail or judgement.*[9]

This is useful advice in looking at music from outside the European classical tradition as well. In widening our perspective, we can understand that the categories of monophony, heterophony, polyphony, and homophony provide a workable model for understanding texture in music, but that this model must be flexible.

ADDITIONAL LISTENING

JOHANN SEBASTIAN BACH'S ORGAN FUGUE IN G MINOR (BWV 578)

This is an excellent example of a four voice fugue. The composition was written for solo organ. In the exposition, the subject first appears in the highest voice played with the organist's right hand. This theme then enters in progressively low pitch areas. While the theme is being stated, the parts that have already come in continue on with additional contrapuntal material; the only time you hear the theme by itself is in the very beginning of the piece. When the fourth voice enters with the subject in the bass, the texture is at its thickest.

After the exposition, episodes containing elements of the theme alternate with restatements of the theme itself. The first episode begins after the bass part states the subject. This short episode contains a four note pattern or sequence that also reappears later in the composition. The theme is then restated, shared by the tenor and soprano voices. The composer modulates and the theme is played again in the middle voice.

Another short episode follows that is marked by a three note sequence in the upper and middle voices. The theme can then be heard clearly in the bass part followed by another short episode. The theme is heard again in the highest voice. The last episode begins with the four note sequence noted earlier and then builds in intensity to the final restatement of the theme in the lowest part. The piece ends with a strong final cadence and ritard or slowing down.

VIVALDI'S "SPRING" CONCERTO (FIRST MOVEMENT)

The opening tutti (A) presents two three-measure themes which are both repeated. The first solo section (B) is an interplay between the solo violinist, first violinists, and second violinists. The three violin parts with their repeated notes, trills, and their quick melodic fragments are meant to suggest bird song.

Here the texture becomes polyphonic as the three voices echo each other and pass melodic motifs back and forth. The absence of the lower instruments (violists, cellists and harpsichordist) creates a thin and light texture dominated by the three melodic parts.

After this section, Vivaldi repeats the second theme, bringing the texture back to homophony. For the rest of the movement, Vivaldi alternates between the thick texture of the whole ensemble and the thinner texture of solo sections.

The following Figure maps out the tutti and episode sections of the entire first movement.

Listening Guide: "Allegro," (first movement)
Antonio Vivaldi, *Spring Concerto*

	Time
A. Tutti—opening two themes	
B. Episode one: solo violin, violins, violas: bird song	0:32
Tutti (repeat of second theme)	1:09
C. Tutti: gentle breezes and streams	1:16
repeat of theme two	1:42
D. Episode two: thunder and lightning: solo violin with sparse accompaniment in form of slow descending notes	1:49
Tutti (second theme in minor key)	2:19
E. Episode three: solo violin, violins, violas with long notes on cello, polyphonic, bird song	2:27
Tutti (new material)	2:45
short passage with solo violin and harpsichord leading back to tutti	2:55
Tutti	3:09

[Lettered sections (A–E) represent lines of text upon which
Vivaldi based his music.]

STUDY QUESTIONS

1. How do you define the role of texture in music?

2. Define the four main categories of musical texture. — p.169

3. What musical textures are prevalent in Irish traditional music? P172

4. What is the prevailing texture in the steel band? P. 175

5. What is the history of salsa? What instruments comprise a typical salsa band?   p.178-179   ↑ P.180

6. What kinds of instruments are found in a Central Javanese gamelan?

7. Why is it difficult to categorize texture in Central Javanese gamelan music?

8. Describe a typical Balinese beleganjur group.

9. What is a fugue?   p.187

10. How does the texture change in the first movement of Vivaldi's "Spring" Concerto?

REFERENCED SOURCES

1. Slobin, Interview. 1997
2. Reck, 1977: 312.
3. Locke, 1996: 86.
4. Stuempfle, 1995: 10.
5. Ibid: 23–26.
6. Manuel, 1995: 83.
7. Bakan, 1998.
8. Kolneder, 1970: 91.
9. Swain, 1987: 39.

CHAPTER 9

HARMONY

About This Chapter

This chapter provides an introduction to the basic features of the Western harmonic system, and chronicles its development from the European church music of the Middle Ages. It also describes the usages of Western harmony in non-classical musics such as folk and jazz. Harmony's natural basis in the overtone series can be heard in both Western and non-Western traditions, such as that of the Central African mbira. But some traditions run counter to this tendency, cultivating harmonies which would sound dissonant to outsiders.

KEYWORDS

consonance/consonant
dissonance/dissonant
drone
interval
key
tonality/tonal
triad

COMPANION RESOURCES

TELEVISION PROGRAM: Harmony

AUDIO SELECTIONS:

44. "The Green Fields of Canada" (excerpt), melody alone and with drone.
45. "Benedicamus Domino" (parallel organum)
46. "Benedicamus Domino" (melismatic organum, c.1125).
47. "Benedicamus Domino" (melismatic organum, c.1175).
48. "Dominator Domine."
49. "Super Flumine Babilonis."
50. "The Green Fields of Canada."
51. "Chemutemgure."

People in many parts of the world enjoy hearing and producing musical harmony. The combined sound of congenial tones makes melodies more colorful and meaningful, and adds momentum to rhythmic patterns. Producing music together in harmony, people enact a powerful social ideal, blending their voices and actions in an engaging embodiment of social accord, agreement, or *consonance*. Some people have a knack for improvising harmony in group singing; but even those who can't make up a harmony can determine whether or not someone else's harmony sounds right to them. Some musical genres, which differ substantially in other factors, are quite similar in their judgments of harmonic consonance. But these perceptual agreements can change when cultural factors come into play, and some people relish harmonies that sound all wrong to others.

Harmony is defined as the simultaneous sounding of two or more pitches, and it is directly related to texture. It can refer to the simultaneous combinations of tones generated by polyphony, or to the chords or drone accompanying a melody in a homophonic texture. By separating out harmony as a distinct subject, we are, in effect, refocusing our lens to look at music in a different way. For example, when we focus on the overall texture of polyphony, we are looking at the interplay of simultaneous melodies; when we focus on harmony, we are picking out the individual *intervals*—the various combinations of tones—which are created, moment by moment, by this melodic interplay. Generally, a consonant interval is one which sounds pleasant, involving compatible tones. A *dissonant* interval sounds edgy, or restless: listeners may find it unpleasant, wanting it to change, or resolve, to a consonant one.

Why is there so much agreement around the world about what kinds of intervals are consonant or dissonant? The answer may lie in the overtone series, which also directly affects musical timbre. Regardless of a sound's pitch and timbre, the overtone series itself always has the same basic structure. The overtones vibrate in specific mathematical relationships to the fundamental pitch—1:2, 2:3, 3:4, 4:5, and so on. The lowest ratios in this series produce the intervals, which are perceived almost universally as consonances: octaves, fifths, fourths, and thirds. Higher ratios produce intervals which are usually considered dissonances: seconds, sevenths and tritones (see Appendix 2).

In actual practice, these intervals are tuned many different ways in various cultures. Relatively few musical tuning systems involve the exact mathematical relationships found in the overtone series. For example, a carefully-tuned Javanese gamelan or African mbira may produce thirds and fifths which sound out of tune to a Western musician. But Western tuning systems may sound just as disagreeable to a non-Western musician. These preferences are culturally constructed; they are not based on objective mathematical facts. Still, the general relationships between the fundamental overtone ratios and the perception of consonant intervals—however they may be locally tuned—suggests a possible reason for the preference for octaves, fifths, fourths, and thirds in so much of the world's music.

Although harmonic practices can be found in many parts of the world, only in the West have musicians developed a vocabulary for describing them in analytic terms. Western composers have worked with explicit harmonic concepts and practices for more than a millennium, developing a detailed theoretical system. Since other cultures do not have such specific ways of describing their harmonic usages, the Western system will provide the terms and concepts for our investigation of the world of harmony. But there is no reason to assume that Europeans in the Christian Era were the first people to discover the appeal of producing music in simultaneous intervals; such practices could be as old as music itself.

DRONES

One type of harmonic practice found in many parts of the world is the use of a *drone*: one or more constant, unchanging pitches providing a backdrop accompaniment for melodies and rhythms. A drone can be a long unchanging tone, like the drone of a bagpipe, or it can be rhythmically articulated: for example, in some folk song traditions in Eastern Europe one singer sings a melody with words, while another sings the same words to a constant drone pitch. Another kind of articulated drone involves the rhythmic reiteration of one note—often on a stringed instrument—to support a melody with both a harmonic and a rhythmic basis.

In some traditions a drone is considered an essential part of the music. For example, in North Indian classical music the drone instrument *tanpura* sounds the primary note of the raga (sa) as well as a secondary note (ma or pa). All of the musicians, including the tabla player, tune their own pitches very carefully to the drone. With melody instruments and voices, this involves concentration on the fine-tuning of subtle microtones—intervals even smaller than half-steps.

Demonstrates the difference between the sound of an Irish melody played alone and with a drone. Notice how the presence of the drone creates a sense of tension and resolution in the musical phrase, as some melody notes sound dissonant with it while others have a consonant sound.

The tanpura provides a constant drone as the player plucks each of the four strings in order over and over again. Their gently buzzing sounds, caused by the open strings vibrating against cotton threads placed on a sloping bridge, spill over each other in an ever-shifting web of consonant sound. For some, this drone has a spiritual significance, representing the pulsing but essentially balanced and unchanging flow of the universe. Plucked instruments like the sarod and sitar often provide a drone as well: each has a special set of drone strings tuned to the tanpura, and the player strums rhythmic accents while playing melodic compositions or improvisations on the melody strings.

THE TANPURA

Other traditions place great importance on the presence of a drone, though it may not be accorded the same kind of significance as that of the tanpura. Scottish Highland bagpipers, for example, would never perform without sounding their drone pipes. But in some traditions a drone may be considered optional. For example, a performance of traditional Irish music will only include a constant drone if an uilleann piper is present. Further, this type of bagpipe includes a stop key which enables the piper to turn off the drones at will and perform on just the chanter, the melody pipe.

THE SCOTTISH HIGHLAND BAGPIPE

© Copyright Edinburgh University Collection of Historic Musical Instruments.

A drone may be considered a comparatively simple form of harmony, since it does not change in pitch. But the combination of a melody with a drone causes a succession of harmonic tensions and resolutions, a concept which is the basis of any harmonic system. As we will see, the earliest codified harmonic practices of Europe involved slowing down old plainchant melodies and ornamenting them with quicker melodic figurations which emphasized consonance—in effect, turning the chants into slowly changing drones and decorating them with melodic ornamentations. It is likely that the medieval church musicians had heard drones before, and were adapting a common usage to a new purpose. We will now turn our attention to the story of the growth of this harmonic tradition, a story which begins in medieval Europe.

■ THE DEVELOPMENT OF WESTERN CLASSICAL HARMONY

The Middle Ages

Chanting in voices blending happily together, they sang , "Blessed is he who cometh in the name of the Lord." And we in our humble way, relying on the unquestioned authority of the men of old, observe the same practice with due solemnity: on the holy festival of Palm Sunday we divide into two groups, singing with melodious voices and crying our "Hosanna" with two bodies of singers, in joyful and triumphant melody. Aldhelm, Bishop of Sherborne [640–709].[1]

Does this seventh-century passage describe a harmonic practice? We don't know for sure: the writer may simply have been describing antiphonal singing—the two groups alternately singing the same chant, perhaps overlapping at times—rather than a conscious harmonic "blending" of different tones. No one knows how long Europeans sang in harmony before they started to leave unambiguous evidence of it. A passage from the ninth century seems to provide more solid documentation:

When one hears two strings at once, and one of them sounds a low note and the other a high one, and the two sounds are mixed in one sweet sound, as if the two voices had blended into one, then they are making what one calls a consonance. Regino of Prüm [d. 915].[2]

It is possible that this writer was merely describing octave doubling, but if so, one might ask why he felt it necessary to define consonance. As in many other cultures, the consonance of the octave might have been so obvious that no one needed to point it out. A twelfth-century passage is more decisive, clearly distinguishing practices observed in Wales and Britain from other group singing styles.

When [the Welsh] make music together, they sing their tunes not in unison, as is done elsewhere, but in parts with many simultaneous modes and phrases. Therefore, in a group of singers (which one very often meets within Wales) you will hear as many melodies as there are people, and a distinct variety of parts; yet, they all accord in one consonant and properly constituted composition. In the northern districts of Britain, beyond the Humber and round about York, the inhabitants use a similar kind of singing in harmony, but in only two different parts, one singing quietly in a low register, and the other soothing and charming the ear above. This specialty of this race is no product of trained musicians, but was acquired through long-standing popular practices. Giraldus Cambrensis, Descripto Cambriae [1198].[3]

Notice that these harmonic traditions were oral ones; notational conventions and theoretical models came later, as ways of describing and codifying what some musicians were already doing by ear. As far as we know, the first explicit theoretical system of harmony involved adding a new decorative layer to the singing of the old plainchant melodies of the Christian Church: a development which was called *organum*.

Organum (c.900–1200)

Consonance is the judicious and harmonious mixture of two tones, which exists only if two tones, produced from different sources, meet in one joint sound, as happens when a boy's voice and a man's voice sing the same thing, or in that which they commonly call organum. Hucbald [c.840–c.930].[4]

A fifth doubling of the plainchant excerpt heard in **audio #36**.

In the above passage, the writer was distinguishing between two kinds of consonance in medieval church music: that of singing in octaves, "when a boy's voice and a man's voice sing the same thing," and that of singing in other intervals, a practice which, by the tenth century was known as *organum*. Organum began as a simple doubling of plainchant at the interval of a fifth or fourth above or below the melody. There was no need to notate or think in any detailed way about this practice: one simply sang the same melody, starting at a different pitch. The result was an enrichment of the overall sound of the chant, not the addition of a separate melody.

Rooted in this practice, some chanters improvised more complex variations using a practice called *melisma*—singing several pitches on one syllable. They started by singing a fifth or fourth above or below the melody, but then moved to other acceptable intervals—fifths, fourths, octaves, and unisons—on various succeeding chanting tones, filling in some connecting or ornamental melodic figures along the way. This may be considered the beginning of European religious polyphony, music in which two or more melodies are combined simultaneously, later known as *counterpoint*.

EXAMPLE 1: TWO-VOICE ORGANUM, C. 1125

Example 1 is most likely a written-out improvisation from around 1125, showing one way of producing a two-voice organum which involves more than a simple parallel doubling. This is an ornamentation of the plainchant excerpt given in Chapter 8.

EXAMPLE 2: TWO-VOICE ORGANUM, C. 1175 (NOTRE DAME)

Be_____

ne_____

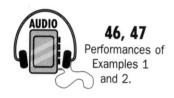

AUDIO

46, 47
Performances of
Examples 1
and 2.

Example 2, a later example of two-voice organum (c.1175) shows a more ornate treatment of the same plainchant. Given the complexity of this style of elaboration, scholars believe that it is not a written-out improvisation but a fully composed embellishment of the chant. The upper voice accompanies the first four chanting tones with a fifth, octave, unison, and fifth, respectively; but it fills in these intervals with so much ornamental detail in the form of little melodic and rhythmic sequences that the basic chant must be sung very slowly. This style of organum was developed at the Cathedral of Notre Dame in Paris, and is associated with a composer named Leonin—one of the first European composers whose name has been preserved.

It is no accident that the development of organum in religious music came at the same time that the visual artists of the church started to explore depth and perspective. Just as these painters and sculptors were pursuing a more vivid portrayal of holy figures, the church musicians were becoming interested in a more nuanced performance of sacred chant. The human figure was still central visually, as the basic chant was musically, but certain aesthetic qualities were beginning to be considered appropriate for holy images and rituals.

As these trends continued to develop, the next few centuries saw deepening depictions of human experiences and emotions by visual artists like Giotto and writers such as Chaucer and Dante. The expressive capabilities of harmony were broadened as well, as composers developed ways to combine more than two tones at a time. Although the word was not in use at the time, composers were beginning to use *triads*: three-note chords which combined the consonant intervals of the third and the fifth.

Early Triadic Harmony (c.1200–1400)

Master Leoninus [Leonin] was generally known as the best composer of organum, who made the great book Magnus Liber *of organa for Mass and Office for the enhancement of the Divine Service. This book was in use until the time of the great Perotinus [Perotin], who shortened it and substituted a great many better* clausulae, *because he was the best composer of discant and better than Leoninus. Moreover, this same Master Perotinus wrote excellent compositions for four voices. . . replete with artful musical turns and figures, as well as a considerable number of very famous pieces for three voices. . . . The book, or rather books, of Master Perotinus have remained in use in the Choir of the Church of Our Blessed Virgin in Paris [i.e., Notre Dame] until the present day.* "Anonymous IV" [c.1272].[5]

As thirteenth-century composers became interested in composing for more than two voices or parts, they started to make more use of a richer concordant sound: a fifth could be subdivided with a third, producing a pleasing three-note consonance which was later called a *triad*. The two most common triads take their names from their lower thirds: a major triad has a major third—an interval comprising four half steps—on the bottom, and a minor triad has a minor third, comprising three half steps, on the bottom. Both of these triads involve a subdivided perfect fifth, so all their intervals are consonant, and they sound harmonically stable to Western ears. Triads with more compicated vibrational relationships, like the "diminished" and "augmented" triads, are considered restless and dissonant in the West (see Appendix 2).

Though they did not articulate the concept of triads in theoretical language, thirteenth-century composers began to use them in their music as ways of preserving an overall harmonious sound while interweaving more than one melody in addition to the basic plainchant, called the *tenor* when used in this way. Such religious compositions became known as *motets*.

EXAMPLE 3: MOTET, C. 1225; ASTERISKS SHOW OCCURRENCES OF TRIADS

A performance of a Motet from Notre Dame, c. 1225.

Example 3 is a motet from Notre Dame, probably from around 1225, in the style of Perotin. Triads appear in this piece, though not very often, and almost never on a strong beat.

This kind of piece required a more detailed level of craft, as composers sought to construct individual melodies (referred to as *contratenor*, *triplum*, and *motetus*, in the quotation below) which were both pleasing in themselves and concordant in their combination. Also, a regular rhythmic pulse was necessary to keep all the melodies together, and this pulse was organized into "rhythmic modes," somewhat similar to the more modern concept of meter. A late fourteenth-century musician described the compositional process in craftsman-like terms:

> *First take for your tenor any antiphon or repository or any other chant from the book of Office chants; and its words should accord with the theme or occasion for which the motet is being made. And then take the tenor and arrange it and put it in rhythm according to what will be revealed below about perfect and imperfect mode: perfect mode is when there are three beats per note of the tenor and imperfect mode is when there are two. And when the tenor is well laid out, if you wish to make a motet in four parts, your next step is to arrange a contratenor and put it in rhythm over the tenor.*

> *And when this is done, take the tenor again, and the contratenor if you are composing in four parts, and arrange a third part, the* triplum, *over them, so that it concords well with the tenor and contratenor. And if all of the above is to work in the best way possible, then divide the tenor into two segments, or four, or as many as you like; and complete one section over the tenor according to the above rules, and each part should be shaped in this way, from first to last. And this is what is known as setting out a motet. Aegidius of Murino,* Tractatus cantus mensurabilis *[c.1400].*[6]

This writer's pragmatic demeanor is particularly striking when he describes the final step, matching the desired text to the music. "Sometimes it will be necessary to stretch many notes over a few words in order to make the setting come out right," he advises, "and sometimes many words must be squeezed into a small amount of time. Just fit it together any way you can."

But this routine approach was not the only one. Composers like Guillaume de Machaut (d. 1377) and Francesco Landini (c. 1325–97) reveled in the wealth of possibilities suggested by the new harmonic practices. Their works demonstrate some of the most agile and creative minds in the history of Western composition, as they experimented with new sounds and new ideas. In this time of burgeoning creativity, the austerity of the medieval period was giving way to an increasing involvement with emotion and passion, and European artists in all fields were finding new and richer ways to express the world of human feeling.

The Renaissance (c. 1400–1600)

This growing concern with human experiences fed into cultural developments which were so far-reaching that many of the people involved felt that a turning point had been reached. Inspired by the humanism of the Greek and Roman classics—compared to the severity of the medieval emphasis on contemplation of the divine—many artists and thinkers declared a rebirth (renaissance) of cultural values. These values were both intellectual and aesthetic, and were seen as restoring the importance of human thought and feeling to their rightful places in social life.

Academies were founded for study and discussion of the classics and contemporary issues, and changing attitudes towards the arts created an atmosphere in which music, visual art, and literature expanded and flourished. An account of the dedication of the Cathedral of Santa Maria del Fiore in Florence on Annunciation Day in 1436 provided a vivid picture of the importance and value of music in the early Renaissance:

> First there was a great line of trumpeters, lutenists, and flutists, each carrying his instrument, trumpet, lute, flute, in his hands, and each dressed in red clothing. Meanwhile, everywhere there was singing with so many and such various voices, such harmonies exalted even to heaven, that truly it was to the listener like angelic and divine melodies; the voices filled the listeners' ears with such a wondrous sweetness that they seemed to become stupefied, almost as men were fabled to become upon hearing the singing of the sirens.
>
> I could believe without impiety that even in heaven, yearly on this most solemn day that marks the beginning of human salvation, the angels sing thus, the more ardently to give themselves up to the celebration of this festive day with sweet singing. And then, when they made their customary pauses in singing, so joyous and sweet was the reverberation that mental stupor, now claimed by the cessation of those sweet symphonies, seemed as if to regather strength from the wonderful sounds.
>
> But at the Elevation of the Most Sacred Host, the whole space of the church was filled with such choruses of harmony and such a concord of diverse instruments that it seemed (not without reason) as though the symphonies and songs of the angels and of divine Paradise had been sent forth from the heavens to whisper in our ears an unbelievable celestial sweetness. Wherefore at that moment I was so possessed by ecstasy that I seemed to enjoy the life of the Blessed here on earth; whether it happened so to others present I know not, but concerning myself I can bear witness. *Giannozzo Manetti*[7]

The music for the moment of Elevation at this event was probably Guillaume Dufay's motet "Nuper rosarum flores," which was composed for the occasion. Dufay (c. 1400–1474) and Josquin Desprez (c. 1440–1521) were two of the most accomplished and creative composers of the early Renaissance, and they were decisive in developing and establishing its harmonic innovations. Particularly in Josquin's music, four-voice harmony was refined into a system which provided the foundation of Western harmony writing for at least five centuries.

This system enabled composers to place increased emphasis on triads. The thirteenth-century three-voice motet we have seen used triads, but they were by no means prevalent; to some extent they were even just conveniences to smooth out the upper voice lines, rather than specifically sought-after sounds. The four-voice style perfected by Josquin afforded much more opportunity to subdivide fifths with thirds while maintaining smooth melodic lines, creating a rich triadic sound which, he felt, lent itself to deeper representations of emotional states. And with four voices, a composer could double what was later called the *root*—the bottom note of the triad—to create a feeling of harmonic "rootedness" and strength.

Another practice which reinforced the triadic sound was the abandonment of parallel octaves, unisons, and fifths—the very practice which enhanced the feeling of a central melody in organum. Now all of the melodic lines were truly equal, and colorful harmonies could paint sonic pictures of human experiences. Musical qualities could support the emotions evoked by the words being sung, in stark contrast to the attitude toward texts expressed by Aegidius.

Further Developments

The second half of the Renaissance saw waves of religious change which influenced harmonic practices. Fueled by humanism and the widespread abuses of power in the Catholic church, the Reformation spread across Europe, splintering Christianity into factions. Reformers like Martin Luther (1483–1546) believed in supplanting the authority of Rome and allowing all people to participate in worship by holding services in their own languages.

Similarly, Luther believed in congregational singing, empowering nonspecialists to glorify God through music. For his hymns, or *chorales*, Luther borrowed folk tunes and composed new ones in a similar style, harmonizing them in four-voice settings which could be sung by everyone. Though he admired the works of Josquin and Dufay, he was convinced that egalitarian participation in sacred music addressed a higher religious goal. Other reformers, such as Jean Calvin (1509–64), believed that even simplified harmonic practices evinced vanity and secularism, and promoted the practice of congregational singing in plain, unharmonized clarity.

Responding to the Reformation, the Catholic church moved to clean up internal corruption, enforce piety, and simplify musical practices. The Counter-Reformation eschewed flamboyant polyphonies and harmonies, encouraging religious ardor rather than aesthetic display. "The whole plan of singing in musical modes should be constituted not to give empty pleasure to the ear," declared a Catholic decree in 1562, "but in such a way that the words may be clearly understood by all, and thus the hearts of listeners be drawn to the desire of heavenly harmonies, in the contemplation of the joys of the blessed."[8]

Avoiding the severity of the Reformation's musical goals but adopting some of its moderating convictions, the Counter-Reformation supported composers whose music was considered both refined and inspiring, including Giovanni Gabrielli (c.1533–85) and Giovanni Pierluigi da Palestrina (c. 1525–94).

Example 4 shows a psalm setting from 1580. This composition demonstrates four-part triadic harmony writing in an elegant style which was considered well-suited to such musical and religious values.

Many composers at this time worked with a variety of secular forms as well, including the *madrigal* and the older *chanson* (originally a secular version of the religious motet), and many dance and functional genres. In both sacred and secular musics of the later Renaissance, judicious use of dissonance became an important expressive device. But dissonance was still subordinate to consonance, and rules for the proper usage of dissonances—includ-

A performance of a Setting of Psalm 137 by Mikotaj Gomótka.

EXAMPLE 4: SETTING OF PSALM 137 BY MIKOTAJ GOMÓTKA, 1580

ing the ways they must be prepared and resolved—were codified. A passage from a 1558 treatise describes this approach:

> As I have said, every composition, counterpoint, or harmony is composed primarily of consonances. Nevertheless, for greater beauty and charm dissonances are used, incidentally and secondarily. Although these dissonances are not pleasing in isolation, when they are properly placed according to the precepts given, the ear not only endures them but derives pleasure and delight from them. They are of double utility to the musician. The first has been mentioned: with their aid we may pass from one consonance to another. The second is that a dissonance causes the consonance that follows it to sound more agreeable. The ear then grasps and appreciates the consonance with greater

pleasure, just as light is more delightful to the sight after darkness, and the taste of sweets more delicious after something bitter. . .

Though I have said that in composing we use consonances primarily, and dissonances incidentally, it must not be thought that these dissonances can be placed in counterpoints or compositions without rule or order, as is sometimes done, for confusion would result. Care should be taken to use them in an orderly, regular fashion, so that all may turn out well.Gioseffo Zarlino [1517–90] in Institutioni harmoniche.[9]

By the time this treatise was written, usages of consonance and dissonance and conventions of part writing had been firmly established. Although a comprehensive theoretical language had not yet crystallized, a basic harmonic system was solidly in place—one which would be used in manifold forms and genres for centuries. But as we will see, new developments continued to enrich harmonic practices, as composers strove to depict human emotions and experiences ever more vividly.

The Baroque Era (c.1600–1750)

The beginning of the Baroque Era in music was marked by the development of what some musicians called the "second practice," as differentiated from the "first practice" of the Renaissance. Throughout European culture, the importance of human feeling in the arts was continuing to increase: authors like Miguel de Cervantes and William Shakespeare were delving ever deeper into the intricacies of the emotions, and painters like Michelangelo da Caravaggio and Peter Paul Rubens were producing sensuous and dramatic works, full of color and movement. Similarly, the second practice in music was an advancement of expression over mere decorousness, an exaltation of spirit over formality. For some, the ultimate musical embodiment of these goals was opera, a new theatrical form involving dramatic tales staged in musical settings.

Of course, the second practice had its detractors. "Would you know what an Opera is?" wrote a French courtier to the English Duke of Buckingham. "It is an *odd medley of poetry and music, wherein the poet and musician, equally confined one by the other, take a world of pains to compose a wretched performance*" (Seigneur de Saint-Évremond [c. 1610–1703], quoted in Hayward, ed. 1930:206; emphasis original). In 1600, a conservative Italian musician published an attack on the harmonic innovations of Claudio Monteverdi, who is now considered the first outstanding composer of opera and early Baroque music:

> *Such composers, in my opinion, have nothing but smoke in their heads if they are so impressed with themselves as to think they can corrupt, abolish, and ruin at will the good old rules handed down from days of old by so many theorists and excellent musicians, who are the very ones from which these modern musicians have learned awkwardly to put a few notes together. . .*
>
> *Of course I recognize that new discoveries are not only a good thing but a necessary one. But first tell me why you want such clashes as they have written? If you would answer, "I wish them to be heard clearly, but not so as to offend the ear," then why not prepare them in the conventional way, as reason dictates? Now, even if you want dissonances to become consonances, they will always remain the opposite of consonant; they are naturally always dissonant and can become consonant, therefore, only if consonances become dissonances . . .*
>
> *Compositions like these, then, are the product of ignorance. For such composers it is enough to set up a great roar of sound, an absurd confusion, an array of defects, and it all comes from the ignorance which keeps them benighted. Giovanni Maria Artusi.*[10]

Monteverdi's response to Artusi—discreetly issued under the name of his brother—provides an elegant exposition of the intentions of the second practice:

> *My brother says that his works are not composed at random, for, in this kind of music, it is his goal to make the words the mistress of the harmony and not its servant, and it is from this point of view that his work should be judged. But in the event Artusi takes a few details, or, as he calls them "passages" from my brother's madrigals, without any regard for the words, which he ignores as if they had nothing to do with the music. By judging these passages without their words, my brother's opponent implies that all merit and beauty lie in following exactly the rules of the First Practice, in which the harmony is mistress of the words. . .*
>
> *"Second Practice". . . is that style which is chiefly concerned with the perfection of the setting; that is, in which harmony does not rule but is ruled, and where the words are mistress of the harmony. This is why my brother calls it "second" rather than "new," and "practice" rather than "theory," for its understanding is to be sought in the process of actual composition.*[11]

One of the chief harmonic innovations ascribed to Monteverdi is the use of certain dissonant chords which are now called *seventh chords*. A triad—a fifth subdivided by a third—can also be seen as two simultaneous thirds, the top note of one providing the bottom note of another. Adding another third to the top of the triad produces a seventh chord, a four-note chord consisting of three simultaneous thirds, the top note of the chord a seventh above the bottom one.

This seventh is a dissonant interval, and previously it was subject to careful regulation: it had to be both approached and resolved by stepwise melodic motion. In fact, in the past the seventh chord had not been considered a chord at all, but merely a dissonant intermediary between one triad and another. Monteverdi pioneered the use of this chord as a powerful expressive device, underscoring moments of strong emotion in the words of his madrigals, operas, and even religious works. His new usage soon became standard: although the seventh was still considered a dissonance which must resolve in a prescribed way, downward stepwise into the next chord, this chord became an important aesthetic tool for Western composers.

Continuo and Figured Bass

A key feature of opera is the *aria*, a solo song in which a character expresses an emotional state. The solo voice must be clearly heard, so the words can be understood. A rich accompaniment with several melodic lines would undermine this imperative, and partly as a response to this situation a practice arose of writing just two parts: the vocal melody and a bass line. But these composers were not interested in a simple two-voice texture, which would have sounded too austere and old-fashioned to them. Instead, the bass line was meant to be played as a *continuo*, with improvised chords provided by a chordal instrument, such as a lute or harpsichord. Such instruments could provide both the bass line and the chords, or the bass line could be played separately, often on a low instrument like the bass viol, the predecessor of the modern cello.

To insure that the improvised chords would fit with both the melody and the bass line, the continuo parts included "figures," numbers which showed what intervals should be played above each bass note. Although musicians at the time would not have described the practice in this way, the figures showed what triads the improviser should use at each point in the accompaniment.

Figured bass writing was by no means limited to vocal music. The idea of a basic two-voice texture filled in with continuo improvisation became one of the most important models of the Baroque era. Many instrumental pieces were written just as a melody with a figured bass, and the listener's ear was drawn to an appreciation of how these two voices interacted, accompanied by a continuo improviser. Even pieces written for orchestra were usually supported in performance by a continuo player, whether or not the composer specifically indicated one. The practice of improvising accompaniments by reading figured bass lines became widespread among the players of chordal instruments, a necessary skill for both careerists and amateurs.

Understanding Baroque Harmony

Around the beginning of the Baroque era, the concept of *tonality* began to supplant the older concept of mode. In various usages the term mode had referred to rhythmic or melodic practices; tonality was a concept that specifically referred to harmonic practices. Like most theoretical concepts in music, it did not arise as an abstract idea, but as a way of understanding and codifying existing musical practices.

Tonality involves the idea that a given piece of music exists in a major or minor *key*, a specific harmonic world which contextualizes individual chords and melodies. So, for example, if a piece is in the key of C major, then the pitch C is the fundamental, or *tonic* pitch—the appropriate pitch to end a melody on with a satisfying feeling of resolution and repose. Similarly, the C major triad is the tonic (or I) chord—the triad which imparts the strongest feeling of rest at the end of the piece. Other notes and triads fall into place around the tonic. For example, the triad a fifth above the tonic is known as the *dominant* (or V), and is considered to exert a strong pull toward the tonic. In this manner, a key becomes a system of harmonic tension and release, ebb and flow, lending a richer level of drama to the "story" told by a melody (see Appendix 2).

Through the end of the nineteenth century, all Western composers used this basic harmonic system. To be sure, there were many additions to it, but the core principles remained intact; for the most part, composers of the Classical and Romantic eras were involved with other kinds of innovation. In the early twentieth century some composers began to feel that the old harmonic system had run its course and was no longer sufficient to their needs.

Some sought to modernize the system by replacing its rules with a new approach to concepts like "key," while others developed "atonality" and other systems and practices intended to replace the tonal system. Although some Western classical composers consider such developments inevitable, others continue to derive fresh ideas and sounds from elements of the tonal system. And as we will see, Western classical composers are by no means the only musicians who are doing this.

■■■ OTHER APPLICATIONS OF WESTERN HARMONY

Western Folk and Popular Musics

We cannot assume that the learned church and court composers of Europe were the first people to discover triads. Since they were the first to develop sufficiently detailed notations, their usages are the earliest for which we have concrete evidence. But while nothing proves conclusively that early folk musicians made use of triads, nothing proves that they did not.

The twelfth-century description of Welsh folk singing quoted earlier demonstrates that a multitude of improvised vocal parts sounded concordant to the writer; this may well indicate the use of triads, though they were not identified as such. With their simple vibrational relationships, the intervals of triads tend to sound agreeable to most people, so there is further reason to suppose that an imaginative musician or group might discover this pleasing sound without exposure to the musical practices of elite institutions. Particularly in vocal music, intuitive harmonic practices may have developed long before such usages were notated.

Instruments afforded further opportunities to enhance monophony. Harps, lutes, guitars, and other multi-stringed instruments could be played both melodically and chordally; anyone who could afford or build such in-

IRISH UILLEANN PIPES AND FIDDLE

struments could produce harmonic accompaniments to songs and dance tunes. Such practices seem to have developed early on in the oral traditions of Mediterranean countries. In several parts of Europe, "ground basses," melodic phrases which were repeated over and over again as a bass line, served as the foundation for many early folk and popular melodies; for example, the medieval song "Greensleeves" is a melody set to an older ground bass sometimes known as "Romanesca." But in general, folk and popular musicians have tended to start with a melody or song, working out harmonic accompaniments which fit concordantly with the notes of the tune.

Although few rural or street musicians would have had the chance to hear religious and court music in the medieval period, succeeding eras brought more interaction between institutional and vernacular cultural forms. There can be no doubt that some cross-pollination occurred between folk and court musics in the Renaissance. We have early notations of folk tunes which were played for courtly dances and entertainments, and it is just as possible that melodies and practices from the court found their way into oral traditions. And as public performance became increasingly important for classical music in the eighteenth and nineteenth centuries, the harmonic practices of composers became accessible to a broader range of the populace. Melodies from operas became standard fare for some folk and popular musicians, who included chordal accompaniments whenever possible.

In the nineteenth century, melodeons and accordions spread throughout Europe. These portable organs could provide chordal music as well as producing melodies, and their loud, full tone made them ideal for outdoor and large group occasions. In Ireland, "regulators" were added to the uilleann pipes: keyed drone pipes which lay across the piper's lap and sound only when one of their keys is struck, usually by the player's wrist. The keys are arranged so that with one broad wrist stroke a piper may strike the keys of more than one regulator to sound a triad—or the keys may be struck separately.

You hear the judicious use of regulators—following a rendition accompanied only by a drone—in a performance of an Irish slow air.

Today Western folk and popular performers have access to a wide variety of chordal instruments, from pianos to synthesizers and samplers. While they seldom make use of all of the harmonic practices of Baroque composers, many players of these instruments work with basic concepts of Western harmony: they use numerals or letter names to refer to chords in a given key, they match their chords to accented melody notes, and generate bass lines which fit harmonically with both the melody and chords. Sometimes groups even work out counter-melodies which interweave harmonically with the main melody, following the same basic rules for usages of consonance and dissonance which were developed in the Renaissance.

Early Western Influences Abroad

In some parts of the world people were exposed to Western harmony through hymns taught by missionaries. Traditions of Western-influenced harmony singing are found throughout Africa and in much of Polynesia, sometimes as adaptations of older practices. Adrienne Kaeppler described a Tongan example of such acculturation:

> *Melodic rendering of poetry was often done polyphonically in two main parts—fasi, or melody, and a laulalo, a drone—both sung by men. Up to four additional parts decorated the fasi. These were two women's parts described as high and low contralto, and two men's parts sung above and below the fasi. Today, much of this polyphony has been replaced by Western harmony, in which a more melodic bass has replaced the drone and a soprano fasi, usually an octave above the men's fasi, has been added.*[12]

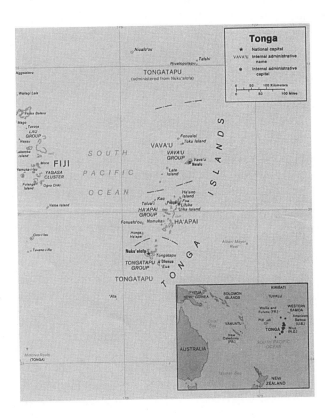

European practices have also been spread through less well-meaning endeavors. The early *conquistadors* and Spanish colonists, for example, brought European musical instruments and usages to many parts of the New World. In what is now generally known as Latin America, a vast array of musical genres arose evincing a blending of European harmony, Native American practices, and the polyrhythmic musics of the Africans who were enslaved by the colonists. Some of the modern-day descendants of this blending—such as salsa and reggae—have gained wide international audiences, influencing other popular musics around the world.

African-American and Recent Popular Musics

In the slavery era, some African-Americans merged indigenous African harmonic practices with European ones. By the 1920s, when African-American musics were first recorded, distinct harmonic hybrids had already developed in blues, religious music, and the music which would later be called jazz. At that time, African American musics involved even more use of seventh chords than the popular musics of Europeans and European Americans, particularly in vocal melodies.

Later blues musicians essentially worked with the same harmonic traditions, but jazz musicians developed more and more complex usages. Seventh chords became the rule rather than triads, and more thirds were added to the top of seventh chords, creating ninth and even eleventh chords. While classical composers also used such chords for certain effects, jazz musicians employed them as part of a standard harmonic language for both composition and improvisation. Unlike folk and popular musicians, who started with a given melody and worked out appropriate-sounding harmonies, jazz musicians worked most intensely with chord progressions themselves, as the basis for composing and improvising.

Meanwhile, the fundamental sound of blues harmonic practices was feeding into the development of popular forms like rhythm & blues and rock & roll. Often with sevenths added, blues cycles of I, IV, and V chords became the harmonic basis of much of American popular music. As recordings of this music spread across the globe, the sound of Western harmony began to influence young musicians in many diverse cultures.

Around the world, most of today's popular music attests to the influence of Western harmony. Triads generally prevail in group arrangements and the dominant-tonic relationship can be heard almost everywhere. The emergence of new musial forms that share a harmonic basis is a unifying factor. Whether the collective genre is known as "zouk," "afropop," or "world beat," the harmonic sound is familiar to the ears of all listeners. This is not to say that ethnic identities and musical creativity have disappeared—indeed, popular musics are sometimes powerful vehicles for such concerns. Indigenous instruments, languages, and musics have been combined in ingenious ways with electric guitars and keyboards. These hybrid musics are grounded in local experience and place, but often reflect the interconnectedness of the global market.

Reggae offers a good example: Musicians in the urban ghettoes of Jamaica were greatly influenced by African-American rhythm & blues, Anglo-American popular music, Afro-Protestant hymns, and indigenous Rastifarian music. The new reggae sound that emerged in the 1960s also had a strong ideological message that resonated with many other oppressed groups around the world. The moral concerns, self respect, and revolutionary nationalism voiced by reggae artists such as Bob Marley, Bunny Wailer, and Peter Tosh helped to make reggae one of the first global popular musics. While reggae itself was a hybrid, new musical styles developed by fusing the reggae beat, message, and basic harmonic progressions with indigenous styles and instruments all over the world.

▬ NON-WESTERN HARMONY

Although Western harmony has spread to many parts of the world, other harmonic practices exist, uninfluenced by the West. Still, in most cases the harmonies people are drawn to are based on the primary intervals of the overtone series which, in the West, are combined to make triads: the fifth and third, and their inversions, the fourth and sixth.

For example, while the balungan instruments of a Central Javanese gamelan produce a single central melody, elaborating instruments like the gendèr often add these concordant intervals in performance, as do the composed countermelodies of the rebab and male chorus. The polyphonic *kora* and *balafon* musics of West Africa are based on these intervals, as is the Central African *mbira* tradition discussed below. And in many parts of the world people have discovered the compelling sound of melodies sung or played in parallel thirds or fifths. Theodore Levin described such a practice in an Islamic ceremony in Central Asia:

> *At the appropriate moment, the men joined the mullah as a chorus that at first sounded heterophonous and disorderly, as though each chanter had begun from his own starting pitch without regard for the other chanters. But a structure quickly became apparent: some of the men were holding more or less accurately the interval of a fifth below the reciting tone and moving the fifth in parallel to the melody as it rose and fell. As they chanted thirty-three repetitions of lâ ilâha illâ' llâh, and a hundred repetitions of illâ' llâh, they nodded their heads gently from side to side. The harmony that had begun as a fifth re-emerged as a third, a fourth, a seventh, and, still later, an octave.[13]*

But there are also traditions which run counter to this trend, savoring the piquant sound of seconds. Bosnian ganga singers, for example, regard these close intervals as bell-like: complex and vibrant. Mirjana Lausevic explained:

> *What people are looking for when singing ganga . . . is physical experience of the sound. And the way they find that is by singing together. Once their whole bodies start resonating and buzzing from this interval of the second, that is the desirable interval that they are looking for. So what they are dealing with is not some external concept of pitches. It is [a] very internal or internalized concept of sound that you are physically experiencing. . . . And the reason this interval is considered a consonance, really, is because it's [the] most physically pleasurable. It's the interval which you can physically experience in a very pleasant way through the buzz in your ears, through the buzz in your chest.[14]*

Levin noted a similar practice in a Central Asian work-song tradition, in which groups of men or women alternate sung couplets:

> *While the chant had a dominant reciting tone, some of the girls sang the reciting tone a bit flat, creating a rich body of beating tones. . . . The singers made it clear that their dissonance was not accidental and not the result of an inability to tune a unison. We had heard other songs [there] in which a unison was kept well tuned. On the contrary, judging by the gusto with which they put their faces close together and shouted out the antiphonal couplets, they clearly reveled in their collective dissonance. Nur Muhammad, a graduate of a specialized music school, agreed. "They love seconds here," he told us, "But try to sing that kind of dissonance through solfège. You can't do it; it's very difficult."[15]*

Whatever specific qualities are valued, many people have been drawn to the simultaneous sounding of tones, and several cultures have developed systems of preferences which govern such activities. While they may not may not make them explicit in words, musicians and listeners understand them implicitly. One such system has grown up around the Central African instrument known as *mbira*.

Zimbabwe: Mbira Music

There are many different kinds of mbira in Zimbabwe and other parts of Africa, but they all share certain structural features. Individual metal strips or keys, each tuned to a specific pitch, are fastened together in such a way that the performer, holding the instrument with both hands, can strike some keys with the left thumb and forefinger, and some with the right. These keys can be retuned or adjusted by the performer, and several different "chunings" or tuning systems may be consciously employed for various pieces. The keys are mounted on or inside a soundboard or resonator, such as a wooden box, a tortoise shell, or a hollowed-out calabash.

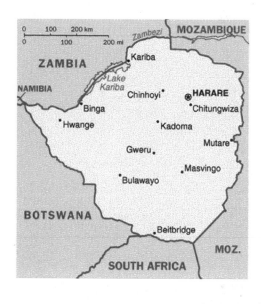

Although mbira players may not subscribe to a body of music theory which resembles that of the West, some musicians have developed conceptual systems relating to their musical materials. For example, according to Paul Berliner, the mbira player Mubayiwa Bandambira characterized the individual keys of his instrument in specific ways: *benzi*, which "frightens you or makes you start, makes you feel awake; makes the heart feel wild like a mad person; makes you dance wildly; has a sharp voice which leads the mbira," *gadzanga*, which "controls the excited feeling of the *benzi* . . . controls the high pitches, cools the feeling down to normal; settles the piece and holds it together," *tida*, which "shouts from far away, sings aloud; makes people feel like singing to it; makes you raise your voice in song," and so on.[16]

Bandambira's culture is the Shona, who are believed to have lived in Zimbabwe since the tenth century. In the Shona's primarily agrarian culture, music has always played important and diverse roles—from the court traditions and war songs of the past, to the work, recreational, and religious traditions of the present. The mbira is an instrument of primary importance to the Shona: its name reflects its crucial function in the *bira* ceremony of ancestor worship, and it is often played for pleasure as well. The Shona value its potential for musical complexity, noting that it can sound like a group of instruments all by itself, and mbira players are considered especially skillful musicians.

THE MBIRA

Harmony in Mbira Music

Mbira music involves repeating polyrhythmic cycles which musicians use to structure their performances. Depending on the mood and skill of the performer, a performance of a given piece may include extensive improvisation. As the mbira player Ephat Mujuru told Berliner, "If I feel like it, I will play one piece all night long. Listen to what I am playing and then come back in a half hour and I'll be playing altogether differently [on the same piece]."[17]

Part of the basis for improvisation is the underlying harmonic structure of each piece; this structure also makes it possible for two or more mbira players to improvise together. Ernest Brown explains that in Zimbabwe

> *you don't have the word for "chord." And you don't have an explicit body of musical theory. But you learn the music by imitation. And . . . if you play notes that are not in the chord, your teacher will tell you, or someone in the audience will tell you, or they'll throw a stick at you [laughs]: you don't do that. They'll say "Here, leave that alone. Don't play that note here." And they'll show you: "Here, play this one." And if you analyze what they're telling you to play, they're telling you to play the notes that are within the chord. So they're hearing . . . the relationship of tones to each other.*[18]

EXAMPLE 5: "CHEMUTMGURE": HARMONIC STRUCTURE AND BASIC POLYRHYTHMIC CYCLE

Example 5 shows the basic polyrhythmic cycle of the mbira piece "Chemutemgure" ("The Wagon Driver") Notes with upward stems are played by the right thumb and forefinger; those with downward stems are played by the left. The two hands alternate quickly, striking simultaneous tones only once in each measure. The second line shows the underlying harmonic structure. You can see the relationship between the two lines: for the most part, the basic polyrhythmic cycle uses the pitches of the underlying harmonic structure, occasionally adding pitches which subdivide an octave with a fifth, or subdivide a fifth with a third. Improvisations on the cycle primarily involve such intervals, so that the underlying structure is always observed. As in so many parts of the world, Zimbabweans clearly feel that octaves, fifths, fourths, thirds, and sixths are pleasing musical sounds, the proper components of both harmonic structure and its elaboration.

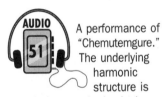

A performance of "Chemutemgure." The underlying harmonic structure is played alone at the beginning and ending of the performance.

■■■ CHAPTER SUMMARY

Just as most of the world's rhythmic preferences correspond to the two- and three-part structures and cycles of the natural world, so most harmonic preferences reflect the simple vibrational ratios at the bottom of the overtone series. And just as rhythmic syncopation can heighten musical interest and excitement, the use of dissonance can enhance the experience of consonance. Whether such practices are explicitly codified or subjectively developed, the agreeable feelings generated by singing and playing instruments in simultaneous intervals are a fundamental part of making music in many parts of the world. And, consciously or not, harmony enacts a powerful ideal of social consonance: voices combined in musical concord replicate the dynamic relationships of individuals in a harmonious society.

STUDY QUESTIONS

1. What intervals sound consonant to most people? Why?

2. What is organum? How did it develop?

3. How did Western harmonic practices develop in the Renaissance and Baroque eras?

4. How has Western harmony influenced other traditions?

5. How do these non-Western harmonic practices compare to the Western system?

   — Bosnian ganga

   — Zimbabwean mbira

REFERENCED SOURCES

1. *The New Oxford History of Music*, Vol. II: 272.
2. Weiss and Taruskin, eds. 1984: 60.
3. Robertson and Stevens, eds. 1960: 246–7.
4. Reese, 1940: 253.
5. Weiss and Taruskin, eds. 1984: 62.
6. Ibid.: 66–7.
7. Ibid.: 81–2
8. Reese, 1959: 449.
9. Translated as Zarlino, 1968: 53–4.
10. Weiss and Taruskin, eds. 1984: 171–2.
11. Ibid.: 172–3.
12. Kaeppler, 1980: 136.
13. Levin, 1996: 236.
14. Lausevic, interview 1997.
15. Levin 1996: 231, 233.
16. Berliner, 1981: 57.
17. Ibid.: 53.
18. Brown, interview 1997

CHAPTER 10

FORM: THE SHAPE OF MUSIC

About This Chapter

How does a composer or an improviser hold an audience's attention over an extended period of time? What gives a piece or a performance a sense of wholeness, coherence, or unity? In this chapter we explore musical form, the component of music that specifically refers to how it is structured and shaped over time. Form refers to the organization of all the musical elements in a piece or performance, including rhythm, melody, dynamics, texture, and timbre, and how they are held together. In every culture, music is governed by rules that lay out standardized shapes and arrangements which occur in performance. The creativity of composers and performers is reflected in how they manipulate these standardized structures to manifest their own individual expression.

KEYWORDS

alap
binary form
gat
genre
jhala
jor
sonata
sonata form
tan
ternary form

COMPANION RESOURCES

TELEVISION PROGRAM: Form: The Shape of Music

AUDIO SELECTIONS:

52. "The Plains of Boyle"
53. "Hé Mandu" Waulking song from Scotland
54. "Lay Down Body"
55. "Pure Religion"
17. "The Comet"
14. Beethoven's Symphony No. 5 in C minor, First Movement
56. "Penitentiary Blues"
57. "Woman Blues"
58. "Rag Kamod"

The expressive arts can be divided into those that can be perceived in a moment and those that unfold over time. We can view a painting or sculpture and see the entire work in a matter of seconds. Music, dance, and theater, on the other hand, develop before us. These arts create an experience that is comparable to a journey that takes place over time. The structure of the journey—how it moves from beginning to end—can be described as its form.

While we might think of melody and rhythm as the basic building blocks of music, form may be viewed as the architecture of music. According to Gage Averill, musical form refers to the total organization of all individual parts:

> *When we talk about form, we're talking about the shape that a piece or performance of music takes from beginning to end. Included in this is a notion that a piece has a beginning, an end, and some kind of way of dividing the piece or structuring the piece from moment to moment. Human beings are pattern seeking creatures and we want to understand a larger unit as being made up of smaller units.*[1]

In a general sense, form refers to the organization of all the musical elements in a piece or performance, including rhythm, melody, dynamics, texture, and timbre, and how they are held together. We can look at the overall structure of an entire symphony, the form of its individual movements, and the smaller constructions that make up each movement. Mary Jo Pagano suggests that a composition's overall form is similar to an architect's plan for an entire building:

> *The form is like a blueprint in the same way that an architect might decide whether he's going to make a skyscraper or whether he's going to make a little log cabin. They're different blueprints.*[2]

The smaller or inner forms can be thought of as the rooms of the building—individual movements or sections that make up the whole. In a song with many verses, for example, we can look at the form in its entirety or the makeup of one stanza with music and text.

In every culture, music is governed by rules that lay out standardized shapes and arrangements which occur in performance. The creativity of composers and performers is reflected in how they manipulate these standardized structures to manifest their own individual expression. They work within genres—a term that refers to general types, categories, and styles of music, such as reggae, alternative rock, Bosnian ganga, and opera—of which form is an integral part. A genre includes the preferred timbres, textures, texts, as well as forms used, while form itself just indicates the structure of a performed entity. A given form may actually be common to many genres, as we will see later with call-and-response and the blues.

Musical forms may be entirely predetermined and predictable, or they may be malleable in various ways. Fiddle tunes in the Anglo-Irish tradition, for example, fall into the former category. They are a closed form, meaning that they are composed pieces of set length. Most tunes are divided into two sections that are each eight measures long. Many other kinds of compositions have general sections, but the length of these may vary widely from one piece to the next. Sonata form, a recipe for composition developed in Europe during the nineteenth century, is one such example. The three sections—exposition, development, and recapitulation—are governed by certain rules, but the content, instrumentation, and length of each section was left up to the individual composer.

Other forms are even more open-ended: the general structure is predetermined, but what happens in performance is not. As will be shown below, the twelve bar blues is a good example of a song form that is expanded in performance. Each verse has a chord progression of fixed length that is repeated over and over again, but the number of times that the pattern is repeated is not usually planned. A single blues tune may be played for five minutes or for thirty minutes depending on the inspiration of the performers. The form—built from the consecutive repetition of the chord progression—serves as the springboard for the performers' improvisations.

North Indian classical music performances provide an even more flexible example of form, in which rules determine the relative order of events, but not the length or most of the musical content. The ways in which a performer introduces, expands, and develops a short pre-composed composition in a certain raga are both dictated by tradition and completely individual. The overall structure is preordained, but the details are flexible.

Some forms involve even less overall delineation: rather than presenting a fixed chain of events, however general, they furnish a pool of possibilities. These open forms necessarily involve improvisation, as one or more musicians make spontaneous decisions in performance. Much of African music involves open forms. In group performances, one musician is often the decision-maker who signals the other musicians to move from one section to another. This kind of spontaneous composition is generative: musicians have a stock of musical material that they can put together differently in each performance.

Beginnings and Endings

While forms vary significantly from culture to culture or within one culture, all music contains a beginning, ending, and the musical events that occur in between. In many cultures, the structural framework of a piece or performance includes a distinctive beginning and ending. David Reck describes the importance of these opening and closing sections:

> Beginnings are, after all, the first things we hear in a musical performance or a piece; they grab us by the scruff of the neck or gradually, subtly, pull us into the magical happenings of sounds. Endings are what we are left with, a last (and maybe lasting) impression. Together, they are the extremities of a musical island in a sea of time.[3]

As discussed later in the chapter, North Indian classical music performances characteristically begin with a slow opening section called "alap" in which the performer outlines the pitches and mood of the raga. In Javanese gamelan, a short introductory phrase called the "buka" played on one instrument formally begins the composition. In Western classical music, there are many examples of introductions and preludes that range in length from a few bars of music to a whole movement.

In many cultures, formulaic patterns or sequences signal the end of a section or performance. In Western classical and popular music, these patterns are called *cadences*. Cadences are composed of chords that move toward resolution and which evoke a sense of conclusiveness. As shown in the previous chapter, this resolution, signified by the return to the tonal center, is most often achieved by the sequence moving from the V (dominant) chord to the I (tonic) chord.

In the music of North India, a "tihai" (a melodic sequence repeated three times) often marks the conclusion to a performance. Expanded endings can also be used to form a complete section, such as the codas found in Western classical music genres. A coda, meaning literally "tail" in Italian, can be either a concluding passage or section of a composition that is added to augment or heighten the sense of finality.

Other conventions are also used as ending devices. In many cultures, a slowing down of the tempo indicates the conclusion of a piece. In Javanese gamelan compositions, for example, all the instrumentalists slow down together, pause as the final gong strikes, and then come in together to play the last note. In many kinds of popular music, performers commonly end by repeating the last line of a song over and over again as they gradually fade out.

Repetition, Contrast, and Sections

While musical beginnings and endings are important cornerstones of composition or performance, equally important are the events that move and develop the music from start to finish. How does a composer or an improviser hold her audience's attention over an extended period of time? What gives a piece or a performance a sense of wholeness, coherence, or unity? In many musical traditions, the techniques used employ varying degrees of repetition and contrast. Repetition jogs the memory of the listener and helps to establish guideposts throughout the performance, while contrast creates interest and anticipation.

Repetition can take place on many levels, ranging from the restatement of a single motif, theme, passage, or rhythmic pattern, to the recapitulation of whole sections. The use of repetition as a structuring device differs from culture to culture. In many African drumming traditions, for example, interlocking percussion patterns are played over and over again in performance. In the Anglo-Celtic ballad tradition, the music stays the same from verse to verse while the text changes in order to tell a story; repetition also occurs in the metrical and rhyming scheme of each line of a single verse. Japanese traditional music, described by Tomie Hahn, on the other hand, is often structured like a narrative, moving from beginning to end with little large scale repetition:

> *Form in Japanese music is based primarily on narrative, where the narrative actually takes you through the piece rather than the repetition of a melody. This really greatly contrasts with Western music or other styles of music around the world where the statement of a melody which comes back again and again is integrated throughout a piece. In Japanese music it is actually quite unusual to have the exact repetition of a melody. I think this is really quite close to the way social life is in Japan where it would be very offensive to say the same thing again and again to one person . . . So this [technique of musical composition] somewhat mirrors speech in Japanese social life.[4]*

The use of contrast also occurs on many levels in composition and performance. While much of the classical music in eighteenth- and nineteenth-century Europe and America relied on structural principles balancing repetition and contrast in order to produce symmetry and unity, twentieth century composers have refused to be bound by the same aesthetic and analytical principles. Some have rejected the notion of form as a pre-planned structure. Chance music—a compositional technique developed in the 1950s in which certain elements of a piece were left up to chance in performance—is just one method of composition that often develops more through contrast than repetition. According to composer George Perle, "varieties of programmed chaos have been a regular part of the avante-garde scene for a long time."

In talking about form, we tend to look at the larger structures in a composition or performance—the overall plan and the pieces that are used to put it together. In this function, the term often indicates discrete sections that can be expressed by the use of letters. For example, music in a two-part structure—defined as binary form—is made up of an A section and a B section. Music in a three-part form in which the first and third sections are identical (ternary form) is built on a pattern of A B A. If one main theme or section alternates with different themes or sections, the resultant form can be labeled as A B A C A D A, etc. While this terminology arises from European and American usage, it can be used as a model to discuss music from many traditions.

Binary form is perhaps the most common of musical structures found in many diverse cultures all over the world. In Irish traditional dance music, for example, most of the tunes have a two part or A B structure. As stated above, the two sections are the same length—eight measures long—and each is usually repeated. The resultant form in performance becomes A A B B—the A section is played twice followed by the B section played twice. The entire tune is then repeated again in exactly the same format. Musicians may repeat the tune as many times as they want, although typically, tunes are played through three or four times, at which point the musicians may switch to another tune.

In many song traditions, a standardized pattern of musical lines and lyrics make up a verse or A section. Some song forms, including many that are found in the Anglo-American tradition, have only one section. Examples include Christmas carols such as "Silent Night" or "Joy to the World." Other songs have a B section that functions as a chorus. While the lyrics change for each repetition of the A section, the words for the B section stay the same. This binary form is often called verse/chorus. A well known song in verse/chorus form is "Jingle Bells."

In the following section, we explore another binary form that is found in many cultures around the world. Call and response is both a structure and a way of performing. It balances the individuality of one performer with the collective unity of a group. In the remainder of the chapter we will discuss form in Western classical music, the blues, and in the classical music of North India.

When listening to the hornpipe "The Plains of Boyle" played by Jerry O'Sullivan, Brian Conway, and Pat Kilbride, you can hear how the regularity of the phrases makes it easy to follow the changes and repeats. Each section is made up of two phrases of four measures. Note the high degree of repetition that occurs because of the repetition of section and the repetition of the whole tune. Because the music is traditionally linked to dance, this regularity of phrase and section is essential in keeping the dancers on track and in time.

CALL AND RESPONSE

Call-and-response form replicates social interaction, structuring music as a kind of stylized conversation. Sometimes this dialogue is a literal question-and-answer format in song: "Ain't that a groove?" James Brown repeatedly sings in his 1960s hit of the same title. "It's so groovy!" the chorus of female backup singers enthusiastically replies. "Do you love me?" he reiterates towards the song's end, his voice rising in pitch and intensity. "Yes, I love you!" the women faithfully assure him each time.

Sometimes the form involves imitation. For example, Native North American stomp dances are often structured around an improvising leader who sings short rhythmic phrases which are repeated immediately by the dancers (**Example 1**). A call-and-response "conversation" may be abstract, as in the alternation of vocables in Example 1; it can be playful, like the refrain of "Ain't That a Groove," and it can be an intrinsic part of spiritual expression, as in many religious practices throughout the world. What unites all these examples is the basic two-part form: a "call" which presents a musical and/or verbal idea, and a "response" which replies to the call.

EXAMPLE 1: CHEROKEE STOMP DANCE LED BY LUMAN WILDCAT (EXCERPT)

Occasionally call-and-response form can be heard in a solo performance. Blues musicians often alternate sung lines with melodic phrases played on their instrument, creating a sense of two voices: one which sings the song, and another which continuously comments on or compliments it. Some solo songs are structured as dialogues, like the classic Scottish ballad "Lord Randall," in which the first half of each verse presents the questions of a dying young man's mother, and each second half furnishes his replies. But for the most part the inherent reciprocal nature of call and response is embodied by the interaction of two or more participants. Often the call is performed by a soloist who may be improvising to some extent, and the response is performed by a group. A few examples will give a general sense of the many approaches to and functions of this ubiquitous musical structure.

Work Songs

Group work songs are often cast in call-and-response form. In such cases the overall rhythm provides the proper pace for the job at hand. The leader—usually chosen for a spirited voice and perhaps an ability to improvise—spurs the work along and keeps the workers' motions synchronized. The group's participation eases the monotony of their tedious and tiring task and often gives them more strength, power, and focus to get the job done.

Sea shanties, work songs sung by sailors in earlier times, were often in call-and-response form: the workers could pause for breath as the "shanty-man" sang a line, and then they would bellow their choral response while hauling the halyards or pushing the capstan. In such cases the leader did not participate in the manual task: his work was to sing strongly, sustaining the men's morale with boasts about their ship and crew, jokes about others, and references to the pleasures they would seek out when the ship reached land.

A performance of this waulking song.

Example 2 shows the basic repeating form of a women's work song from the Hebrides Islands off the western coast of Scotland. This is one of many songs used for "waulking": a communal process of beating newly-woven woolen cloth on a table to make it denser, a necessary practice for these cold, windswept islands. As the women pound the cloth rhythmically, this song—each verse a few lines of text framed by vocables—allows them to imagine flying away to an idealized castle and lover (**Example 3**).

EXAMPLE 2: "HÉ MANDU" SUNG BY MRS. KATE MacLEOD AND CHORUS (1ST VERSE)

EXAMPLE 3: "HÉ MANDU" FULL TEXT

verse 1:

<u>group</u>:	Hé mandu	(vocables)
<u>solo</u>:	'S truagh nach digeadh	Alas, that this does not
<u>group</u>:	hé mandu	(vocables)
<u>solo</u>:	siod 'gham iarraidh	come to fetch me:
<u>group</u>:	hé mandu	(vocables)
<u>solo</u>:	gille 's litir	a messenger and a letter,
<u>group</u>:	hì ri oro	(vocables)
	each is diollaid	a horse and a saddle
	hé mandu hì ri oro hó ró hù ó	(vocables)

following verses:

If I had the sparrow's wing,

the bird's' power of flight, the wild duck's foot,

I would swim across the narrows,

the Sound of Islay, the Sound of Orkney.

I would go into the castle

and I would bring my sweetheart out;

I would not ask whose she was.

My Donald was well-reared—

not on green pond water

but on the milk of brown-haired women.

Religious Usages

As call and response can unify spirits and hands in work, so it can also unify hearts and souls in worship. Sometimes such moments are built into key parts of a ritual: "Lift up your hearts," the celebrant sings or speaks in some versions of the Christian liturgy. "We lift them up unto the Lord," the congregation responds. "Let us give thanks unto the Lord our God," the celebrant continues. "It is meet and right so to do" the group confirms. In such cases the soloist embodies spiritual leadership, and the responding group articulates communal affirmation. In other cases the soloist may act more like a prompter, as in the practice of "lining out" hymns and psalms which survives today in parts of Europe and America: a soloist sings each line first, and then the congregation repeats the line all together. Or a soloist might present a narrative of a religious experience, while the recurring group response personifies support and encouragement, as in the next example.

African-American religious music has always involved call-and-response form, from the ring shouts dating from the slavery era to the gospel music of today. In a ring shout, the caller, or "songster," sits beside the "sticker," who rhythmically beats the floor with a broom handle. Standing behind them, the "basers" provide polyrhythmic handclapping and vocal responses. The "shouters" also respond, as they move in a counter-clockwise ring with shuffling steps. This tradition has been documented since the slavery era, and has survived despite numerous historical attempts to purge southern Black

churches of what some people considered an inappropriate form of worship. In fact, the ring shout derives from African practices rather than European ones, which is probably what upset the reformers.

Example 4 shows the basic repeating pattern for a traditional ring shout which survives in some African-American communities on the sea islands off the coast of South Carolina and Georgia. After a brief introduction the pattern is established: the leader improvises his calls with traditional lines depicting a peaceful death ("you ought to lay down body, get your rest") and a mighty resurrection on judgment day ("tombstone's moving, grave is a-birthing, soul is rising"). Matching the story, the unchanging response and rhythm intensify, in a powerful celebration of the soul's victory (**Example 5**).

A performance of this ring shout.

EXAMPLE 4: "LAY DOWN BODY" SUNG BY THE McINTOSH COUNTY SHOUTERS (EXCERPT)

EXAMPLE 5: "LAY DOWN BODY" FULL TEXT

Introduction:	Lay down body, lay down a little while
Songster's lines:	This old body, oh, is tired
	Lay down body, this old body
	Old soul and body is so tired
	Old soul and body need resting
	You oughta lay down body, get your rest
	You don't worry, lay down body
	Lay down body, you don't worry
	My Lord'll wake you, oh, when He calls
	Soul and body
	Tombstone's moving, grave is a-bursting
	Soul is rising, oh body, weary body
	You'll be happy, a happy end
	Sing oh hallelujah
	You'll be happy, problems be over
	My problems over, my problems over
	I made it home, I made it home
	I made it home at last (etc.)

Musical "Conversations"

Throughout the world, many musical genres involve some version of call-and-response form. While some examples involve the alternation of a soloist with an essentially unchanging group part, call and response is also used as a technique within composition or improvisation to suggest dialogue—a musical conversation. Such musical interactions can be partially or entirely verbal, or they can be completely non-verbal.

As noted earlier, some songs are dialogues set to music, and opera—Western and non-Western—abounds with examples of pre-composed musical conversations. Improvised verbal musical conversations are rarer, but they can be found. For example, when competing rappers perform contemporary versions of "the dozens," their spontaneous rhymed insults are addressed to each other. In parts of Africa, the rhythms and relative pitches of local tone languages can be replicated on instruments, producing "speech" which can be understood by cultural insiders; in such cases, interplay between such instruments—or between instruments and human voices—can result in a fully verbal musical interchange. The African ethnomusicologist and musician Francis Bebey cited an example from Gabon in which a xylophone "converses" with young female dancers.[5]

Xylophone:	Hey there, girls!
Dancers:	Yes!
Xylophone:	Where are you from?
Dancers:	We are from Endoumsang, from Nseme Nzimi's family. You can tell from his eyes that he is sad and would be capable of dying from hunger right next to a pile of sugar cane.
Xylophone:	Aha?
Dancers:	Aha!
Xylophone:	A poor country . . . ?
Dancers:	Is one where a man must rely on his flocks to live.
Xylophone:	The sin of adultery . . . ?
Dancers:	You forgive your brother if he steals from you, don't you?
Xylophone:	Cocoa leaves . . . ?
Dancers:	I made a mat from some this evening.
Xylophone:	An evil place . . . ?
Dancers:	Is where you never meet the man you love.
Xylophone:	Spinster's letters . . . ?
Dancers:	Never mention men.
Xylophone:	Aha?
Dancers:	Aha!

Reverend Gary Davis's guitar sometimes finishes phrases for him, "sings" a phrase while he speaks it, and, prompted by his command "talk to me," responds with an energetic musical affirmation of the need to "have that pure religion" before you can cross the river Jordan into heaven. Yet another level of "conversation" occurs in each of the song's verses, with Davis accosting a sinner—"Where you goin' old liar?"—and speaking the sinner's response: "Goin' to tell some lies."

Sometimes musical "conversations" are only partially verbal, involving a singer and an instrument which may replicate speech or song, or which is played in a way that produces abstract responses to the singer's words. Such practices were common in early jazz bands: as the singer took a breath between phrases, one or more instruments filled the intervening beats with short improvised lines which often bore a direct relationship to what was just sung. Some solo performers create this kind of call-and-response "conversation" between their voices and their own accompanying instruments.

Musical call and response can also be entirely non-verbal. One concrete example is pre-arranged signaling—such as when the lead drummer in an African ensemble plays a rhythmic phrase which means "switch to the next section"—but some other examples are more abstract, suggesting a real non-verbal conversation between two or more musicians. Jazz is a music built for this kind of interaction: a fully-engaged jazz musician is listening to every other musician who is playing at the moment, and all of the improvisations—solo or backup—affect each other. The American pianist Tommy Flanagan described this phenomenon in piano duo recordings he has made:

> You don't know what the other player is going to play, but on listening to the playback, almost every time, you hear that you related your part very quickly to what the other player played just before you. It's like a message that you relay back and forth. . . . Or, if we're switching off every eight bars, there will be something in my eight bars that's related to the last part of the soloist before me. . . . You want to achieve that kind of communication when you play. When you do, your playing seems to be making sense. It's like a conversation.[6]

Such unrehearsed interactions may be heightened by the musicians' reactions to unexpected occurrences. The American ethnomusicologist and musician Paul Berliner describes such an occasion: "Once when Benny Bailey finished a solo a few measures early at a performance at the Jazz Showcase, pianist Jodie Christian spontaneously filled in the progression with a melodic phrase comprising a series of large, descending intervals, which saxophonist Jackie McLean immediately seized for the opening of his own solo."[7]

This is call and response at its most minute and extemporaneous level, as improvising musicians react to each other with split-second timing, creating a moment of collective composition. The example pushes the boundaries of the form a bit—the "call" in this case was simply an unexpectedly early ending to a solo, and the pianist's fill-in could be described as a response that the saxophonist treated like a call by responding to it—but we can see that it is built on the same basic principles as the more straightforward examples we have looked at. Whether in work, worship, or pleasure, call-and-response form can unify and synchronize minds, hearts, and voices in powerful idealizations of human interactions.

FORM IN WESTERN CLASSICAL MUSIC

There are many kinds of form in Western classical music, but as violinist Timothy Ying states, the music is most often organized around the idea of "things repeating and things developing":

> Essentially they all take the same tack that something has to happen over time, and you have various things that will come back and repeat. And those repetitions are signals for your ear, they are the sign points for structure. So whether it's a sonata form, whether it's a binary or ternary form, these aural sign points are what indicate to you when the various sections occur. . . . It's a constant conflict between repeating something that you know and changing it—what's the same and what's different.[8]

TIMOTHY YING

As stated earlier in this chapter, form can be analyzed on different levels ranging from the structure of an entire work to the form of one verse. In this discussion of form, we will examine form as a mold or recipe which composers use to shape their compositions.

Binary Form

Binary form is also used to structure compositions in the Western classical tradition. Many instrumental pieces from the Renaissance and Baroque periods, for example, are composed as dance forms that fall into a two part structure. The pavane, galliard, minuet, sarabande, gavotte, gigue, and contredanse were popular dances that provided models for composition. Some of these pieces were used for dancing while many others were meant only for listening. Like Irish traditional dance music, these compositions often have repeated A and B sections usually of the same length that can be abbreviated as:

l: A :l l: B :l in which everything between the l: :l signs is repeated.

While the form is actually A A B B in performance, it is also called binary form.

The dance suite became a popular genre in the Baroque period (1600–1750). Suites were written for many of the orchestral and chamber ensembles of the period, as well as for solo harpsichord and lute. Each suite had at least several movements, each in binary form and based on a particular dance. Composers used the standardized dance forms of the period to write stylized music that was essentially for listening. Each dance in the suite was distinguished by its meter, special rhythms, and tempo. The sarabande, for example, was a slow dance in 3/4 that often had a marked accent or emphasis on the second beat of the measure; the gavotte was characterized by a long upbeat of two quarter notes and performed at a moderate tempo.

Although the order of the dances was left up to the individual composer, the general method was to place dances with contrasting rhythms and tempos next to each other—a slow stately sarabande would be followed by a sprightly bourée. Many suites ended with gigues, a fast and lively dance thought to have derived from the Irish jig. Other dance forms included the allemande, courante, minuet, and siciliana.

The Baroque trio sonata and solo sonata were two other multi-movement genres in which binary form was used. Trio sonatas were actually written for four instruments: two upper range melody instruments such as violin, flute, or oboe, one bass instrument, and harpsichord. The solo sonatas were usually performed with three instrumentalists: a solo melody instrument with continuo accompaniment from harpsichord and cello or bassoon. Johann Sebastian Bach wrote some sonatas meant to be performed by one instrument—beautiful compositions for solo cello, violin, and flute.

Like the dance suites, many of the movements of the trio sonata or solo sonata were modelled on dances in binary form. Other sonatas had several contrasting movements that were designated by their tempi; a common plan was slow—fast—slow—fast. Georg Phillipp Telemann, Bach, and George Frideric Handel were Baroque composers who wrote many sonatas and trio sonatas for various combinations of the popular instruments of the day, including the recorder, flute, violin, oboe, bassoon, and cello.

Ternary Form

As discussed earlier, ternary form refers to music in a three part structure that follows a pattern of A B A. The A sections contain exactly the same music while the B section contains contrasting material. There are many examples of ternary form in both the classical and popular repertoires. "Twinkle Twinkle Little Star" is an example of a song in ternary form.

The thirty-two bar song form is found in nearly all songs derived from Western European musical traditions, including art songs, folk songs, jazz tunes, and rock. In performance, the thirty-two bars are derived from four eight measure sections—A A B A. Musicians play the A section twice, the B section—called the bridge in popular music—once, and then go back to the A section again. This pattern of A A B A lays out the framework for the song.

In "The Comet," the thirty-two bar pattern is repeated over and over again as the musicians improvise within the set structure of the form. The rhythm, chord structure, and the length of the song keep the musicians together as they take turns improvising.

Sonata Form

Sonata form—also known as sonata-allegro form and not to be confused with a sonata—is one of the most important forms of the Classical and Romantic periods and remains in use today. It was developed in the eighteenth century and used by many composers, including Haydn, Mozart and Beethoven. The form was often employed as the first movement of a long work, such as a symphony, sonata, concerto, piano trio, or string quartet. Like ternary form, sonata form falls into three sections, called the *exposition, development,* and *recapitulation,* but in this case, the recapitulation is not an exact repeat of the exposition.

Sonata form is a recipe or mold and a method of composition that composers employ. While the overall structure is subject to clearly articulated rules and procedures, the musical content is left completely up to the individual composer. In sonata form, each section plays a different function in developing the piece:

> *There is a progression of events that happen. So just like in a novel you've got a structure, some kind of conflict, and then the conflict escalates. And finally you reach a crisis point, and then there's some kind of resolution. We all feel great after the resolution.*[9]

In the exposition section, the composer introduces or "exposes" the most important musical material in the form of themes and motives. Expositions must have at least one theme presented in the tonic key. Every exposition then has a change of key or modulation in which a new theme or themes may be introduced. The most common modulation is to the dominant. The exposition is often repeated in performance.

In the development section, composers get to develop the ideas from the exposition, and as Mary Jo Pagano states, it's the development section that allows composers to be creative:

> *The development section is probably one of the reasons why composers really favor this form because it gives them a chance to explore tonal possibilities. . . . It's a way of trying on different coats so to speak. Sometimes a composer will take themes—it can be the first theme, the second theme, or parts of that theme, and explore them and develop them, turn them upside-down, put them in different*

keys, develop the ideas. At the end of the exposition becomes a point of great tension. Right after that tension we resolve to the recapitulation.[10]

The recapitulation begins with a return of the first theme in the original key, a return home after the journey through the development section. The recapitulation is literally a "recap," a restatement of musical material from the exposition. This section resolves the tension of the development section. A coda may occur at the end of the recapitulation.

The above examples demonstrate only a few of the many musical forms found in the Western classical idiom. We will now examine form in an important popular American genre known as the blues.

▬ TWELVE-BAR BLUES

Sometimes a musical form seems to take on a life of its own, well beyond the time and place in which it originated. From its beginnings among poor African-Americans in the southern United States around the late nineteenth-century, twelve-bar blues form has spread to just about every corner of the earth where guitars are played. It has served as the foundation for tender love songs, searing rock anthems, defiant social protests, and advertising jingles. Teenagers have danced to it in urban parks in Tokyo, adults have cherished it in rural road houses, and stockbrokers have sipped martinis to it in posh nightclubs. The visionary electric guitarist Jimi Hendrix learned his instrument by playing it, and Elvis Presley, the Beatles, and the Rolling Stones all began their careers with it. It is vigorous today, with a good number of thriving blues clubs, dedicated performers, and a loyal audience.

Like most song forms, twelve-bar blues is strophic: it is made up of stanzas (or verses), and each stanza uses the same overall musical structure. Musicians define this particular form by referring to its repeating stanzaic structure of twelve bars. A bar (or measure) of music is a steady grouping of beats; each of the twelve bars of this form is a group of four beats. These bars are further grouped into three phrases of four bars each.

The basic harmonic structure of the form is shown in **Figure 1**: the first phrase remains with the I chord (perhaps briefly going to the IV chord in the second bar); the second phrase begins with a strong statement of the IV chord, then returns to I for its second half; and the V chord marks the beginning of the third phrase, which characteristically moves to the IV chord before resolving to I for its second half. Often musicians finish the cycle with a reference to the dominant V chord to emphasize the return to I at the start of the next cycle (or at the resolution at the end of the song). There are a few other blues harmonic patterns, and a larger number which might be called "bluesy," but this twelve-bar form is by far the most widely-used structure in blues.

Blues lyrics are usually couplets, two lines which rhyme and form a complete sentence. These couplets can fit into the twelve-bar form in various ways, but the most common is what is called AA'B verse form. In this form, the first line of the couplet (A) is sung during the cycle's first phrase and is repeated with musical variation (A') in the second phrase; the third phrase carries the second line of the couplet (B).

Beethoven's Symphony No. 5 in C minor, first movement, provides a good example of sonata form. *[Additional listening information is at the end of the chapter.]*

"Penitentiary Blues" is a twelve-bar blues with an AA'B verse structure. For the last verse Hopkins uses a formal device known as "stop time": the beginning of the cycle is interrupted for his conversation with his mother and father, while his guitar punctuates the exchange with a single repeated motif; then the cycle resumes as the guitar plays the IV chord. Although the result is a verse with more than twelve bars, musicians think of this practice as a modification of the standard twelve-bar form: "stop time" literally means briefly stopping the cycle and then resuming it.

FIGURE 1: 12-BAR BLUES HARMONIC STRUCTURE

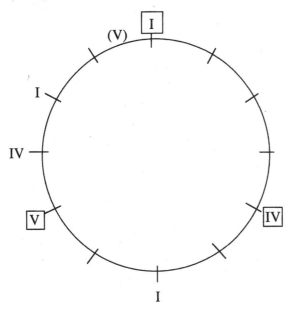

The full story of blues is also the story of African-Americans in the twentieth century. It encompasses all of the rural and urban troubles and migrations, and the hope, despair, anger, and pleasure of thousands of individuals. Our brief introduction to this story begins shortly after the turn of the century, in a place that was still reeling from the effects of a slavery era and a Civil War: the southern United States.

Early Blues

Although W. C. Handy referred to himself as "The Father of the Blues," he was not the form's originator—he was one of the first people to make a comfortable living with it. Handy himself told a story of his chance meeting with blues, "the weirdest music I had ever heard," in a Mississippi train station in 1903. Gertrude "Ma" Rainey, another popular entertainer who was sometimes billed as "The Mother of the Blues," recalled her first encounter with blues in a small town in Missouri around 1902, describing the sound as "strange and poignant."

Such references make it clear that blues singing was already widespread in the southern United States well before the first blues recordings were made in the early 1920s. By that time blues songs and instrumentals—mostly using the twelve-bar pattern—could be found in at least two distinct types, which might be referred to as "vaudeville" and "downhome."[11] Since many vaudeville performers, including Handy and Rainey, first heard blues from downhome musicians, it makes sense to begin by investigating this rural style.

BESSIE SMITH

Source: Courtesy Library of Congress.

Downhome Blues

Slavery had been abolished in 1863, but in the early twentieth century blacks in the southern United States were still kept at the bottom of society. The tenant farming system enforced poverty and debt, "Jim Crow" laws locked in segregation, blacks had no legal rights, and they were regularly harassed by police and other whites. For most, there was no escape from a system which required hard labor from dawn to dusk all week excepting Sundays. Saturday night was a time of celebration: barbecues, conviviality, and "juke joints," black-operated shacks where one might find homemade whiskey, fried fish, gambling, music (often blues), and dancing.

Sunday mornings were for church services, which also featured music, but of a different kind. Still, although many preachers condemned blues as "the Devil's music," both the juke joint and the church involved ceremonies of renewal and symbols of group bonding. Their ritual leaders—preacher and blues singer—even used similar rhetorical conventions. And through their different worldviews, both institutions taught the same basic message: "treat people right."[12]

Many of the earliest downhome blues recordings from this period must be understood as truncated improvisations rather than as through-composed "pieces." 78 rpm technology required a break in the music every two or three minutes, when the recording disk ran out of space. Sometimes blues songs were issued on two sides of a record, labeled "Part 1" and "Part 2," but usually the musicians just recorded a two-to-three minute version of each song. In their natural contexts, these songs could be performances lasting a half hour or more: a musician with a strong ability to improvise verbally and instrumentally could keep a song going as long as his or her imagination held out without becoming repetitive, pleasing both dancers and listeners.

As Jeff Titon has demonstrated, a song's identity usually involved a basic melody and accompaniment, though these could be quite flexible, and a "foundation stanza" which gave the song its title and general subject. Linked to this in the singer's mind were one or more "supporting" stanzas, which directly related to the theme, and perhaps the imagery, of the foundation stanza. Finally, the singer knew and could call forth spontaneously a large number of "unlinked" stanzas, which may have little or no direct relevance to the subject of the foundation stanza, but which fit in well with the melody, rhythm, and character of the song.[13]

For example, Charley Patton's 1929 recording of "Pony Blues" (**Example 6**) begins with the foundation stanza, establishing the song's title, theme, and imagery. In local slang at that time, a "rider" was a lover; elaboration of the horse/rider metaphor is a hallmark of this song's lyrics, and it is also expressed musically as Patton imitates the clopping of horse's hooves on his guitar. The second stanza is unlinked: its humorous portrayal of someone trying to make a phone call may well just function here as a good vehicle for singing a higher melody which Patton alternates with the tune of the preceding stanza. A supporting stanza follows, presenting a further development of the horse/rider imagery. The next three stanzas are less directly supportive, though they deal with themes in love relationships: first an ironic expression of preference for women of mixed race (Patton was comparatively light-skinned himself), then a starkly contrasting depiction of a heartbreaking moment of farewell, and finally a supremely nonchalant parting shot.

Charley Patton performed at juke joints and parties in the Mississippi Delta region, an area rich in both fertile farmland and blues. From contemporary accounts, we know that he was a consummate improviser, able to stretch a song well beyond the three-minute recording limit. He recorded "Pony Blues" around the beginning of his recording career, and it appears from his use of unlinked and semi-supporting stanzas that he was improvising to a certain extent. By the next year, when he recorded some of his most powerful songs, he clearly had begun to form his songs more consciously into three-minute compositions when recording them.

EXAMPLE 6: "PONY BLUES" TEXT

> Hitch up my pony, saddle up my black mare
> Hitch up my pony, saddle up my black mare
> I'm goin' find a rider, baby in the world somewhere
>
> Hello central, 'tsa matter with your line
> Hello central, matter now with your line
> Come a storm last night, tore the wires down
>
> Bought a brand new Shetland, man already trained
> Brand new Shetland, baby already trained
> If you get in the saddle, tighten up on your rein
>
> And a brownskin woman like somethin' fit to eat
> Brownskin woman like somethin' fit to eat
> But a jet black woman, don't put your hand on me
>
> Took my baby to meet the mornin' train
> Took my baby, meet that mornin' train
> And the blues come down, baby like showers of rain
>
> I got somethin' to tell you when I gets a chance
> Somethin' to tell you when I get a chance
> I don't want to marry, just want to be your man

Vaudeville and Jazz Blues

Vaudeville singers used many different song forms, but blues were often featured, largely because blues records were selling particularly well at the time. Vaudeville blues were usually in twelve-bar form with AA'B stanzas, involving call and response between a solo female singer and one or more male instrumentalists. The words were seldom improvised, so the observations above about downhome blues stanza relationships do not apply here, except as possible elements of the creative processes of vaudeville songwriters.

A concurrent New Orleans-based African-American genre which had ties to the vaudeville style, and eventually replaced it, became known as jazz. Jazz instrumentalists often used twelve-bar blues form as a basis for improvising, and for structuring songs and instrumental compositions.

Later Developments

At the time of the first recordings some general blues performance styles had already developed. Vaudeville and jazz musicians toured extensively, further spreading their styles across the country. By comparison, downhome styles

"Woman Blues," recorded in 1944, demonstrates how a creative musician can use the twelve-bar form to create an elaborate improvisation with playfully shifting moods.

remained more local and less commercially successful. But in the early 1940s more and more southern blacks were migrating to northern industrial centers, looking for better work and a better life. In response to these new environments—and, sometimes, new technologies—a new blues style began to take shape.

From Downhome to Uptown

One of these southern migrants was McKinley Morganfield, known to his friends as Muddy Waters, an outstanding young local musician who moved from the Mississippi Delta region to Chicago in 1943. He met other migrant musicians there (almost all working as laborers, like himself), and began performing with them on weekends. A new blues sound was developing in Chicago, influenced to some extent by jazz groups, and also by a technological development: the electric guitar.

Although some technological innovations—such as steel resonators and strings—had already increased the volume of the guitar, it was still an instrument that could not be combined successfully with louder instruments like the piano, trumpet, and drum set. With the advent of electric instruments, jazz guitarists could play in a full band—horns, piano, and all. Muddy Waters, with his subtle melodic guitar technique often augmented with a slide bar or "bottleneck," was among the first downhome-style musicians to exploit the electric guitar's ability to mix nuanced solo playing with other instruments.

Microphones and sound systems offered a similar potential for the voice, and these new possibilities fit perfectly with a popular attraction to the jazz "rhythm section"—the combination of piano, bass, and drums which provided a driving beat and solid harmonic basis. Among Waters and his colleagues, the "Chicago blues" style developed: a powerful group sound involving an electric guitar played melodically, a rhythm section (perhaps with a second electric guitar replacing or augmenting the piano's role), amplified voice, and perhaps an amplified harmonica as well.

The Chicago blues style spread across America, with hit records by Muddy Waters and others. When a new generation took it on in the late 1950s and early 1960s, a number of new branches developed, all using twelve-bar blues form to various extents: some brief, bland developments like the twist and surf music, and some longer-lived, more vital ones like rhythm & blues. Early rhythm & blues musicians such as Chuck Berry, Little Richard, and Jerry Lee Lewis used twelve-bar blues form extensively, often speeding it up to a feverish pace. Many of the "British invasion" groups of the early 1960s started out by imitating Chicago blues recordings, and several of the later "psychedelic" groups, such as the Grateful Dead and Hot Tuna, featured extended arrangements of twelve-bar blues songs.

Today the Chicago style and some of its offshoots are the mainstays of a widespread "blues revival." Though these styles are not often heard in the most commercially-oriented venues, they have devoted audiences in smaller institutions and festivals, and talented young musicians continue to fill the shoes of their elders.

Bebop and Cool Jazz

In the 1930s and 1940s blues was still essentially an African-American genre. By contrast, jazz was increasingly claimed by white audiences as "American" (that is, not necessarily black) music. "Big bands"—groups with carefully scored "swing" arrangements for multiple brass and reed instruments along with a rhythm section—played the popular music of the day, often with white leaders and singers, and white Broadway composers wrote hit songs which capitalized on jazz idioms.

To some young African-Americans in the early 1940s, mainstream jazz was a music that could no longer articulate their world, which was still one of social and economic marginalization. A subculture began to develop, with young black men wearing berets, goatees, and outrageously baggy "zoot suits," speaking "hip talk" with unique words and phrases, and playing a new form of jazz: *bebop*. Pioneered by the saxophonist Charlie Parker, the trumpeter Dizzy Gillespie, and others, bebop was both intellectual and visceral, serious and irreverent, meticulous and wild.

The mainstream jazz establishment was outraged, in some of the same ways that the popular-music establishment of the 1980s railed against rap music and the hip-hop subculture:

> *To a certain extent, this music resulted from conscious attempts to remove it from the danger of mainstream dilution or even understanding. For one thing, the young musicians began to think of themselves as serious musicians, even artists, and not performers. . . . This attitude certainly must have mystified the speak-easy-Charleston-Cotton-Club set of white Americans, who had identified jazz only with liberation from the social responsibilities of full citizenship. It also mystified many of the hobbyists, who were the self-styled arbiters of what Afro-American music should be. Most of the jazz critics and writers on jazz (almost all of whom, for obvious reasons, were white) descended on the new music with a fanatical fury. The young musicians were called "crazy" (which stuck in the new vernacular), "dishonest frauds," or in that slick, noble, patronizing tone that marks the liberal mind: "merely misguided."*[14]

Bebop was fast and virtuosic; most people couldn't figure out how to listen or dance to it. Like hip talk, it was full of unfamiliar idioms. But just as hip talk was based on the grammatical substructure of standard English speech, so bebop was built on the foundations of jazz: choruses and bridges, alternation of improvising soloists, and even common forms, including twelve-bar blues. Some admirable recorded examples of bebop versions of twelve-bar blues include Charlie Parker's "Billie's Bounce," "Bloomdido," and "Now's the Time."

At one point in his all-too-brief career, Parker hired a young trumpet player named Miles Davis to fill in for Gillespie. Davis proved equal to this daunting task, and went on to become one of the most prolific innovators in the history of jazz. Bass player Calvin Hill recalled that "in the old days when I used to buy records, I was always into Miles, whatever Miles came up with. Like, you could hardly wait for the newest Miles Davis record to come out because you knew he was going to come out with something different. You just couldn't wait. You'd go out and buy the record and rush home and put it on and see what was new."[15] In the 1950s "what was new" included a genre which came to be known as *cool jazz*.

While bebop emphasized vigorous dynamism and technical wizardry, cool jazz portrayed more finely-nuanced moods, elevating introspective thoughtfulness over dazzling displays of virtuosity. Like most innovations, it was not universally accepted right away. At first, one of the jazz musicians Berliner interviewed "'hated Miles Davis's cool jazz playing,' with its dark sound and minimal use of vibrato. Whenever a Davis record came on the radio, he turned it off immediately."[16] But this musician, and many others, were soon won over. As LeRoi Jones (now Amiri Baraka) wrote: "[Davis] had a deep connection to the basic blues impulse, and he could insinuate more blues with one note and a highly meaningful pause than most cool instrumentalists could throughout an entire composition."[17]

Sometimes Davis and other cool jazz players did more than "insinuate" blues: occasionally they even based their music on the old twelve-bar form. Two excellent recordings of Davis and his band improvising on the twelve-bar blues cycle are "Bags' Groove" and "Freddie Freeloader."

Later jazz styles tended to use twelve-bar blues form less, almost as if bebop and cool jazz had finally summed up all that could be said with it. But these older styles are still played by many musicians, and to many the ultimate test of a jazz player's technical skill is still whether he or she is able to "play bop." Although twelve-bar form is not currently involved in the forefront of jazz innovation, it is something that unites all jazz musicians. In situations where instrumentalists "meet on the stand"—that is, they have never played together until they find themselves sharing the stage somewhere—one of the quickest and most effective ways to get to know each other musically is to improvise together on a form they all know: the twelve-bar blues.

FORM IN THE CLASSICAL INSTRUMENTAL MUSIC OF NORTH INDIA

Like the blues and jazz, North Indian classical music develops primarily through improvisation. Musicians elaborate on a small amount of precomposed material, which is often in binary form. While jazz and blues musicians commonly base their improvisations on harmonic progressions, North Indian musicians focus on melody, following the rules of the particular raga which they are singing or playing. Their overall performance falls into distinct predetermined sections that, while individually shaped by the musician, are subject to traditional rules of form.

Modern performances of North India classical instrumental music typically include the following sections: 1) a three-part alap (improvisation), 2) a two-part slow or medium tempo gat (composition), 3) improvisations based on the gat, 4) a fast gat, and 5) improvisations based on the fast gat.

The alap itself is divided into three parts: 1) the alap proper, in free rhythm; 2) the *jor,* in which a medium-tempo pulse is established; and 3) the *jhala,* in which the pulse accelerates. The alap is accompanied only by a drone played on the plucked *tanpura.* The gats and gat-based improvisation are accompanied by tabla, and performances typically include one or more tabla solos, in which the drummer takes "center-stage," accompanied by the soloist, who for the time being marks time by repeating the first line of the gat.

The gat itself usually includes two parts: the *sthayi*, which explores the lower and middle octaves of the player's range, and the *antara*, which goes into the upper octave. The soloist's gat-based improvisations include rhythmic play, called *layakari*, and fast, virtuosic passages, called *tans*.

To help you understand the overall form of the performance, we are including a chart (Figure 2) which shows the timing of the various sections. Minutes and seconds are shown above the horizontal boxes; the nature of each section is described within its box. Listening to the recorded example, you can observe the musical form of Buddhadev Das Gupta's improvised alap, jor, and jhala, each of which may be divided into coherent melodic "limbs." Each limb focuses on a somewhat different set of notes, shaping the playing like paragraphs in an essay. In writing, the content of a paragraph is the subject matter addressed by the author; in alap, the content is a set of notes and melodic motives.

Buddhadev Das Gupta plays "Rag Kamod" on the plucked sarod, accompanied on tabla by Ray Spiegel and on tanpura by Ira Landgarden. The performance includes alap, jor, jhala, a medium tempo gat, improvised rhythmic play, tans, a fast gat, and tabla solos. This nine and one-half minute exposition is complete, but brief; a full concert performance might last for an entire hour. The soloist—in this case, Buddhadev Das Gupta—can tailor his improvisations to suit his mood and fit the available time.

FIGURE 2: "RAG KAMOD" (AUDIO 58) PERFORMED BY BUDDHADEV DAS GUPTA

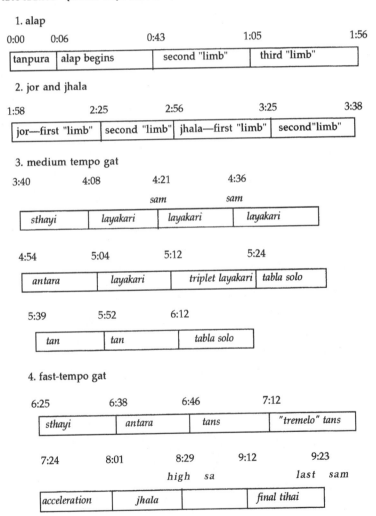

"In my beginning is my end" would be an appropriate description of the form of North Indian classical music. Every performance begins and ends with the keynote, sa. Each exposition begins slowly, gradually revealing the melodic character and mood of the raga. Compositions, which serve as a point of departure and return for episodes of rhythmic play (layakari) and virtuoso passage-work (tans), gradually increase in tempo, building to a series of climaxes of rhythmic and melodic tension before the final return to sa and *sam,* the respective beginnings of the raga and tala.

▬ FLEXIBLE AND OPEN FORMS

As we have seen, Western composers have worked with structures like sonata form, in which the general sections—exposition, development, and recapitulation—are fixed, but the content and length of these may vary widely from one piece to the next. Similarly, a North Indian *alap* improvisation usually

A WEST AFRICAN DRUM ENSEMBLE

follows a preset overall shape, but performers will fill out that shape in different ways on different occasions, taking more time with one section and less with another, or expanding or contracting the overall length. The overarching structures of the sonata or alap are foreordained, but the details are malleable. The former requires the imagination of a composer while the latter is shaped in performance by the imagination of the improviser.

As stated earlier in the chapter, some forms involve even less overall delimitation: rather than presenting a fixed order of sections or events, however general, they furnish a pool of possibilities. These "open" forms necessarily involve improvisation, as one or more musicians make spontaneous decisions in performance. Much of African music involves open forms, and we have seen that a solo mbira player may improvise on a basic harmonic structure for as long as sufficient inspiration is maintained. In group performances, one musician is often the leader, the decision-maker who signals the other musicians to move from one possibility to another. In West African drum ensembles, open group forms are usually directed by a lead drummer.

Lead Drumming in West Africa

A West African lead drummer performs several functions. He improvises infectious rhythms which inspire and enliven the musicians and dancers. He keeps the tempo under control, ensuring that the music does not slow down or speed up. In some cases, he may "speak" through replication of the varying pitches and rhythms of a local tone language, drumming out proverbs, salutations, praises, or encouragements. And when accompanying an improvising solo dancer, he artfully matches his drumming to the individual characteristics of the dancer. The master Ghanaian drummer Alhaji Ibrahim Abdulai described such practices to the American ethnomusicologist John Chernoff:

> Immediately a dancer comes to us, we give him his beat. Because already we know the type of his dance, we just play in accordance with his feet and the movement of his body, and we get him. . . . But when we are playing alone and there are no dancers, and I keep on changing the beat, that means that I am talking with the drum. When a dancer comes to look and not to dance at any particular moment when I am drumming, then he knows what I am doing. That dancer knows what I am saying with my drum.[18]

Another important function of the lead drummer is literally to lead the music and dancing with predetermined signals. A given ensemble piece involves a basic polyrhythmic cycle and a fundamental dance step, but there are also various other cycles and steps which may alternate with the central ones. Specific rhythmic patterns played by the lead drummer tell the musicians and dancers when to begin and end the whole performance, and when to switch into an alternative polyrhythm and/or step and when to switch back. The lead drummer is entrusted with a kind of spontaneous generation of form.

MICHAEL WIMBERLY

JALAL SHARRIFF

NAFISA SHARRIFF AND MADOU DEMBELE

A PERFORMANCE OF "MANDIANI"

EXAMPLE 7: "MANDIANI"

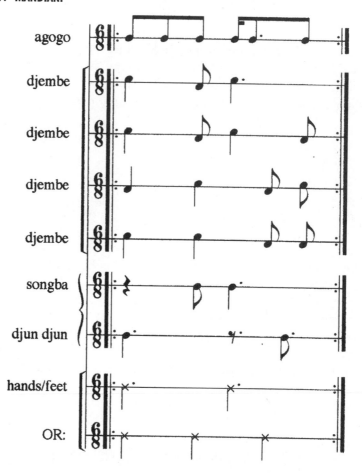

A PERFORMANCE OF "MANDIANI"

Example 7 shows the basic polyrhythmic cycle of "Mandiani," a West African drum ensemble piece with an open form. Performed in Mali, Guinea, and Senegal, it is named for a great musician of the past, and invokes his spirit as a blessing. The *agogo* bell and the low *djun djun* and *songba* drums provide an unchanging basis, while various patterns may be played on *djembe* drums.

Flexible and Open Forms in Jazz

This performance of "Mandiani" may be viewed as a kind of call-and-response form: the leader's signals provide the call, and the others respond in specific ways. Some jazz performances are structured similarly: while the piece's chord progression sets a basic form, a leader may determine how many times the progression is repeated, who solos and for how long, and when the group switches between composed and improvised sections. Alternatively, musicians may make such decisions through group consensus, either before or during a performance. Particularly creative and cohesive groups might even spontaneously depart from a piece's chord progression together, using the composed form as a flexible point of departure and return. The saxophone player Lee Konitz recalled such moments when he played in pianist Lennie Tristano's group:

> When we would play "All the Things You Are," we would get to the point where the music was moving so intensely that the music would start to leave the song form, the actual structure of the song. We might get involved with one tonal area and just stop the progress of the song right there and play freely in that area. That could just stretch out as completely as we would want it to go and then return to the song. This was a note-to-note kind of playing. It was an impressionistic utilization of the song.[19]

Sometimes jazz musicians are involved with practices which are even more open, perhaps dispensing with chord progressions and compositions altogether, allowing the overall form to be determined largely by consensus during each performance. This kind of spontaneous generation of form, which arose during the 1950s and early 1960s, is generally referred to as free jazz. Repudiating the formal conventions which to many seem synonymous with jazz, free jazz players seek to create an extemporaneous music which is unfettered by predetermination. For example, the saxophonist Gary Barz spoke of improvising on chord patterns which he made up as he went along:

> You just keep going on and on; it's one long melody. I don't think it's that different from how I ordinarily play because it's the same music, just another type of song, really, where you don't have the structure set up before you play. So, you work out your own structure as you play, really taking improvisation to the epitome.[20]

Other jazz musicians found free jazz intriguing, but difficult to enter into. One unnamed musician confided to Paul Berliner, "I'd get up to solo and I wouldn't know what to do; to play chord changes or to ignore them—just play colors, textures. Sometimes, I'd let a whole chorus go by without playing, turn around, and walk off the stage."[21] But some found a stimulating challenge in free jazz playing. The drummer Ronald Shannon Jackson recalled playing with the saxophonist Albert Ayler, who even wanted to work with free rhythm in his group:

> He'd say, "Fill all that space out. I don't care how you do it, but do it." He didn't want any space or holes in the music. He wanted to hear rhythms all over. The only thing he'd tell me was, "No time, I don't want to hear ching-ka-ching-ka-ding—no bebop.". . . There was a pulse to the music because of the melody being played, but not the

kind of pulse you were normally listening for. The time-feeling was more suspended, like waves that moved along with the song.[22]

To some people, the notion of free jazz is unacceptable: such music can no longer be called jazz. To others, it can be some of the most powerful music-making imaginable: the music is so completely linked to the moment of its performance that it contains all the exhilaration of a dramatic voyage of discovery. Drummer Keith Copeland described a particularly unusual performance by the now-legendary saxophonist John Coltrane, in which the improvisational intensity caused the pianist and bass player to stop playing, leaving drummer Elvin Jones with Coltrane "just blowing up and down, an endless flow, [while Jones] remained in back of him just bashing, slashing, and crashing away. . . . Trane and Elvin played at such an energy level all the time that it scared you to death the whole time you were listening to them. It was just a constant conversation between them, all the time."[23]

Open and flexible forms can enact social values such as enlightened leadership, group consensus, and individual expression. Since they always involve some level of improvisation, they also underline the immediacy of here-and-now experience. No two performances will be identical, so open forms cannot be thought of as finished works of art; rather, they are dynamic processes which are revealed only through each unique realization.

▰▰ CHAPTER SUMMARY

Form is one of the most important components of music, determining the parameters and shape music takes in performance. It can be perceived on many levels, from the internal structure of a brief song to an hour-long performance of one raga. Whether the form is pre-set, as in the first movement of the Beethoven's Fifth Symphony, or open-ended, as in the North Indian sarod performance, forms are governed by rules that are understood and shared by composers, performers, and listeners within a particular culture. Forms are reflections of existing models that are shaped and molded differently by each individual musical creator. Musical forms will continue to evolve as composers and improvisers seek to create new meanings and new ways of ordering time in the music they create.

ADDITIONAL LISTENING

AUDIO #14: BEETHOVEN'S SYMPHONY NO. 5 IN C MINOR, FIRST MOVEMENT

The famous first theme or motive of the exposition occurs in the opening four measures. A continuation, based on this opening motive, follows and then the motive itself repeats (0:17). A further continuation of the theme is marked by a long crescendo. The French horn announces the bridge (0:42) that will move the music to the second theme (0:46). Played by the strings and woodwinds it has a lyrical feeling which is in direct contrast to the first theme. The end of the exposition section is based on the opening theme (1:14). The entire exposition then repeats (1:24).

The development section begins with the opening theme played on the French horn in a new key (2:49). There is a development of the continuation of the theme and then a powerful passage based on the same rhythm of the continuation (3:12) The bridge theme is played and developed (3:26). The bridge theme is then fragmented: the strings play two notes followed by the woodwinds playing two notes (3:38). The fragmentation continues with the two sections alternating one note (3:46). A loud passage based on the opening theme runs directly into the recapitulation that begins with the opening motive (4:11).

After the recap of the opening motive and continuation, there is suddenly a slow oboe cadenza (4:30). After a second continuation, the French horn announces the bridge leading to the second theme (5:04). While the strings and winds play this theme, the timpani is playing the rhythm of the first theme. The coda begins with a series of repetitions of the continuation (5:47) and a new march-like theme (6:16). Finally the first motive is played loudly with brass (6:57), followed by a continuation of the theme, and a strong conclusion.

STUDY QUESTIONS

1. How is form in music different from form in the visual arts?

2. On how many levels can you describe a composition's form?

3. What is binary form? List three different genres that are structured in binary form.

4. Describe some of the contexts in which call and response is used.

5. What is sonata form?

6. What is the basic blues structure? How do musicians use that structure in performance?

7. What are the typical sections of a contemporary North Indian classical instrumental performance?

8. How is the performance of free jazz different from playing the blues?

REFERENCED SOURCES

1. Averill, interview 1997.
2. Pagano, interview 1997.
3. Reck, 1977: 405–406.
4. Hahn, interview 1996.
5. Bebey, 1975: 88.
6. Berliner, 1994: 369.
7. Ibid.: 375.
8. Ying, interview 1997.
9. Ibid.
10. Pagano, interview 1997.
11. Titon, 1994: xvi-iii.
12. Ibid.: 18–20, 29.
13. Ibid.: 33–8.
14. Jones, 1963: 188.
15. Berliner, 1994: 276.
16. Ibid.: 277.
17. Jones, 1963: 209.
18. Chernoff, 1979: 110–1.
19. Berliner, 1994: 379.
20. Ibid.: 225.
21. Ibid.: 276.
22. Ibid.: 337.
23. Ibid.: 338.

CHAPTER 11

COMPOSERS AND IMPROVISERS

About This Chapter

In this chapter, we examine how composers and performers create music. We look at the methods, training, and resources that composers and improvisers from different cultures use to create pieces and performances. We also discuss the role of the composer and improviser in culture. Creative musicians are typically involved with characteristic forms, molds, and styles that serve as the raw materials from which they fashion their own unique compositions or improvisations. With each new creative act, composers and improvisers situate themselves in relation to the tradition of which they are a part.

KEYWORDS

composition
improvisation
riff
taqasim

COMPANION RESOURCES

TELEVISION PROGRAM: Form: Composers and Improvisers

AUDIO SELECTIONS:

59. *Great Southern Spirits* by Stephen Leek: "Kondalilla" (3rd movement).

60. "Amelia" by Bob McQuillen.

61. "San Juan Pueblo Cloud Dance Song" by Peter Garcia, Sr.

58. "Rag Kamod"

62. 'Ud Taqasim in Maqam Nahawand.

In common usage, the two nouns in this chapter's title are treated as opposites. Music is either "composed," from the Latin *componere,* to put together, or "improvised," from the Latin *improvisus,* unforeseen. Composers carefully plot out their pieces, either on paper or in their minds, while improvisers produce their music extemporaneously, not knowing exactly what will happen until the very instant of their performance. But sometimes an improvisation can be seen as an "instant composition," a composition as a "frozen improvisation." For most creative musicians, composition and improvisation are related processes which might even flow seamlessly into each other. To understand the ways that such musicians really work with their materials, the conceptual duality must be replaced by something more like a continuum.

If we try to find the farthest poles of this continuum, we might end up with some forms of electronically-mediated music on the "composed" side: pieces which exist on tape as finished performances which will always be identical; the acoustics and sound equipment of any given playback situation provide "unforeseen" elements, but they cannot be viewed as human improvisation. On the "improvised" side, it is hard to imagine a human performance in which absolutely nothing has been even vaguely "put together" beforehand—unless one counts what a pre-toddler might do to a table with a spoon; the child may be responding to inborn tendencies toward rhythm, but since these are unconscious they cannot be regarded as willful composition.

Even music which is fully written out in a complex notational system— a Chopin piano prelude, for example—involves "unforeseen" elements in performance: the feelings of the pianist at the time of performance, the particular instrument involved, the general temperament of the audience, and the specific occasion can inspire a sensitive musician to a slightly different interpretation each time. Though the pianist will never change the notes or other indications—phrasing, dynamics, and so on—which Chopin specified, these subtle differences in performance belong, in spirit, to the realm of improvisation.

By the same token, music which is completely improvised, such as free jazz, involves a number of elements which are "put together" beforehand: the musicians are all drawing on their extensive experience with improvising, alone and in groups, and they have learned how to make open forms work in musically satisfying ways. Again, this kind of practical background may not constitute what most people would call a "composition," but it informs the musical activities in similar ways to those of a pre-composed improvisational format.

Moving closer to the center of the continuum, one may find many examples of musics which combine elements of the two. Performances of both Hindustani classical music and jazz usually involve much more improvisation than composition, but the improvisations are structured in pre-determined ways. Jazz musicians improvise on the basis of the harmonic cycle of the composition. Hindustani musicians work within the pre-established norms of raga and tala, as well as in overall improvisational formats such as alap, jor, and jhala. Central Javanese gamelans perform compositions, but several of the instruments are characteristically played in semi-improvisational ways within a set of learned parameters. West African drum ensembles also perform set compositions, but these pieces involve some latitude for many of the players to improvise, and a great deal of room for improvisation by the lead drummer who can even change the overall shape of the performance by signaling sectional changes.

Folk musicians perform composed pieces too, but in some cultures they are most highly-respected when they are able to nuance and embellish them in different ways each time. The Irish *sean-nós* singer Joe Heaney often said "I never sing a song the same way twice," but just as frequently he declared "I always sing songs exactly the way my father did." This apparent contradiction is resolved when one realizes that his father also never sang them the same way twice!

Compositions often begin as improvisations, as a musician experiments with musical ideas in order to weigh possibilities and make final decisions. Some Western composers have produced pieces called "impromptus," specifically indicating their origin in improvisation, and bebop composers often drew from their improvisations on older harmonic cycles in composing new pieces. The outstanding French Newfoundland fiddler and composer Emile Benoit described such a process to Colin Quigley:

> *So I used to play for dances an' all that. We had no radio, no television, or nothing like that. So, I used to get tired. You gets tired [of] the same thing all the time, eh? You'll find,* fatiguer, *the same song. Same reel or same air. You gets tired. You want to hear something new. So I start makin' up things, eh, air, changing air, and all that. So [the dancers say], "Chee, where you heard that?"... Well from that, well you plays that for a while, then gets tired of it. Then try something again. That's the way it goes, oui? Yes, but after a while, you does that for years and years, eh? Well, you're getting pretty smart at it, oui? The same like go to school, oui? Getting your grade twelve. Same thing.*[1]

Conversely, performers in improvisational traditions like jazz, Arabic, and Hindustani classical music often employ compositional concepts as they endeavor to construct a coherent musical "story" on the spot, with a feeling of a beginning, middle, and end which work together in a satisfying way.

Both composition and improvisation can be collaborative efforts. Some "free" jazz groups, like the Art Ensemble of Chicago, have developed performing styles in which collective improvisation is not necessarily based on prearranged formal considerations: group dynamics and audience energy may lead them into completely unexpected musical adventures shaped only by spontaneous interplay at the moment of performance.

In Maoist China, the state-ordered practice of composition by committee resulted in music whose significance was more ideological than artistic. But some musical groups, like the rock band Rusted Root, value a kind of communal composition in which a member brings ideas to a rehearsal and the whole group contributes to the final shaping of the piece: the outcome, they feel, is a shared musical utterance whose power is enhanced by its embodiment of the group's cooperative energy.

In some cultures creative musical processes can involve a non-human element, and the concept of music may extend to the sounds of birds, whales, wind, and waterfalls. As we will see, some Native American groups maintain that songs can come from supernatural sources. In some cultures, songs can come directly from nature or from dreams. The Western concept of "talent" fits interestingly with such beliefs that musical creativity is rooted in more than conscious intelligence. The concept is not found in all cultures: for example, when James Koetting asked the master Ghanaian musician William Alban Ayipaga Connelly whether he believed in talent, Connelly replied negatively, categorizing the concept as *jùjú*: magic, or—to him, at least—superstition.[2]

Whatever its provenance, musical creativity involves a response to various kinds of flexible or rigid considerations—rules, norms, tendencies—which are embedded in culture. The following investigation of some of these influences will provide a foundation for more detailed case studies.

THE MUSICAL SYSTEM

Although composers and improvisers work in the present, they are grounded in the past: formally or informally, they are part of a musical system. This foundation includes practical knowledge of the instruments or voices they are composing for or improvising with, their own capabilities and those of any other musicians involved, and sometimes notational systems as well. Some musics require an understanding of a theoretical system, such as Western harmony or the Arabic maqam system. All musical creativity involves certain implicit and explicit considerations which are fundamental to the tradition on which the composer or improviser chooses to build. In one way or another, the creative musician is usually involved with characteristic forms, materials, and styles.

Form

As we have seen, form is a crucial element in the compositional process. A composer may begin with a fragmentary musical idea, but before long, questions of overall form must be addressed: Should this idea be developed as a theme? Should it lead to something else? Should it return? Sometimes form itself is the first factor a composer determines.

For example, an eighteenth-century Western composer might decide or be commissioned to write in sonata form. This composer's training and experience would suggest coming up with a lively first subject and a contrasting second subject, both of which have some potential for development. Improvising at an instrument, the composer would soon arrive at two compatible subjects, and could get right to work. Especially prolific composers like Haydn and Mozart must have worked this way, letting form generate composition to a certain extent.

Concerns about form are equally important to improvisers. Knowing the harmonic cycle which underlies a given piece, jazz musicians structure their improvisations to fit with it in varying ways: form allows them to know where they are, and where they are going. Similarly, Hindustani tabla players build their improvisations within the framework of the tala cycle. Such improvisers may consciously work with larger forms too, determining how many tala or chord cycles they will improvise on and fashioning longer improvisations accordingly. Some tabla players are so adept at mental mathematics that they can plan a cross-rhythmic improvisation that will span several tala cycles and end at precisely the right moment, and jazz musicians can "go out," momentarily seeming to defy the chord pattern but then re-synchronizing with it in a musically compelling way. In such cases, form plays an important role in the generation of improvisational ideas.

Materials

Materials may be less concrete than forms, but no less important in influencing musical creativity. As we have seen, ragas specify certain melodic possibilities, prohibiting others. An improvising Hindustani or Arabic musician works with both the potential of the raga or maqam—explicit but flexible materials which exist only in the mind—and the dictates of overall musical form.

Jazz musicians work with implicit materials in similar ways, improvising within musical norms which identify and differentiate the melodic, rhythmic, and harmonic character of jazz from other musics. Improvisational materials can be more specific as well. For example, *gendèr* players in Central Javanese gamelans know predetermined sets of melodic patterns which are appropriate for particular musical moments, but they may spontaneously make selections from these sets, weaving them into their previous and prior selections.

Jeff Titon proposed the concept of "preforms" to describe how blues musicians improvise: "A preform carries the connotation of something roughly sized or shaped, but not finished. Stored in its rough state, it is given whatever final shaping is necessary as it is fit into the accompaniment. Among musicians, the repository for these preforms often is called a "bag"; and what it contains is preforms for the patchwork quilt of variation."[3] Titon compares this process to many daily activities, showing how the manipulation of flexible materials is a common human experience. The idea of preforms fits well with the concepts of raga and maqam—the latter are simply more explicit versions of the same kinds of activities.

Composers also work with materials which may be implicit or explicit. Explicit materials like raga and maqam are essential considerations for composers in their traditions. While most of the world's musical systems do not have a theoretical language for their conceptualization, they still involve implicit materials which are somewhat comparable to explicit ones. A folk musician composing a dance tune, for example, knows the form the tune must take in order to be appropriate for the particular dance, but also knows implicitly how to make the tune idiomatic, so that it is compatible with the whole repertory. Under traditional circumstances, a Scottish fiddler will not compose a melody that sounds Polynesian; and to those deeply involved with the music, Scottish tunes even sound identifiably different from those of neighboring traditions in England and Ireland.

Style

A creative musician's style may be thought of as both a personal and a local phenomenon. Long before Western classical music was thought of as one unified system, various national and local styles were acknowledged: French music, Italian music, Viennese music, music of the Cathedral of Notre Dame, and so on. Early blues were also thought of as local: East Texas style, Mississippi Delta style, New Orleans style, etc.

People in any sizable area differentiate between local styles in various ways. Composers and improvisers are always aware of their stylistic roots, whether they see them as belonging to a particular geographic region or to a particular lineage of musicians. Beethoven considered himself a stylistic descendant of Handel and Haydn, as well as a participant in the local musical style of Vienna. Miles Davis knew that his stylistic influences involved older bebop players, along with the musicians he knew and worked with in contemporary jazz genres.

In some cases a creative musician also develops a personal style—perhaps more than one over time. Such developments can be controversial: an especially idiosyncratic personal style may not be accepted immediately, or at all. Still, creative musicians often place a high value on finding their own "voice," and many listeners respond positively to a composer or improviser's unique musical personality. But this is not a universal value: some musics place a higher premium on creativity which does not celebrate the individual but honors the group, by producing new sounds that fit perfectly with old ones. In such cases a musician is not encouraged to develop a personal style, but to carry the unadulterated tradition from past to future, replenishing it with congenial new material.

THE INNER WORLD

In addition to their foundation in pre-established musical systems, composers and improvisers respond to their own inner worlds. Such a response might largely involve a wish to uphold and supplement a beautiful tradition, as in the cases just mentioned. But it also might include a wish to connect deeply with one's own feelings, to express one's emotions, responses to nature, and so on. It might even involve a wish to assert oneself, to make others stop and listen, perhaps bringing them into a new kind of awareness. The impulse to create often springs from some combination of such desires, which in turn influence aspects of the creative musician's work.

Emotion

Emotions of sorrow, love, and indignation have been the wellsprings of countless songs. In various parts of the world, funereal mourning is an improvised tradition. The bereaved have heard others perform it, but do not compose what they will chant or sing over the deceased—the words and melody just come when the mourner's emotional state summons them. For the Kaluli in Papua, New Guinea, "song that moves men to tears" and "weeping that moves women to song" are among the highest cultural values, as Steven Feld has noted.[4]

Perhaps the most influential song in all of gospel music, "Precious Lord, Take My Hand," was composed by Thomas A. Dorsey as he grieved over the death of his wife. One of the deepest of Irish love songs, "Eileanóir a Rúin," is said to have sprung spontaneously from the lips of the eighteenth-century poet Carrol Dálaigh when he first saw the beautiful young woman who was to become his wife. And one of the signal songs of the 1960s antiwar movement, "The Big Muddy," was written by Pete Seeger in response to his rage over the squandering of life in Vietnam. A Netsilik Eskimo vividly described to explorer Knud Rasmussen how songs rise from the emotions:

> *Songs are thoughts, sung out with the breath when people are moved by great forces and ordinary speech no longer suffices. Man is moved just like the ice floe sailing here and there out in the current. His thoughts are driven by a flowing force when he feels joy, when he feels fear, when he feels sorrow. Thoughts can wash over him like a flood, making his breath come in gasps and his heart throb. Something, like an abatement in the weather, will keep him thawed up. And then it will happen that the words we need will come of themselves. When the words we want to use shoot up of themselves—we get a new song.[5]*

Emotions can be expressed through music in more abstract ways too. To some extent, Beethoven's "Eroica" symphony grew out of the inner turmoil created by his increasing deafness, musically portraying feelings of heroism and triumph, morbidity, and a final embracing of the multifaceted beauty of life. A portrayal of changing emotions in a composition or improvisation can seem to tell an abstract story, communicating the complexities of the musician's inner world. Trumpeter Bobby Rogovin described how he listens to improvisers to Paul Berliner:

> I thought of the soloist's lines like the way we talk sentences, and I heard all the emotion in them. . . . He's saying this now; he's saying that next. He's sad there. He's getting a little cocky here. He gets a little happy there. He builds up here. He relaxes there. Things phrased in a certain way have a certain meaning. . . . Miles is really good at this. It's not so much the notes he plays as the way he plays the notes.[6]

Another trumpeter, Adolphus "Doc" Cheatham, told Berliner that "if a guy plays a beautiful solo and he's playing from the heart or he's talking with his horn, we say, 'He's telling a story.' If he's playing bad, we say, 'He plays like he's got rocks in his blood.'"[7]

Impressions

Sometimes creative musicians are prompted by inward associations with elements of the outside world. Many composers have drawn inspiration from nature, sometimes alluding to this association explicitly, as with Claude Debussy's evocation of the sea, *La Mer*. A striking Native American example of a more specific impression from the natural world comes from a member of the Washo Peyotists, as reported by Alan Merriam:

> When I was a child in Carson Valley I used to go out in the fields at night during a thunder storm to listen. Lightning and thunder had a special fascination for me, and I still dream about it. I remember how the sounds of thunder seemed to strike against Job's Peak and then glance off and go rolling northward like the sounds which had followed and swallowed up "the old lady and the old man" [mythological creatures in the Washo creation tale]. While the thunder was rolling away I could hear him singing a song; his voice was that sound thunder makes when it echoes among the mountains. I can remember that song, and I can sing it. I have sung it ever since I was a child. It is my song.[8]

The music of the Kaluli draws extensively from bird songs, which have a special emotional and cosmological significance for them.[9] The Hindustani raga system includes many relationships of ragas with elements of the natural world—specific seasons, birds, flowers, and so on—which may guide the improviser to bring out the raga's inner essence.

Sometimes compositions or improvisations are inspired by other kinds of impressions. For example, Emile Benoit described a musical idea that came to him in an airplane:

> I got the sound of the wings, eh? I was in the hind seat, in behind the wing, eh? And listening to that [makes a high-pitched nasal hum], you know, a sound [makes the sound again]. And I didn't sing it, but I

had that [sound in mind], you know? So I took the violin and I played it. It was easy, easy to play and I play it right low. After a little while I got it and then I open up [laughter]. Jeez cripes, they started getting up. They started getting up from their seats. . . they wanted to know what was going on [laughter]. So . . . I went up, [the steward] put me on the [intercom] for fifteen minutes. Played. They all went, sat down in their seat [laughter]. So I played the Flying Reel, so I told them there that I just compose it. . . . . Yeah, it was all right.[10]

Creative musicians may also be stimulated by other artists. Some Western composers have been inspired by literary works, such as Richard Strauss's orchestral "tone poem" based on Friedrich Nietzsche's *Also Sprach Zarathustra*, and musical settings of poems are clearly responses to the poets' original utterance.

The realm of visual art has prompted some compositions, like Modest Musorgsky's *Pictures at an Exhibition*. Other musics can provide potent associations too: jazz musicians may consciously evoke the older world of blues in their improvisations, and Western classical composers sometimes purposely echo their own local folk musics. Sometimes actual people are alluded to, as when a jazz musician quotes a phrase associated with Louis Armstrong or Charlie Parker, or when a rap arrangement includes samples from recordings by James Brown.

■■■ THE OUTSIDE WORLD

Most creative musicians want their work to be received by other people; therefore their work is influenced by considerations of context and communication. Pre-toddler spoon-banging may be considered a kind of expression, but it is not particularly edifying as communication. And while it may be acceptable in the family kitchen, it is normally not welcome in a musical event. In order to bring elements of their inner world forward, composers and improvisers need to be fluent in the musical "language" understood by their listeners, and they must take into consideration the particular time and place for their work.

Situation

The situation or context in which a performance takes place is an important factor for most composers and improvisers. A jazz musician improvising at a nightclub frequented by serious jazz aficionados feels more freedom to explore a wide range of ideas than one who is playing for a socializing crowd at a wedding reception: the former audience wants to listen closely to creative musicians, while the latter simply wants to hear pleasant background music, perhaps something they can dance to. Film composers must supply what the director wants to accompany a given scene, tailoring their music to split-second requirements. A Hindustani musician may find it necessary to perform shorter improvisations for non-Indian audiences, who cannot follow the nuanced intricacies of slowly unfolding a raga. Such situations do not destroy creativity, but they certainly limit it, and some composers and improvisers cannot—or will not—adapt to such limitations.

By contrast, a church congregation may be in exactly the right frame of mind to be attentive to, and moved by, a complex sacred composition or an extended vocal improvisation. A concert-hall or jazz-club audience offers a secular analogy: they have come for a contemplative experience, and are eager to hear music which will stimulate their minds and hearts. In such situations, creative musicians know that they can work with musical subtleties in a variety of ways.

Creative musicians might be even more immediately connected with their audiences, supplying what is needed for particular kinds of direct involvement—such as dancing. As mentioned earlier, composers of social dances must know the proper form and rhythm required for particular dances; and in some traditions improvisers may work very closely with dancers. The master Ghanaian drummer Alhaji Ibrahim Abdulai described such a process to John Chernoff:

> *Steady changing music is the feeling of the drummer, that is, the particular one who is drumming, that's what he feels. As he is drumming, sometimes people are also dancing. He watches their feet and how they take their feet for the dance. He watches the movement of the body and the feet, and as the dancer takes his steps in the dance, he will drum according to it. That is why I told you earlier that I had wanted you to call the Takai drummers and dancers for you alone to study, because there is one particular man who is very good at dancing, and you will see how he will be taking his feet. There is also one particular drummer who really watches that man. When the dancer lifts his feet and moves his body, then that man will play the music according to the movement of the body. Then you will see how clearly it comes together and how it changes according to how he dances. If he starts moving his feet and his body, the drummer will drum according to his movements. Immediately he stops, you will see that the one drumming in tune with him will also stop. Then you will see how it is his dance movements which bring the changes of the drumming.[11]*

Tradition and Innovation

With each new creative act, composers and improvisers situate themselves in relation to their tradition. As mentioned earlier, some traditions are very conservative, and the creative musician is judged by strict standards. If a Hindustani musician attempts to add new elements to a raga, most listeners will hear the innovation as a violation: the musician is clumsy, or tasteless. But if that musician produces new ways of working *within* the raga's traditional structure, audiences may be delighted.

Some genres are more accommodating to innovation. Musicians like John Coltrane and Ornette Coleman pushed the boundaries of jazz in visionary ways, and are now considered to be very important figures in jazz history. Western classical music in the twentieth century has been the scene of constant innovation, with some composers creating whole new musical systems and even new definitions of music. The serial procedures of Arnold Schönberg, the chance operations of John Cage, and the mathematical applications of Milton Babbit—to cite just a few examples—have been hailed as momentous innovations by some, while others find their music merely bewildering.

Inventing a new musical language involves a communicative risk: will anyone understand it? In an essay originally titled "The Composer as Specialist"—notoriously retitled by its publisher "Who Cares If You Listen?"—Babbit staked out his territory:

> *I dare to suggest that the composer would do himself and his music an immediate and eventual service by total, resolute, and voluntary withdrawal from this public world to one of private performance and electronic media, with its very real possibility of complete elimination of the public and social aspects of musical composition. . . . Admittedly, if this music is not supported, the whistling repertory of the man in the street will be little affected, the concert-going activity of the conspicuous consumer of musical culture will be little disturbed. But music will cease to evolve, and, in that important sense, will cease to live.*[12]

Indeed, at the present time music such as Babbit's survives only with institutional support. It has not been accepted by the general public: its language truly is that of the "specialist," who, throughout his essay, Babbit contrasts with the "layman" who cannot be expected to comprehend advanced developments in musical composition.

Innovation is a courageous act, and composers and improvisers often must grapple with its consequences. Coltrane and Coleman were not widely accepted by jazz audiences at first, but they did not capitulate to popular taste, and eventually many listeners and other musicians came to value their contributions. Still, major innovation is not the only form of creativity, and many musicians and listeners place the highest value on music which can be appreciated and enjoyed by a wide musical community. Emile Benoit described the pleasure of having one of his compositions accepted at a dance:

> *Another time I composed . . . [a piece], "Farewell," it's called. . . . I played it to a party and jeepers, fancy, everybody liked it, you know, eh? And Joe Farwell, him, he got on the floor and he danced, well, it's just as well to say all night. We start seven o'clock, we finish two o'clock in the morning. For every dance on the floor, and that's all I played, that's all I played all night, "Farewell." Yeah. . . . And after that . . . I went out with a horse and a couple of my family come with me too, and when we came home [it] was right calm, eh. And the moon shining so bright. Oh, beautiful. I used to hear people, eh? [sings melody of "Farewell Reel"]. Now, [it] was the tune called Farewell, eh? [whistles tune]. They know that because I played it all night [laughter]. So after that when they goes to the times, they go on "Give us Farewell."*[13]

Whether they choose to reach out to many people, to a small number of cognoscenti, or even to keep their music entirely to themselves, creative musicians make decisions about connections between their inner and outer worlds and position themselves in some relationship to the past and present. For more detailed examples of composing and improvising within particular traditions, we now turn to a few case studies.

THE ROLE OF THE COMPOSER IN WESTERN CLASSICAL MUSIC

We have discussed Western classical music throughout this book, but how can we really define it? In some senses, this is a difficult question to answer. It is "Western" historically, in that it developed in Europe; but it is performed and replenished with new compositions from all over the world, and not only by people of European ancestry. One could even argue that it is not ultimately European in origin, since so many of its practices and instruments were brought to Europe long ago from parts of western Asia and northern Africa, areas which are sometimes loosely referred to in the West as "the Middle East" and "the Near East."

It is not easy to define "classical" either: it might actually make the most sense to define it by what it excludes—folk and popular musics—though occasionally that distinction becomes problematic, as when a classical soloist or group performs music composed by a folk or popular musician, or vice versa. One salient feature is the degree of its dependence on written notation; as a rule Western compositions—including those for "non-classical" ensembles, such as jazz or marching bands—must be written out before they can be performed.

Although today people tend to think of Western classical music as a unified category, this idea is comparatively recent and arises largely from the changing social situations in which the music has thrived. Generally, we can say that the system is rooted in the institutional religious and court practices of medieval Europe. It appears that for some time the musics of the church and the court were quite separate. Sacred music was sung by soloists or unison groups: a particularly well-known example today is the repertory referred to as Gregorian Chant or plainchant. Court music involved an array of functional, entertainment, and dance musics, related in various ways to local folk musics, but generally involving the conscious refinement and embellishment that suited an aristocratic atmosphere.

The Composer Before 1900

By the thirteenth century these traditions were already starting to mix in some places, with court composers using sacred chant melodies as the basis for composing secular music, and church composers borrowing compositional ideas from the world of court music. While some composers continued to specialize in music for one venue or the other, by the middle of the fifteenth century many composers were employed to write both sacred and secular music.

Subsequent decades saw the rise of opera and the consequent development of a third important venue, the theater. Apart from certain works by earlier composers—mainly choral, keyboard, or lute works—the music of what is now called the Baroque era is the earliest music that is still often heard in conventional Western classical performances. A number of pieces by some of this era's composers, including Antonio Vivaldi, George Frideric Handel, and Johann Sebastian Bach, are quite well known today.

These composers, like others before them, were mostly supported by the patronage of church or court. Composition was regarded as a craft that was often handed down in families. Composing was a job in which individual artistic expression had to be tailored to fit the needs and requirements of both patron and performance situation. Whether the context was a party at court requiring chamber music, a royal birthday celebration, or a regular church service, composers were required to provide new compositions for each event. They also functioned as performers and conductors, as well as teachers and organizers. As Cantor of St. Thomas's Church in Leipzig, Johann Sebastian Bach not only had to write a new cantata (a major work for soloists, chorus, and orchestra) almost every week, but he had to notate it in parts, rehearse the musicians, conduct it in performance, and organize the music for the other churches in town.

Although Baroque composers notated most of their music, it was common practice to leave room for the musicians to improvise in performance. Composers were not required to write out each ornament and note as musicians were expected to know where and how to correctly embellish the music. The most obvious form of improvisation occurred in the continuo part, which was written just as a figured bass line. Harpsichordists or organists played the notated line with their left hand, often supported on this same line by bass instruments such as the cello or bassoon, while improvising a part based on the appropriate chords with their right hand.

These improvisatory practices gradually died out after the Baroque period. Although Mozart was a fabulous improviser, his music is completely notated. The score became the complete blueprint for performance and performers were left little room for real improvisation. The cadenza was the one place that performers were given free rein. Typically occurring in concertos featuring a single instrument and orchestra, the soloist's cadenza was and is often a lengthy passage occurring near the end of a movement. This moment gives the soloist a chance to display virtuosity and brilliance while the other instruments are silent. As the cadenza climaxs and ends, the orchestra then comes back in to finish the piece.

During the Classical period (roughly 1750–1825) a growing public concert world started to play a much greater role in the music's social maintenance. While some composers—such as Franz Josef Haydn—still relied mainly on courtly patronage, others—including Mozart, Beethoven, and Franz Schubert—relied partly or entirely on public venues and private patronage for financial support. Accordingly, their music developed in ways which were congenial to public concert settings, with listening audiences who wanted to experience a more dramatic range of expression. Orchestras and opera companies grew larger, and the works written for them became longer and appealed to wider audiences. Works for smaller ensembles also grew longer, and similarly more diverse in their expressive range. Instruments were developed to produce fuller, richer tones, and wider dynamic and pitch capabilities.

Such trends continued as public patronage became even more important in the Romantic period (roughly 1815–1900), with the massive operas of Richard Wagner, Giuseppe Verdi, and Giacomo Puccini; the fervent symphonies of Robert Schumann, Johannes Brahms, and Gustav Mahler; and in the increasingly virtuosic chamber works of many composers. While most of these composers wrote sacred music as well, after the Baroque era it was increasingly unlikely that a composer would be regularly employed to provide a new church piece every Sunday. Sacred musical traditions generally became more conservative (with occasional exceptions, such as the monumental Requiem Masses of Verdi and Brahms), and religious institutions sponsored the creation of new musical works less often.

The role and function of the composer also changed during the nineteenth century as a separation developed between composer, performer, and conductor—they were no longer certain to be the same person. Both composition and conducting became more specialized activities. Beethoven was probably the first composer to make his living solely from composing. Regarded as a genius in his own lifetime, he is also viewed as the first truly independent artist who followed his own muse. Subsequent composers came to be regarded as visionaries and artists rather than craftsmen—each engaged in creating his or her own unique expression.

Twentieth-Century Trends

Around the beginning of the twentieth century composers such as Claude Debussy, Bela Bartók, Arnold Schoenberg, and Igor Stravinsky started to push classical music well beyond many of its prevailing formal and harmonic conventions. The cataclysmic social and political events surrounding the two World Wars were mirrored in all the arts by an increasing abandonment of standard practices, in a conviction that a new artistic order must accompany a new world order, along with a sense that older practices were unredeemably tainted by the wrongs of the past.

IGOR STRAVINSKY

Much of twentieth-century classical music has involved such a rejection of previous norms of tonality, melody, and harmony in the search for new techniques and sounds. Some of these techniques have included the use of electronic instruments and computers, the use of ambient and chance sounds, the invention of new instruments, and the incorporation of non-Western musical elements. Twentieth century composers have taken, and continue to take, a variety of individual approaches to musical creation, making use of what has gone before while perpetually forging new paths. Some, including the Australian composer Stephen Leek, have experimented with the use of improvisation in their compositions.

Leek is one of the best known composers in Australia today, as well as founder of Australian Voices, a choir devoted to performing vocal works by contemporary Australian composers. Although his scores are entirely notated, most of his compositions allow for some improvisation, either in structure, rhythm, texture, or form. By allowing this type of freedom, Leek believes that his music is given new life and expression in every performance. He also feels that his approach allows for dynamic collaboration between composer and performer:

I actually build into my scores elements so that the performances are never the same, so the performer has the opportunity to have input into decision making along the process of the performance of the piece. It could be for instance that they are given pitch materials and they're asked to extend the durations or choose the durations. It could be they are not given any pitch material at all, but given the rhythmic structure. . . . And that for me provides a really exciting medium where it's not just me as the immortal composer, but (I am) part of a process which comes alive during every performance.[14]

STEPHEN LEEK

A performance of "Kondalilla."

"Kondalilla," the third movement of Leek's four movement choral work, *Great Southern Spirits,* provides one example of his use of improvisation within a portion of a composition. In the opening he gives the sopranos specified pitches, but allows them to put them into any rhythmic framework:

> *The sopranos open the movement with information which is provided in a box which they can interpret and repeat ad lib, by deciphering the information that's there and making choices about where they place the material, how long the material occurs, how thick the texture becomes they have some input into the polyphony of the piece. . . . Sometimes it might be quite thin, sometimes there might be silence, sometimes there might be quite a dense sort of sound. . . . They decide how the tension is created and released.[15]*

While Leek has been quite successful in getting recognition and support throughout Australia for his work, other composers have not been as lucky. In many cases, experimental music has proved disastrous for public patronage: feeling assaulted by unpleasant and seemingly incomprehensible new music, audiences largely have withdrawn their support. Most orchestras and opera companies have been forced to become very conservative in their programming, offering relatively few performances of new music. If it were not for the support of academic institutions and private foundations, much of this innovative music could not survive today.

At this moment, the Western classical performance world is still dominated by works from the Classical and Romantic periods. Both musicians and audiences often favor these works, and a typical short list of "the great composers" would largely comprise those from these two periods, with less from the Baroque era and the twentieth century and still fewer from pre-Baroque times. Still, there are thriving performance scenes for "early music" and "contemporary music," each with its own public and private patronage systems.

Although their role in society has changed over time, contemporary composers continue to write new music that keeps the Western classical tradition growing and dynamic as they recharge, rejuvenate, and reshape music materials into their own individual artistic creations. Some, such as Phillip Glass, Steve Reich, Lou Harrison, and Gordon Gottleib, are greatly influenced by non-European traditions. According to composer Gerald Shapiro, the process depends on what has gone before—all the music and techniques of previous composers—as well as the composer's own training and inspiration:

> *I think what I'm writing is one long piece and that I chop off a section of it and I give it out. And every piece has something of the material that came before. Every piece is an intersection. I live a life. I have children, I have parents, a wife. I'm happy. I'm sad. Something is going well. Something is going poorly. I work as a teacher of composition. I discuss how to shape different intervals and different chords into effective wholes. . . . Two separate lines are happening. . . . There's a technical study that's going on. I'm learning all the time about music, and studying new ways of using techniques. And I'm living a life and learning all the time what's in my heart, you know, what's in the world around me. And each piece represents a special intersection between those two things.[16]*

▬▬ COMPOSITION AND THE FOLK PROCESS: NEW ENGLAND CONTRA DANCE MUSIC

While music in the Western classical tradition has been created, for the most part, by known composers, Euro-American traditional or folk musics are often anonymous. Even though individual composers originally conceived these songs and instrumental pieces, their work entered a common body of repertory in generic forms, in which the composers' names are forgotten over time. The music is often transmitted orally from musician to musician; each performer in the chain personalizes it as it becomes part of his or her repertory. There is no single definition of music that is considered "folk" or "traditional," but typically, traditional music genres have great meaning for a community and have been passed down from one generation to the next.

Although authorship in many folk genres is obscured and old repertoire is cherished, new compositions help to keep a tradition dynamic. In the contemporary contra dance world, for example, both old tunes and new tunes intermingle in performance. Composers work within established parameters of tune structure, but create new melodies. Because of recordings and publications, some composers now get credit for their tune creations, although many tunes still enter the common repertory anonymously. Since performers improvise on tunes during dances, compositions tend to get slightly altered as they are passed from musician to musician. We now look at this tradition in more detail.

Music Repertory

As discussed in Chapter 2, contra dances are thought to have originated in England before the sixteenth century and imported to America in the seventeenth and eighteenth centuries. The dances have always been closely associated with the music used for their accompaniment. The current music repertory is drawn primarily from a pool of Irish, Scottish, French Canadian, and Cape Breton fiddle tunes—reels, jigs, marches, and hornpipes. There are thousands of tunes in this repertory, many dating back to the eighteenth century.

Published tune collections have long been part of the Anglo-Celtic-American fiddle tune tradition and new ones continue to be published. These collections, at least up until the last twenty years, typically presented the tunes with no acknowledged composer. Instead, the tunes, were (and are) considered part of the "folk tradition," unowned by any single composer. Because oral transmission—passing the music on directly from musician to musician—plays such an important role in the maintenance of the tradition, tune authorship is less valued than in many other musical genres. While tune names sometimes indicate the name of the composer ("Coleman's Jig" for example), most do not. Tunes are felt to be "owned" by the musicians who play them.

Nevertheless, new compositions have been an integral part of the contra dance repertory, as they have been in other fiddle tune traditions. In Cape Breton, Novia Scotia, for example, composing is characteristic among fiddlers. According to a study by Virginia Garrison, about one quarter of the musicians she interviewed had written a tune, while a few became known as prolific composers.[17] Peter Cooke found a similar situation in the Shetland Islands where he reported that composing is also an important part of the fiddling tradition. While most musicians compose a few tunes, a minority consider themselves, and are considered by others, as composers.[18]

Bob McQuillen

Bob McQuillen is reputed to be the most prolific composer in the New England contra dance scene. Although he got his start playing dance music in the 1940s, he didn't begin composing until 1972. The tune "Scotty O'Neill" was written in memory of one of his students who died in a motor cycle accident. He gradually started composing more tunes after this first attempt, most of which were written for and dedicated to special people in his life, including friends, fellow musicians, callers, and children. He published his first book of tunes entitled *Bob's Notebooks* in 1975 and released his tenth in 1994. These books are self published and distributed by McQuillen himself and a number of folk music stores. He always sends a complimentary copy to each person for whom he's written a tune in that particular volume.

McQuillen said that he writes tunes because he loves both the process of writing and of meeting people for whom he wants to write a tune:

> *I'm going to 1500 next. I'm going to keep on. I can see no way that I'm going to stop writing the tunes. The tunes are too much fun. It's a fun trip to do, it's a neat thing. I love doing it. And as long as there are people I enjoy meeting and have relation with in the music scene, why I'm going to find people I'm going to want to write a tune for.[19]*

McQuillen stated that he has no desire to put an individual stamp on his tunes. Instead he says that he is writing to fit into the "New England tradition" that is a composite repertory of anonymous fiddle tunes from different origins:

> *It can sound a lot of different ways because we use here in New England lots of different ethnic origins in our music. We've got the Scottish thing, well the Cape Breton style I'll put it that way. . . . Then we have the Irish thing and then we have the French thing from Canada. And then we have, I don't know whether to call it just naturally New England. . . . So those things are all old New England tunes and so I can make a tune so that it sounds French, or I can make it in the Irish tradition with the endings and inflections. . . . I can do all this different stuff that would fit into the tradition. And so that's what I emulate.*

> *I'm just doing my thing the best that I can and as far as my stamp, I don't have a stamp. There are others who say to me, "That sounds like a McQuillen tune . . . but I don't know what that means. . . . All I know is that I do my thing and this is how it comes out and if they call that a McQuillen style, well that's what it is. . . . I just plain write them.[20]*

A performance of "Amelia."

While McQuillen says that relatively few of his 1000 tunes have been performed extensively, some have become part of the collective contra dance repertory, including "Amelia," "The Dancing Bear," "The Boys of Antrim," "Mary Elders Jig," and "Spring Song."

In explaining how these tunes became part of the folk tradition, he cites the circulation of his books as the primary reason:

> I just put out a book and somebody played it and they liked the sound of it and it went on. . . . I started putting these damn books out and they just went round and round and round. And I keep putting them out, so pretty soon people are starting to look at it. And especially if they got their tune in there.[21]

McQuillen draws much of his inspiration for composing from the people around him. His tunes—taken as a unique body of repertoire—create a whole community of people who have been recipients of their own Bob McQuillen tune. Other composers in the contra dance scene have different approaches to their work, but this pattern of personalizing tunes after people and places is a common theme in the composing process.

Nevertheless, McQuillen suggests that he is less interested in having his tunes be labeled "McQuillen" tunes, but prefers that they get played enough to be considered part of the "folk tradition." His attitude reflects a value system that honors the group over the individual by producing new sounds which fit perfectly with old ones.

▬ COMPOSITION IN NATIVE AMERICAN CULTURES

The indigenous peoples of America have developed many musical genres which are conservative, but not closed: while new compositions are valued, and sometimes even required, they follow the conventions of the tradition. Of course, many Native Americans are involved with genres that mix indigenous elements with ideas from popular and other musics. But since this kind of mixing is a global phenomenon, here we will concentrate on the older Native American traditions and the concepts and practices through which their practitioners continually replenish their repertories: the process of recombining traditional materials, sometimes as a collaborative effort, and the influence of the supernatural.

Numerous indigenous cultures exist throughout North and South America, each with its own traditions; the present examples are drawn from the Great Plains and southwestern desert regions of the United States.

Recombining

What makes a new song acceptable within a conservative tradition? One might approach this question by asking its opposite: what would make a new song unacceptable? One answer is ineptitude, the composer simply proving unequal to the aesthetic task of generating a pleasing product. A further answer involves the materials of composition: a new piece will not be accepted if it is not made up of the appropriate elements, properly used. Established repertories consist of pieces which employ predominantly traditional components in traditional ways, and a new addition to such a repertory must do the same.

This kind of compositional process has been called *recombining*.[22] Like an author using the common words and structures of a language to produce a new literary work, the composer employs the tradition's characteristic materials, recombining them in a new way which still adheres to its organizational models. In genres like Hindustani, Western classical, and Arabic musics these materials and models are explicitly codified and taught; in many other traditions they are implicit, acquired only through immersion in the repertory. In the words of an Eskimo song recorded by Laura Boulton:

> *All songs have been exhausted.*
> *He picks up some of all*
> *And adds his own*
> *And makes a new song.*[23]

For example, when Judith Vander asked "Do you ever make up handgame songs?" the Shoshone singer Helene Furlong replied "Yeah, try to put two and two together, or page number 1 with page 21."[24] Responding to a similar question, the Shoshone singer Lenore Shoyo said, "Yeah, I had to work at it. So I sat home all day thinking of a song. And I keep getting mixed up. I had a hard time, but I finally got it together."[25] Putting "page number 1 with page 21," "getting mixed up," and "finally [getting] it together" articulate the process of recombining: reordering traditional elements and mixing them until they come together in a satisfying way.

Composing in this manner can also be a collaborative undertaking. Furlong's brother Wayland described this kind of process to Vander:

> WAYLAND: *"It's some songs put together on the end and some songs that was this year's and altogether mixed."*
> JUDY: *"You said that C. helped too?"*
> WAYLAND: *"Yes, he added little bits here and there. So it was really the two of us."*
> JUDY: *"Do you usually do that when you make up a song?"*
> WAYLAND: *"Most generally. That was the first time that C. and I ever made up a song together. Most of the time it's with Helene."*[26]

The kachina dance songs of the Hopi are cooperatively composed for each annual performance occasion, following traditional musical and textual regulations. In some cases a number of men from the kachina cult sit together and collectively work out a new song. In other cases a male member of the cult provides a preliminary composition which he then presents to the group. They have no obligation to accept it. If they accept it they are free to alter it. The composer may even request this, if he is unsatisfied with part of it.

Similarly, the music for the Cloud Dance of San Juan Pueblo is freshly composed each year, following its own set of traditional rules. The example given here was composed by Peter Garcia, Sr. and then submitted to a group of song composers for any changes they might deem necessary.

AUDIO 61

A performance of "San Juan Pueblo Cloud Dance Song," part 2.

"San Juan Pueblo Cloud Dance Song" by Peter Garcia, Sr., part 2.
Translation by the composer.

Verse 1:
Sun blueish Lake, its surrounding areas, from there the sacred Koshares began to come out—on top of the lake, they began to jump about. (repeat)

> **Chorus 1:**
> Over there from the Laguna Lake, the summer Kachina Boys began to come out. Over there from the Laguna Lake the summer Kachina Girls started to come, with their corn-producing process and with their wheat-growing process, here at this place they arrived. [repeat Verse 1 and Chorus 1]
>
> **Verse 2:**
> It is from here, San Juan Village, the Keres way, the Parrots ways, humming bird boys in their own way are enjoying their ways of life. It is from here, San Juan Village, the Keres way, the Parrots ways, humming bird girls in their own way are sounding their sacred horns.
>
> **Chorus 2:**
> Over there from the Laguna Lake, the summer Kachina Boys began to come out. Over there from the Laguna Lake the summer Kachina Girls started to come, with their rain-making process and with their water-producing process, here at this place they arrived. [repeat Verse 2 and Chorus 2]

San Juan and Hopi are both Pueblo cultures, and they share several features. Like the Hopi kachina dances, the San Juan Cloud Dance is concerned with rain and crop fertility; Garcia's lyrics refer to kachina boys and girls and to koshares, the sacred clowns, invoking their power. Pueblo cosmology recognizes an inherent duality in creation, and Pueblo song texts often have parallel constructions referring to the male and female sides of this duality, as in this example. Also typical of Pueblo songs, the verses and choruses are framed by sections sung with vocables. Garcia has worked within the accepted traditional models, recombining their elements to produce a new song that fits in well with the existing repertory.

The Supernatural

Some Plains cultures have traditionally placed great importance on the "vision quest," a solitary search for spiritual power which often has involved travel and fasting over several days. In a state of physical weakness and heightened consciousness, the seeker would experience visions which might not be exclusively visual: they could include voices, and songs. Usually some kind of agent would be involved-a spirit being who brings the song and presents it to the receiver. A Flathead described such an experience to Alan Merriam:

> There was a guy who was looking for power once, and he heard a guy coming from a long way off, singing a song. He finally met the guy, and the guy was singing a stick game song. He told the young feller, "When you get to be a certain age, you can use that song for the stick game." The young man remembered the song until the time he came to use it.[27]

Songs from supernatural sources contain personal power. The "young feller" now had a song which belonged to no one else, and he could use it for his own spiritual and physical strengthening.

Another of Merriam's Flathead examples did not involve a formal vision quest, but involved an intensified emotional state:

When someone is discouraged or he doesn't know what to do, he may be sitting around his tipi and a spirit comes to tell him what to do. Sometimes he can hear the singing from way far off, and hear it approaching. Before daylight he hears the spirit coming, always from the East. The tipi always faces east, with its ears up. [The ears refer to the open smoke flaps of the tipi.] The spirit comes from afar and hits the ears; then it comes down the ears and stands in front of the person. It tells him what to do, and it sings the song. As it comes toward the tipi it has been singing the song many times as it comes.[28]

In this case the man's tipi was a participant in the process: his home—an extension of himself—received the spirit first, through its "ears."

Visions and songs may arrive without invitation. Another Flathead man told Merriam of being briefly left alone in the wilderness with his young sister when he was "eight or nine" years old. His sister suddenly saw a grizzly bear approaching them, and alerted her brother. A vision ensued:

I went out of my head. I was way up on top of a mountain. People were dancing, singing, playing stick game, cards. I looked around and it was me singing. Then I went out again. I was on another mountain and the same people were there doing the same thing. The grizzly bear took me back each time, and this happened on four mountains. The people all had otter skins around their heads. All the animals were singing and dancing in there. It was always me singing.[29]

As in many visions, the agent here was a powerful animal, who transported the boy to four similar locations (perhaps symbolic of the four directions, north, south, east, and west). Animals can provide an effective link to the supernatural, providing a bridge between human consciousness and the unknown world beyond.

Merriam arrived at some interesting ideas about the Flathead examples he encountered, which are worth bringing up here. Rejecting the notion of "unconscious composition," he pointed out that in his examples

one aspect of the process seems to be repeated again and again. This is the fact that the song, which the petitioner will later learn, is first heard from far away; the being who is singing it comes closer and closer, singing constantly, until it finally actually appears. Without desiring to stretch a point too far, it seems quite likely that this formalized supernatural-song pattern refers symbolically to the process of composition. That is, the song is dimly heard (dimly formulated) at first, and then becomes clearer and clearer as the supernatural being approaches (as the petitioner gains a stronger sense of the structure of the song he is, in fact, composing) . . . [In other examples] it is significant to note that although the pattern of slow approach is not suggested, there is substituted a type of situation in which the individual is subjected to a number of repetitions of the songs he will learn . . . while the people would hotly deny the interpretation presented here, it seems likely that hallucination and composition are closely connected in the manner suggested.[30]

While outsiders may judge such a rational approach to be more "realistic" than an insider's viewpoint, the Native American conception is worthy of nuanced understanding. Important clues can be found in descriptions of personal experiences like that of Angelina Wagner, who told Vander about a Sun Dance song in her repertory:

> *My mother, she found that song. When the sun was coming out and she came into our kitchen and then she heard that song. She was sleeping the first time she heard that song, so she start in singing that song. And when she sang that song, well, she thought that it was a prayer song. Something mentioned to her that it would be a prayer song. That's the way they do, too, for the Ghost Dance songs. It's got meanings to them or something like that, to somebody who found that song. So she got up and was singing that song, and she went in there to the room where my dad was sleeping; and she sang that song for him and my dad just caught that song all at once [the sign of a true visionary song]. He just sang it once, and he knew that song and that's what they sing. And my dad sang that song 'cause it was my mother's song. The old man said, "Well, if it's given to you, maybe it's been a blessing for you."* [31]

Notice the verbs Wagner used for song acquisition: "found," "heard," "caught," and "given." These are the words heard again and again among Native Americans describing such experiences. They point to the concept that the song already exists, in a realm beyond consciousness. In extraordinary moments, such a song can be "found" and "caught," "given" and "heard." The first pairing recalls the experiences of successful hunting; the second suggests a bestowal to a worthy recipient. To many Native Americans the two readings are not only compatible, but intertwined.

While Wagner's father was not an agent of this song's provenance, he played an important role in confirming its authenticity as a vision song. It was well-received, and became an integral part of the Sun Dance ritual. Another of Vander's Shoshone examples—this time from a "dream" at a peyote meeting—combines the phenomenon of wife/husband confirmation with visualization and animal agency (or, in this case, insect agency):

> *We had a meeting one time a long time ago, and this fireplace was still there in front of the cabin. . . . There was a butterfly flying right on top of it, and it was humming this certain song. It was a real pretty song; my mother was asleep, and she started humming that same song that my dad was thinking about and he was seeing. You know, you can't visualize somebody seeing a song, but he did. He seen that song as well as it coming to his mind. This butterfly was fluttering around that song just like that song right over that fireplace. And he seen it. See, this is his dream, or he seen it, visualized it. All of a sudden he just woke up and started singing that song. And my mother was thinking about that same song.* [32]

Native American conceptions of song acquisition through connections to the supernatural world do not require rational explanations; their validity for the cultures in which they are valued suffices for our respect. But whether one embraces an indigenous or Western analytic viewpoint, songs of supernatural provenance are songs of power: they are not trivial. In this connection, we may observe that tales are also told of Western composers who were supernaturally stimulated, perhaps in visions, for one or more of their compositions. Composers like Bach and Mozart are sometimes referred to as "divinely inspired," particularly for their sublime religious masterpieces. Such Western concepts also involve the idea that extrahuman energies can contribute to both musical generation and power.

■ IMPROVISATION IN NORTH INDIAN CLASSICAL INSTRUMENTAL MUSIC

In the Western classical traditions, the "labor" of music-making is usually divided between separate individuals who perform the distinct roles of composer, conductor, vocalist and instrumentalist. The composer creates a musical score, the conductor makes important decisions about tempo and interpretation and directs the actual performance, and the singers and instrumentalists read the score, follow the conductor's signals, and create the sounds which the audience hears in a concert hall or on a recording or broadcast.

In North Indian classical music, one individual commonly performs all of these functions in a single performance. If the solo performer is an instrumentalist, he probably has learned to sing the same music that he plays on the sitar, sarod, violin, sarangi, flute, or shehnai, because Indian instrumental music in large measure imitates the style of vocal music. In concert, the soloist spontaneously chooses the repertory to be performed, sets the tempo, and sings or plays a program in which she composes large portions of the performance on the spur of the moment. Accompanists follow the directions of the soloist, who combines at once the roles of composer, conductor, and performer.

The musician's improvisations are guided by the conventions of raga (melodic mode), tala (rhythmic cycle), and the forms of a variety of vocal and instrumental genres. We may regard the basic forms of Indian music as a sort of mold into which the musician pours the performance of a particular raga. Thus, the performer's improvisation is not absolutely free. He must always maintain the basic character of the raga, fit his playing into the rhythmic framework of the tala, and present more or less in order the different portions of a complete classical performance. The overall form, and to a large extent, the melodic content of his exposition, is dictated by tradition, but he is free to fill the mold according to his own spontaneous inspiration.

On a microscopic level, the soloist may improvise even when playing the pre-composed gat in a sitar or sarod recital. Ornamentation, in the form of added grace notes or slight variations in rhythm and melody, is a constant factor in the style of many players and singers. Such subtle variations are so common that most Indian musicians might not even think of them as improvisation. In the player's mind, a few correctly added grace notes do not "change" the composition at all, and improvisation occurs not in the playing of the gat, but in other portions of a performance: the introductory alap, jor, and jhala, and the layakari (rhythmic play) and tans (fast passages) which follow the opening statement of the gat.

Alap, Jor, and Jhala

The principle function of a player or singer's introductory alap is to establish the mood and outline the melodic features of the raga being performed. The first step is to present the key-note sa. The next step is to fill in the lower and middle octaves of the soloist's instrumental or vocal range, proceeding through a series of improvised melodic "limbs," each of which helps to reveal the important notes and melodic gestures of the raga being performed. After the leisurely alap is complete, the player proceeds to the jor and then the jhala, in which a pulse is first established and then accelerated, giving rhythm an increasingly prominent place in the performance.

Gat, Layakari, and Tans

Rhythm becomes still more important when a player renders a gat (instrumental composition), set in a rhythmic cycle such as the sixteen-beat teental. During the alap, jor, and jhala, the instrumentalist improvises within the limits imposed by the raga being performed. Once the gat has been introduced, all improvisations must also be tailored to fit within the tala structure, dovetailing perfectly with the first few notes of the gat, which serve as a point of departure and return for episodes of rhythmic play (layakari) and fast passages (tans). Layakari and tans can be short, taking only a few beats of a single tala cycle, or extended, continuing for several cycles.

Buddhadev Das Gupta presents a complete performance of Rag Kamod, including alap, jor, jhala, slow and fast gats, layakari, and tans. The form chart given in Chapter 10, page 249 is a useful "roadmap" to the composed and improvised sections of this performance.

[Additional listening analysis is at the end of the chapter.]

▬ IMPROVISATION IN ARABIC MUSIC

In Arabic art music, instrumental improvisations called *taqasim* may either be extended items in a recital, or short introductions to, or bridges between, composed pieces. In either case, the taqasim provides an opportunity for the soloist to display both his virtuosity and his knowledge of the *maqamat* (melodic modes) of Arabic music.

The form of the taqasim, melodic improvisation in free rhythm, appears to have a relationship to the *tajwid* form of Qur'anic chant, and to "a broad generic continuum in which the taksim is one vehicle for the expression of *tarab* (musical rapture or ecstacy)"[33] Taqasim therefore seems to have a close connection with both orthodox and less conventional forms of Islamic worship.

Each taqasim is structured in a way that both reveals the essential melodic characteristics of the maqam being rendered, and allows the improviser to explore relationships with other maqamat. Like a raga, each maqam has a particular set of notes which provide a basic vocabulary for improvisation and composition. A performer will begin his taqasim by focusing on a small group of notes, gradually expanding to include and highlight different aspects of the maqam. Movement through the octave, and especially into higher and lower octaves, often involves the use of accidentals—sharps, half-sharps, flats, or half-flats—which are part of the melodic "personality" of the mode.

After the initial maqam in a taqasim has been introduced, the performer may begin to modulate—moving from one maqam to another. Musicians commonly conceive of the maqamat in groups of related modes, and musical mastery requires a thorough knowledge, not only of the maqam with which a

Instrumentalist Simon Shaheen plays a taqasim on the 'ud, an unfretted, plucked instrument related to the European lute and guitar. He is accompanied by Michel Merhej on the tambourine or daff.

[Additional listening analysis is at the end of the chapter.]

performance begins, but of the entire modal landscape which might be traversed in the course of an improvisation. Skillful modulation demonstrates the artist's grace and ingenuity, and players who excel in this aspect of taqasim are greatly admired by knowledgeable listeners.

▆▆ IMPROVISATION IN JAZZ

Jazz has undergone many transformations during the nearly one century since its birth in New Orleans. The product of the interplay of African, European, and American musical traditions in the urban south, jazz originated with African-American composers and performers and has since become a truly international genre.

Jazz performance is essentially the art of improvising within a certain set of stylistic limits. Within those parameters, the musician speaks a particular musical "language," with its own vocabulary and grammatical conventions. This language, a synthesis of African, European, North American, and Latin American musical elements, is constantly evolving, as new musicians contribute their own, individual dialects to the mix.

Among the features of West African music that informed the development of jazz, improvisation over a texture of repeating ostinatos was a key element. The "time-line" which is maintained by the bell in an Ashanti or Ewe drumming ensemble, has its analog in the "groove" established by a jazz drummer on his high-hat cymbal, and the repeating tonal and rhythmic patterns in the accompaniment part played by a Mande *kora* player has its parallel in the pulsations of the "walking bass" in a jazz ensemble.

Over these repeating patterns, jazz vocalists and instrumental soloists improvise virtuoso passages which both reach back to African vocal and instrumental traditions and also express an exuberant individualism which seems entirely American. The later development of "free jazz" in the playing of musicians like Ornette Coleman in the 1960's, in which all the members of an ensemble were given license to improvise as "soloists" simultaneously, seems a particularly boisterous expression of an American ideal—that of a society free of the constraints of rigid convention and "old-world" social hierarchies.

Form

In the traditional forms which pre-date, and have persisted through and beyond the era of "free jazz," jazz musicians typically begin their performances by playing an item from the "standard" repertory, often the melody of a popular song, with an eight-bar "A" section played twice, an eight-bar "B" section called the "bridge," and a concluding "A" section which often has a different and more "final" sounding conclusion than the original "A." After playing this thirty-two measure melody once or twice, a jazz soloist or ensemble begins several rounds of improvisation.

These improvisations may fall anywhere on a continuum from recognizable variations on the original melody to highly abstract melodic statements which bear no resemblance to the tune which served as a point of departure. Wherever the improvisation falls on this continuum, however, it must fulfill two requirements: 1) it must conform to the harmonic sequence of the original melody, and 2) it must "fit" rhythmically into the usually thirty-two bar form of the song.

Language

The language of jazz includes several elements. All players share, first of all, a common harmonic vocabulary, consisting of the various chords which can be constructed in the key in which the song is written. Among these chords, there is a hierarchy, somewhat like the "pitch hierarchy" in a raga or maqam.

The "I" chord, built on the keynote of the song, usually serves as the first and (especially) the last chord in a song—it is the home base, to which all improvisations ultimately return. The "V" chord, built on the fifth scale degree of the key in which the song is written, is second in importance to the "I" chord; the final cadence or harmonic resolution in a song usually consists of motion from "five" to "one." This cadence is usually preceded by the "II" chord, built on the second degree of the scale; "II-V-I" is the most commonly heard harmonic progression in traditional jazz, particularly at final cadences.

These chord symbols are often written above the notated melody in "lead sheets" which serve as a score for learning or performing jazz compositions. The chord symbols provide guidance both to the improvising soloist and to the accompanists, who improvise their accompaniment by deciding how to "voice" the chords (high or low, broad and lush or thin and sparse), and how to fit them rhythmically into the structure of a measure.

In addition to a common harmonic language, jazz musicians also share a vocabulary of melodic motifs or "riffs," popular melodic fragments inherited from previous generations of players. In some cases, a large repertory of such motifs can be traced to a single influential musician, like the seminal bebop saxophonist, Charlie Parker. Other riffs, like the commonly heard walking bass line associated with boogie-woogie piano-playing, are part of the legacy of anonymous musicians in oral tradition.

JAZZ IMPROVISATION

Musicians adopt these riffs, break them up, and re-combine them in a never ending stream of improvisation, employing them just as people use cliches ("How do you like them apples?" "Is that so?" "Well I never!") in everyday speech.

Finally, each jazz musician must create his or her own vocabulary of personal motifs, a repertory of original riffs that become a distinctive trademark of his or her improvisational style. In each player's improvising, we will hear her use of the common harmonic language, the employment of favorite motifs from players who have influenced the individual, and hopefully some original riffs which carry the artistic "signature" of a performer who has begun to create a personal dialect within the larger language of jazz.

▬ CHAPTER SUMMARY

In looking at musical creation on a continuum, we have examined ideas of composition and improvisation in several traditions. Many musics involve at least some element of both composition and improvisation in their conception or performance. As we have seen, musical creativity is linked to various kinds of flexible or rigid considerations—rules, norms, tendencies—which are embedded in culture.

Some of these responses are rooted in learned techniques related specifically to musical tradition, while others are drawn from other aspects of culture and the environment. Although composers and improvisers work in the present, they are grounded in the past. They are part of a musical system that gives them the necessary materials and tools (instruments) to work with. It is from these raw materials that composers and improvisers fashion their own unique creations.

ADDITIONAL LISTENING

AUDIO #58 IMPROVISATION IN RAG KAMOD: A BRIEF ANALYSIS

Buddhadev Das Gupta begins his alap in a brief gesture which ends on Sa (C) at 0:06. He reveals the "minister-note" Re (D) at 0:10 and then slides up to the "king-note" Pa (G) at 0:13. During the remainder of the first "limb," which concludes on Sa at 0:42, he sketches the crooked motion of Rag Kamod in a series of short, zig-zagging gestures.

In the portions of alap, jor, and jhala which follow, Buddhadev Das Gupta continues to show the basic melodic contours and pitch hierarchy of Rag Kamod as he moves first through the lower octave, then the middle and upper octaves, and then gives an increasing emphasis to pulse and rhythm.

In the sections of rhythmic play and fast tans that follow Buddhadev Das Gupta's exposition of the composed gat (beginning at 3:40), his improvisations conform not only to the melodic contours of Rag Kamod, but to the rhythmic structure of the sixteen-beat cycle known as teental. His first episode of rhythmic play, beginning at 4:15, takes one cycle of teental, concluding at 4:28. Other episodes of layakari follow. The tempo increases at 5:45, and he plays his first fast tan at 5:51. This short tan occupies only eight beats, one-half cycle of teental, concluding at 5:56. At 6:00 he plays a longer tan, which takes 28 beats or one and three-quarters cycles, ending the medium tempo gat at 6:20.

Improvised tabla solos are interspersed between the sarod layakari and tans. The medium tempo gat is followed by a fast gat, with more layakari, tans, and tabla solos.

AUDIO #62. SIMON SHAHEEN PLAYS A TAQASIM ON THE 'UD

Simon Shaheen begins his improvisation in maqam Nahawand, which sounds very much like the C harmonic minor scale, using the notes C, D, E-flat, F, G, A-flat, and B natural. At 0:35 in the recording, "A" is raised to its natural position, signaling a shift in focus to the octave note (c) rather than the lower tonic (C). At 0:52, Mr. Shaheen plays G-flat, a characteristic accidental note in maqam Nahawand.

At 1:04, we hear the first modulation, to maqam Bayyati on G. The tonic note moves from C to G, and the notes A half-flat, B-flat, and E half-flat are introduced. In this modulation and in the two which follow, continuity is provided by the continued use of tones already introduced, while interest is stimulated by the introduction of new, unanticipated notes.

At 1:44, Mr. Shaheen makes a second modulation, to maqam Saba on G. The tonic remains at G, and c-flat and g-flat are introduced. At 2:07 he starts to return to maqam Nahawand, first by introducing a transitional moment with A natural and F sharp. Then the B natural is returned along with A-flat, and we are back in maqam Nahawand. Finally, at 2:52, the taqasim ends in the same maqam in which it began.

STUDY QUESTIONS

1. What is the difference between composition and improvisation?

2. What are some of the improvised elements in the performance of a composition that is completely notated?

3. What are some of the composed elements in jazz performance?

4. What is the "folk process?"

5. Describe some examples where composers are influenced by nature and the supernatural.

6. Describe an Arabic taqasim.

REFERENCED SOURCES

1. Quigley, 1995: 18.
2. Koetting, 1992: 84.
3. Titon, 1978.
4. Feld, 1982.
5. Rasmussen, 1931: 321.
6. Berliner, 1994: 258.
7. Ibid.
8. Merriam, 1964: 180.
9. Feld, 1982.
10. Quigley, 1995: 68–90.
11. Chernoff, 1979: 110.
12. Babbit, 1958: 126–7.
13. Quigley, 1995: 19.
14. Leek, interview 1997.
15. Ibid.
16. Shapiro, interview 1997.
17. Garrison, 1985: 206.
18. Cooke, 1986: 24–7.
19. McQuillen, interview 1993.
20. Ibid.
21. Ibid.
22. Cowdery, 1990: 92ff.
23. Boulton, 1954: 5.
24. Vander, 1988: 183.
25. Ibid.: 227.
26. Ibid.: 131.
27. Merriam, 1964: 168.
28. Ibid.
29. Ibid.: 169.
30. Ibid.: 168–9.
31. Vander, 1988: 66–7.
32. Helene Furlong, in ibid.: 141.
33. Feldman, 1993: 1–9.

CHAPTER 12

MUSIC AND TECHNOLOGY

About This Chapter

In this chapter we explore the interconnections between music and technologies. We learn that music has always involved technology, which extends human faculties beyond those of the unaided body. Several key concepts are presented: musical instruments enhance our melodic and rhythmic capabilities, and sometimes are imbued with notable cultural significance; sound amplification technology extends the capacity of our ears, and sound recording and reproduction can even be seen as an augmentation of our memory, enabling us to store and re-listen to musical performances, as well as an extension of our physical location in time and space. The chapter concludes by describing developments in electronic instruments and recording studio techniques that have opened a wide range of possibilities for creative musicians.

KEYWORDS

gong ageng
indie
synthesizer
overdubbing
soundscape
cassette culture
sampler

COMPANION RESOURCES

TELEVISION PROGRAM: Music and Technology

AUDIO SELECTIONS:

64. "Little Cabbage"

Music and technology have always been closely intertwined. Music from a radio or stereo system comes to our ears through twentieth-century technology. Earlier technologies, such as those of instrument building, also shape our experience of music. Musical technology develops along with music itself, the one constantly suggesting new ideas to the other.

Technology involves extending human capacities beyond those of the unaided body and mind. Some percussion instruments, like Australian Aboriginal clapping sticks, enhance the abilities of clapping hands, producing a louder, sharper sound and alleviating the pain of constantly striking the palms. Instruments like the flute and violin expand the capacity of the voice to produce melody, providing attractive sonorities and extended range and volume, and requiring less stamina than continuous singing.

More recent technologies offer an augmentation of the ears through electronic amplification, and of the memory through sound recording and storage. Sound reproduction technologies even extend our physical location in time and space, enabling us to hear music produced on the other side of the earth, perhaps before we were born.

Until the mid-twentieth century, most people believed that only humans could conceive of and produce extensions of the body. Now we know that some animals, such as chimpanzees, are capable of making and using certain kinds of tools. Still, technology—like music—is an essential part of being human, and an investigation of the relationships between these two subjects reveals the ways in which we bring our ingenuity to our expressive capacities, connecting our rational and emotional worlds. We will begin with our most fundamental use of technology in music, extending our bodies by manipulating other objects to produce sound.

■■■ MUSICAL INSTRUMENTS

Clapping or singing, rhythm or melody—no one knows which came first in human history. Both activities require only the human body. But as soon as something beyond the body was used, the idea of a musical instrument was born, and musical technology came into being. It is a fair guess that the first instruments were idiophones, since any hard objects can be struck together to make a sound. Melody-producing instruments involve more sophisticated technological developments.

We do not know when this kind of development first occurred, but a new discovery may push the date farther back than anyone previously thought. In a recent archeological investigation of a Neanderthal campsite, a bone fragment was found which looks like a flute: holes had been carved in it that closely resemble the fingerholes of flutes. Researcher Robert Fink has shown that the holes of this bone fragment would, if it indeed was a flute, produce a close approximation of a musical scale based on the overtone series. If this artifact was a flute—and some researchers feel that its relationship to the overtone-series scale proves this conclusively—it would be the oldest musical instrument known, somewhere between 43,000 and 82,000 years old.[1]

A flute involves relatively simple technology: basically, it is a tube with holes cut into it. The fife played by African-American musicians like Othar Turner is just a piece of cane stalk, cut to the desired length and reamed out with a hot poker, with one hole for blowing and five or six for the fingers. Similarly, the Japanese shakuhachi is a selected piece of hollowed-out bamboo with carefully-spaced finger holes, though it also involves further developments: a thumb-hole on the back, a specifically-shaped mouthpiece that allows it to be end-blown, and a lacquered interior.

Medieval European end-blown flutes, known as flageolets, incorporated similar technological developments, and European makers of both flutes and flageolets began to experiment with keys as well. A keyed bass recorder is an example of a technologically-advanced flageolet. The modern Western flute—a metal instrument with holes which are covered by padded keys rather than bare fingers, and with myriad extra keys for trills and accidentals—is a product of some of the latest developments in industrial technology.

A basic idiophone is also technologically simple. Many found objects already make a satisfying sound when struck, and others can be modified in uncomplicated ways—by hollowing-out or shaping—to produce a more desirable percussive sound.

Other instruments involve comparatively complex technology even in their simplest forms. A skin-headed drum requires at least three different materials: one for the resonator, one for the head, and one to attach the head to the resonator. The idea of one or more stretched strings is similarly complex, involving ways to adjust and maintain string tension, provide a resonating structure, and—in the case of fiddle-like instruments—to design and construct an effective bow.

MODERN FLUTE MAKING

The modern piano involves an even more complicated combination of technological developments. A stretched string can be set in vibrating motion, producing a tone. Stretched strings of varying length, weight, or materials can produce higher and lower tones. Such strings can be attached to a frame, like a harp, so one person can play them melodically, rhythmically, and chordally. This frame can be mounted on a resonator, like a zither, increasing the strings' volume and enhancing their timbre. The strings can be struck, making a more vibrant sound than plucking. They can also be dampened, so intricate playing does not become jumbled as the strings resonate over each other. A keyboard mechanism can operate one striker and damper per string, enabling the player to strike several strings at a time with an automating damping system which can be overridden by a foot pedal. And finally, this mechanical apparatus can be carefully adjusted to provide a wide range of dynamic subtlety. While we may not realize it when we enjoy the sound of piano music, we are listening to the operation of a complex technological marvel.

But musical instrument technology can involve more than just tool-making, just as musical instruments themselves can be more than mere sound-producing equipment. Instruments are imbued with cultural meaning, and the processes of creating them can be similarly significant. For example, Mantle Hood documented a process of drum making in Ghana which included offerings, libations, and formal speeches made to a selected tree before it was felled to provide the drum's hollowed-out resonator.[2] Another example of the intersection of technology and culture is the traditional process of making a *gong ageng*, the lowest and most important gong in a Central Javanese gamelan.

Gong Smithing in Central Java

Primary among the instruments of any gamelan is its largest gong, the gong ageng, *which sounds at the beginning and end of a composition, and accentuates other significant musical events, sometimes separated in performance by several minutes. Only the most skilled of musicians play the* gong ageng; *its deep reverberation and meaning can be fully savored only when it is struck precisely at the right moment and with precisely the right feeling. A* gong ageng *can inspire such deep respect that it is often given a formal, poetic name, such as "The Venerable Tempted to Smile," "The Venerable Aromatic Rain," or "The Venerable Honeyed Thunder," and it is by this name that its gamelan is known. Elaborate arrangements of food and incense are regularly laid out as offerings next to the gong stand and some even feel that it is through the gong ageng that one is able to hear the voice of the Almighty.*[3]

An instrument of surpassing spiritual power, the gong ageng is not to be rolled off an assembly line at a factory. Central Javanese gong-smiths have not availed themselves of twentieth-century technology: their art is practiced in much the same way it was done a hundred years ago. The process of making one gong ageng can easily occupy thirteen men, alternating to avoid exhaustion, for three full days or more.

Over a blazing fire fed by a goatskin bellows, copper is melted and tin is mixed in, carefully observing the required proportions, to make bronze. When the alloy is ready, it is poured into a pre-heated mold. Now the great energy of the workers must flow: bellows are pumped as the disk is heated in the fire until it is glowing red, and as soon as it is taken out and laid on an anvil the hammering begins. Up to five smiths, standing closely together around the fiery disk, must supply a torrential burst of pounding with their nine-kilogram hammers as it is slowly turned.

Soon the disk must be rushed again to the fire, while the smiths rest from their burst of strenuous activity. As this process is repeated again and again, the disk slowly takes the necessary shape for a beautiful-sounding instrument. Finally, it is ready to be cooled by sudden immersion in a pool of water. The completion of the instrument will involve meticulous fine-tuning.

This process, involving such vigorous and sustained activity and resulting in an instrument of such cultural import, is considered to require great spiritual power. Traditionally, gong smiths approached their work only on auspicious days, after purification through meditation and fasting. To protect themselves from the spiritual dangers of presuming to control the elemental forces of wind, fire, and water, they assumed mythological personas when inside the forge. With the head smith ritually transformed into the great Javanese hero Panji, and the other workers changed into Panji's family and servants, extraordinary spiritual strength was summoned for the momentous task of producing an instrument of transcendent power.

While other instrument makers are seldom equated with mythic heroes, they are often highly respected as masters of their craft. And even if an instrument is not explicitly treated as an embodiment of spiritual power, it can still inspire wonder through its uncanny capacities. Instruments extend the body, but they also extend people's ability to communicate their abstract, heartfelt inner world. An instrumentalist becomes a kind of superhuman, with enhanced powers of expression. And recent developments in electronic technology have broadened such possibilities even further.

ELECTRONIC MUSICAL TECHNOLOGY

Electronic applications have extended musical technologies in several ways. Sound amplification and recording have transformed both the ways music is made and its potential for access by audiences. Electronic sound-producing and processing devices have widened the range of possibilities for performers and composers. Developments in electronic musical technologies are rapid and complex, and their impact is felt all over the world. We now turn to an investigation of some of these developments and their cultural implications.

Sound Amplification

In the mid-twentieth century a new enhancer of musical sound was developed, involving not an echoing resonator but a microphone, amplifier, and loudspeaker. Electronic amplification made it possible for music to be heard at greater distances, over ambient sounds such as conversations, or at a more stimulating volume for dancing. It also enabled softer instruments to play with louder ones without being drowned out. Further, previously incongruous performance styles could be mixed: for example, a singer like Bing Crosby could croon gently into a microphone and still be audible over a piano, drums, and even horns.

This capacity for increased volume has had widespread cultural impact. The potential for mixing indigenous acoustical instruments with amplified ones has spawned a prodigious growth of new popular musical genres throughout the world. For example, Christopher Waterman has shown how the ability to combine electric guitars and amplified voices with traditional Yoruba "talking drums" led to the development of modern *jùjú* in Nigeria. With this fusion of old and new technologies, *jùjú* became a music which combines traditional Yoruba musical and social values with an infectious contemporary sound.[4]

Loud music both embodies and enacts power. Nineteenth-century European composers demonstrated this fact by increasing the size of their orchestras, just as instrumentalists and vocalists of that era developed increased capacities for resonance and dynamics. This connection between musical volume and its affective power is also evident in the aesthetics of today's popular music.

Amplification in Performance: Rock and Heavy Metal

As we have seen, the earliest usages of amplification in music facilitated the inclusion of softer instruments with louder ones, and made it possible for a singer to be heard over a fuller accompaniment. Soon amplification came to be used for an entire group, enabling performance in larger spaces. But in today's popular music, volume is also an affective choice. Combined with other kinds of electronic sound processing, volume enhances the power of the music's emotional expression, addressing the listener not only through the ears, but through the whole body. In his study of heavy metal music, Robert Walser notes that:

> Heavy metal relies heavily on technology for its effects, not least for this sheer volume of sound, impossible until recent decades. But reverb and echo units, as well as sophisticated overdubbing techniques, have also become important to metal performance and recording. Such processing can expand aural space, making the music's power seem to extend infinitely. . . . Loudness mediates between the power enacted by the music and the listener's experience of power. Intense volume abolishes the boundaries between oneself and such representations; the music is felt within as much as without, and the body is

seemingly hailed directly, subjectivity responding to the empowerment of the body rather than the other way around.[5]

A significant component of this affective use of amplification is controlled distortion. In most cases, distortion—the noisy buzzing caused when a loudspeaker is driven with more volume than it was built to handle—is considered undesirable in sound amplification and reproduction. But in the late 1950s, rock musicians began experimenting with using the sound deliberately, as a timbre which symbolized power. Walser points out how this timbral change functions symbolically:

Not only electronic circuitry, but also the human body produces aural distortion through excessive power. Human screams and shouts are usually accompanied by vocal distortion, as the capacities of the vocal chords are exceeded. Thus, distortion functions as a sign of extreme power and intense expression by overflowing its channels and materializing the exceptional effort that produces it.[6]

Indeed, the most characteristic use of distortion in rock and heavy metal is in the sound of the "lead" guitar, which provides melodic lines recalling—and sometimes purposely imitating—the human voice.

Unlike the late-1950s electric guitarists who slashed loudspeaker cones for a distorted sound, rock musicians since then have relied on electronic processing devices which produce distortion without endangering their equipment. Other processing devices produce other sonic effects, like the "wah-wah" pedal used by Jimi Hendrix and other 1960s musicians.

While some musicians revel in the range of such possibilities for electronic processing, others feel that they can go too far. A rock musician interviewed by Leslie Gay criticized a guitarist for having "too many knobs between the guitar and the amp's speaker," later explaining that "every electronic thing adds some muck to the sound and deteriorates the fidelity, hindering the directness of the 'feel' of the guitar."[7] Commenting on this perception, Gay noted that musical expression which is "obstructed by the technology, rather than controlled by the musician, not only obscures communication between musician and audience but also disconnects the musical instrument from the musician."[8]

Whether it works for or against expression and communication, electronic amplification and processing are involved in many musical performances today. But amplified sound is not only heard in performance settings. It is also part of what R. Murray Schafer termed our "soundscape," the audible environment in which we live.[9] Amplified music can be found in Western soundscapes in the form of barely-noticed music playback in retail environments, or as a neighbor's too-loud radio, but Western soundscapes include much less amplified music than some Eastern ones, such as those of Indonesia.

Amplification in the Soundscape: Indonesia

Western visitors to Java—and other parts of Indonesia—are likely to notice within hours of their arrival how different the soundscape is from their own. . . . The new arrival will inevitably be startled out of slumber at 4:30 or 5:00 in the morning with sounds of the call to morning prayer blasting from large and powerful speakers in the

mosques. . . . Traffic movement in daylight hours is heavily punctu-
ated with honking horns. . . . Small trucks advertising films, concerts,
or even herbal medicines are equipped with loud speakers and screech
out a combination of recorded popular dang-dut *music and "live"*
announcements at ear-splitting levels of amplification.[10]

Java is one of the most densely populated places on earth, and in its urban soundscapes a chaos of loud sounds is commonplace. This daily
cacaphony is exacerbated by layers of amplified music, issuing not only from
advertising trucks, but also from shops and cafes.

But in some cases the Javanese actively cultivate this kind of multi-musi-
cal soundscape. "The large public celebrations occasioned by important holi-
days in Java are characterized by a kaleidoscopic variety of overlapping
sounds," R. Anderson Sutton pointed out. Strolling slowly through such an
event with his tape recorder running, Sutton captured "an overlapping of
sound streams that, without any editing on my part, gives the impression of a
tape collage. For example, I passed by a shadow puppet performance—with
full, live gamelan accompaniment, amplified voices of female singer and puppeteer—and with these one hears a host of 'other' sounds from the fair, including recorded popular music."[11]

Sutton noted that comparable Western events are carefully scheduled and
physically laid out so that "musical sounds do not intrude upon one another,
even at a festive event where undivided attention toward the musical sounds
is not expected." To explain the difference, he referred to the Javanese word
ramé, which "translates as busy, noisy, congested, tangled—but in a positive
sense."[12] The word derives from a Sanskrit word meaning "beautiful," and
one can appreciate the beauty of ramé in the complex patterns of a Javanese
batik textile prints, or in the intricate polyphonic textures of gamelan music.
Multiple amplified sound systems at a public celebration enable a boisterous
enactment of this indigenous concept, which is considered appropriate for a
festive atmosphere.

Amplified music in the soundscape can also involve social power. Edward
Herbst describes an event in Bali in which certain visiting dignitaries had
come to a temple courtyard to witness a rare performance of a dance-drama
accompanied by the gentle sound of long bamboo flutes. This performance
was suddenly rendered inaudible by "a blaring noise, so it seemed to all
around, coming from a loudspeaker somewhere." The many other courtyards
of the temple were searched to find the loudspeaker, and its cable was traced
to "a little old man in the *jeroan pura,* inner courtyard of the temple, inton-
ing the *kawi* verses, as he had no doubt done countless times before, in that
same place, but then only heard by a few nearby friends and passersby bringing their offerings":

We learned that some kind of power play was being enacted and that
whoever was in control of the microphone was not willing to delimit
his newly acquired technology. The visiting dignitaries could not con-
vince the possessors of the amplifier to turn down the volume. Now,
it turns out that intravillage rivalries had been going on since colonial
times, in which performance forms were already being incorporated
into the struggle for power and social order. The amp and speaker
happened to be a new instrument of power and dominance in this dy-
namic between several kinship groups and political persuasions.[13]

Although Indonesia is officially Muslim (excepting Bali, which is Hindu), older animistic beliefs are often just below the surface, and they can interact with the superhuman quality of amplified music in various ways. "Once when I felt unusually tired at my gamelan teacher's house," Sutton recalls, "he suggested I lie down and sleep for a little while. His wife ushered me into one of the bedrooms and turned on the radio at near full volume—not to keep me awake, but to make me feel secure. With loud sounds around, I would not feel lonely or, worse, empty. Emptiness represents vulnerability to the spirit world, which is ever waiting to catch human beings unaware."[14]

One Javanese musician described to Sutton the exhilaration of amplifying his own voice: "a kind of modern magic (*gaib*), as he put it."[15] But such "magic" is not necessarily perceived as benign. In the sacred shadow puppet theater forms of Java and Bali, the *dalang* puppeteer is considered far more than an entertainer. A dalang embodies and expresses great spiritual power, both through manipulation of the puppets and through an extraordinary range of vocal subtleties in heightened speech and song. The now-common practice of amplifying the dalang's voice raises spiritual concerns among some, like those interviewed by Herbst in Bali:

> *While several* dalangs *have expressed to me their feelings of a need to keep the interest of their less-focused contemporary audience, many recognize a difficult trade-off with the sound blaring from a loud-speaker, rather than the body of the* dalang, *changing the corporeal and spiritual nature of performance. In my recent discussions with* dalangs, *several have pondered whether the* dalang *is losing his real voice, and whether* kawi suara *(the transcendent, spiritual voice of the* dalang) *can exist in such a disembodied, detached form. In a discussion I had in 1992 with two prominent* dalangs, *one even went so far as to say that loudspeakers could be the death of* kawi suara.[16]

This example raises the issue of cultural pollution, in which use of Western technology clashes with deep indigenous aesthetic and spiritual values. Like Westerners, some people in other cultures are eager to embrace technological developments, while others worry that essential human qualities are lost in the process—like the electric guitarist with "too many knobs." But as our other Indonesian examples have shown, sound amplification can also present opportunities for reinforcing cultural values, uniting the old and new in ways which affirm indigenous principles. The same kinds of possibilities are afforded by another important technological development: sound recording, the ability to store and reproduce musical performances.

Sound Recording

While the development of music writing and the printing press had widespread effects on the transmission and storage of music, musical notation can only be used by specialists. And such notations do not really present a musical experience, except for skilled and imaginative music readers. They are more like sets of instructions for recreating music, rather than actual "pictures" of sound. Before the end of the nineteenth century music existed only in live performance: it vanished into the air the instant it was produced, never to be heard again.

This situation has changed dramatically with the advent of sound recording. Not only can we hear a piece more than once, we often can choose from several different performances of it, selecting our favorite and listening to it whenever we wish. With lightweight, portable playback machines and headphones, we can also listen to it in any location. We can even record music ourselves, and send it wherever we please. And digital recording technology enables us—in theory, at least—to produce sonic archives which will never deteriorate.

Of course, sound recording has not always been so sophisticated and accessible. The first sound recording device, called the phonograph, was developed in 1877 by the American inventor Thomas Edison. This hand-cranked machine directed sound through a mouthpiece and vibrating diaphragm to a needle which etched grooves into tinfoil wrapped around a turning cylinder. The recording was played back by a similar mechanism working in reverse, with a paper cone amplifying the vibrating diaphragm. One could only play these recordings a few times before the tinfoil became useless, and their scratchy sound was hardly something one would listen to for aesthetic pleasure.

Improvements followed, beginning with replacement of the hand crank with a clockwork device, insuring the steady turning of the cylinder. The replacement of tinfoil with wax cylinders provided some improvement in sound and durability, but not much. The recordings were still scratchy and pinched-sounding, and they still deteriorated fairly quickly.

Still, some scholars were immediately drawn to the invention's potential for documenting and storing musical performances—if not for aesthetic pleasure, at least for study. Wax cylinder recordings of Native American and other oral-tradition musics were made as early as 1889, by people who would later be considered among the founders of the field of ethnomusicology. Not least among these was the visionary Hungarian composer Béla Bartók, who traveled around eastern Europe making hundreds of wax cylinder recordings of folk musicians. Back home at his writing desk, Bartók meticulously transcribed these recorded performances, producing some of the most detailed notations the world had ever seen. Despite the care he lavished on these transcriptions, he declared that the only true "notations" of these performances were the grooves etched on the cylinder itself!

In 1887, the German inventor Emile Berliner patented the first device which recorded sound on a disc rather than a cylinder. Originally marketed as a toy for children, it began to generate wider interest. Unlike cylinders, which could not be duplicated, a metal plate could be made from the original disc, and this plate could be used to stamp out reproductions. Commercial enterprises arose, and sound recordings became consumer goods. At first the playback apparatus was a novelty item for the rich: a phonograph cost almost $200 in the American currency of the 1890s. But by the turn of the century the price had come down to $25, and more people could enjoy this new form of entertainment. Recordings of humorous and dramatic monologues and scenes could be purchased, as well as popular tunes and songs. Soon American record companies were also targeting ethnic immigrant groups and African-Americans with songs in their own languages or dialects.

By the early 1900s, the quality of sound reproduction had become sufficient to interest lovers of classical music, and records of opera arias and short chamber works appeared. Advertising for these products stressed the fidelity

A RECORDING STUDIO

of the sound, with images like the Victor dog listening intently to "his master's voice" issuing from the playback horn of a phonograph.

The advertisements worked. Half a million phonographs were sold in the United States in 1914, two million in 1919. Packaged in a handsome cabinet, the phonograph became a desirable piece of parlor furniture, often providing more entertainment than the piano. Less elaborate models could be purchased by less affluent people, and some record companies started to record rural blues and country music, expanding the audience for sound recordings to poorer but more numerous customers.

These early recordings were made by aiming instruments and voices toward a giant horn which directed the sounds to the diaphragm and needle recording apparatus. Softer instruments were placed closest to the horn, and sometimes small amplifying horns were affixed to instruments like the violin, in an attempt to balance the overall sound. To record a full orchestra, certain players sometimes had to run up to the horn for their solo passages, then return to their seats to rejoin the ensemble sound. Despite these difficulties, the resulting recordings were immensely popular, and sound recording and reproduction flourished.

Notwithstanding the many economic, political, and social upheavals of the ensuing years, sales of sound recordings and playback equipment have continued to grow. The flourishing recording industry has become a very lucrative business for the biggest companies. Some critics fear that a few vast multinational corporations now control music entirely, ruthlessly deciding what people will hear and selling it to them. But while this may be the case for some consumers, alternatives are not always hard to find.

Although a small number of major corporations control most of the recording industry, independent recording companies—known as "indies"—have long played important roles in the overall picture. Indies have always targeted more limited audiences, often specializing in the music of a particular ethnic group or region. The "majors" have notoriously worked to eliminate competition by buying out indies or wooing away their constituencies. In general indies continue to fill the needs of specialized audiences while the majors continue to concentrate on music that has a wider following. As Peter Manuel has noted, the burgeoning indie scene in the United States "illustrates that in a society sufficiently affluent that minorities can own independent recording companies, the music industry may come to offer a relatively satisfactory balance and coexistence between dominating, homogenizing majors, and smaller, marginal indies."[17] But what about less affluent societies, where indies cannot even begin to compete with majors on the same playing field?

Cassette Culture

In a groundbreaking study, Manuel coined the term "cassette culture" to describe independent sound recording "in the context of a new world order with new potentialities for decentralization, diversification, autonomy, dissent, and freedom."[18] Small cassette indies have arisen throughout the world, finding niches in which they can prosper. Cassettes are relatively inexpensive to produce in mass quantity, so they can be sold more cheaply than records or CDs. Cassette playback systems are also comparatively inexpensive, and many are both durable and portable.

A cassette-producing indie can be established almost anywhere. Some third world cassette-based indies involve little more than a technician, one or two microphones, and a bank of tape-copying machines. Local musical styles can be featured, tailored to local populations, without the headaches of operating a centralized recording company and targeting a wide audience with expensive advertising. Manuel discusses how these grassroots companies can ignore broad cultural demographics and distribute exactly what their specialized audience wants to hear, directly to them:

> In Israel, rock misrahi *associated with Oriental Jews, although scorned by Ashkenazis and the state radio stations, has enjoyed ample dissemination by cassettes. Similarly, while air play on the Egyptian state radio was once a prerequisite to any sort of musical renown, singers such as Ahmad 'Aduwe have become stars via cassettes, in spite of being shunned by radio gate-keepers. . . . The Turkish state music bureaucracy, although contemptuous of the Arab-influenced pop genre* arabesk, *has been unable to curb its popularity, as cassettes of it abound. Sri Lankan pop* baila *has similarly flourished almost exclusively on cassettes, with taxi drivers playing essential roles as disseminators via their car stereos. Even in the United States, cassettes have established niches as vehicles for regional synchretic genres; one example is "Jawaiian," a Hawaii-based fusion of reggae and Hawaiian pop music.*[19]

These are but a few examples of popular musics which thrive in the world of cassette culture, despite their neglect by major recording companies and radio stations. Small cassette companies play an increasing role in religious music as well. In India, playing a cassette of devotional music can become a part of religious rituals, and the availability of cassette recordings of songs relating to particular deities and sects can help to cement a minority community which is otherwise threatened by the more homogeneous devotional music of the mass media.

Cassette culture can also nurture local folk musics, in some cases even contributing to a revival of endangered musics. Manuel quotes the founder of a small cassette company in northern India:

> My friend, an agriculturalist, points out that a different fertilizer may be needed for every hundred yards of land, because here there is a potassium shortage, there a nitrate shortage. But the big fertilizer companies just make a general product, and the crops suffer. It's the same with folk music. [A famous popular singer]'s songs will sell, because they're melodious, well-produced, and extensively promoted, but the special heart and soul of a region—only a local can convey that. Especially for the little guy, who's illiterate, who only knows his own little dialect—if he hears his own little dialect sung on the media, by a local who knows the soul of a region, he is so happy. With regional music, even people who sing out of tune can make hits, because they have soul.[20]

Such a featuring of regional style can have an opposite effect, one of homogenization, when it is the product of a larger enterprise: the widespread dissemination of one local style can prompt neglect of others, even by their practitioners. As Jerry O'Sullivan explains, in Ireland "prior to the radio and the phonograph, learning music was done very, very locally. Keep in mind that going back only a hundred years ago or so . . . most people never got beyond their little village and you could tell where somebody was from just by listening to them play—you wouldn't even have to hear them speak."[21] In the 1920s, a number of Irish musicians made recordings in the United States, including Michael Coleman, a masterful fiddler who played in the style of Killavel, a small town in County Sligo.

O'Sullivan notes that Coleman's impressive recordings "traveled back to Ireland and they changed fiddle playing style. People tried to imitate Coleman whether they were from Sligo or whether they were from Cork or Donegal. It was no longer the case that you could tell where somebody was from by listening to them. That was the beginning, that this was starting to be homogenized."[22]

The smaller technology and audience of the cassette-producing indies are less apt to cause a situation where recording one local style causes the neglect of others. Indeed, these indies tend to encourage regional styles, both rewarding local musicians and reinforcing the identity of their audiences.

Some cultural critics envision a grim future of "cultural gray-out" in which the wonderfully varied regional musics of every corner of the earth will be abandoned one by one until the majors rule the musical taste of the world. To be sure, recordings and performances by some pop music stars are in demand almost everywhere. But thanks in part to cassette culture, grassroots music-making has not been overwhelmed, and in some cases both local tradition and hybrid innovation are flourishing more than ever before. Like much technology, sound recording and dissemination is neither good nor bad in itself; it is a versatile tool which can be used for many purposes. Yet another potential use of electronic musical technology involves the creation of music itself.

Electronic Technology and Creative Musicians

Before the twentieth century almost every musical experience had to involve one or more live performers singing or playing a musical instrument. The few exceptions were mechanical instruments like music boxes and barrel organs: modifications of conventional instruments that could be "played" by a rotating mechanism powered by a clock-like spring apparatus or a hand cranking device. Such machines were largely considered novelties, providing little inspiration for serious creative musicians. But as technologies changed, new opportunities were recognized for expanding the scope of musical creativity.

From the very beginning of the twentieth century, the development of electronic sound-producing devices inspired some inventors to create musical instruments with the new technology. An early example, which can still occasionally be heard today, is generally known as the "theremin" after its Russian inventor, Leon Theremin, who called it the "etherophone" when he created it in 1920.

The theremin makes a memorable visual impression: standing before something which looks like a radio receiver with two antennae, the performer's hands move gently through the air, controlling pitch and volume by the spacial relationship of hands to antennae. Writing in the *New York Times* in 1967, Harold C. Schoenberg described its sound as "not unlike an eerie, throbbing voice," or like "a cello lost in a dense fog and crying because it does not know how to get home." The instrument may be recalled as a swooping sound heard on some 1960s popular recordings, or carrying the melody in the original "Star Trek" theme music.

Most early electronic instruments were used either to play conventional music or to produce special effects. Like mechanical instruments, they were seldom viewed as devices which could significantly expand the scope of musical creativity. Still, a few composers started to explore the potential of electronic applications in their work, including a young American named John Cage.

Composers and Electronic Music

"Every film studio has a library of 'sound effects' recorded on film," Cage wrote in 1937. "With a film phonograph it is now possible to control the amplitude and frequency of any one of these sounds and to give it rhythms within or beyond the reach of the imagination. Given four film phonographs, we can compose and perform a quartet for explosive motor, wind, heartbeat, and landslide."[23]

While such ideas were largely considered little more than amusing novelties at the time, and still are by some people, other statements in the same essay now sound visionary:

The special function of electrical instruments will be to provide complete control of the overtone structure of tones (as opposed to noises) and to make these tones available in any frequency, amplitude, and duration. . . . The composer (organizer of sound) will be faced not only with the entire field of sound but also with the entire field of time. . . . No rhythm will be beyond the composer's reach. . . . Before this happens, centers of experimental music must be established. In these centers, the new materials, oscillators, turntables, generators, means for amplifying small sounds, film phonographs, etc., available for use [sic].[24]

Such centers were indeed established, and composers like Cage began exploring the potentialities which new technology offered to creative musicians. In 1957, Cage described the range of ideas enabled by the technological developments which were currently available:

Given a minimum of two tape recorders and a disk recorder, the following processes are possible: 1) a single recording of any sound may be made; 2) a rerecording may be made, in the course of which, by means of filters and circuits, any or all of the physical characteristics of a given recorded sound may be altered; 3) electronic mixing (combining on a third machine sounds issuing from two others) permits the presentation of any number of sounds in combination; 4) ordinary splicing permits the juxtaposition of any sounds. . . . But advantage can be taken of these possibilities only if one is willing to change one's musical habits radically.[25]

While Cage was among the pioneers of composing with recording technology, he was interested in working with the broadest range of sonic possibilities, including doing unconventional things with conventional instruments. His early experiments with "prepared piano" involved placing items like bolts and leather strips between the strings of a grand piano, resulting in an increased timbral palette for the pianist: a new technological development for a nineteenth-century instrument. Cage also made use of electronics as instruments in live performance: for example, one of his pieces from the early 1950s is a composition for twelve radios.

ALVIN LUCIER

Throughout his long career, Cage used technological developments to explore new sonic possibilities, often challenging the very definition of music in the process. Inspired by Cage and his contemporaries, a number of composers have pursued the ever-increasing potential of electronic applications. Some have also followed Cage in rejecting the idea of musical aesthetics; but others, like Alvin Lucier, bring a new kind of sonic poetics to their work.

For example, Lucier's *Music on a Long Thin Wire* involves a very simple electronic setup: a thin wire stretched across a room between the poles of a large magnet, vibrated by a single oscillator, and amplified through loudspeakers. The whole system becomes a delicate, ever-changing feedback loop which can be "played" by manipulating the oscillator and amplifier. "A short length of wire would look like a laboratory experiment," he said in an interview, "but if you thought of it as a sound sculpture, your imagination could take that wire down the length of a room. I had to be prepared for not knowing what it was going to sound like, although in my imagination I knew. I had an intuition that it would sound amazing."[26] Lucier's aesthetic approach is clear in his description of fellow composer David Rosenboom "playing" the wire:

> I was struck by the sensitivity with which he tuned the system. It seemed that the more he reduced the power, the more effectively it vibrated. It was paradoxical. I guess there's a natural plateau above which the wire refuses to handle more power; below that point, it accepts what comes into it and interesting things start to happen. At one point, David achieved a state in which the wire would start and stop vibrating of its own accord; it would go through long cycles of marvelously complex harmonic changes.[27]

Lucier's long thin wire is a kind of electronic musical instrument, notable for its structural simplicity. More complex electronic instruments had started to appear in the early 1960s, as people strove to ease the laborious task of working with separate sound generators and processors, and splicing magnetic tape. These new instruments, called synthesizers, combined sound generators and processors in one interlinked system, along with "sequencers": devices which enabled the placing of sonic events in time. Using a bank of knobs and a keyboard, composers and musicians could now perform electronic music in real time, rather than relying on tape recorders.

Synthesizers proved extremely versatile. While they could be used to streamline the work of electronic composers, synthesizers could also be played as keyboard instruments, and some jazz and popular musicians started to use them in this way.

More recently, digital technology has made it possible to integrate non-electronic sounds through "sampling": converting sounds into digital codes which can be electronically processed. Now both electronic and natural sounds—from voices to acoustical instruments to "explosive motor, wind, heartbeat, and landslide"—can be processed in a single keyboard instrument, putting any sound literally at the musician's fingertips. Samplers and synthesizers can also be programmed through connection to a computer, enabling performances well beyond the capacity of a human keyboard player.

With the availability of electronic samplers, synthesizers, and computer applications, many composers no longer work at a piano with manuscript paper and pencil. This new way of composing heightens awareness of the ways that available technology can influence musical creativity. Gerald Shapiro has grappled with the ways technology can affect his work:

GERALD SHAPIRO

One way of making a piece is to make the piece on a synthesizer and record as you go on the computer. No notation: playing, playing, I don't like this, I don't like that, try it again, record again on the computer as a sequence. Little by little I began to realize that the music I wrote was very shaped by the technology I was using to write it. The process became sort of passive: way more listening, and way less writing, it was slowed down and I was losing track of the shaping of it. So I switched over to paper and pencil again. And then after a while I switched back again. And after a while it began to seem that I could work either way interchangeably.[28]

Synthesizers and samplers have expanded the idea of what a musical instrument can be, and even of what a creative process can be. A further expansion of these concepts involves using the recording studio as an instrument in itself: a single interlinked system which can be used creatively to produce new music, rather than simply to document a performance.

Studio Production

As the word indicates, a sound "recording" was first conceived as a record—as accurate as possible—of a sonic event, comparable to a film record of a visual event. But just as film can now be edited and manipulated for myriad "special effects," sound recording studios can produce music which goes well beyond the possibilites of a live performance.

The development of "stereophonic" (stereo) recording in the mid-twentieth century brought about a significant shift in the way recording technology can be used. For early one-track "monaural" recording on magnetic tape, sound collected by a microphone was transformed through a tape recorder's "recording head" into a stream of magnetic information on a moving tape. Played back, this informational "track" was read by a "playback head" and transformed back into sound. Stereo recording involves two microphones, two recording heads, and two parallel tracks on the tape. Played back through two separated speakers, these two simultaneous tracks place the recorded sounds in space, according to their original proximity to each of the two microphones.

Stereo recording added depth and clarity to the reproduced sound of a live performance. But the use of more than one parallel track on a tape suggested a new idea, which became known as "overdubbing." Tape recorders were developed which could record on one track while playing back the other. Music could be recorded on one track, the tape could be rewound, and then more music could be recorded on the other track, while listening to the first to synchronize with it. Played back together, the two tracks would sound as if they had been recorded at the same time.

Using this process of overdubbing on tapes with several tracks, musical layers could be added at will. One singer's voice could be recorded singing any number of simultaneous tracks, resulting in the formerly impossible sound of a one-person vocal group. Musicians could "play together" without even being present in the studio at the same time. For example, a drummer and bassist could record a rhythm track and a guitar track could be overdubbed later. First used extensively in popular music, overdubbing produced musical experiences which never existed in real time.

Combined with electronic sound processing, such as adding echo and other effects, overdubbing moved sound recording from mere documentation into a new realm of creative potential. In the late 1960s, popular music albums started to present sonic experiences which seldom merely replicated the sound of live performances. Imaginary sonic worlds could be constructed, and recording became an expressive form in its own right, no longer a simple reproduction of a musical event. The technological realm of the electronic music composer was merging with that of the popular entertainer.

More recent developments have expanded this connection, as sampling technology has fed into the development of rap music production. In this genre, often the studio itself is the "instrument" which accompanies the rapping. Production crews like Public Enemy's "Bomb Squad" assemble carefully-crafted polyrhythmic accompaniments. Robert Walser describes the creative process of the Bomb Squad's Hank Shocklee:

> *Shocklee's compositional method is to combine pre-recorded sounds, drawing on his collection of over nineteen thousand recordings. Like other producers, he must find just the right sounds for each piece, which sometimes requires layering, for example, four different bass drum sounds from different records to make one new sound. The samples must be delicately balanced, and the sequences are carefully fine-tuned to simulate the nuances of live performance. All of this means that it is often more work to build tracks out of samples than it would be to compose and arrange for live musicians.*[29]

This procedure almost seems to subvert the technological ease promised by sythesizers and samplers. Indeed, Shocklee's creative process recalls that of the early electronic composers like John Cage, as does his musical philosophy: he explained to Mark Dery that "We believed that music is nothing but organized noise. You can take anything—street sounds, us talking, whatever you want—and make it music by organizing it."[30]

Building on such developments in rap production, composers in other popular music genres like new age and techno are constructing virtual musical worlds. As digital technology becomes less expensive, more and more people have access to a range of creative possibilities which were once only available to composers in a handful of electronic music centers. Sophisticated music production can even be done in one's home.

A techno piece by the American composer Thomas Ross, who has converted a room in his house into an electronic production studio. It includes digitally-sampled voices and acoustical instruments, as well as electronically-generated sounds.

CHAPTER SUMMARY

Some people assume that as technology improves, music gets better. To them the piano, with its wider pitch and dynamic range, is an improvement of the harpsichord, just as the more versatile keyboard sampler is an improvement of the piano. But this is a simplistic view of culture. Expressive culture does not merely get better or worse: it changes with its overall cultural context, mirroring every development. Today, use of recent technology may be a matter of taste: a musician may choose a wooden flute, for example, out of a preference for its sound, even if it is harder to find than a modern metal one. As a composer who works with both electronic and conventional media, Gerald Shapiro expresses a long-range view of music and technology:

All instruments have developed technologically, and it slowly, slowly changes. The important thing to remember is it doesn't get better. Technology gets better, but the music of the Middle Ages is as compelling, is as good, as the music of the twentieth century—and I know some would say, better. There's no progress in music or any of the arts, but there is change, and that change is certainly driven as much as anything by changes in technology.[31]

STUDY QUESTIONS

1. What are examples of musical technologies?

2. What are examples of technologically simple instruments? What are some more complex ones?

3. How does instrument technology articulate cultural values?

4. What is the cultural significance of amplification in popular music?

5. What is a soundscape? How does the idea relate to the concept of *ramé* in Java?

6. What is cassette culture? How does it relate to the overall music industry?

7. How do creative musicians use electronic sound technology?

REFERENCED SOURCES

1. Fink, 1997.
2. Hood. 1971: 273.
3. Quigley, 1998.
4. Waterman, 1990.
5. Walser, 1995: 45.
6. Ibid.: 42.
7. Quoted in Gay, 1998: 82.
8. Ibid.: 85.
9. Schafer, 1977.
10. Sutton, 1996: 251–2.
11. Ibid.: 257.
12. Ibid.: 257, 258.
13. Herbst, 1997: 135.
14. Sutton, 1996: 258.
15. Ibid.: 264.
16. Herbst, 1997: 136.
17. Manuel, 1993: 25.
18. Ibid.: 3.
19. Manuel, 1993: 33.
20. Ibid.: 193.
21. O'Sullivan interview, 1997.
22. Ibid.
23. Reprinted in Cage, 1987: 3.
24. Ibid.: 4–6.
25. Ibid.: 9.
26. Lucier and Simon, 1980: 164.
27. Ibid.: 167.
28. Shapiro interview, 1997.
29. Walser, 1995: 196.
30. In Dery, 1990: 83.
31. Shapiro interview, 1997.

WESTERN NOTATION

The musical examples in this book are written in Western notation, a system that has been evolving since early medieval times. The basic conventions of this system—its ways of showing pitch and rhythm—are not hard to learn. Pitch is read vertically, just as we might think of tones as being relatively high or low; and rhythm is read from left to right, just as we may think of time proceeding in this direction as we read sentences.

Indicating Rhythm

Rhythmic durations are indicated with three kinds of symbols: note heads, stems, and flags. The left-hand side of **Example 1** shows the five rhythmic symbols most commonly used. The *whole note* is an open note head with no stem or flag, and the *half note* is like a whole note, but with a stem. The

EXAMPLE 1

quarter note is a shaded note head with a stem, and the *eighth note* is like a quarter note, but with a flag. The *sixteenth note* is like an eighth note, but with two flags. Stems and flags may point up or down; as a rule, they point upward when the note head appears in the bottom half of the staff, and downward when the note head appears in the top half.

Just to the right of each of these notes you can see the corresponding *rest*. A rest is a silence. Silences are an important part of much music, and often it is necessary to show exactly how long a particular voice or instrument is silent.

The right-hand side of Example 1 shows how these rhythmic durations relate to each other through subdivision. A half note is exactly one-half as long as a whole note, a quarter note is one-half as long as a half note, and so on. Notice that the names of these durations indicate their relationships: two half notes take the same amount of time as one whole note, four quarter notes take the same amount of time as one whole note, and so on. As you can see, notes with flags may be connected with *beams* to show how they are grouped together. The single flags of eighth notes become single beams, and the double flags of sixteenth notes become double beams.

There is one further symbol: a dot placed just to the right of a note indicates that that note's duration is increased by *one half* of whatever it indicated by itself. **Example 2** shows two aspects of this convention. While one regular quarter note equals the duration of two eighth notes, one *dotted* quarter note equals the duration of *three* eighth notes—the dot increases the quarter note's duration by one half. Also, just as two quarter notes equal the duration of one half note, two *dotted* quarter notes equal the duration of one *dotted* half notes—increasing a note's duration by one half also increases its subdivisions by one half.

EXAMPLE 2

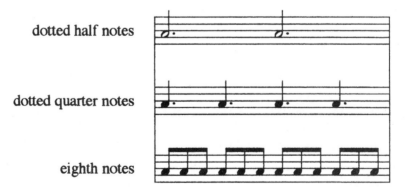

dotted half notes

dotted quarter notes

eighth notes

Finally, in music these durations are often found in regular rhythmic groups. These groups are shown by *bar lines* and *time signatures*. **Example 3** is in 4/4 time, indicated by the time signature at the beginning and the bar lines throughout. The top number in the time signature shows how many beats or pulses constitute a bar, or *measure*; in this case, there are four beats per measure. The bottom number indicates what rhythmic duration constitutes a beat; in this case, the number "4" refers to a quarter note. So in Example 3 a measure consists of the duration of four quarter notes—which, as we have seen, is the same duration as one whole note, two half notes, and so on.

EXAMPLE 3

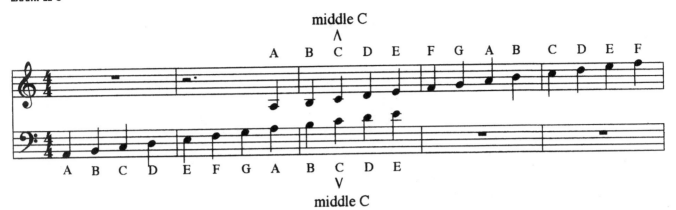

Indicating Pitch

The rhythmic symbols in all of these examples are shown on a five-line *staff*. This is necessary to show the difference between the whole-note rest and the half-note rest: the whole-note rest hangs down from the fourth line from the bottom, while the half rest, identical in shape, sits on top of the third line from the bottom. But the main reason for using the five-line staff in music notation is to indicate pitch along with rhythm.

A *clef* is used at the beginning of every line of notation to show what pitches are indicated by the lines of the staff. The *treble clef*, seen at the beginning of the top line of Example 3, designates the second line from the bottom as the pitch G above middle C, by spiraling around that line. *Middle C* is a pitch roughly in the middle of the full pitch range of a piano or orchestra; in the treble clef, middle C is the note which appears on the first *ledger line* below the staff. As you can see, ledger lines are used to indicate pitches above or below those contained by the staff itself. A letter name from A through G is assigned to each line (or ledger line) and to the space in between each line. The treble clef is used for relatively high-pitched sounds: women's voices, or instruments like the violin and flute.

The *bass clef*, seen at the beginning of the bottom line of Example 3, is used for lower-pitched sounds: men's voices, or instruments like the cello and bass. This clef designates the fourth line from the bottom as the pitch F below middle C. An overlap between the bass and treble clefs is shown in the middle of Example 3: the A on the top line of the bass clef is exactly the same pitch as the A on the second ledger line below the treble clef, and so on. Notice that middle C is one ledger line above the bass clef, and one ledger line below the treble clef.

Instruments with a very wide pitch range, like the piano and organ, are notated on two parallel staves like those in Example 3, one with a treble clef and one with a bass clef. Sometimes other clefs are used; for example, viola notation usually uses a clef which designates the third of the five staff lines as middle C.

The notes shown in Example 3 correspond to the pitches sounded by the white keys of the piano. **Example 4** shows one octave of the piano keyboard, from C to C. If you play the notes shown here on the white keys of a real piano, you will hear an ascending *major scale*.

EXAMPLE 4

C D E F G A B C

The black keys produce tones which lie between the pitches of some of the white keys. If you play all of the keys in sequence, you will hear a *chromatic scale*. The intervals between the pitches of a chromatic scale—those between each adjacent key, including black keys—are all *half steps*.

Two half steps make a *whole step*. When you play only the white keys of the piano, some of the intervals are whole steps—the ones with black keys in between—and some are half steps—the ones without intervening black keys. The interval between C and D is a whole step: there is another key between them. The interval between E and F is a half step: they are adjacent keys.

The pitches of the black keys are indicated with *sharp* and *flat* signs. The sharp sign (#) indicates that a pitch is raised by a half step. The black key between C and D could be written as C#. The flat sign (b) indicates that a pitch is lowered by a half step. The black key between C and D could also be written as Db. The choice between indicating that key as C# or Db depends on the key in which the music is written, or the context of the particular passage. **Example 5** shows two different ways of writing the chromatic scale: ascending, with sharps, and descending, with flats. In general, it works best to use sharps in an ascending passage, and flats in a descending passage. If you think of the C on the left of Example 4 as middle C, Example 5 would indicate the pitch of each of the keys moving from left to right, then right to left.

EXAMPLE 5

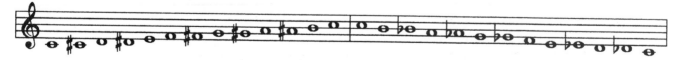

Sharps and flats are assumed to apply throughout a measure. For example, if a G# is written at the beginning of a measure, any subsequent G in the same range in that measure is assumed to also be G#. This assumption can be cancelled by the use of the *natural* sign. **Example 6** shows a measure with four Gs: the first is raised to G#, the second would be assumed to be G# also, the third is lowered to G natural, and the fourth is lowered further, to Gb.

EXAMPLE 6

There are other signs for indicating pitch and rhythm in Western notation; these are just the ones you will need in order to read the examples in this book. If you have the corresponding audio package, looking at the notated examples while you listen to the music will help you to become familiar with this notation.

THE WESTERN HARMONIC SYSTEM

The basics of the Western harmonic system have been in place since the Baroque Era (c. 1600–1750). The essential interrelated concepts are scale, interval, chord, and key.

A *scale* is a set of available pitches, arranged in stepwise order. Baroque composers worked with two particular *diatonic* scales, each with seven steps: the *major* and *minor* scales. We have seen that the white keys of the piano from C to C produce a major scale. The substitution of two specific black keys changes this scale from C to C to a minor scale. **Example 1** shows these two scales. Incidentally, Western theorists recognize three slightly different kinds of minor scales: the one we are concerned with is called *harmonic minor*, because it is the one most frequently used for harmonic music.

Illustrates the examples in Appendix 2.

EXAMPLE 1

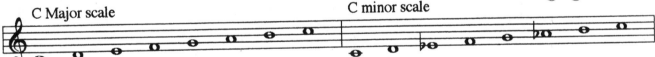

Interval refers to the distance between two pitches, whether they are simultaneous (*harmonic*) or in sequence (*melodic*). The difference between the major and minor scales lies in their different intervals.

Example 2 shows the intervals within one octave, using middle C as the bottom note (you can refer to the piano keyboard in Appendix 1 to visualize these intervals). Interval names involve both their *spelling* and their *quality*. So, for example, the interval from C up to D is one step, spelled as a *second*. If the D is lowered to Db, the quality of the interval is *minor*, so it is called a minor second; if the D is natural, the quality of the interval is *major*, so it is called a major second. A minor second spans one half step; a major second

EXAMPLE 2

spans a whole step—two half steps. Similarly, a minor third spans three half steps, while a major third spans four. This concept holds true for sixths and sevenths as well.

Fourths and fifths are not thought of as major or minor, but as *perfect*, *augmented*, or *diminished*. An augmented interval spans one more half step than its perfect version, while a diminished interval spans one less. A perfect fourth spans five half steps, one more than a major third, so an augmented fourth spans six half steps. A perfect fifth spans seven half steps, so a diminished fifth spans six. Notice that a diminished fifth is the same interval as an augmented fourth, spelled differently. This interval divides the octave exactly in half, and is also sometimes called a *tritone*.

A *chord* results from playing two or more notes simultaneously. Sounded together, each interval in Example 2 forms a two-note chord. Baroque harmony made much use of three-note chords, called *triads*. A triad can be thought of as a fifth which is subdivided with a note which is a third above the bottom note of the fifth, and a third below the top.

Example 3 shows the four triads used in Baroque music. Triads are also named for their quality. A *major* triad has a perfect fifth and a major third on the bottom; this bottom third gives the triad its name. The major triad is the fundamental triad of the major scale, sounding that scale's first, third, and fifth pitches. Similarly, a *minor* triad has a perfect fifth and a minor third on the bottom; it is named for its bottom third, and it is the fundamental triad of the minor scale.

EXAMPLE 3

Diminished and *augmented* triads are named for the quality of their fifths. A diminished triad has a diminished fifth and a minor third, and an augmented triad has an augmented fifth and a major third. These triads were considered dissonant, and their use was carefully regulated in the Baroque era.

In addition to triads, a particular four-note chord was used by Baroque composers. This was formed by adding another third to the top of a triad, creating an interval of a minor seventh with the bottom note. Therefore this chord was called a *seventh chord*. **Example 4** shows a seventh chord based on middle C.

EXAMPLE 4

Baroque harmony involves the *tonal* system, in which chords and scales are heard in relationship to an overall *key*. In the key of C Major, the notes of the C major scale are used for the basic chords, the note C is referred to as the *tonic note*, and the C major triad is called the *tonic chord*. The first triad in Example 3 is the tonic chord in the key of C Major, also called the I chord. A triad built on the next step, D, would be called a ii chord—the lower-case numeral is used to show that this is a minor chord. The iii chord, based on E, is also minor, while the IV and V chords are major. The vi chord is minor, and the chord based on B is diminished, written vii°. The most commonly-used seventh chord is based on the V chord; this seventh chord is written as V7.

Example 5 shows two fundamental sequences of chords, called *progressions*, in the key of C Major. The first progression is the harmonic backbone of the key: I-V7-I. The I chord establishes the key, and the V7 is considered to exert a strong harmonic pull back towards the I (more so than the V chord without the seventh). The second progression includes the IV chord, and shows the plain V chord followed by V7 and I.

EXAMPLE 5

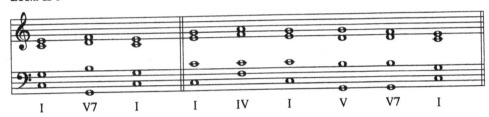

| I | V7 | I | I | IV | I | V | V7 | I |

The notes of the chords in this example are not close together as they have been in previous examples: they are distributed among four "voices" as they might be in a four-part chorale. So, for example, in the first chord the *root*, the bottom note of the triad, appears in the bass voice, and also an octave up in the alto; the fifth appears in the tenor, and the third is in the soprano. Notice that the seventh of the V7 chord, in the soprano, always resolves by moving downward into the next chord.

These progressions show the basic structures of tonal music. Tonal pieces almost always begin with the I chord and end with the progression V7-I (or just V-I). In between, they may go anywhere else in the key—to the ii chord, the vi chord, and so on. But these chords are always heard in their relationship to the overall key, which is defined by the I chord.

The basic chords in the key of C Major can all be played on the white keys of the piano; no sharps or flats are used. But other keys require the use of sharps or flats in order to maintain the proper interval relationships. For example, the key of G uses white keys for all of the notes except its seventh, F. The seventh note in a major key must be just a half step below the tonic note, so the F must be consistently written as F#. To avoid having to include the sharp sign every time the note F is written, composers use a *key signature* just after the clef sign on each line of music. The key signature shows the consistent tonal framework of a piece, just as the time signature shows its consistent rhythmic organization.

Example 6 shows the same progressions written in Example 5, but this time they are in the key of C minor. C minor requires a key signature of three flats, showing that E, A, and B are flatted unless indicated otherwise. In this example the note B is in fact raised, using a natural sign. This is because we are using the harmonic minor scale, which involves a raised seventh degree.

EXAMPLE 6

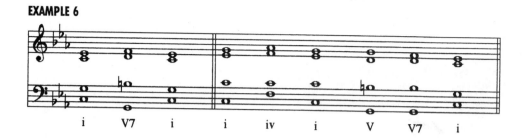

This Appendix provides enough information for you to understand the examples in this book, but there is a great deal more to be said about the Western tonal system. An introductory music theory course is the best way to gain a fuller understanding of Western harmony.

GLOSSARY

acculturation—the learning of music (or other cultural elements) from a culture other than ones own.

aerophone—an instrument in which air is the principal means of vibration, such as a flute, oboe or trumpet.

affective memory—recollections which have a powerful emotional effect on us.

alap—the slow opening section in a North Indian classical music performance in which the performer outlines the pitches, melodic contour, and mood of the raga.

amplitude—volume: the loudness or softness of the sound.

aural transmission—learning by hearing.

authenticity—the quality or state of being authentic or genuine. In early music, faithfulness to the conventions of original performance traditions. A problematic term when talking about music and performance practice.

ballad—a narrative song.

bebop—a jazz genre emphasizing virtuosic instrumental playing and innovative harmonic ideas, which developed in the early 1940s as part of an emerging subculture among young African-Americans.

binary form—a musical form having two sections (AB).

blues (see also "twelve-bar blues")—generally, certain song forms and performance practices which originally developed among rural African-Americans in the southern United States in the early twentieth century.

bol—(Hindi; literally "word") mnemonic syllables used by North Indian drummers in memorizing repertory for the drums known as tabla or pakhawaj. Kathak dancers from North India also use bols in memorizing rhythmic patterns and choreography.

call and response—a musical form involving regular alternation between a "call" which often is a semi-improvised solo, and a "response" which often is performed by a non-improvising group.

cassette culture—the world of independent sound recording, dissemination, and reception by way of audio cassettes.

céilí—(Irish) a) a dance event with Irish traditional music; b) informal entertainment including Irish traditional music, singing, dancing, and storytelling, usually occurring in the home.

chordophone—an instrument with one or more strings stretched between fixed points, such as a violin, guitar, or harp.

clave—a basic rhythmic pattern which provides the framework for Cuban and some other Latin American musics, sometimes played on the two sticks known by the same name.

colotomic—used by Javanese gamelan scholars to explain the regular subdivisions of the repertory's cyclic structure, and indicating the instruments which punctuate a particular point or points in the cycle.

composition—a piece of music that is planned out before performance.

compound meter—rhythmic groupings in which the beat is subdivided by three pulses: 6/8, 12/8, and so on. The term is also used for meters with odd numbers of beats (other than 3) such as 5/4, 7/8, and so on.

concerto—a large orchestral work scored for orchestra and a solo instrument, generally in three movements.

consonance (adj. consonant)—two or more simultaneous pitches which sound pleasing or restful together; a subjective designation.

continuo—in European Baroque music, the notation or performance of a figured bass—a bass line with figures indicating where pitches were to be played over it. The term also indicates the instruments used to play the continuo part, such as the harpsichord, organ, and cello.

cool jazz—a jazz genre developed by certain veteran bebop musicians in the 1950s, which emphasizes finely nuanced moods.

culture—a group's shared ways of experiencing, participating in, and making sense out of their world. In addition to the arts, culture includes languages, religions, belief systems, social organization, necessary skills, and everyday habits.

development—the middle section of sonata form, involving elaboration and invention based on material from the exposition section.

diatonic—designates seven-tone scales constructed of five whole- and two half-steps, such as the major and minor scales (as opposed to the chromatic scale).

dissonance (adj. dissonant)—two or more simultaneous pitches which do not sound consonant; a subjective designation.

drone—one or more pitches which are constantly sounded as background in a performance.

duple meter—consistent groupings of two beats; may be simple or compound.

duration—the length of time that a musical sound lasts.

dynamics—intentional changes of amplitude or volume in performance.

early music—generally, European repertory dating from the Middle Ages through the mid-18th century.

electronic transmission—the use of electronic media such as sound and video recordings, television and radio broadcasts, and computers in the learning process.

electrophone—an instrument which produces its sound electronically.

enculturation—the process of learning one's cultural traditions, including the informal acquisition of musical knowledge.

ethnomusicology—the academic study of music in relation to culture.

exposition—a) the first section of a fugue in which the theme is "exposed" at staggered intervals in all the voices; b) the first section of a movement in sonata form.

form—the overall structure of musical composition or improvisation.

fleádh cheoil—traditional Irish music and dance competitions held at the local, regional, and national levels.

free jazz—a jazz genre which arose in the 1950s and early 1960s, which involves solo or group improvisation with little or no predetermination of the result.

frequency—rate of vibration, measured in cycles per second. Our ears perceive frequency as pitch.

fugue—imitative polyphonic compositions usually built on a single theme.

functional memory—the aspect of memory that has to do with remembering when, where, and how to do things.

fundamental—the tone which forms the basis for an overtone series; the pitch we can identify and reproduce.

funk—an American popular music genre which arose in the mid-1960s, emphasizing polyrhythmic instrumental arrangements and vocal styles derived from soul and gospel.

gamelan—a general term used in various parts of Indonesia which is translated as "musical ensemble" or "orchestra." Such ensembles involve sets of instruments tuned to each other (and not to any standard "objective" pitch, like Western instruments). These instruments might be made of bronze, bamboo, wood, or other materials.

ganga—a vocal genre from Bosnia, characterized by very close harmonies. This loud and powerful music is meant to be sung outdoors by groups of either men or women.

gat—(pronounced "gut") in North Indian classical music, an instrumental composition set in tala (a metric cycle).

genre—general types, categories, and styles of music, such as reggae, alternative, rock, Bosnian ganga, and opera.

gong ageng—the largest gong in a Central Javanese gamelan.

gospel—an African-American Christian genre which involves blues-based vocal styles and rhythmic and harmonic accompaniment.

guru-sishya parampara—the master-disciple tradition in India.

harmony—the simultaneous sounding of more than one pitch.

head—a jazz composition, consisting of a melody which serves as a point of departure for improvisation.

heterophony—occurs when two or more musicians simultaneously sing or play the same melody in different ways. These differences can range from small discrepancies in unison singing—such as in a church congregation—to more pronounced variations in ornamentation or rhythm.

Hindustani (also Hindusthani)—of or pertaining to North India. North Indian classical music (or raga sangit) is called Hindustani classical music; South Indian raga sangit is called Carnatic classical music.

homophony—a form of polyphony in which one or more simultaneously occurring parts function as a support for a dominant part.

idiophone—an instrument which is sounded by the substance of the instrument itself. Examples include bells, gongs, and shakers.

improvisation—music that is composed at the time of performance.

indie—an independent recording company.

interval—the distance between two pitches.

jhala—in North Indian classical instrumental music, the third section in a three-part introductory alap, in which the tempo accelerates but no tala cycle (meter) is established. Also, the technique of playing fast, tremelo-like jhala passages on instruments, applied not only to the third portion of an introductory alap, but also to the final, very fast portion of the performance of a fast gat in tala.

jor—in North Indian classical instrumental music, the second section in a three-part introductory alap, in which a medium tempo pulse is introduced but no tala cycle (meter) is established.

key—a specific harmonic world which contextualizes individual chords and melodies in a Western tonal composition or performance; a given piece is considered to be "in" a particular key even if it includes modulation, and it usually begins and ends with that key's tonic chord.

koto—a long zither with movable bridges and thirteen strings from Japan.

maqam—a) the modal melodic systems of Arabic and Turkish classical music, practiced in Turkey (where it is spelled makam), northern Africa, and the Middle East; b) one of the modes of Arabic or Turkish classical music.

material culture—an anthropological term referring to any and all physical manifestations of culture. In music, material culture includes musical instruments, notation, music books, recordings, microphones, amplifiers, performance costumes, etc.

mbira—a metal-keyed idiophone in the general class of instruments known as lamellaphones, distributed widely throughout sub-Saharan Africa. Also called sanzi, likembe, kalimba, and thumb piano.

measure—the basic unit of meter consisting of strong and weak beats that occur within one bar.

media landscape—all of the musical "territory" made available to a musician or music student by the available media, including sound and video recordings and broadcast performances.

melisma—singing several pitches on one syllable.

melody—the singable part of music; a line or rising and falling pitches which presents an abstract musical "story."

membranophone—an instrument which vibrates by means of a tightly stretched skin or membrane, such as a drum.

metallophone—a metal keyed xylophone.

meter—a recurrent pattern that groups pulses into strong and weak beats.

mnemonic—assisting or designed to assist memory

mode—a) a particular, scale-like group of notes, generally including seven pitches within an octave, used to generate melodies; b) one of the European church modes from which the term takes its name. Many modal systems involve characteristics such as pitch hierarchy and signature motifs in addition to a scale-like ladder of pitches.

modernization—the process whereby a music retains its traditional essence, but becomes part of the contemporary world and its set of values.

modulation—the process of moving from one keynote or tonic to another in the course of a composition or improvisation. In Western music, modulation refers to changes of key, affecting the process of harmonic progression; in Arabic music, it refers to changes of maqam.

monophony—a term referring to texture, meaning music in one part.

motet—a European sacred polyphonic composition from the Middle Ages or Renaissance, or a later composition growing out of the earlier motet tradition.

motif, motive—a short melodic or rhythmic fragment which repeats, perhaps with some variation.

movement—a complete musical composition which serves as part of a larger work, such as a symphony or concerto.

narrative—a song that tells a story.

octave—the interval which is comprised of the seven scale degrees (doh through ti) plus the next note (doh) of the diatonic scale, which is an "eighth" or octave above the starting pitch. Pitches an octave apart are sometimes considered to share an identity, as when men and women sing the same melody in different octaves. Physically, each successively higher octave is double the frequency of the previous one (A=220 cycles per second, a=440 cycles per second, and so on).

opera—a theatrical form involving dramatic tales staged in musical settings.

organology—the study of musical instruments, the "organs" used to produce musical sound

organum—the earliest notated polyphonic music of Europe (900–1200 CE) involving a plainchant melody and one or more additional melodic parts.

oral transmission—the process of learning through imitation directly from a carrier of a musical tradition.

ostinato—a repeating rhythmic and/or melodic pattern.

overdubbing—the process of recording tracks at different times and then playing them back simultaneously.

overtone series—the fundamental pitch and a simultaneously sounding series of progressively higher overtones present in one tone. The fundamental pitch is the actual note sung or played and it is usually the tone we can identify and hear most clearly. The combination of fundamental with the particular overtones that sound along with it help to create the timbre or tone color of a particular sound or tone.

pitch—the vibrating frequency, commonly described as the highness or lowness of a sound.

plainchant—the oldest known form of European Christian music, involving monophonic settings of sacred texts.

polyphony—generally used to describe any multi-part musical tradition. Polyphony results when two or more lines of music are played or sung simultaneously.

polyrhythm—the simultaneous sounding of multiple rhythmic patterns.

primary sources—in early music, original scores or facsimiles, and literary, iconographic, and organological sources (musical instruments) contemporary to the music itself.

program music—an instrumental work that is narrative or descriptive, often based on a non-musical form, such as a painting or poem.

pulse—regularly occurring beats of equal weight.

raga—a) one of the modes used to generate melodies in Indian classical music. Each raga is characterized not only by a scale-like set of pitches, but by a pitch hierarchy and particular melodic motifs and "paths," as well as extra-musical characteristics; b) the concept of melodic mode in Indian classical music.

rap—an African-American popular music genre involving spoken rhymes over polyrhythmic beats, which developed in the late 1970s as part of the emerging subculture known as hip hop.

recapitulation—the final section of sonata form, in which all or part of the exposition is repeated without the exposition's decisive modulation.

reception—how music is received by its audience.

rhythm—the time element in music.

riff—in jazz, a short motif or melodic gesture which is used as a "building block" in creating improvisations.

ritual—recurring functional activities that focus minds and energies through their formal repetitiveness, reinforcing feelings and actions which are valued by the individual and community. In common usage, ritual often refers to life-cycle events and religious ceremonies.

root—the bottom note of a triad.

rumba—an African-American popular music and dance genre which developed in Cuba in the 1860s.

salsa—a pan-Latino popular music genre which developed in New York City in the mid-twentieth century.

sam—(pronounced "sum") the first beat in a North Indian tala cycle.

sampler—an electrophone which records, processes, and reproduces sound through digital technology.

sangit—in India, a Sanskrit term signifying "music," whose original meaning also encompassed dance as well as vocal and instrumental music.

scale—a collection or row of pitches, often subdividing the octave into a series of steps.

sean-nós—an Irish repertory and singing style which literally means "old way." Generally applied to traditional singing in Irish, a Gaelic language.

secondary sources—writings by modern scholars about a musical tradition.

seventh chord—a four-note chord consisting of a triad and an additional third.

shakuhachi—a Japanese endblown flute that is made from a bamboo stalk and root.

simple meter—rhythmic groupings in measures of two, three, or four beats.

sine wave—a simple sound wave which involves no overtones, just a fundamental, visually represented as a reversed "S" on its side.

son—the most popular twentieth century Cuban music and dance genre.

solfege—in the Western classical tradition, syllables that used to indicate pitches or steps of the diatonic scale—doh, re, mi, fa, so, la, and ti.

sonata—a musical composition in several movements often scored for a solo keyboard or for a small ensemble.

sonata form—a form used from the Classical period on, often as the first movement for a symphony or other large orchestral work.

soundscape—the audible environment.

South Asia—the geographical and cultural area comprised of the modern nations of Pakistan, India, Bangladesh, Nepal, and Sri Lanka.

stereo (stereophonic)—a method of sound recording and playback which uses two simultaneous recording tracks to reproduce sounds in spacial relationships.

syncopation—the accenting of off-beats or weak beats.

syncretic—blending congenial elements from different cultures to produce hybrid musical forms.

synthesizer—an electrophone which integrates electronic sound production and processing.

tala—a) repeating rhythmic cycles in the classical musics of India; b) the concept of rhythm in Indian classical music.

tan—in North Indian classical music, a very fast passage. An important part of improvisation, in which a singer or instrumentalist displays technical virtuosity as well as melodic and rhythmic imagination.

taqasim—in Arabic classical music, instrumental improvisations that may either be extended items in a recital or short introductions to, or bridges between, composed pieces.

tempo—speed, how quickly or slowly music is performed. Tempo refers to the velocity of the basic pulse of a performance, rather than rhythmic density.

ternary form—a musical form having three sections; the third section is a repeat of the first.

texture—the organization of music into one or more simultaneously sounding parts, and the ways in which these different parts relate to each other.

theme—a musical idea, such as a melody or rhythmic pattern, which is used as the basis for musical invention.

timbre—tone color; technically, the complexity and shape of sound waves.

tonal—an adjective describing music composed according to the conventions of the Western harmonic system.

tonality—a "key" in the Western harmonic system; for example, the tonality of D major.

tonic—the keynote of a piece composed in the tonal system of Western classical and popular music. By analogy, the term is used to refer to the keynote or finalis in a number of modal and melodic systems.

topical—having to do with topics and social issues of the day.

track—a single sequence of recorded sound.

triad—a three-note consonance which may be conceptualized as a fifth subdivided by a third or as a stack of two thirds.

twelve-bar blues—the most widely used form associated with blues, involving a specific harmonic pattern and certain characteristic verse forms.

vibrato—a minute fluctuation of both volume and pitch in every sustained note.

vocable—musical syllables that are sung but have no literal meaning. Examples include jazz scat-singing, Irish lilting, and the tarana compositions of North Indian classical singing.

Westernization—the process whereby a formerly non-Western music changes through the accretion of Western elements.

written transmission—the use of notation and/or theoretical texts in musical learning.

REFERENCED AND ADDITIONAL SOURCES

Preface

Referenced Source

Blacking, John. 1987. "A Commonsense View of all Music": Reflections on Percy Grainger's *Contribution to Ethnomusicolgy and Music Education*. Cambridge: Cambridge University Press.

CHAPTER 1. SOUND, MUSIC, AND THE ENVIRONMENT

Referenced Sources

Alekseev, Eduard, Kirgiz, Zoya, and Levin, Ted. 1990. "Program Notes." *Tuva Voices From the Center of Asia*. Washington D.C.: Smithsonian Folkways C-Sf 40017.

Baily, John. 1997. "Afghan Perceptions of Birdsong." *The World of Music* 39/2:51–59.

Brown, Ernest. 1997. Interview for *Exploring the World of Music*, Pacific Street Films.

Campbell, Patricia J. 1981. *Passing the Hat: Street Performers in America*. New York: Delacorte Press.

Crafts, Susan, Cavicchi, Daniel, and Keil, Charles. 1993. *My Music*. Hanover: Wesleyan University Press.

Ellis, Catherine. 1980. "Aboriginal Music and Dance in Southern Australia." *The New Grove Dictionary of Music and Musicians*, edited by Stanley Sadie, 1:722–728. London: MacMillan.

Feld, Steven. 1982. *Sound and Sentiment: Birds, Weeping, Poetics, and Song in Kaluli Expression*. Philadelphia: University of Philadelphia Press.

Laušević, Mirjana. 1997. Interview for *Exploring the World of Music*, Pacific Street Films.

Levin, Theodore. 1997. Interview for *Exploring the World of Music*, Pacific Street Films.

Levin, Theodore. 1997. Unpublished Project Description.

Lipsitz, George. 1994. *Dangerous Crossroads: Popular Music, Postmodernism and the Poetics of Place*. London: Verso.

Nettl, Bruno. 1978. *Eight Urban Musical Cultures: Tradition and Change.* Urbana, IL: University of Illinois Press.

Redman, Josh, 1997. Interview for *Exploring the World of Music,* Pacific Street Films.

Rice, Timothy. 1994. *May It Fill Your Soul: Experiencing Bulgarian Music.* Chicago: University of Chicago Press.

Rose, Tricia. 1994. *Black Noise: Rap Music and Black Culture in Contemporary America.* Hanover: Wesleyan University Press.

Seeger, Anthony. 1992. "Ethnography of Music." *Ethnomusicology: An Introduction,* edited by Helen Myers. New York: Norton.

Seeger, Anthony. 1987. *Why Suyá Sing.* Cambridge: Cambridge University Press.

Shapiro, Gerald, 1997. Interview for *Exploring the World of Music,* Pacific Street Films.

Slobin, Mark. 1997. Interview for *Exploring the World of Music,* Pacific Street Films.

Slobin, Mark. 1996. "Bosnia and Central/Southeast Europe." *Worlds of Music.* New York: Schirmer.

Tanenbaum, Susie J. 1995. *Underground Harmonies: Music and Politics in the Subways of New York.* Ithaca: Cornell University Press.

Waterman, Christopher Alan. 1990. *Jùjú: A Social History and Ethnography of an African Popular Music.* Chicago: University of Chicago Press.

CHAPTER 2. THE TRANSFORMATIVE POWER OF MUSIC

Referenced Sources

Berliner, Paul. 1994. *Thinking in Jazz.* Chicago: University of Chicago Press.

Blacking, John. 1973. *How Musical Is Man?* Seattle: University of Washington Press.

Brown, Ernest. 1997. Interview for *Exploring the World of Music.* Pacific Street Films.

Cohen, John. 1982. *Gypsies Sing Long Ballads.* [video] New York: Cinema Guild.

Cowan, Jane. 1990. *Dance and the Body Politic in Northern Greece.* Princeton: Princeton University Press.

Cowdery, James R. 1990. *The Melodic Tradition of Ireland.* Kent, OH: Kent State University Press.

Daniel, Yvonne. 1995. *Rumba: Dance and Social Change in Contemporary Cuba.* Bloomington, IN: Indiana University Press.

Dennis, David B. 1996. *Beethoven in German Politics 1870–1989.* New Haven: Yale University Press.

DiSpirito, Jim. 1997. Interview for *Exploring the World of Music.* Pacific Street Films.

Dunson, Josh. 1965. *Freedom in the Air: Song Movements of the Sixties.* New York: International Publishers.

Fox, Matthew (ed.) 1987. *Hildegard of Bingen's Book of Divine Works,* translated by Ron Miller. Santa Fe: Bear & Company.

Frith, Simon. 1987. "Toward an aesthetic of popular music." *Music and Society,* edited by Leppert and McClary. Cambridge: Cambridge University Press.

Glabicki, Michael. 1997. Interview for *Exploring the World of Music*. Pacific Street Films.

Glassie, Henry. 1982. *Passing the Time in Ballymenone*. Philadelphia: University of Pennsylvania Press.

Greenway, John. 1953. *American Folksongs of Protest*. Philadelphia: University of Pennsylvania Press.

Heilman, Samuel. 1987. *The People of the Book*. Chicago: University of Chicago Press.

Herbst, Edward. 1997. *Voices in Bali*. Hanover, NH: Wesleyan University Press.

Kotzsch, Ronald. 1992. "Invitation to a Ball." *Country Dance and Song Society News* 108:10.

Laušević, Mirjana. 1993. Personal communication to Author.

Lord, Albert B. 1960. *The Singer of Tales*. Cambridge: Harvard University Press.

McAllester, David P. 1996. "North America/Native America." *Worlds of Music*. New York: Schirmer.

McCarthy Brown, Karen. 1991. *Mama Lola: A Voudou Priestess in Brooklyn*. Berkeley: University of California Press.

Manuel, Peter. 1988. *Popular Musics of the Non-Western World*. New York: Oxford University Press.

Merriam, Alan P. 1977. "Definitions of 'Comparative Musicology' and 'Ethnomusicology': An Historical-Theoretical Perspective." *Ethnomusicology* 21/2:189–204.

Morton, Robin. 1973. *Come Day, Go Day, God Send Sunday*. London: Routledge & Kegan Paul.

Nettl, Paul. 1967. *National Anthems*, translated by Alexander Gode. New York: Frederick Ungar Publishing Company.

Reese, Gustave. 1940. *Music in the Middle Ages*. New York: Norton.

Rouget, Gilbert. 1985. *Music and Trance*, translated by Brunhilde Biebuyck. Chicago: University of Chicago Press.

Slobin, Mark. 1993. *Subcultural Sounds*. Hanover: Wesleyan University Press.

Storr, Anthony. 1992. *Music and the Mind*. New York: Ballantine Books.

Takaki, Ronald. 1993. *A Different Mirror: A History of Multicultural America*. Boston: Little, Brown, and Company.

Titon, Jeff Todd. 1997. "Ethnomusicology and Values: A Reply to Henry Kingsbury." *Ethnomusicology* 41/2:258–60.

Turnbull, Colin. 1962. *The Forest People*. New York: Touchstone.

Wiess, Piero, and Taruskin, Richard. 1984. *Music in the Western World*. New York: Schirmer.

Additional Sources

Denisoff, Serge. 1971. *Great Day Coming*. Urbana: University of Illinois Press.

Heilbut, Tony. 1971. The *Gospel Sound: Good News and Bad Times*. New York: Simon and Schuster.

Lomax, Alan. 1967. *Hard Hitting Songs for Hard-Hit People*. New York, Oak Publications.

CHAPTER 3. MUSIC AND MEMORY

Referenced Sources

Breen, Marcus. 1994. "I Have a Dreamtime." *World Music: The Rough Guide.* London: The Rough Guides.

Brown, Howard Mayer. 1976. *Music in the Renaissance.* Englewood Cliffs: Prentice-Hall.

Cohen, John. 1997. Interview for *Exploring the World of Music,* Pacific Street Films.

Herreid, Grant. 1997. Interview for *Exploring the World of Music,* Pacific Street Films.

Hobsbawm, Eric (ed.). 1989. *The Invention of Tradition.* Cambridge: Cambridge University Press.

Kilbride, Pat. 1997. Interview for *Exploring the World of Music,* Pacific Street Films.

Levin, Theodore. 1997. Interview for *Exploring the World of Music,* Pacific Street Films.

Lowenthal, David. 1985. *The Past is a Foreign Country.* Cambridge: Cambridge University Press.

Moulden, John. 1994. *Thousands are sailing: a brief song history of Irish emigration.* Portrush, Northern Ireland: Ulstersongs.

O'Sullivan, Jerry. 1997. Interview for *Exploring the World of Music,* Pacific Street Films.

Peterson, Nicolas. 1970. "Buluwandi: A Central Australian Ceremony for the Resolution for Conflict."*Australian Aboriginal Anthropology,* edited by Ronald M. Berndt. Australian Institute for Aboriginal Studies: 200–215.

Perlman, Marc. "Early Music Talk Begins to Heat up Again," NY: The New York Times, June 18, 1998:29.

Pope, Isabel. 1980. "Encina, Juan del." *The New Grove Dictionary of Music and Musicians,* edited by Stanley Sadie, 6:159–161. London: MacMillan.

Ronström, Owe. 1996. "Revival Reconsidered." *The World of Music* 38/3: 5–20.

Seeger, Anthony. 1987. *Why Suyá Sing: A musical anthropology of an Amazonian people.* Cambridge: Cambridge University Press.

Shipper, Paul. 1997. Interview for *Exploring the World of Music,* Pacific Street Films.

Slobin, Mark. 1997. Interview for *Exploring the World of Music,* Pacific Street Films.

Takaki, Ronald. 1993. "Emigrants from Erin." *A Different Mirror: A History of Multicultural America.* Boston: Little Brown and Company.

Tunney, Paddy. 1991. *The Stone Fiddle.* Belfast: Appletree Press.

Wild, Stephen. 1997. Interview for *Exploring the World of Music,* Pacific Street Films.

Zajac, Tom. 1997. Interview for *Exploring the World of Music,* Pacific Street Films.

CHAPTER 4. TRANSMISSION: LEARNING MUSIC

Referenced Sources

Das Gupta, Buddhadev. 1997. Interview for *Exploring the World of Music,* Pacific Street Films.

DiSpirito, Jim. 1998. Interview for *Exploring the World of Music,* Pacific Street Films.

Erlin, Liz. 1998. Interview for *Exploring the World of Music,* Pacific Street Films.

Glabicki, Michael. 1998. Interview for *Exploring the World of Music,* Pacific Street Films.

Henry, Edward O. 1989. "Institutions for the Promotion of Indigenous Music: The Case for Ireland's Comhaltas Ceoltoiri." *Ethnomusicology* 33/1: 67–96.

Laušević, Mirjana. 1997. Interview for *Exploring the World of Music,* Pacific Street Films.

Merriam, Alan. 1964. *The Anthropology of Music.* Evanston: Northwestern University Press.

Pagano, Mary Jo. 1997. Interview for *Exploring the World of Music,* Pacific Street Films.

Redman, Josh. 1997. Interview for *Exploring the World of Music,* Pacific Street Films.

Rice, Timothy. 1994. *May It Fill Your Soul: Experiencing Bulgarian Music.* Chicago: University of Chicago Press.

Spiegel, Ray. 1997. Interview for *Exploring the World of Music,* Pacific Street Films.

Ying, Timothy. 1997. Interview for *Exploring the World of Music,* Pacific Street Films.

Additional Sources

Booth, Gregory D. 1986. *The Oral Tradition in Transition: Implications for Music Education from a Study of North Indian Tabla Transmission.* Ph.D. dissertation, Kent State University.

Kippen, James. 1988. *The Tabla of Lucknow.* Cambridge: Cambridge University Press.

Miner, Allyn. 1993. Sitar and Sarod in *the 18th and 19th Centuries.* Wilhelmshaven: Noetzel.

Ruckert, George. 1991. *The Music of the Baba Allauddin Gharana as Taught by Ali Akbar Khan at the Ali Akbar College of Music.* Ali Akbar Khan, general editor. New York and St. Louis: East Bay Books.

Shankar, Ravi. 1968. *My Music, My Life.* NY: Simon and Schuster.

CHAPTER 5. RHYTHM

Referenced Sources

Evans, David. Nd. *Gravel Springs Fife and Drum* (Film). Center for Southern Folklore.

Hahn, Tomie. 1997. Interview for *Exploring the World of Music.* Pacific Street Films.

Jones, Bessie. 1987. *For the Ancestors: Autobiographical Memories,* edited by John Stewart. Urbana: University of Illinois Press.

Kerman, Joseph. 1987. *Listen.* New York: Worth Publishing.

Koetting, James T. 1992. "Africa." *Worlds of Music.* New York: Schirmer.

Palmer, Robert. 1992. "James Brown." *The Rolling Stone Illustrated History of Rock & Roll,* edited by Anthony DeCurtis and James Henke, with Holly George-Warren. New York: Random House.

Redman, Josh. 1997. Interview for Exploring the World of *Music*. Pacific Street Films.

Roberts, John Storm. 1972. *Black Music of Two Worlds*. Tivoli, NY: Original Music.

Searles, Julie. 1990. Personal communication with Author.

Additional Sources

Daniel, Yvonne. 1995. *Rumba: Dance and Social Change in Contemporary Cuba*. Bloomington and Indianapolis: Indiana University Press.

Deva, B. Chaitanya. 1981. *An Introduction to Indian Music*. New Delhi: Publications Division, Ministry of Information and Broadcasting, Government of India.

George, Nelson. 1988. *The Death of Rhythm & Blues*. New York: Plume.

Jones, Bessie, and Bess Lomax Howes. 1987. *Step It Down: Games, Plays, Songs, and Stories from the Afro-American Heritage*. Athens, GA: University of Georgia Press.

Kippen, James. 1988. *The Tabla of Lucknow*. Cambridge: Cambridge University Press.

Manuel, Peter. 1995. *Caribbean Currents: Caribbean Music from Rumba to Reggae*. Philadelphia: Temple University Press.

Marre, Jeremy. 1982. *The Spirit of Samba: Black Music of Brazil*. [video] *Beats of the Heart*. Harcourt Films.

McGowan, Chris, and Ricardo Pessanha. 1991. *The Brazilian Sound: Samba, Bossa Nova, and the Popular Music of Brazil*. New York: Billboard.

Powers, Harold S. 1980. "India, subcontinent of." *The New Grove Dictionary of Music and Musicians,* edited by Stanley Sadie, 9:69–141. London: MacMillan.

Rose, Tricia. 1994. *Black Noise: Rap Music and Black Culture in Contemporary America*. Hanover, NH: Wesleyan University Press.

Ruckert, George. 1991. *The Music of the Baba Allauddin Gharana as Taught by Ali Akbar Khan at the Ali Akbar College of Music*. Ali Akbar Khan, general editor. New York and St. Louis: East Bay Books.

Shankar, Ravi. 1968. My Music, My Life. New York: Simon and Schuster.

Wade, Bonnie C. 1979. *Music in India: The Classical Traditions*. Englewood Cliffs, NJ: Prentice-Hall, Inc.

_____. 1984. *Khyal: Creativity Within North India's Classical Music Tradition*. Cambridge: Cambridge University Press.

Walser, Robert. 1995. "Rhythm, Rhyme, and Rhetoric in the Music of Public Enemy." *Ethnomusicology* 39/2:193–217.

CHAPTER 6. MELODY

Referenced Sources

Bhatkhande, V. N. 1979. *Hindustani Sangeet Paddhati: Kramik Pustak Malika, Part IV*. Hathras, India: Sangeet Karyalaya.

Conway, Brian. 1997. Interview for *Exploring the World of Music,* Pacific Street Films.

Cowdery, James R. 1990. *The Melodic Tradition of Ireland*. Kent, OH: Kent State University Press.

Das Gupta, Buddhadev. 1997. Interview for *Exploring the World of Music*, Pacific Street Films.

Feldman, Walter. 1993. "Ottoman Sources on the Development of the Taksim." *Yearbook for Traditional Music* 25:1–28.

Hull, Eleanor. 1912. *The Poem-Book of the Gael*. London: Chatto and Windus.

Marcus, Scott Lloyd. 1989. *Arab music theory in the modern period*. Ph.D. dissertation, University of California, Los Angeles.

O'Sullivan, Jerry. 1997. Interview for *Exploring the World of Music*, Pacific Street Films.

Powers, Harold S. 1980. "Mode." *The New Grove Dictionary of Music and Musicians*, edited by Stanley Sadie, 12:376–450. London: MacMillan.

Redman, Josh. 1997. Interview for *Exploring the World of Music*, Pacific Street Films.

Seeger, Pete. 1997. Interview for *Exploring the World of Music*, Pacific Street Films.

Shaheen, Simon. 1997. Interview for *Exploring the World of Music*, Pacific Street Films.

Shields, Hugh. 1993. *Narrative Singing in Ireland*. Dublin: Irish Academic Press.

Shiloah, Amnon. 1995. *Music in the World of Islam: A Socio-cultural Study*. Detroit: Wayne State University Press.

Stubbs, Frederick. 1997. Interview for *Exploring the World of Music*, Pacific Street Films.

Touma, Habid Hassan. 1977. *La Musique Arabe*, translated by Christine Hetier. Paris: Editions Buchet/Chaste.

_____ 1996. *The Music of the Arabs*, translated by Laurie Schwartz. Portland: Amadeus Press.

Wade, Bonnie C. 1979. *Music in India: The Classical Traditions*. Englewood Cliffs, NJ: Prentice-Hall.

_____ 1984. *Khyal: Creativity Within North India's Classical Music Tradition*. Cambridge: Cambridge University Press.

Wright, Owen. 1980. "Arab music." *The New Grove Dictionary of Music and Musicians*, edited by Stanley Sadie, 12:514–525. London: MacMillan.

Additional Sources

Danielou, Alain. 1987. *Northern Indian Music (The Main Ragas)*. New Delhi: V. K. Publishing House

Deva, B. Chaitanya. 1981. *An Introduction to Indian Music*. New Delhi: Publications Division, Ministry of Information and Broadcasting, Government of India.

Kaufmann, Walter. 1968. *The Ragas of North India*. Bloomington: Indian University Press.

Shankar, Ravi. 1968. *My Music, My Life*. NY: Simon and Schuster.

CHAPTER 7. TIMBRE: THE COLOR OF MUSIC

Referenced Sources

Adriaansz, W., 1980. "Japan iv, 2: Instruments." *The New Grove Dictionary of Music and Musicians*, edited by Stanley Sadie, 9:526–536. London: MacMillan Press.

Bebey, Francis. 1969. *African Music: A People's Art*. New York: Lawrence Hill & Company.

Berliner, Paul. 1981. *The Soul of Mbira*. Berkeley: University of California Press.

Dournon, Geneviève. 1992. "Organology." *Ethnomusicology: An Introduction*. New York: Norton.

Fujie, Linda. 1996. "East Asia/Japan." *Worlds of Music*. New York: Schirmer.

Hahn, Tomie. 1997. Interview for *Exploring the World of Music*, Pacific Street Films.

Jourdain, Robert. 1996. *Music, The Brain, and Ecstasy*. New York: William Morrow and Company.

Kippen, James. 1988. *The Tabla of Lucknow*. Cambridge: Cambridge University Press.

Knight, Roderic. 1976. "Notes." *Kora Music from the Gambia played by Foday Muso Suso*. New York. Folkways FW 8510.

Kartomi, Margaret. 1990. *On Concepts and Classifications of Musical Instruments*. Chicago: The University of Chicago Press.

Levin, Ted. 1997. Interview for *Exploring the World of Music*, Pacific Street Films.

Locke, David. 1996. "Africa/Ewe, Mande, Dagbamba, Shona, BaAka." *Worlds of Music*. New York: Schirmer.

Malm, William. 1959. *Japanese Music and Musical Instruments*. Rutland, VT: Charles E. Tuttle.

Miner, Allyn. 1993. *Sitar and Sarod in the 18th and 19th Centuries*. Wilhelshaven: Noetzel.

Reck, David. 1977. *Music of the Whole Earth*. New York: Charles Scribner's Sons.

Redman, Josh. 1997. Interview for *Exploring the World of Music*, Pacific Street Films.

Scholes, Percy. 1978. *The Oxford Companion to Music*. Tenth Edition. Oxford: Oxford University Press.

Shaheen, Simon. 1997. Interview for *Exploring the World of Music*, Pacific Street Films.

Stubbs, Frederick. 1997. Interview for *Exploring the World of Music*, Pacific Street Films.

Touma, Habib Hassan. 1996. *The Music of the Arabs*. Portland: Amadeus Press.

Wright, Owen. 1980. "Arab Music." *The New Grove Dictionary of Music and Musicians*, edited by Stanley Sadie, 12:376–450. London: MacMillan Press.

Additional Sources

Charry, Eric. 1994. "West African Harps." *Journal of the American Musical Instrument Society* 20:5–53.

Manuel, Peter. 1988. *Popular Music of the Western World*. New York: Oxford University Press.

Waterman, Christopher. 1990. *JùJú: A Social History and Ethnography of an African Popular Music*. Chicago: University of Chicago Press

CHAPTER 8. TEXTURE

Referenced Sources

Bakan, Michael. 1998. "Walking Warriors: Battlegrounds of Culture and Ideology in the World of Balinese Gamelan Beleganjur." *Ethnomusicology* 42:3.

Kolneder, Walter. 1970. *Antonio Vivaldi: His Life and Work.* Berkeley: University of California Press.

Locke, David. 1996. "Africa/Ewe, Mande, Dagbamba, Shona, BaAka." *Worlds of Music.* New York: Schirmer.

Manuel, Peter. 1995. *Caribbean Currents: From Rumba to Reggae.* Philadelphia: Temple University Press.

Reck, David. 1977. *Music of the Whole Earth.* New York: Charles Scribner's Sons.

Slobin, Mark. 1997. Interview for *Exploring the World of Music*, Pacific Street Films.

Stuemplfe, Stephen. 1995. *The Steelband Movement.* Philadelphia: University of Pennsylvania Press.

Swain, Jay. 1987. *Sound Judgements.* San Francisco: San Francisco Press.

Additional Sources

Aho, William R. 1987. "Steel Band Music in Trinidad and Tobago: The Creation of a People's Music." *Latin American Music Review* 8/1:26–55.

Bartholomew, John. 1980. *The Steel Band.* London: Oxford University Press.

Boggs, Vernon. 1992. *Salsiology.* New York: Greenwood.

Herbst, Edward. 1997. *Voices in Bali: Energies and Perceptions in Vocal Music and Dance Theater.* Hanover, NH: Wesleyan University Press.

Hill, Donald R. 1993. *Calypso Calaloo: Early Carnival Music in Trinidad.* Gainesville, FL: University Press of Florida.

Lindsay, Jennifer. 1992. *Javanese Gamelan: Traditional Orchestra of Indonesia.* 2nd ed. New York: Oxford University Press.

Sutton, R. Anderson. 1991. *Traditions of Gamelan Music in Java: Musical Pluralism and Regional Identity.* Cambridge: Cambridge University Press.

Tenzer, Michael. 1991. *Balinese Music.* Berkeley, CA: Periplus.

CHAPTER 9. HARMONY

Referenced Sources

Berliner, Paul. 1981. *The Soul of Mbira.* Berkeley and Los Angeles: University of California Press.

Brown, Ernest. 1997. Interview for *Exploring the World of Music*, Pacific Street Films.

Hayward, John, ed. 1930. *The Letters of Saint Évremond.* Loundon: Routledge.

Kaeppler, Adrienne. 1980. "Polynesian Music and Dance." *Musics of Many Cultures: An Introduction*, edited by Elizabeth May. Berkeley and Los Angeles: University of California Press.

Laušević, Mirjana. 1997. Interview for *Exploring the World of Music*, Pacific Street Films.

Levin, Theodore. 1996. *The Hundred Thousand Fools of God*. Bloomington and Indianapolis: Indiana University Press.

The New Oxford History of Music. 1954. London: Oxford University Press.

Reese, Gustave. 1940. *Music in the Middle Ages*. New York: Norton.

Reese, Gustave. 1959. *Music in the Renaissance*. New York: Norton.

Robertson, Alec, and Stevens, Denis, eds. 1960. *The Pelican History of Music*. New York: Penguin.

Weiss, Piero, and Taruskin, Richard, eds. 1984. *Music in the Western World: A History in Documents*. New York: Schirmer.

Zarlino, Gioseffo. 1968. *The Art of Counterpoint*, translated by Guy A. Marco and Claude V. Palisca. New Haven: Yale University Press.

Additional Sources

Blacking, John. 1973. *How Musical Is Man?* Seattle: University of Washington Press.

Roberts, John Storm. 1972. *Black Music of Two Worlds*. Tivoli, NY: Original Music.

CHAPTER 10. FORM: THE SHAPE OF MUSIC

Referenced Sources

Averill, Gage. 1997. Interview for *Exploring the World of Music*, Pacific Street Films.

Bebey, Francis. 1975. *African Music: A People's Art*, translated by Josephine Bennett. Brooklyn, NY: Lawrence Hill Books.

Berliner, Paul. 1994. *Thinking in Jazz*. Chicago: University of Chicago Press.

Chernoff, John M. 1979. *African Rhythm and African Sensibility*. Chicago: University of Chicago Press.

Hahn, Tomie. 1996. Interview for *Exploring the World of Music*, Pacific Street Films.

Jones, LeRoi. 1963. *Blues People*. New York: Morrow Quill.

Pagano, Mary Jo. 1997. Interview for *Exploring the World of Music*, Pacific Street Films.

Palmer, Robert. 1981. *Deep Blues*. New York: Penguin.

Perle, George. 1990. *The Listening Composer*. Chicago: University of Chicago Press.

Reck, David. 1977. *Music of the Whole Earth*. New York: Charles Scribner's Sons.

Titon, Jeff Todd. 1994. *Early Downhome Blues: A Musical and Cultural Analysis*. Urbana, IL: University of Illinois Press.

Ying, Timmy. 1997. Interview for *Exploring the World of Music*, Pacific Street Films.

Additional Sources

Barlow, William. 1989. *Looking Up at Down: The Emergence of Blues Culture*. Philadelphia: Temple University Press.

Locke, David. 1987. *Drum Gahu: The Rhythms of West African Drumming*. Crown Point, IN: White Cliffs Media Company.

CHAPTER 11. COMPOSERS AND IMPROVISERS

Referenced Sources

Babbit, Milton. 1958. "Who Cares If You Listen?" *High Fidelity* 8/2:38–40, 126–7.

Boulton, Laura. 1954. "The Eskimos of Hudson Bay and Alaska." Notes to Folkways Records FE4444 (LP).

Chernoff, John Miller. 1979. *African Rhythm and African Sensibility*. Chicago: University of Chicago Press.

Coker, Jerry. 1964. *Improvising Jazz*. Englewood Cliffs: Prentice-Hall, Inc.

Cooke, Peter. 1986. *The Fiddle Tradition of the Shetland Isles*. Cambridge: Cambridge University Press.

Cowdery, James R. 1990. *The Melodic Tradition of Ireland*. Kent, OH: Kent State University Press.

Feld, Steven. 1982. *Sound and Sentiment*. Philadelphia: University of Pennsylvania Press.

Feldman, Walter. 1993. "Ottoman Sources on the Development of the Taksim." *Yearbook for Traditional Music* 25:1–28.

Garrison, Virginia. 1985. Traditional and Non-Traditional Teaching and Learning Practices in Folk Music: An Ethnographic Field Study of Cape Breton Fiddling. Ph.D. dissertation, University of Wisconsin.

Koetting, James. 1992. "Africa/Ghana." *Worlds of Music*, edited by Jeff Todd Titon. New York: Schirmer.

List, George. 1997. "Hopi Kachina Dance Songs: Concepts and Context." *Ethnomusicology* 41/3:413–32.

McQuillen, Bob. 1993. Interview with the Author.

Marcus, Scott Lloyd. 1989. *Arab music theory in the modern period*. Ph.D. dissertation. University of California, Los Angeles.

_____. June 1998. E-mail communication with authors.

Merriam, Alan P. 1964. *The Anthropology of Music*. Evanston, IL: Northwestern University Press.

Miner, Allyn. 1993. *Sitar and Sarod in the 18th and 19th Centuries*. Wilhelmshaven: Noetzel.

Shiloah, Amnon. 1995. *Music in the World of Islam: A Socio-cultural study*. Detroit: Wayne State University Press.

Nettl, Bruno. 1974. "Thoughts on Improvisation, a Comparative Approach." *Musical Quarterly* 60:1–19.

Titon, Jeff Todd. 1978. "Every Day I Have the Blues: Improvisation and Daily Life." *Southern Folklore Quarterly* 42:85–98.

Touma, Habid Hassan. 1996. *The Music of the Arabs,* translated by Laurie Schwartz. Portland: Amadeus Press.

Quigley, Colin. 1995. *Music from the Heart: Compositions of a Folk Fiddler*. Athens, GA: University of Georgia Press.

Rasmussen, Knud. 1931. *The Netsilik Eskimos: Social Life and Spiritual Culture*. Copenhagen: Report on the Fifth Thule Expedition 1921–24, Vol. VIII, No. 1–2.

Wade, Bonnie C. 1973. "Chiz in Khyal: The Traditional Composition in the Improvised Performance." *Ethnomusicology* 17/3:443–459.

_____. 1979. *Music in India: The Classical Traditions*. Englewood Cliffs, NJ: Prentice-Hall, Inc.

_____. 1984. *Khyal: Creativity Within North India's Classical Music Tradition*. Cambridge: Cambridge University Press.

Vander, Judith. 1988. *Songprints: The Musical Experience of Five Shoshone Women*. Urbana, IL: University of Illinois Press.

Additional Sources

Deva, B. Chaitanya. 1981. *An Introduction to Indian Music*. New Delhi: Publications Division, Ministry of Information and Broadcasting, Government of India.

Ruckert, George. 1991. *The Music of the Baba Allauddin Gharana as Taught by Ali Akbar Khan at the Ali Akbar College of Music*. Ali Akbar Khan, general editor. New York and St. Louis: East Bay Books.

Shankar, Ravi. 1968. *My Music, My Life*. New York: Simon and Schuster.

CHAPTER 12. MUSIC AND TECHNOLOGY

Referenced Sources

Cage, John. 1937. "The Future of Music: Credo." Reprinted 1987 in *Silence*. Middletown, CT: Wesleyan University Press.

_____. 1957. "Experimental Music." Reprinted 1987 in *Silence*. Middletown, CT: Wesleyan University Press.

Dery, Mark. 1990. "Public Enemy: Confrontation." *Keyboard* (September):81–96.

Fink, Robert. 1997. *Neanderthal Flute*. Saskatoon: Greenwich.

Gay, Leslie C., Jr. 1998. "Acting Up, Talking Tech: New York Rockers and Their Metaphors of Technology." *Ethnomusicology* 42/1:81–98.

Herbst, Edward. 1997. *Voices in Bali: Energies and Perceptions in Vocal Music and Dance Theater*. Hanover, NH: Wesleyan University Press.

Hood, Mantle. 1971. *The Ethnomusicologist*. Kent, OH: Kent State University Press.

Lucier, Alvin, and Douglas Simon. 1980. *Chambers*. New York: Columbia University Press.

Manuel, Peter. 1993. *Cassette Culture: Popular Music and Technology in North India*. Chicago: Chicago University Press.

_____. 1988. *Popular Musics of the Non-Western World: An Introductory Survey*. New York: Oxford University Press.

O'Sullivan, Jerry. 1997. Interview for *Exploring the World of Music*, Pacific Street Films.

Quigley, Samuel. 1995. "Gong-Smithing in Twentieth-Century Surakarta." *Asian Art and Culture* 8/3.

Schafer, R. Murray. 1977. *The Tuning of the World*. New York: Alfred A. Knopf.

Shapiro, Gerald. 1997. Interview for *Exploring the World of Music*, Pacific Street Films.

Sutton, R. Anderson. 1996a. "Interpreting Javanese Electronic Sound Technology in the Contemporary Javanese Soundscape." *Ethnomusicology* 40/2:249–268.

Sutton, R. Anderson. 1996b. "Asia/Indonesia." *Worlds of Music*. New York: Schirmer.

Wallis, Roger and Krister Malm. 1984. *Big Sounds from Small Peoples: The Music Industry in Small Countries*. New York: Pendragon.

Walser, Robert. 1993. *Running With the Devil: Power, Gender, and Madness in Heavy Metal Music*. Hanover, NH: Wesleyan University Press.

_____. 1995. "Rhythm, Rhyme, and Rhetoric in the Music of Public Enemy." *Ethnomusicology* 39/2:195–218.

Waterman, Christopher. 1990. *Jùjú: A Social History and Ethnography of an African Popular Music*. Chicago: University of Chicago Press.

Additional Sources

Frith, Simon, and Andrew Goodwin, eds. 1990. *On Record: Rock, Pop, and the Written Word*. New York: Pantheon.

Rose, Tricia. 1994. *Black Noise*. Hanover, NH: Wesleyan University Press.

Sterne, Jonathan. 1997. "Sounds Like the Mall of America: Programmed Music and the Architechtonics of Commercial Space." *Ethnomusicology* 41/1:22–50.

Wicks, Keith. 1982. *Sound and Recording*. New York: Warwick Press.

ABOUT
THE AUTHORS

Dorothea Hast received the Ph.D in ethnomusicology from Wesleyan University in 1994. She has conducted field research on traditional music and dance in New England, Ireland, and India. Her most recent trip to Ireland in 1998 was funded by a faculty development grant from Southern Connecticut State University. Her writings include articles for *Dance Research Journal, The Garland Encyclopedia of World Music, The New Grove Dictionary of Music and Musicians,* and the *Encyclopedia of New England Culture.* She was Director of Content and Writer for the television series, *Exploring the World of Music.* She has taught at Colgate University, Northeastern University, and the University of North Carolina at Greensboro, and currently teaches both at Wesleyan University and Southern Connecticut State University.

James Cowdery received the Ph.D. in ethnomusicology from Wesleyan University in 1985. He has taught at Wesleyan University, Brown University, New York University, and Sarah Lawrence College, and he served as Editor of *Ethnomusicology,* the Journal of the Society for Ethnomusicology, from 1995 to 1998. His writings include *The Melodic Tradition of Ireland* (Kent State University Press) and articles and reviews for *Ethnomusicology, The UCLA Journal of Dance Ethnology,* and *The Garland Encyclopedia of World Music.*

Stan Scott received the Ph.D. in ethnomusicology from Wesleyan University in 1997. He has received four fellowships to conduct field research and study music in North India: a Fulbright-Hays fellowship in 1984–5, an American Institute of Indian Studies senior fellowship in 1989-90, and Colgate University faculty research fellowships in 1995 and 1996. A specialist in North Indian classical singing and Bengali folk music, he has performed in major concert halls in India and the United States. His second area of research is Irish traditional music; he has conducted field research in Ireland and performed at the Willie Clancy School, the Clare Festival of Traditional Singing, and on Irish national radio. He has taught at Colgate University, Clark University, Wesleyan University, Central Connecticut State University, and Simon's Rock of Bard College, and teaches North Indian classical singing at Brown University.

THE COOPERATIVE WRITING PROCESS

The three authors worked together closely on this book, discussing all aspects of it and contributing ideas throughout. Each section was initially written by one of us, and then finalized through group participation. The basic authorship is outlined by chapter as follows:

Hast: 1: whole chapter, except for "Music in Urban Environments." 2: "Music and the Creation of Community," "The Power of Music in Worship," "Music and Healing." 4: "Learning Irish Traditional Music." 5: "Introduction." 6: "Melody in Irish Music." 7: whole chapter, except for "Timbre in Indian Classical Instrumental Music," and "Timbre in Vocal Music." 8: "Introduction," "Trinidad: The Steel Band," "Texture in Western Classical Music." 10: "Introduction," "Form in Western Classical Music." 11: "The Role of the Composer in Western Classical Music," "Composition and the Folk Process."

Cowdery: 1: "Music in Urban Environments." 2: "Introduction." 5: "Polyrhythm in the African Diaspora." 6: "Introduction." 8: "Latin America: Salsa," "Indonesia: The Central Javanese Gamelan," "Balinese Gamelan Beleganjur." 9: whole chapter. 10: "Call and Response," "Twelve Bar Blues." 11: "Introduction," "The Role of the Composer in Western Classical Music," "Composition in Native American Cultures." 12: whole chapter.

Scott: 2: "The Political Power of Music." 3: whole chapter. 4: whole chapter, except for "Learning Irish Traditional Music." 5: "Introduction," "Rhythm in South Asian Classical Music." 6: "Melody in Arabic Music: Maqam," "North Indian Classical Music." 7: "Timbre in Indian Classical Instrumental Music," and "Timbre in Vocal Music." 10: "Form in the Classical Music of North India." 11: "Improvisation in North Indian Classical Instrumental Music," "Improvisation in Arabic Classical Music," "Improvisation in Jazz."